"I like the layout and design. The reading level is easy, yet not condescending. The book is engaging. There is wonderful information presented in a concise, understandable, practical, usable manner. It is such a **positive and practical text.** Compared to other texts, **I'd give it a definite thumbs up.**"

Jeanine Long, Southwest Georgia Technical College

"[S]tudents with every type of learning style will be able to learn and apply the concepts in [this text] in a lasting manner."

Lanita Legan,
Texas State University

"User-friendly, interesting to read… full of tips and strategies students can use."

Katherine Hansen,
Minnesota State University

"I think the text is excellent and **supports lifelong learning.** The writing style… suggests a conversation between the text and its reader. **Clear, 'fresh,' comprehensive and focuses on the 'whole' student.** Sound theoretical base."

Christine A. Lottman, University of Cincinnati

"*Keys to Success* is an invaluable resource. It walks the reader through transitioning to college and **demonstrates how to build intelligence that will help in all college classes.**"

David G. Horn, Student, Denison University

"I like the message that **success is earned and takes work – that message seems clearer in this text than many others.**"

Jean E. Abshire, Indiana University Southeast

"Unlike other textbooks that focus on lecturing with a certain heaviness, Carter's *Keys* is more interactive. Never once while reading did I feel discouraged; rather, *Keys* inspired and encouraged me to take the next step in my academic career with confidence."

Laura Daugherty, Student, University of Colorado—Boulder

**CAROL CARTER** was a C student in high school. During her senior year, she got a wake-up call when her brother told her that she had intelligence, but she wouldn't go far in life unless she believed in herself enough to work hard. She began college knowing she was "behind the 8-ball" in terms of her skills. What she lacked in experience, she made up for with elbow grease and persistence. She maximized her strength as an interpersonal and intrapersonal learner. The work paid off and she graduated college with honors and a desire to help other students.

Carol is committed to helping students turn on their brains, get motivated, and discover their abilities. As president of her own company, LifeBound, she teaches study, interpersonal, and career skills to middle school and high school students in order to help them become competitive in today's global world. She trains and certifies coaches in academic coaching skills, and focuses on at-risk students with her volunteer teaching at the federal prison and her LifeBound work in the Denver housing projects. "All students are at risk for something whether it is academic, emotional, social, or economic," says Carol. "If each of us is allowed to be human and accept our flaws, we can overcome our limitations and be the best for ourselves and others."

Carol also speaks on educational topics nationally and internationally, and is pictured here with some students at the Aziza Schoolhouse in Phnom Penh, Cambodia. Her first book, *Majoring in the Rest of Your Life*, launched her writing career and opened the door to her work on the *Keys to Success* series.

**JOYCE BISHOP** has taught college students for more than 20 years. After struggling with a learning disability as a student, she focused on her visual and logical-mathematical learning abilities and went on to earn a Ph.D. in psychology. Right now, she is in her dream job as Staff Development Coordinator at Golden West College, training other faculty in effective teaching and learning strategies and also in how to teach online. For five years Joyce was voted "favorite teacher," and she was Teacher of the Year for 1995 and 2000.

Joyce and her husband, Dave, a former high school principal, started a program 17 years ago for girls who have no family support or whose families are unable to help them through school. Since that time, the Pathways to Independence nonprofit foundation has sent 215 young women to college, and 175 have graduated into gainful employment. While the girls have come from backgrounds as diverse as prison, extreme poverty, abuse, or psychological disorders, Joyce and Dave have been their champions. This photo is of Joyce with one of her Pathways graduates, Valerie, who obtained her degree in nursing and is now working at a major university hospital as a pediatric nurse. "It is so inspiring to see what these girls do with their lives," says Joyce, "once they know that they can do anything."

**SARAH LYMAN KRAVITS** lives the strategies for success that she writes about. As an author and mother of three children aged 8, 5, and 2, she faces the challenges of time management, goal achievement, and fulfilling responsibilities (not to mention eating right and getting enough sleep). In her writing and research, she works to keep up with technology and the growth of knowledge. In her relationships with work colleagues all over the country as well as with friends and family, she strives for integrity, effective communication, productive teamwork, and, most of all, flexibility. Creativity also plays a dominant role. Along with her husband, an actor on Broadway and a musician, she promotes creative ideas and actions in the home (and needs lots of creativity in order to manage children's strong wills and unique personalities).

Unlike Carol and Joyce, Sarah thrived in school from an early age based on her strength in verbal-linguistic and logical-mathematical learning. A few years after graduating from the University of Virginia as a Jefferson Scholar, she worked as program director for LifeSkills Inc., a nonprofit organization that aims to further the career and personal development of high school students. This work led her into coauthoring her first student success text and the realization that she was driven to empower students to reach their goals. "Lifelong learning is the essential success skill," says Sarah. "I would happily trade places with my readers to have the chance to challenge my mind in a college classroom again. Learning gives you a chance to go beyond just thinking about your dreams so that you can make them happen."

# KEYS TO SUCCESS

## Building Analytical, Creative, and Practical Skills

**Sixth Edition**

CAROL CARTER

JOYCE BISHOP

SARAH LYMAN KRAVITS

PEARSON

Prentice
Hall

Upper Saddle River, New Jersey
Columbus, Ohio

**Library of Congress Cataloging-in-Publication Data**

Carter, Carol.
Keys to success: building analytical, creative, and practical skills / Carol Carter, Joyce Bishop,
Sarah Lyman Kravits. — 6th ed.
p. cm.
Includes bibliographical references and index.
ISBN-13: 978-0-13-600504-9 (pbk.)
ISBN-10: 0-13-600504-7 (pbk.)
1. College student orientation—United States—Handbooks, manuals, etc. 2. Study skills—Handbooks, manuals, etc.
3. College students—United States—Life skills guides. 4. Career development—United States—Handbooks, manuals,
etc. I. Bishop, Joyce (Joyce L.), 1950– II. Kravits, Sarah Lyman. III. Title.
LB2343.32.C37 2009
378.1'70281—dc22

2007042348

**Vice President and Executive Publisher:** Jeffery W. Johnston
**Executive Editor:** Sande Johnson
**Developmental Editor:** Charlotte Morrissey
**Managing Editor:** Pamela D. Bennett
**Project Manager:** Kerry J. Rubadue
**Production Coordination:** Thistle Hill Publishing Services, LLC
**Editorial Assistant:** Lynda Cramer
**Design Coordinator:** Diane C. Lorenzo
**Cover Designer:** Candace Rowley
**Cover Image:** Jupiter Images
**Operations Specialist:** Susan Hannahs
**Director of Marketing:** Quinn Perkson
**Marketing Manager:** Amy Judd
**Marketing Coordinator:** Brian Mounts

This book was set in Sabon by S4Carlisle Publishing Services. It was printed and bound by R.R. Donnelley/Willard.
The cover was printed by Phoenix Color Corp./Hagerstown.

Credits and acknowledgments appear on page 423, which constitutes an extension of the copyright page.

**Pearson Prentice Hall**™ is a trademark of Pearson Education, Inc.
**Pearson**® is a registered trademark of Pearson plc
**Prentice Hall**® is a registered trademark of Pearson Education, Inc.

Pearson Education Ltd.
Pearson Education Singapore Pte. Ltd.
Pearson Education Canada, Ltd.
Pearson Education—Japan

Pearson Education Australia Pty. Limited
Pearson Education North Asia Ltd.
Pearson Educación de Mexico, S.A. de C.V.
Pearson Education Malaysia Pte. Ltd.

10 9 8 7 6 5 4 3 2 1
ISBN-13: 978-0-13-600504-9
ISBN-10:   0-13-600504-7

# DEDICATION

We dedicate the sixth edition of *Keys to Success* to the memory of the students and faculty at Virginia Tech who were victims of the tragic campus shootings on April 16, 2007. May their unfulfilled goals and dreams inspire students everywhere to push harder to grasp their own dreams and to believe in education as the answer and the hope.

# CONTENTS

# FOREWORD

## by the Student Editors

College is a time of self-discovery and growth, a time to understand how education serves you in school and out, a time to chart the course for your future. The knowledge you gather will change the way that you see yourself, society, and the world. Through this knowledge, you can find and travel your own path in life.

We have each had our unique struggles in finding our paths. We have worked at becoming better students, we have tried to stay dedicated in the face of challenges, we have adapted to people and academic subjects, and we have kept a lot of balls in the air as we worked to manage our academic, work, and personal lives. Through it all we picked up on some helpful strategies that we want to share with you.

**Stay on top of your time.** Most students have to stretch to make time for classes, homework, and studying. Your course schedule has to fit into your family time, work schedule, and social life. Remember not to overload yourself and spread yourself too thin among all of your responsibilities, and make sure to prioritize your course work. And study for tests ahead of time—tests sneak up on you quickly, and cramming doesn't always work (we know this from experience).

**Examine choices carefully.** Unlike high school where you more or less followed a standard curriculum, you now have much more freedom to make choices about nearly every aspect of your education, including your major, classes, instructors, and even schedules. Make sure that you are prioritizing the classes you need. Meet with academic advisors and instructors, look at your needs and strengths, and take time to make the choices that work best for you.

**Connect with people and organizations.** Befriend your classmates because college relationships are special and also because those relationships will often help you learn the material better than you would learn it on your own. Get involved with organizations to expand your horizons, give back to others, and enhance your résumé (or grad school application).

**Use your resources.** Math and language labs, computer labs, tutors, advisors, libraries and librarians, and instructors are all there to help you and make your college experience the best that it can be.

This class will help you lay the foundation that will carry you through to your degree and on to your professional life. *Keys to Success* has helped us learn, grow, and make effective choices now, and has given us tools to keep growing in the future. Now it is your turn—use it well, and best wishes for an incredible college experience.

**DARREN LOVE**
**COURTNEY MELLBLOM**
**CHERYL WHITLEY**

v

# REAL PEOPLE, REAL PERSPECTIVES

## Peer-to-Peer Perspectives from Students

# Perspectives from Academics and Workplace Professionals

# BRIEF CONTENTS

## CHAPTER 8
## RESEARCHING AND WRITING: GATHERING AND COMMUNICATING IDEAS 240

## PART III
## CREATING LIFE SUCCESS 279

## CHAPTER 9
## RELATING TO OTHERS: COMMUNICATING IN A DIVERSE WORLD 280

## CHAPTER 10
## PERSONAL WELLNESS: TAKING CARE OF YOURSELF 310

## CHAPTER 11
## MANAGING MONEY AND CAREER: REALITY RESOURCES 344

NOTE: Every effort has been made to provide accurate and current Internet information in this book. However, the Internet and information posted on it are constantly changing, so it is inevitable that some of the Internet addresses listed in this textbook will change.

# PREFACE

Many students beginning college—or returning after many years—wonder if they have what it takes to succeed. What is the recipe for success in college and beyond? Does a top SAT score, straight-A report card, or high IQ predict success? Do low grades or scores signal that you'll stumble?

Among the ideas presented by the many people who have researched this question, one approach stands out from the rest. Psychologist Robert Sternberg coined the term *successful intelligence* to indicate that intelligence is much, much more than the kind of "book smarts" that can be measured by IQ or similar tests. Rather, it is the ability to use a combination of **analytical, creative,** and **practical** abilities to reach your most important goals.

What are the analytical, creative, and practical processes that underlie intelligence?

### This Is Intelligence: Analysis

Analytical intelligence is highly valued as a crucial component of academic success. More commonly known as critical thinking, it is the ability to assess, analyze, compare, and evaluate information.

### This Is Intelligence: Creativity

Creative intelligence is the ability to innovate, generate a variety of ideas in response to problems, or think out of the box. It also involves shifting perspectives and risk taking.

### This Is Intelligence: Practical Application

Practical intelligence is more than "street smarts" or common sense. It also includes an awareness of oneself and others in situations and the translation of that knowledge into action. It is developed primarily through experience, observation, and practice.

## *Keys to Success* Focuses on Successful Intelligence

Why is successful intelligence such an effective theme for a student success text? Here are some key reasons:

- It delivers strategies that work for *all kinds of students,* not just those with strong analytical skills who tend to do well in school.

- Research proves that teaching and learning with successful intelligence *improves achievement* across cultures, socioeconomic status, age, and gender.[1]

- It recognizes that *intelligence is dynamic* and can be developed, which *encourages lifelong learning,* a key ingredient for success in the modern world.

- It *promotes goal achievement* in college and beyond, supporting our tried-and-true emphasis on success in college, career, and life.

Having introduced successful intelligence as its theme in the fifth edition, *Keys to Success* takes its integration to new heights this time around, with tools in each chapter to help you build analytical, creative, and practical intelligence:

- **NEW!** At the beginning of the chapter, a mind map preview surveys the successful intelligence skills you will be working on.

- **REVISED!** Throughout the chapter, **Get Analytical, Get Creative,** and **Get Practical** exercises build those specific skills in the context of chapter material.

- **NEW!** As you finish the chapter, a **Successful Intelligence Wrap-Up** hits the high points of what you explored and accomplished.

- **NEW!** Chapters 1 and 12 contain a **pre- and post-course assessment** to help you measure yourself as a "self-activator" who will put successful intelligence strategies into action.

- **REVISED!** Each end-of-chapter exercise set begins with **Successful Intelligence: Think, Create, Apply,** an exercise that synthesizes the three aspects of successful intelligence by applying them to chapter content.

- **NEW!** Each chapter has a link to Successful Intelligence Connections Online, an audio feature on the text's Companion Website that will help you apply successful intelligence to specific chapter topics.

## *Keys to Success* Features Help You Grow

Complementing the successful intelligence theme, additional features of this text will help you achieve your goals in college, career, and life.

**Practical Strategies and Advice.** Practical intelligence is in high demand in college and in the workplace. Instructors and students all over the country said they wanted more practical advice and application—and here it is in the form of topics and text features:

- Reflecting psychologist Daniel Goleman's latest research on **social intelligence** as well as his ongoing work with **emotional intelligence,** *Keys to Success* offers practical tools to help you master your feelings and make the most out of your relationships with others. New material on social intelligence, and expanded material on emotional

1. E.L. Grigorenko, L. Jarvin, and R.J. Sternberg, "School-Based Tests of the Triarchic Theory: Three Settings, Three Samples, Three Syllabi." *Contemporary Educational Psychology,* 27, April 2002, pp. 167–208.

intelligence, is highlighted in chapters 1, 4, and 11, and both social and emotional intelligence are referenced throughout the text.

- Near the beginning of each chapter, Real Problems, Practical Answers offers advice from a peer, an instructor, or a professional in response to a student question.

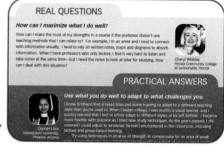

- In this information age, **information literacy** is crucial for success. Chapter 4 has a new analytical thinking example showing different ways in which to critically evaluate information, and chapter 8 contains an updated segment on research, with comprehensive information about evaluating any kind of material you encounter in the library or on the Internet.

- Test taking and time management are high on the list of important practical skills. At the end of each of the three parts in *Keys to Success*, **Get Focused! features** help you build these crucial skills.

- At the end of every third chapter, a Personal Triumph case study showcases an extraordinary student who overcame adversity to achieve success. Accompanying these stories are art pieces created by students who have overcome challenges of their own.

A Text-Wide Focus on How You Learn. This text gives you tools to find out how you learn best, as well as strategies for applying this information in practical ways:

- The first of **chapter 3's self-assessments** helps you explore your strengths in eight ability areas that psychologist Howard Gardner calls the **multiple intelligences:** verbal-linguistic, logical-mathematical, bodily-kinesthetic, visual-spatial, interpersonal, intrapersonal, musical, and naturalistic. The other, the MBTI-based **Personality Spectrum,** helps you explore how you relate to others.

- In chapters 5 through 11, you will find Multiple Intelligence Strategies grids with strategies, related to a chapter topic, geared toward each of the eight intelligences. Enhanced for this edition, each grid has a new column that demonstrates possible ways to apply multiple intelligence-based strategies to a particular academic discipline (each chapter features a different discipline).

- Beyond the Multiple Intelligence Strategies grids, material in other chapters (particularly chapters 9 and 11) shows how you can apply what you know about how you learn to situations such as career exploration and communication.

End-of-Chapter Exercises. In addition to the **Successful Intelligence: Think, Create, Apply** synthesis exercise, the end-of-chapter exercises promote development of a skillset necessary to compete in a knowledge economy and global marketplace: group problem solving (**Teamwork: Create Solutions Together**), journaling and practical writing (**Writing: Journal and Put Skills to Work**), and preparing for a successful career (**Personal Portfolio: Prepare for Career Success**).

## *Keys to Success* Is Better Than Ever

The new edition of *Keys to Success* includes improved presentations of critical college, career, and life success topics. Highlights include the following:

- **Quick Start to College** has been focused even more tightly on helpful information to get you in the groove as you begin school.

- An overhaul of **chapter 1 (Welcome to College)** involves an expanded introduction of successful intelligence, three successful intelligence self-assessments, and careful selection of supporting topics such as academic integrity and working with others.

- **Chapter 3 (Learning How You Learn)** is newly streamlined in its explanations of multiple intelligences and the personality spectrum, more clear in its treatment of the accompanying assessments, and more practical in helping you apply what you learn from the assessments to school, work, and life.

- **Chapter 4 (Critical, Creative, and Practical Thinking)** has been strengthened to help you understand and use the different aspects of successful intelligence.

- Study skills enhancements in **chapters 5 through 8 (Reading and Studying; Listening, Note Taking, and Memory; Test Taking; and Researching and Writing)** include revised coverage of SQ3R, memory, and test taking; new material on text notes and highlighting and on combining text and class notes; and a streamlined writing chapter with a new writing sample.

- The latest health and fitness information appears in **chapter 10 (Personal Wellness)**, notably in the sections on eating well, immunizations, staying safe, and drugs.

- **Chapter 11 (Managing Money and Career)** has a new emphasis on the most practical money management and career planning advice.

## *Keys to Success* Is Your Tool for Life

Broadening your definition of intelligence may change how you view your abilities and what you expect of yourself in college, in the workplace, and in your personal life. Successful intelligence can empower you with tools you never knew you had. Take action with what you learn about yourself and success in this text. Think and act analytically, creatively, and practically in the coming years as you work hard to achieve your goals and find a learning path that is uniquely your own.

Students and instructors: Many of our best suggestions come from you. Send your questions, comments, and ideas about *Keys to Success* to Carol Carter at *caroljcarter@lifebound.com*. We look forward to hearing from you, and we are grateful for the opportunity to work with you.

# ACKNOWLEDGMENTS

## *Keys to Success*, Sixth Edition: An Exceptional Development Process

When we introduced the theme of Robert Sternberg's *Successful Intelligence* with the fifth edition of *Keys to Success,* our users let us know that we had something special happening. Our goal for the sixth edition became the enhancement of this cutting-edge theme, with particular attention to its practical application in college, the workplace, and life.

To that end, Prentice Hall enlisted the involvement of Glenn and Meg Turner of Burrston House in our revision process. The Burrston House instructor and student focus groups, as well as instructor contacts who responded to extensive surveys, brought to us an extraordinary wealth of information about our materials and about what students and instructors need today. Glenn and Meg synthesized this information and presented insightful views that greatly informed the revision process.

With the Burrston House participants, our excellent team of reviewers who gave extensive feedback, and three savvy student editors, we received input on both text and design from more than 80 individuals on the revision of this sixth edition. *Keys to Success,* Sixth Edition, has risen to new heights in large part due to their efforts, and we are immensely grateful. We also especially thank our editor Sande Johnson for her advocacy and her driving this process to such a successful conclusion, and our developmental editor Charlotte Morrissey for somehow providing both in-depth content feedback as well as minutely detailed process management.

Finally, we thank Robin Baliszewski, Jeff Johnston, and Prentice Hall President Tim Bozik for their support and vision of what *Keys to Success* can accomplish.

**Chicago Focus Group**
Deryl Davis-Fulmer, Milwaukee Area Technical College
Valerie Jefferson, Rock Valley College
Georgia Kariotis, Oakton Community College
Antoinette McConnell, Northeastern Illinois University
Jacqueline Robinson, Milwaukee Area Technical College
Manuel Salgado, Elgin Community College
Arturo Vazquez, Elgin Community College
Tania Wittgenfeld, Rock Valley College

**Denver Focus Group**
Martha Martin
Joe Ritchie, University of Central Florida
Karen Schulz, University of Baltimore
Rose Stewart-Fram, McLennan Community College
Cheri Tillman, Valdosta State University

**Ft. Lauderdale Focus Group**
Raishell Adams, Palm Beach Community College–Palm Beach Gardens
Susan Bierster, Palm Beach Community College–Lake Worth
Kobitta Chopra, Broward Community College
Alice Godbey, Daytona Beach Community College
Roselee Helfand, Broward Community College

Cynthia Johnson, Palm Beach Community College–Lake Worth
Frank Kurtz, Broward Community College
Nick Nunes, Daytona Beach Community College
Amoy Reid, Broward Community College
Cathy Seyler, Palm Beach Community College–Palm Beach Gardens
Pamela Shaw, Broward Community College–South Campus
Ione Turpin, Broward Community College
Joy Vaughan-Brown, Broward Community College

**Los Angeles Focus Group**
Dirk Baron, California State University–Bakersfield
Rodolfo Frias, Santiago Canyon College
Howard Masuda, California State University–Los Angeles
Caron Mellblom-Nishioka, California State University–Dominguez Hills
Nadia Mendoza, California State University–Fullerton
Robert Roth, California State University–Fullerton
Cheryl Spector, California State University–Northridge

**Orlando Focus Group**
Christy Cheney, Valencia Community College–East Campus
Patsy Frenchman, Santa Fe Community College
S. Renee Jones, Florida Community College at Jacksonville–North Campus

Dana Kuehn, Florida Community College at
    Jacksonville–Deerwood Center
Charlene Latimer, Daytona Beach Community College–Deland
Kristina Leonard, Daytona Beach Community
    College–Flagler/Palm Coast
Jenny Middleton, Seminole Community College
Alan Pappas, Santa Fe Community College
Terry Rafter-Carles, Valencia Community College–Orlando
Tracy Stuck, Lake Sumter Community College–Leesburg Campus
Debbie Warfield, Seminole Community College

**Student Focus Group Attendees**
*Golden West Community College:* Marcos Cerda, Fidelio Cruz,
    Matthew Hendrickson, John Robledo, Vuthuyen Nong, Mayra
    Pena, Isabel Torres, Phuong Le, Nicole Cossani, Clara Moreno
*Los Angeles Harbor College:* Antonio Velasquez, Wanda Taylor
*California State University, Los Angeles:* Lydia C. Blanco

**Sixth Edition Reviewers**
Dirk Baron, California State University–Bakersfield
Lynn Berkow, University of Alaska
Mary Carstens, Wayne State College
Patrick Clarke, Southern Utah University
Colleen Courtney, Palm Beach Community College
Jacqueline Crossen-Sills, Massasoit Community College
Carolyn Darin, California State University–Northridge
Billy Davis, Florida Community College at Jacksonville-South
    Campus
Jean Gammon, Chattanooga State Technical Community College
Katherine Hansen, Minnesota State University-Mankato
Madeline Hart
Noreen Lace, California State University–Northridge
Lanita Legan, Texas State University
Linda Lemkau, North Idaho College
Christine A. Lottman, University of Cincinnati
Judith Lynch, Kansas State University
Patricia A. Malinowski, Finger Lakes Community College
Howard Masuda, California State University–Los Angeles
Gladys Montalvo, Palm Beach Community College
Nanci C. Nielsen, University of New Mexico–Valencia Campus
Carolyn Patterson, Texas State Technical College–West Texas
Allison Perrin, South Plains College
Kim Smokowski, Bergen Community College
Rose Stewart-Fram, McLennan Community College
Cheri Tillman, Valdosta State University
Ronald Weisberger, Bristol Community College

**Reviewers for Previous Editions**
Peg Adams, Northern Kentucky University
Veronica Allen, Texas Southern University
Fred Amador, Phoenix College
Angela A. Anderson, Texas Southern University
Robert Anderson, The College of New Jersey
Manual Aroz, Arizona State University
Glenda Belote, Florida International University
Todd Benatovich, University of Texas at Arlington
John Bennett Jr., University of Connecticut
Ann Bingham-Newman, California State University–Los Angeles
Mary Bixby, University of Missouri–Columbia
Barbara Blandford, Education Enhancement Center at
    Lawrenceville, NJ
Jerry Bouchie, St. Cloud State University
D'Yonne Browder, Texas Southern University
Mona Casady, Missouri State University
Kara Craig, University of Southern Mississippi

Leslie Chilton, Arizona State University
Jim Coleman, Baltimore City Community College
Sara Connolly, Florida State University
Janet Cutshall, Sussex County Community College
Valerie DeAngelis, Miami-Dade Community College
Joyce Annette Deaton, Jackson State Community College
Rita Delude, NH Community Technical College
Marianne Edwards, Georgia College and State University
Judy Elsley, Weber State University in Utah
Ray Emett, Salt Lake Community College
Jacqueline Fleming, Texas Southern University
Ralph Gallo, Texas Southern University
Skye Gentile, California State University–Hayward
Bob Gibson, University of Nebraska–Omaha
Jennifer Guyer-Wood, Minnesota State University
Sue Halter, Delgado Community College
Suzy Hampton, University of Montana
Karen Hardin, Mesa Community College
Patricia Hart, California State University–Fresno
Maureen Hurley, University of Missouri–Kansas City
Karen Iversen, Heald Colleges
Laura Kauffman, Indian River Community College
Kathryn K. Kelly, St. Cloud State University
Quentin Kidd, Christopher Newport University
Nancy Kosmicke, Mesa State College
Patsy Krech, University of Memphis
Paul Lede, Texas Southern University
Frank T. Lyman Jr., University of Maryland
Marvin Marshak, University of Minnesota
Kathy Masters, Arkansas State University
Barnette Miller Moore, Indian River Community College
Rebecca Munro, Gonzaga University
Sue Palmer, Brevard Community College
Bobbie Parker, Alabama State University
Curtis Peters, Indiana University Southeast
Virginia Phares, DeVry of Atlanta
Brenda Prinzavalli, Beloit College
Margaret Quinn, University of Memphis
Corliss A. Rabb, Texas Southern University
Eleanor Rosenfield, Rochester Institute of Technology
Rebecca Samberg, Housatonic Community College
Karyn L. Schulz, Community College of Baltimore
    County–Dundalk
Jacqueline Simon, Education Enhancement Center at
    Lawrenceville, NJ
Carolyn Smith, University of Southern Indiana
Joan Stottlemyer, Carroll College
Jill R. Strand, University of Minnesota–Duluth
Toni M. Stroud, Texas Southern University
Cheri Tillman, Valdosta State University
Thomas Tyson, SUNY Stony Brook
Eve Walden, Valencia Community College
Marsha Walden, Valdosta State University
Rose Wassman, DeAnza College
Angela Williams, The Citadel
Don Williams, Grand Valley State University
William Wilson, St. Cloud State University
Michelle G. Wolf, Florida Southern College

**Student Editors**
Darren Love
Courtney Mellblom
Cheryl Whitley

**The rest of the *Keys,* Sixth Edition story—Our heartfelt thanks to these individuals who also facilitated this edition's leap forward:**

- Robert J. Sternberg, Dean of the School of Arts and Sciences at Tufts University, for his groundbreaking work on successful intelligence and for his gracious permission to use and adapt that work as a theme for this edition.
- Those who generously contributed personal stories, exhibiting courage in being open and honest about their life experiences:

    Kevin Abreu, Montclair State University; Beverly Andre, Triton College; Stephen Beck, Learn-to-Learn Company; Joyce Bishop, Golden West College; Peter Changsak, Sheldon-Jackson College; Darrin Estepp, Ohio State University; Rose Stewart-Fram, McLennan Community College; Victoria Gough, Glendale Community College; Ramona Z. Locke, Vice President Senior Financial Consultant, Merrill Lynch Private Client Group; Darren Love, Midwestern University; Parisa Malekzadeh, University of Arizona; Joe A. Martin Jr., Professor of Communications, University of West Florida; Courtney Mellblom, California State Polytechnic University; Raymond Montolvo Jr., University of Southern California; Afsaneh Nahavandi, Arizona State University; Nisar Nikzad, Community College of Denver; Victor Ozuna, San Diego State University; Morgan Paar, Academy of Art College; Morgan Packard, Tulane University; Shyama Parikh, DePaul University; Antoine Pickett, Resident Engineer, Federal Aviation Administration; Randy Ust, University of Mary; Tracy Ust, St. Cloud University; Benjamin Victorica, University of Florida; Cheryl Whitley, Florida Community College; Tonjua Williams, St. Petersburg College

- Cynthia Nordberg, Dr. Frank T. Lyman, Prof. Beth Berry, and Prof. Jennifer Joralmon for their invaluable advice and assistance.
- Student artists Matthew Denman, Jen Fisher, Abigail Holtz, and Elie Sanon for their artwork accompanying the Personal Triumph features and their Personal Triumphs on the Companion Website. Thanks also to Susan Denman, Dana Kuehn, and Linda Russ for their help in securing artwork.
- Martha Martin, for her significant contribution to the new Instructor's Manual and PowerPoints, and Christy Cheney and Terry Rafter-Carles, for their work on the Test Item File and the Companion Website.
- Our production team for their patience, flexibility, and attention to detail, especially Pam Bennett, Candace Rowley, Kerry Rubadue, Angela Urquhart and the team at Thistle Hill, and typesetters S4 Carlisle Publishing Services.
- Our marketing gurus, especially Amy Judd, David Gesell, and Joe Hale, who leads a savvy team of sales directors including Matt Christopherson, Patty Ford, Connie James, and Deborah Wilson.
- The Prentice Hall representatives and the management team, led by National Sales Manager Brian Kibby, who deliver our message to its intended recipients—instructors and students.
- Our families and friends, who have encouraged us, advised us, and put up with our commitments.
- We extend a very special thanks to Judy Block, whose research, writing, and editing work was essential and invaluable.

# SUPPLEMENTAL RESOURCES

## for *Keys to Success*

## INSTRUCTOR SUPPORT

Resources to simplify your life and engage your students:

### Book Specific

| | |
|---|---|
| Instructor's Manual with Test Bank | 0-13-512818-8 |
| PowerPoint CD | 0-13-512878-1 |
| TestGen | 0-13-512858-7 |
| Faculty Development Workshop: Integrating Successful Intelligence | 0-13-514245-8 |

### Online Faculty Training

*Hone your teaching skills and build community with other instructors with the first-of-its-kind* **Keys Online Faculty Training Course** *with author Joyce Bishop!*

Online Instructor Faculty Training—Join the *Keys* author online faculty training sessions, available to all adopters through Course Compass, at your convenience. Ask questions. Share ideas. Troubleshoot. Be part of this collaborative community—learn what other *Keys* adopters are doing; be able to share exercises, syllabi, and teaching strategies; and observe an actual online student success course taught by Joyce Bishop. Request your unique pass code from your local representative.

### Online Resources

*Easy access to online, book-specific* **teaching support** *is now just a click away!*

Instructor Resource Center—Register. Redeem. Login. Three easy steps that open the door to a variety of print and media resources in downloadable, digital format, available to instructors exclusively through the Prentice Hall IRC. Visit **www.prenhall.com** for additional information.

Online Instructor Resources include: Online Instructor's Manual, Test Bank, PowerPoints, Faculty Development Workshops, OneKey Course Cartridge, and more.

Instructor Resource Center

Register today at www.prenhall.com to access instructor resources digitally.

## Online Course Management Through OneKey

*Teaching an online course, offering a hybrid class, or simply introducing your students to **technology** just got a whole lot easier!*

## OneKey

*All you and your students need to succeed. Powered by Blackboard, WebCT, or Course Compass, OneKey is Prentice Hall's course management resource for instructors and students. This platform provides access to online teaching and learning tools—24 hours a day, 7 days a week. OneKey means all your resources are in one place, with one passcode for maximum convenience, simplicity, and success.*

What's Key?

This powerful, ***integrated course management*** resource for *Keys to Success* contains the following:

- Online instructor's resources: Computerized Test Bank, PowerPoints, Instructor's Manual and more
- Pearson's Research Navigator™
- Text-specific Companion Website
- Prentice Hall Planner for Student Success
- Student Reflection Journal for Student Success
- Ten Ways to Fight Hate
- Student Success SuperSite (publisher-provided course website)
- Strategies for Success CD
- Understanding Plagiarism
- Supplemental Videos: Students will be engaged by the video clips on Technology, Math and Science, Managing Money and Career, Learning Styles and Self-Awareness, Study Skills, and Peer Advice, which reinforce the course content.

Visit www.prenhall.com/onekey, and scroll through the gallery option to Student Success for additional information. Note the videos housed on our OneKey sites are now available on DVD, 0-13-514249-0.

## Research Resources

*Reinforce strong **research skills**, encourage **library use**, and **combat plagiarism** with this tool!*

Prentice Hall's Research Navigator—Designed to help students with the research process—from identifying a topic to editing the final draft. It also demonstrates how to make time at the campus library more productive. RN includes 4 databases of credible and reliable source material to get your research process started: The EBSCO/Content Select, *New York Times*, Link Library, and the *Financial Times*. Visit www.researchnavigator.com for additional information.

# Video Resources

*Choose from a wide range of **video resources** for the classroom!*

Prentice Hall Reference Library: Life Skills Pack, 0-13-127079-6, contains all of the following videos:

- Learning Styles and Self-Awareness, 0-13-028502-1
- Critical and Creative Thinking, 0-13-028504-8
- Relating to Others, 0-13-028511-0
- Personal Wellness, 0-13-028514-5

Prentice Hall Reference Library: Study Skills Pack, 0-13-127080-X, contains all of the following videos:

- Reading Effectively, 0-13-028505-6
- Listening and Memory, 0-13-028506-4
- Note Taking and Research, 0-13-028508-0
- Writing Effectively, 0-13-028509-9
- Effective Test Taking, 0-13-028500-5
- Goal Setting and Time Management, 0-13-028503-X

Prentice Hall Reference Library: Career Skills Pack, 0-13-118529-2, contains all of the following videos:

- Skills for the 21st Century—Technology, 0-13-028512-9
- Skills for the 21st Century—Math and Science, 0-13-028513-7
- Managing Money and Career, 0-13-028516-1

Prentice Hall Full Reference Library Pack, 0-13-501095-0, contains the complete study skills, life skills, and career skills videos on DVD.

OneKey Video Pack, 0-13-514249-0, contains Student Advice, Study Skills, Learning Styles, and Self-Awareness, Skills for the 21st Century—Math, Science, and Technology, and Managing Money and Careers videos on DVD.

Faculty Development Video Resources

- Teacher Training Video 1: Critical Thinking, 0-13-099432-4
- Teacher Training Video 2: Stress Management & Communication, 0-13-099578-9
- Teacher Training Video 3: Classroom Tips, 0-13-917205-X

Faculty Development Series Workshops

- Carter: Faculty Development Workshop DVD, 0-13-199047-0
- Faculty Development Workshop on integrating Successful Intelligence, 0-13-514245-8

Current Issues Videos

- ABC News Video Series: Student Success, 2/E, 0-13-031901-5
- ABC News Video Series: Student Success, 3/E, 0-13-152865-3

## Assessment

*Through partnership opportunities, we offer a variety of **assessment** options!*

LASSI—The LASSI is a 10-scale, 80-item assessment of students' awareness about and use of learning and study strategies. Addressing skill, will, and self-regulation, the focus is on both covert and overt thoughts, behaviors, attitudes, and beliefs that relate to successful learning and that can be altered through educational interventions. Available in two formats: Paper, 0-13-172315-4, or Online, 0-13-172316-2 (Access Card).

Noel Levitz/RMS—This retention tool measures Academic Motivation, General Coping Ability, Receptivity to Support Services, PLUS Social Motivation. It helps identify at-risk students, the areas with which they struggle, and their receptiveness to support. Available in Paper or Online formats, as well as Short and Long versions. PAPER Long Form A: 0-13-072258-8; PAPER Short Form B: 0-13-079193-8; Online Forms AB&C: 0-13-098158-3.

Robbins Self Assessment Library—This compilation teaches students to create a portfolio of skills. S.A.L. is a self-contained, interactive library of 49 behavioral questionnaires that help students discover new ideas about themselves, their attitudes, and their personal strengths and weaknesses. Available in Paper, 0-13-173861-5; CD-Rom, 0-13-221793-7; and Online, 0-13-243165-3, (Access Card) formats.

Readiness for Education at a Distance Indicator (READI)—READI is a Web-based tool that assesses the overall likelihood for online learning success. READI generates an immediate score and a diagnostic interpretation of results, including recommendations for successful participation in online courses and potential remediation sources. Please visit www.readi.info for additional information, 0-13-188967-2.

## Diversity

*Teaching tolerance and discussing **diversity** with your students can be challenging!*

Responding to Hate at School—Published by the Southern Poverty Law Center, the Teaching Tolerance handbook is a step-by-step, easy-to-use guide designed to help administrators, counselors, and teachers react promptly and efficiently whenever hate, bias, and prejudice strike.

## Custom Publishing

*For a truly tailored solution that fosters campus connections and increases retention, talk with us about **custom publishing**.*

Pearson Custom Publishing—We are the largest custom provider for print and media shaped to your course's needs. Please visit us at www.pearsoncustom.com to learn more.

# STUDENT SUPPORT

Tools to help make the grade now, and excel in school later.

*We offer an **online study aid** to help students fully understand each chapter's content, assess their knowledge, and apply what they've learned.*

Companion Website—The text-specific website includes an online glossary of key terms, practice quizzes of objective and subjective questions, e-journaling activities, real student stories, and audio files from the authors. Please visit the site for this text at www.prenhall.com/carter.

*Our **Student Success SuperSite** is a one-stop shop for students to learn about career paths, self-awareness activities, cross-curricular practice opportunities, and more! This course-specific, rather than text-specific, website provides materials to supplement your student success course.*

SuperSite—www.prenhall.com/success

*We recognize students may want a **choice** of how their text is delivered.*

CourseSmart eTextbooks Online—Provides an alternative to the traditional print version of the text. The entire book can be purchased in an online format for 50% off the cost. Now students have a choice! Please visit www.coursesmart.com for additional information.

**Where the web meets textbooks for STUDENT SAVINGS.**

*Time management is the #1 challenge students face. We can help.*

Prentice Hall Planner—A basic planner that includes a monthly and daily calendar, plus other materials to facilitate organization (8.5 × 11).

Premier Annual Planner—This specially designed, annual 4-color collegiate planner includes an academic planning/resources section, monthly planning section (2 pages/month), and weekly planning section (48 weeks; July start date), which facilitate short-term as well as long-term planning (spiral bound, 6 × 9).

*Journaling activities promote self-discovery and self-awareness.*

Student Reflection Journal—Through this vehicle, students are encouraged to track their progress and share their insights, thoughts, and concerns (8½ × 11, 90 pages).

*Learning to adapt to the **diverse** college community is essential to students' success.*

10 Ways to Fight Hate—Produced by the Southern Poverty Law Center, the leading hate-crime and crime-watch organization in the United States, this guide walks students through 10 steps that they can take on their own campus or in their own neighborhood to fight hate every day, 0-13-028146-8.

*The **Student Orientation Series** includes short booklets on specialized topics that facilitate greater student understanding.*

S.O.S. Guides—Connolly: *Learning Communities*, 0-13-232243-9, and Watts: *Service Learning*, 0-13-232201-3, help students understand what these opportunities are, how to take advantage of them, and how to learn from their peers while doing so. New to the series is Hoffman: *Stop Procrastinating Now!: 10 Simple & SUCCESSFUL Steps for Student Success*, 0-13-513056-5.

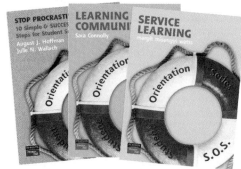

Quick Start to College, with its coverage of some basic information you need at the beginning of your course work, is designed to help you feel more in control as you start this important journey toward the achievement of a college education. As you read, consult your college handbook and/or website to learn about the specific resources, policies, and procedures of your college.

Start by learning what your college expects of you—and what you have a right to expect in return as a consumer of education. Continue on, to explore the people and resources that can help you while you are enrolled. Finally, consider the financial aid possibilities that can help you pay for it all.

## What Your College Expects of You

If you clarify what it means to be a college student right at the start, you will minimize surprises that may be obstacles later on. What is expected of you may be different from anything you encountered in high school or in other educational settings. Because expectations differ from college to college, use the material that follows as general guidelines.

### Follow Procedures and Fulfill Requirements

Understanding and following college procedures will smooth your path to success.

### Registration

Registration may take place through your school's computer network, via an automated phone system, or in the school gym or student union. Scan the college catalog and Web site and consider these factors as you make your selections:

- Core/general requirements for graduation
- Your major or minor or courses in departments you are considering
- Electives that sound interesting, even if they are out of your field

Once you choose courses, but before you register, create a schedule that shows daily class times to see if the schedule will work out. Meet with your advisor for comments and approval.

### Graduation and Curriculum Requirements

Every college has degree requirements stated in the catalog and Web site. Make sure you understand those that apply to you. Among the requirements you may encounter are these:
- Number of credits needed to graduate, including credits in major and minor fields

- Curriculum requirements, including specific course requirements
- Departmental major requirements

## School Procedures

Your college has rules and regulations, found in the college handbook and on the Web site, for all students to follow. Among the most common procedures are these:

**Adding or dropping a class.** This should be done within the first few days of the term if you find that a course is not right for you or that there are better choices. Withdrawals after a predetermined date, except those approved for special cases, receive a failing grade.

**Taking an Incomplete.** If you can't finish your work due to circumstances beyond your control—an illness or injury, for example—many colleges allow you to take a grade of Incomplete. The school will require approval from your instructor and you will have to make up the work later.

**Transferring schools.** Research the degree requirements of other schools and submit transfer applications. If you are a student at a community college and intend to transfer to a four-year school, take the courses required for admission to that school. In addition, be sure all your credits are transferable, which means they will be counted toward your degree at the four-year school.

## Understand Your School's Grading System

GRADE POINT
AVERAGE (GPA)

A measure of academic achievement computed by dividing the total number of grade points received by the total number of credits or hours of course work taken.

When you receive grades, remember that they reflect your work, not your self-worth. Most schools use grading systems with numerical grades or equivalent letter grades (see Key QS.1). Generally, the highest course grade is an A, or 4.0, and the lowest is an F, or 0.0.

In every course, you earn a certain number of college credits, called *hours*. For example, Accounting 101 may be worth three hours. These numbers generally refer to the number of hours the course meets per week. When you multiply each numerical course grade by the number of hours the course is worth, then take the average of all these numbers and divide by the total number of credit hours you are taking, you obtain your **grade point average,** or GPA.

Learn the minimum GPA needed to remain in good standing and to be accepted and continue in your major. Key QS.2 shows you how to calculate your GPA. You can also use Web resources such as www.back2college.com/gpa.htm to calculate your GPA electronically.

KEY QS.1 Letter grades and equivalent numerical grades per semester hour.

| Letter grade | A | A− | B+ | B | B− | C+ | C | C− | D+ | D | F |
|---|---|---|---|---|---|---|---|---|---|---|---|
| Numerical grade | 4.0 | 3.7 | 3.3 | 3.0 | 2.7 | 2.3 | 2.0 | 1.7 | 1.3 | 1.0 | 0.0 |

**KEY QS.2** An example that shows how to calculate your GPA.

| COURSE | SEMESTER HOURS | GRADE | POINTS EARNED FOR THIS COURSE |
|---|---|---|---|
| Chemistry I | 4 | C (2.0 points) | 4 credits × 2.0 points = 8 |
| Freshman Writing | 3 | B+ (3.3 points) | 3 credits × 3.3 points = 9.9 |
| Spanish I | 3 | B− (2.7 points) | 3 credits × 2.7 points = 8.1 |
| Introduction to Statistics | 3 | C+ (2.3 points) | 3 credits × 2.3 points = 6.9 |
| Social Justice | 2 | A− (3.7 points) | 2 credits × 3.7 points = 7.4 |
| **Total semester hours** **Total grade points for semester** | **15** | | **40.3** |

GPA for semester (total grade points divided by semester hours): 40.3 divided by 15 = 2.69
Letter equivalent grade: C+/B−

## Make the Most of Your School's Computer System

A large part of college communication and work involves the computer. In a given day you might access a syllabus online, e-mail a student, use the Internet to tap into a library database, write a draft of an assignment on a computer, and send a paper draft to an instructor electronically. Most dorm rooms are wired for computers, and an increasing number of campuses have wireless networks. Some schools are even moving to a "paperless" system where all student notifications are sent via e-mail, requiring every student to activate an e-mail account and check it regularly. Here are some suggestions for using your computer effectively:

- *Get trained.* Register for an e-mail account at your school and connect to the college network. Take classes to master word processing, data and spreadsheets, and the Internet. You may want to get trained in course management systems such as Blackboard if your school uses one.
- *Use computers to find information.* Frequent the college Web site and use library databases. If they are available, download podcasts of lectures.
- *Be a cautious user.* Save Save your work periodically onto a primary or backup hard drive, CD, or flash drive. In addition, install an antivirus program and update it regularly.
- *Stay on task.* During study time, try to stay away from Internet surfing, instant messaging, visiting Facebook pages, and playing computer games.

One of the most important directives for college students communicating via computer is to *follow guidelines when contacting instructors via e-mail.* When you submit assignments, take exams, or ask questions electronically, rules of etiquette promote civility and respect. Try these suggestions the next time you e-mail an instructor:

- *Use your university account.* Instructors are likely to delete unfamiliar e-mails from their overloaded e-mail in-boxes. "Helen_Miller@yourschool.edu" will get read—but "disastergirl@yahoo.com" may not.
- *Don't ask for information you can find on your own or bother your instructor with minor problems.* Flooding your instructor with unnecessary e-mails may work against you when you really need help.
- *Write a clear subject line.* State exactly what the e-mail is about.
- *Address the instructor by name and use his or her title.* "Hello Professor Smith" or "Hi Dr. Reynolds" is better than "Hey."
- *Be clear and comprehensive.* First, state your question or problem and what you want to achieve. For example, "In my essay, I believe I covered the key points. I would like to meet to discuss your critique." Next, if necessary, support your position, using bullet points if you have a number of support statements. Finally, end by thanking the instructor and signing your full name.
- *Avoid abbreviations and acronyms.* Write as though you were crafting a business letter, not a social e-mail to a friend.
- *Use complete sentences, correct punctuation, and capitalization.* Be sure to reread your e-mail before sending, so that you have a chance to correct any mistakes.
- *Give the instructor time to respond.* Don't expect a reply within two hours. If you hear nothing after a couple of days, send a follow-up note that contains the full text of your first message. A note that simply says "Did you get my last e-mail?" won't be helpful if for any reason your instructor didn't receive or read the first one.

### Get Involved

Extracurricular activities give you a chance to meet people who share your interests and to develop teamwork and leadership skills as well as other skills that may be important in your career. In addition, being connected to friends and a supportive network of people is one of the main reasons people stay in school.

Some freshmen take on so many activities that they become overwhelmed. Pace yourself the first year. You can always add activities later. As you seek the right balance, consider this: Studies have shown that students who join organizations tend to persist in their educational goals more than those who don't branch out.[1]

## Connect with People and Resources

During your first weeks of school—as you navigate through what may seem like a maze of classes and business offices—it is important to know that instructors, administrators, advisors, and a range of support staff are available to help. Groups and organizations also provide support and opportunities to broaden your experience. Tap into the following resources at your school.

## Instructors and Teaching Assistants

The people who teach your courses—instructors and teaching assistants—are your most available human resources at college. You see them from one to five times per week and interact with them more directly than with any other authority on campus. They see your work and, if your class size is small, they hear your ideas and consequently may get to know you quite well. Instructors are potential resources and necessary allies in your education.

What kind of help might you seek from an instructor or teaching assistant?

- Clarification on material presented in class
- Help on homework
- Information about how to prepare for a test
- Consultation on a paper you are working on
- Details about why you received a particular grade on a test or assignment
- Advice about the department—courses, majoring—or related career areas

When you want to speak personally with an instructor for longer than a minute or two, choose your time carefully. Before or after class is usually not the best time for anything more than a quick question. When you need your instructor's full attention, there are three ways to get it: Make an appointment during office hours, send e-mail, or leave a voice mail message.

- *Office hours.* Instructors keep regular office hours. Generally, these appear on your syllabus and are posted on instructors' office doors and on instructors' or departmental Web pages. Always make an appointment for a conference. Face-to-face conferences are ideal for working through ideas and problems (for example, deciding on a term paper topic) or asking for advice (for example, looking for guidance on choosing courses in the department).
- *E-mail.* Use e-mail to clarify assignments and assignment deadlines, to ask questions about lectures or readings, and to clarify what will be covered on a test. Using the e-mailing guidelines presented earlier in Quick Start will increase the likelihood of receiving a positive response. Instructors' e-mail addresses are generally posted on the first day of class and may also appear in your handbook or syllabus.
- *Voice mail.* If something comes up at the last minute, you can leave a message in your instructor's voice mailbox. Make your message short, but specific ("This is Rick Jones from your ten o'clock Intro to Psychology class—I'm supposed to present my project today, but have a fever of 102 degrees"). Avoid calling instructors at home unless they give specific permission to do so.

If you are taking a large lecture course, you may have a primary instructor plus a *teaching assistant* (TA) who meets with a small group of students on a regular basis and grades your papers and exams. You may want to approach your TA with course-related questions and problems before approaching the instructor. Because TAs deal with fewer students, they may have more time to devote to specific issues.

## Academic Advisors

In most colleges, every student is assigned an advisor who is the student's personal liaison with the college. (At some schools, students receive help at an advising center.) Your advisor will help you choose courses every term, plan your overall academic program, and understand college regulations, including graduation requirements. He or she will point out possible consequences of your decisions ("If you put off taking biology now, you're facing two lab courses next term"), help you shape your educational goals, and monitor your academic progress.

Although you are responsible for fully understanding graduation requirements—including credit requirements—and choosing the courses you need, your advisor is there to help you with these critical decisions. You will most likely be required to meet with your advisor once each term; however, you can schedule additional meetings if and when you need them.

MENTOR

A trusted counselor or guide who takes a special interest in helping you reach your goals.

## Mentors

You may find a mentor during college who can give you a private audience for questions and problems, advice tailored to your needs, and support, guidance, and trust. In return, you owe it to a mentor to respectfully take advice into consideration. A mentor might be your advisor, an instructor in your major or minor field, or a resident assistant (RA). Some schools have faculty or peer mentoring programs to match students with people who can help them.

## Tutors and Academic Centers

Tutors can give you valuable and detailed help on specific academic subjects. Most campuses have private tutoring available, and many schools offer free peer tutoring. If you feel you could benefit from the kind of one-on-one work a tutor can give, ask your instructor or your academic advisor to recommend a tutor. If your school has one or more academic centers, you may be able to find a tutor there. *Academic centers*, including reading, writing, math, and study-skills centers, offer consultations and tutoring to help students improve skills at all levels.

## Administrators

Every college needs an administrative staff to operate smoothly and efficiently. One of the most important administrative offices for students is the Office of the Dean of Student Affairs, which, in many colleges, is the center for student services. Staff members there can answer your questions or direct you to others who can help. You will also encounter administrative offices involved with tuition payments, financial aid, and registration, as follows:

- The *bursar's office* (also called the office of finance or accounting office) issues bills for tuition and room and board and collects payments from students and financial aid sources.
- The *financial aid office* helps students apply for financial aid and understand the eligibility requirements of different federal, state, and private programs (see chapter 11 for more details on financial aid).

- The *registrar's office* handles course registration, sends grade reports, and compiles your official *transcript* (a comprehensive record of your courses and grades). Graduate school admissions offices require a copy of your transcript, as do many prospective employers.

## Student-Centered Services

A host of services helps students succeed in college and deal with problems that arise. Here are some you may find.

**Academic computer center.** Most schools have computer facilities that are open daily, usually staffed by technicians who can assist you. Many facilities also offer training workshops.

**Student housing or commuter affairs office.** Residential colleges provide on-campus housing for undergraduate students. The housing office handles room and roommate placement and deals with special needs (for example, an allergic student's need for a room air conditioner) and problems. Schools with commuting students may have transportation and parking programs.

**Health services.** Health services generally include sick care, prescriptions, routine diagnostic tests, vaccinations, and first aid. All clinics are affiliated with nearby hospitals for emergency care. In addition, psychological counseling is sometimes offered through health services or at a separate facility. Many colleges require proof of health insurance at the time of registration.

**Career services.** This office helps students find part-time and full-time jobs, as well as summer jobs and internships. Career offices have reference files on careers and employers; they also help students learn to write résumés and cover letters and search job sites on the Internet; and they hold career fairs and provide space for employers to interview students on campus.

**Services for disabled students.** For students with documented disabilities, federal law requires that assistance be provided in the form of accommodations ranging from interpreters for the hearing impaired to ramps for students in wheelchairs. If you have a disability, visit this office to learn what is offered, and remember that this office is your advocate if you encounter problems.

**Veterans' affairs.** The Office of Veterans' Affairs provides veterans with services including academic and personal counseling and current benefit status, which may affect tuition waivers.

## Resources for Minority Students

The term *minority* includes students of color; gay, lesbian, and bisexual students; and students from underrepresented cultures or religious backgrounds. Along with activities that appeal to the general student population, most colleges have organizations and services that support minority groups, including specialized student associations, cultural centers, arts groups with a minority focus, minority fraternities and sororities, and political-action groups.

Many minority students seek a balance, getting involved with members of their group as well as with the college mainstream. For example, a student may join the Latino Students Association as well as clubs for all students such as the campus newspaper or an athletic team.

# Explore and Apply for Financial Aid

Financing your education—alone or with the help of your family—involves gathering financial information and making decisions about what you can afford and how much help you may need. *The first important step is to never assume you are not eligible for aid.* Almost all students are eligible for some kind of need-based or merit-based financial assistance.

## Types of Aid

Aid comes in the form of student loans, grants, and scholarships.

**Student loans.** As the recipient of a student loan, you are responsible for paying back the amount you borrow, plus interest, according to a predetermined payment schedule that may stretch over a number of years. The federal government administers or oversees most student loans. To receive aid from any federal program, you must be a citizen or eligible non-citizen and be enrolled in a program that meets government requirements. Individual states may differ in their aid programs, so check with the financial office for details. Key QS.3 describes the main student loan programs.

**Grants.** Unlike student loans, grants do not require repayment. They are awarded to students who show financial need and can be funded by federal, state, or local governments as well as private organizations. Key QS.4 describes federal grant programs.

**Scholarships.** Scholarships are awarded to students who show talent or ability in specific areas (academic achievement, sports, the arts, citizenship, or leadership). They may be financed by government or private organizations, schools, or individuals.

KEY QS.3

## Get the details on federal student loan programs.

| LOAN | DESCRIPTION |
| --- | --- |
| **Perkins** | Low, fixed rate of interest. Available to those with exceptional financial need (determined by a government formula). Issued by schools from their allotment of federal funds. Grace period of up to nine months after graduation before repayment, in monthly installments, must begin. |
| **Stafford** | Available to students enrolled at least half-time. Exceptional need not required, although students who prove need can qualify for a subsidized Stafford loan (the government pays interest until repayment begins). Two types of Staffords: the direct loan comes from federal funds, and the FFEL (Federal Family Education Loan) comes from a bank or credit union. Repayment begins six months after you graduate, leave school, or drop below half-time enrollment. |
| **PLUS** | Available to students enrolled at least half-time and claimed as dependents by their parents. Parents must undergo a credit check to be eligible, or may be sponsored through a relative or friend who passes the check. Loan comes from government or a bank or credit union. Sponsor must begin repayment 60 days after receiving the last loan payment. |

## KEY QS.4

# Get the details on federal grant programs.

| GRANT | DESCRIPTION |
|---|---|
| **Pell** | Need-based; the government evaluates your reported financial information and determines eligibility from that "score" (called an expected family contribution, or EFC). Available to undergraduates who have earned no other degrees. Amount varies according to education cost and EFC. Adding other aid sources is allowed. |
| **Federal Supplemental Educational Opportunity (FSEOG)** | Need-based; administered by the financial aid administrator at participating schools. Each participating school receives a limited amount of federal funds for FSEOGs and sets its own application deadlines. |
| **Work-study** | Need-based; encourages community service work or work related to your course of study. Pays by the hour, at least the federal minimum wage. Jobs may be on campus (usually for your school) or off (often with a nonprofit organization or a public agency). |

## Applying for Federal Aid

Anyone who wants to apply for federal aid needs to fill out the Free Application for Federal Student Aid (FAFSA) form either on paper or electronically. The form can be found at your library, at the Federal Student Aid Information Center, through your college's financial aid office or Web site, or via the U.S. Department of Education's Web site at www.ed.gov/finaid.html.

In recent years the FAFSA form has come under fire for its length (8 pages with 101 questions) and complexity, involving detailed and often hard-to-compile financial information. It is easy to be intimidated by the amount of work involved and to simply give up on the process altogether. The U.S. Department of Education, concerned about the low number of eligible students who apply for federal aid, has become aware of this "fear factor" that keeps people from making the most of this resource and is attempting to make the process more user-friendly.

The Department of Education has a new online tool called FAFSA4caster (FAFSA Forecaster). You or your parents can enter financial information into the tool and receive an estimate of the amount of federal aid you would qualify for, as well as an estimate of the amount of money that you would have to put in (the "expected family contribution"). The tool will also store your answers to FAFSA questions and transfer them to the FAFSA form when you make your actual aid application, reducing the form length by about half. Even with these changes, the process can still be challenging, so don't hesitate to ask for help from your financial aid office.

Additional information about federal grants and loans is available in the current version (updated yearly) of *The Student Guide to Financial Aid*. This publication can be found at your school's financial aid office, or you can request it by mail or phone (800-433-3243). The publication is also available online at http://studentaid.ed.gov/guide.

## Managing the Application Process

The key word for success in this process is *early*. Research early; get forms early; apply early. The earlier you complete the process, the greater your chances of being considered for aid, especially when you are applying for part of a limited pool of federal funds granted to your college.

It can take work to locate financial aid opportunities; many aren't widely advertised. Start digging at your school's financial aid office and on the school Web site. Visit your library, bookstore, and the Internet for ideas. Funding guides catalog thousands of financial aid offers, and the Internet features online scholarship search services. Think carefully about what you should apply for and why, and get insight from someone in the financial aid office as you consider the options.

Your role in this process does not stop here. If you do receive aid from your college or elsewhere, follow all the rules and regulations, including remaining in academic good standing and meeting yearly application deadlines (in most cases, you will have to reapply *every year* for aid). Finally, take a new look at what's available to you each year; you may be eligible for different grants or scholarships at various points in your college career.

You are beginning the journey of your college education and lifelong learning. The work you do in this course will help you achieve your goals in your studies, your personal life, and your career. Psychologist Robert J. Sternberg, the originator of the successful intelligence concept that is the theme of *Keys to Success*, said that those who achieve success "create their own opportunities rather than let their opportunities be limited by the circumstances in which they happen to find themselves."[2] Let this book and this course help you create new and fulfilling oppurtunities on your path to success.

## Endnotes

1. Alexander W. Astin, *Preventing Students from Dropping Out*, San Francisco: Jossey-Bass, 1976.
2. Robert J. Sternberg, *Successful Intelligence: How Practical and Creative Intelligence Determine Success in Life*, New York: Plume, 1997, p. 24.

PART

I

# Defining Yourself and Your Goals

# WELCOME TO COLLEGE

## Opening Doors to Success

*"Successfully intelligent people . . . have a can-do attitude. They realize that the limits to what they can accomplish are often in what they tell themselves they cannot do, rather than in what they really cannot do."*

ROBERT STERNBERG

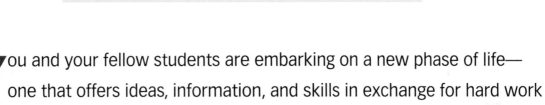

**Y**ou and your fellow students are embarking on a new phase of life—one that offers ideas, information, and skills in exchange for hard work and dedication. The tools you acquire in college will help you succeed in an ever-changing world where technology and the global marketplace are transforming the way you live and work. *Keys to Success* will help you learn successfully, graduate, and reap the personal and professional rewards of a solid education. This chapter gets you started with an overview of how being a "successfully intelligent," responsible, and forward-thinking student will help you face challenges head-on and achieve more than you ever imagined.

*In this chapter you explore answers to the following questions:*

- Where are you now—and where can college take you?  4
- How can successful intelligence help you achieve your goals?  7
- What actions will prepare you for college success?  11
- How can you work effectively with others?  19
- How can the things you learn now promote life success?  23
- Successful Intelligence Wrap-Up  25

### Analytical

- Evaluating your starting point as you begin college
- Analyzing how successful intelligence can help you achieve goals
- Considering how specific actions promote success in college

### Creative

- Creating new ideas about college goals
- Developing a fresh understanding of your ability to grow
- Creating ways to benefit from failure

### Practical

- How to follow the code of academic integrity
- How to work with others effectively
- How to become a lifelong learner

# Where Are You Now—And Where Can College Take You?

Reflect on the road that brought you to this day. You completed high school or its equivalent. You may have built life skills from experience as a partner or parent. You may have been employed in one or more jobs or completed a tour of duty in the armed forces. You have enrolled in college, found a way to pay for it, signed up for courses, and shown up for class. And, in deciding to pursue a degree, you chose to believe in your ability to accomplish goals. You have earned this opportunity to be a college student!

To make the most of college, first understand its value. College is the ideal time to acquire skills that will serve you in the global marketplace, where workers in the United States work seamlessly with people in other parts of the world. Thomas Friedman, author of *The World Is Flat*, explains how the digital revolution has transformed the working environment you will enter after college: "It is now possible for more people than ever to collaborate and compete in real time with more other people on more different kinds of work from more different corners of the planet and on a more equal footing than in any previous time in the history of the world—using computers, e-mail, networks, teleconferencing, and dynamic new software."[1]

This means that you may be doing *knowledge work* and other jobs in conjunction with, or in competition with, highly trained and motivated people from around the world. Reaching your potential has never been

**GLOBAL MARKETPLACE**

An interconnected marketplace, where companies do business without regard to time zones and boundaries, and where companies from all over the world compete directly for business.

## How can I make the transition to college easier?

I grew up in a diverse community and am in the first generation of my family to attend college. In high school, making friends and fitting in was very easy for me. However, I am nervous about the college experience. One reason is that I don't have role models in my family for what college is all about, and another is that the student body at my college has a different cultural makeup than my high school and community. When I tried meeting people on campus the first day I visited, I didn't feel like I made any real connections. What can I do to make the change easier?

Kevin Abreu
Montclair State University
Montclair, New Jersey

# PRACTICAL ANSWERS

## Draw on your strengths, be yourself, and reach out to others.

Rose Stewart-Fram, M.Ed.
Psychology Department
McLennan Community
College, Waco, Texas

In high school you and your friends shared a common culture. You could look on college as a new culture. Draw on the strengths you developed in high school as well as your experiences growing up to help you make new friends, even if it feels awkward while you are making the effort.

My dad was in the military and we moved to a different region of the United States, or even out of the country, *every year.* I had to adapt to new places, new people, new accents, and new customs. I learned to fit in even though I felt like a phony trying to talk like my friends in New Jersey and California. And forget trying to alter my southern accent enough to "pass" in Maine, because that didn't work! So, finally I learned that I had to be myself and hope that people would accept me for who I am, and they did.

I was also a first-generation college student and I felt like a fish out of water, too. I did not have the academic preparation and study skills that I needed. When I was in school, there weren't many support services or remedial classes available to help struggling freshmen. I worked with other students to get notes and to form study groups to study for tests, and I made some terrific friends in the process. If you're strong in academics, tutoring and note taking are great ways to earn extra money and make new friends.

Asking the people sitting next to you in class questions about class notes or different ideas from the lecture is a wonderful way to start a conversation. Also, many colleges have peer-mentoring programs where older students help entering freshmen learn the ropes. By being yourself and using your strengths to help others, you will bridge the cultural gap and become a part of this new culture.

Best wishes on a great first year in college, and many great years to come.

more crucial to your success. You will be up to the task of succeeding in the global marketplace if you do the following:

- Acquire solid study skills
- Commit to lifelong learning and job training
- Persevere despite obstacles
- Perform high-quality work on a consistent basis
- Embrace change as a way of life

## More education is likely to mean more income.

Median annual income of persons with income 25 years old and over, by gender and highest level of education, 2002

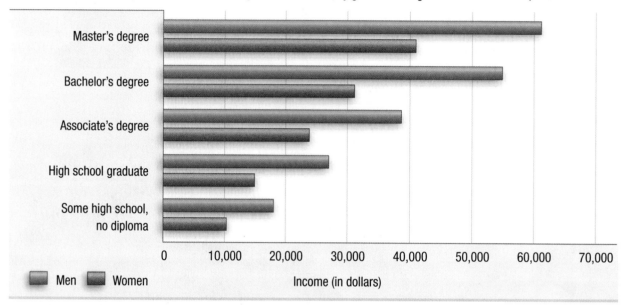

Master's degree

Bachelor's degree

Associate's degree

High school graduate

Some high school, no diploma

0   10,000   20,000   30,000   40,000   50,000   60,000   70,000

Men   Women   Income (in dollars)

*Source:* U.S. Census Bureau, "Income, Poverty, and Health Insurance Coverage in the United States, 2003," *Current Population Reports*, Series P60-226, August 2004.

On a more personal level, college can help you achieve overarching "life success goals:"

**Life Success Goal: Increased employability and earning potential.** Getting a degree greatly increases your chances of finding and keeping a highly skilled, well-paying job. College graduates earn, on average, around $20,000 more per year than those with just a high school diploma (see Key 1.1). Furthermore, the unemployment rate for college graduates is less than half that of high school graduates (see Key 1.2).

**Life Success Goal: Preparation for career success.** Your course work will give you the knowledge and hands-on skills you need to achieve your career goals. It will also expose you to a variety of careers and areas of academic specialty, many of which you may not have even heard of. Completing college will open career doors that are closed to those without a degree.

**Life Success Goal: Smart personal health choices.** The more educated you are, the more likely you are to take care of your physical and mental health. A college education prepares you with health-related information and attitudes that you will use over your lifetime, helping you to practice wellness through positive actions and to avoid practices with the potential to harm.

**Life Success Goal: Active community involvement and an appreciation of different cultures.** Going to college prepares you to understand complex

## More education is likely to mean more consistent employment.

Unemployment rates of persons 25 years old and over, by highest level of education, 2005

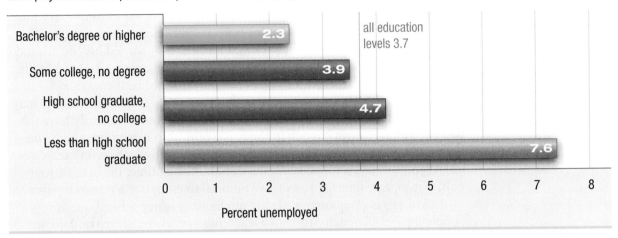

*Source:* U.S. Department of Labor, Bureau of Labor Statistics, Office of Employment and Unemployment Statistics, "Employment and Earnings," January 2005.

political, economic, and social forces that affect you and others. This understanding is the basis for good citizenship and encourages community involvement. Your education also exposes you to the ways in which people and cultures are different and how these differences affect world affairs. As a worker likely to encounter many cultures in the global marketplace, this knowledge will help you succeed.

**Life Success Goal: Self-knowledge.** Being in college gets you thinking about yourself on a big-picture level. What do you do well? What do you want out of life? What can you improve? College gives you the chance to evaluate where you are and decide where you want to be.

This course and *Keys to Success* provide the tools you need to kick off this exploration. Especially crucial is your ability to use *successful intelligence—* your most important goal-achievement tool, and the theme of this text.

# How Can Successful Intelligence Help You Achieve Your Goals?

Think about how you define *intelligence.* Many people view an intelligent person as someone with "book smarts," someone who will excel in high-level analytical courses and go on to a brilliant career in a challenging profession such as science or law. Traditionally, many people have also believed that each individual is born with a fixed amount of intelligence, and that this has a significant effect on success. Another fairly common belief is that standardized tests, such as IQ (intelligence quotient) tests, accurately measure a person's intelligence and are predictors of success.

Psychologist Robert J. Sternberg has an entirely different view of intelligence. His life experiences convinced him that traditional intelligence measurements lock people into poor performances and often do not accurately reflect their potential for life success. When test anxiety caused Sternberg to score poorly on IQ and other standardized tests during elementary school, he delivered exactly what was expected of him—very little. In the fourth grade, when a teacher expected more from him than he had ever shown he could give, she provided a spark that turned his life around.

Sternberg asserts that IQ tests, the Scholastic Assessment Test (SAT), the American College Test (ACT), and other standardized tests measure inert intelligence. He further explains that those who score well on tests may have strong recall and analytical skills, but they do not necessarily have the power to make things happen in the real world.[2] No matter how high you score on a library science test, for example, your knowledge won't serve you unless you can use it to locate, in a short amount of time, the specific journals, books, and Internet resources you need to complete a research paper.

Sternberg is also convinced that intelligence is *not* a fixed quantity; people have the capacity to increase intelligence as they learn and grow. Recent studies support this perspective, showing that the brain continues to develop throughout life if you continue to learn new things.[3] To make this development happen, you need to actively challenge yourself and believe in your ability to grow. Psychologist Carol Dweck says that "people with a growth mindset thrive when they're stretching themselves."[4] Conversely, people who shy away from challenge will experience less growth. Challenge yourself, and your value to yourself and to others will grow.

**INERT INTELLIGENCE**

Passive recall and analysis of learned information rather than goal-directed thinking linked to real-world activities.

## Defining Successful Intelligence

In his book *Successful Intelligence: How Practical and Creative Intelligence Determine Success in Life*, Sternberg focuses on what he calls *successful intelligence*—"the kind of intelligence used to achieve important goals."[5] Successful intelligence better predicts life success than any IQ test because it focuses largely on actions—what you *do* to achieve your goals—instead of just on recall and analysis.

Sternberg uses this story to illustrate the impact of successful intelligence:

> *Two boys are walking in a forest. They are quite different. The first boy's teachers think he is smart, his parents think he is smart, and as a result, he thinks he is smart. He has good test scores, good grades, and other good paper credentials that will get him far in his scholastic life.*
>
> *Few people consider the second boy smart. His test scores are nothing great, his grades aren't so good, and his other paper credentials are, in general, marginal. At best, people would call him shrewd or street smart.*
>
> *As the two boys walk along in the forest, they encounter a problem—a huge, furious, hungry-looking grizzly bear, charging straight at them. The first boy, calculating that the grizzly bear will overtake them in 17.3 seconds, panics. In this state, he looks at the second boy, who is calmly taking off his hiking boots and putting on his jogging shoes.*

  KEYS TO SUCCESS

*The first boy says to the second boy, "You must be crazy. There is no way you are going to outrun that grizzly bear!"*

*The second boy replies, "That's true. But all I have to do is outrun you!"*[6]

This story shows that successful problem solving and decision making require more than book smarts. When confronted with a problem, using *only* analytical thinking put the first boy at a disadvantage. On the other hand, the second boy thought in different ways; he analyzed the situation, creatively considered the options, and took practical action. He asked and answered questions. He knew his purpose. And he lived to tell the tale.

Sternberg breaks successful intelligence into three parts or abilities:

- *Analytical thinking*—commonly known as *critical thinking*—involves analyzing and evaluating information, often in order to work through a problem or decision. Analytical thinking is largely responsible for school success and is measured through traditional testing methods.

- *Creative thinking* involves generating new and different ideas and approaches to problems and, often, viewing the world in ways that disregard convention.

- *Practical thinking* means putting what you've learned into action in order to solve a problem or make a decision—and carrying what you learn from the experience with you to use with future situations. Practical thinking enables you to accomplish goals despite obstacles.

Together, these abilities move you toward a goal, as Sternberg explains:

Analytical thinking is required to solve problems and to judge the quality of ideas. Creative intelligence is required to formulate good problems and ideas in the first place. Practical intelligence is needed to use the ideas and their analysis in an effective way in one's everyday life.[7]

Here are two examples that illustrate how this works.

Learning is not the only benefit of engaging successful intelligence. Using practical and creative skills also contributes to relationship building and a sense of fun in the classroom.

**Successful intelligence in a study group—reaching for the goal of helping each other learn.**

- *Analyze* the concepts you must learn, including how they relate to what you already know.
- *Create* humorous memory devices to help you remember key concepts.
- *Think practically* about who in the group does what best, and assign tasks accordingly.

**Successful intelligence regarding academics—reaching for the goal of declaring a major.**

- *Analyze* what you do well and like to do. Then analyze the course offerings in your college catalog until you come up with one or more that seem to mesh with your strengths.

- *Create* a dream career, then come up with majors that support it. For example, if you want to be a science writer, consider majoring in biology and minoring in journalism.
- *Think practically* about your major by talking with students and instructors in the department, looking at course requirements, and interviewing professionals in fields of interest.

Why is successful intelligence your key to success? It helps you understand how learning propels you toward goals, boosting your desire to learn. It gives you ways to move toward those goals, increasing your willingness to work hard. It helps you to maximize strengths and compensate for weaknesses, leading to a greater ability to capitalize on who you are and what you can do. It also increases your value in school and on the job: *People with highly developed critical, creative, and practical thinking skills are in demand because they can apply what they know to new situations, innovate, and accomplish their goals.*

The three elements of successful intelligence can give all kinds of learners a more positive outlook on their abilities. Students who have trouble with tests and other analytical skills can see that creative and practical thinking also play a significant role in success. Students who test well but have trouble using their knowledge to innovate and make things happen can develop a team approach to success as they work to improve their creative and practical skills. Everyone can find room, and ways, to grow.

## How This Book Helps You Build Successful Intelligence

*Keys to Success* is designed to help you build the analytical, creative, and practical thinking skills that will get you where you want to go in school and in life.

### Chapter Content

Each chapter incorporates successful intelligence with the following:

- A visual overview of the analytical, creative, and practical tools that you will gather in the chapter
- Contextual connections to analytical, creative, and practical thinking
- Accounts and examples from students, professors, and professionals that show how people use various analytical, creative, and practical skills to accomplish goals
- A *Successful Intelligence Wrap-Up* that summarizes the analytical, creative, and practical skills you have explored

In addition, chapter 4—the chapter on thinking—goes into more detail about all three skills.

### In-Chapter Activities

Within the text of each chapter, you will find three activities that help you build your successful intelligence skills:

- *Get Analytical* gives you an opportunity to develop your own analytical skills through your analysis of a chapter topic.

- *Get Creative* prompts you to develop your own creative skills as you think innovatively about chapter material.
- *Get Practical* provides a chance to develop your own practical skills through the experience of applying an idea from the chapter.

In this chapter, these exercises take the form of mini-assessments, tools that will help you get to know yourself as an analytical, creative, and practical thinker. With self-knowledge as the starting point, you will develop your successful intelligence throughout this book. Chapter 12 will provide an opportunity for you to assess yourself once again and consider how you have grown in each area.

### End-of-Chapter Exercises

Here you have the opportunity to combine what you have learned and apply it to important tasks in several ways, as follows:

- *Successful Intelligence: Think, Create, Apply* unites the three aspects of successful intelligence.
- *Teamwork: Create Solutions Together* encourages you to apply various successful intelligence elements to a group setting.
- *Writing: Journal and Put Skills to Work* provides an opportunity to put analysis, creative thoughts, and practical ideas down in words.
- *Personal Portfolio: Prepare for Career Success* builds practical skills and a portfolio of information that promote career success.

Whereas successful intelligence is the overarching framework of how you will achieve college and life goals, many specific elements move you toward those goals day by day. Explore attitudes and actions that prepare you for success.

# What Actions Will Prepare You for College Success?

Preparing for college success is as much a state of mind as it is making sure you take specific actions. The following section points to the basics you need—in actions as well as attitude—to achieve your goals. Always remember that you are your own manager, in charge of meeting your obligations and making decisions that move you toward your goals.

## Be Responsible and Accountable

Your primary responsibility as a student is to pursue academic excellence—to do your very best in every course so that you come away with knowledge and marketable skills. The theme of *responsibility* stands out in how two New Mexico State University students describe the struggle to adjust to college life:[8]

*Angie Miller (majoring in Biology):* The hardest part of my [freshman] courses was that I had to do all my work myself with nobody telling me every day that my homework was due. . . . Also, I felt that there was more

# GET ANALYTICAL!

## Assess Yourself as an Analytical Thinker

For each statement, circle the number that feels right to you, from 1 for "not at all true for me" to 5 for "very true for me."

1. I recognize and define problems effectively.      1 2 3 4 5

2. I see myself as a "thinker," "analytical," "studious."      1 2 3 4 5

3. When working on a problem in a group setting, I like to break down the problem into its components and evaluate them.      1 2 3 4 5

4. I need to see convincing evidence before accepting information as fact.      1 2 3 4 5

5. I weigh the pros and cons of plans and ideas before taking action.      1 2 3 4 5

6. I tend to make connections among pieces of information by categorizing them.      1 2 3 4 5

7. Impulsive, spontaneous decision making worries me.      1 2 3 4 5

8. I like to analyze causes and effects when making a decision.      1 2 3 4 5

9. I monitor my progress toward goals.      1 2 3 4 5

10. Once I reach a goal, I evaluate the process to see how effective it was.      1 2 3 4 5

Total your answers here:      _____

If your total ranges from 38–50, you consider your analytical thinking skills to be *strong.*

If your total ranges from 24–37, you consider your analytical thinking skills to be *average.*

If your total ranges from 10–23, you consider your analytical thinking skills to be *weak.*

*Remember that you can improve your analytical thinking skill with focus and practice.*

material covered in a shorter time period, so it was more study time than in high school.

*Daniel Estrada (majoring in Latin American History and Spanish):* I find that . . . the [classes are] more to my interest since I picked [them].

Now the catch is that it is not up to the instructor to keep you on task. . . . It is left unsaid that it is our responsibility to keep up with the reading, homework, and actually showing up for class.

As a student, you show responsibility by taking a series of small but important actions that are the building blocks of academic success:

- Read assigned material before it is discussed in class.
- Attend class on time and with a positive attitude.
- Complete assignments on schedule.
- Listen attentively, take notes, and participate in discussions.
- Study for exams, either on your own or with others.
- Communicate with instructors and students, and seek help from them if you need it.

A critical responsibility in each class is to thoroughly read your syllabus and refer to it frequently throughout the term. You will receive a syllabus at the first class meeting of each of your courses. Consider each syllabus as a "contract" between you and your instructor, outlining what your instructor expects of you (such as readings, assignments, and class participation) as well as what you can expect from your instructor (availability, schedule of topics, clarification of grading system).

Your syllabus will answer questions about course focus, required and optional reading, schedule of coverage, dates of exams and due dates for assignments, the components of your final grade, and more. Marking up your syllabus in your own way will help remind you of responsibilities, as will "backdating"—in other words, noting in your datebook, calendar, or PDA the interim goals you have to achieve by particular dates in order to complete more involved assignments. For example, if you have a 15-page paper due on October 15, you would enter dates in September and October for goals like choosing a topic, research, first draft, and final draft. Key 1.3 shows a portion of an actual syllabus with important items noted.

Finally, in all of your daily academic tasks, persist until you know exactly what you need to accomplish so that you can complete your work on time. Persistence is the responsible student's master key.

SYLLABUS

*A comprehensive outline of course topics and assignments.*

## Get Motivated

Success is a process, not a fixed mark. Motivation is what keeps the process in motion. Successfully intelligent people find ways to motivate themselves to learn, grow, and work toward what they want. Your challenge as you begin college is to identify and activate the forces that move you forward. These *motivators*—grades, love of a subject, the drive to earn a degree—can change with time and situations.

The primary key to motivation is to continually remind yourself of what you stand to gain from achieving your most important goals. A nursing student at Palo Alto College in San Antonio, Texas, understands how goals relate to motivation: "To stay motivated I will always remember that I am doing this to better myself and to learn what I need to in order to be the best nurse that I can be. Making a commitment and staying true to it is not easy, but I know that an uncommitted person will never finish anything."[9]

PERSISTENCE

*The act of continuing steadfastly in a course of action, even in the face of obstacles or challenges.*

MOTIVATION

*A goal-directed force that moves a person to action.*

**KEY 1.3** A syllabus helps you stay on schedule and fulfill responsibilities.

---

### ENG 122 Spring 2007

**Instructor:** Jennifer Gessner
**Office Hours:** Tue & Thur 12:30–1:30 (or by appointment) in DC 305
**Phone:** 303-555-2222
**E-mail:** jg@abc.xyz

*[How to connect with the instructor]*

**Required Texts:** *Good Reasons with Contemporary Arguments,* Faigley and Selzer
*A Writer's Reference,* 5th ed., Diana Hacker

*[Books and materials to get ASAP]*

**Required Materials:**

- a notebook with lots of paper
- a folder for keeping everything from this class
- an active imagination and critical thinking

**Course Description:** This course focuses on argumentative writing and the researched paper. Students will practice the rhetorical art of argumentation and will gain experience in finding and incorporating researched materials into an extended paper.

**Writer's Notebook:** All students will keep, and bring to class, a notebook with blank paper. Throughout the semester, you will be given writing assignments to complete in this book. You must bring to class and be prepared to share any notebook assignment. Notebook assignments will be collected frequently, though sometimes randomly, and graded only for their completeness, not for spelling, etc.

*[Course coverage, expectations, responsibilities]*

**Grading:**

- Major Writing Assignments worth 100 points each.
- Final Research Project worth 300 points.
- Additional exercises and assignments range from 10 to 50 points each.
- Class participation: Based on the degree to which you complete the homework and present this in a thoughtful, meaningful manner in class.
- Attendance: Attendance is taken daily and students may miss up to three days of class without penalty, but will lose 5 points for each day missed thereafter.
- Late work: All work will lose 10% of earned points per class day late. No work will be accepted after five class days or the last class meeting.

*[How grades are determined for this course]*

**Final Grade:** The average of the total points possible (points earned divided by the total possible points). 100–90% = A; 89–80% = B; 79–70% = C (any grade below 70% is not passing for this class).

**Academic Integrity:** Students must credit any material used in their papers that is not their own (including direct quotes, paraphrases, figures, etc.). Failure to do so constitutes plagiarism, which is illegal, unethical, <u>always recognizable</u>, and a guaranteed way to fail a paper. The definition of plagiarism is "to steal and use (the writings or ideas of another) as one's own."

*[Reflects school's academic integrity policy]*

**Week 4**
2/1      <u>The Concise Opinion.</u>
         HW: Complete paper #1 Rough Draft (5–7 pages double-spaced)

2/3      How Professionals Argue
         HW: <u>Read Jenkins Essay (p 501 of *Good Reasons) and</u> Rafferty
         <u>Essay (p 525)</u>; compare argumentative style, assess and explain
         efficacy of arguments.

**Week 5**
2/15     Developing an Argument
         *Essay Quiz* on Jenkins and Rafferty Essays
         HW: Chap 5 of *Good Reasons;* based on components of a definition of
         argument, write a brief explanation of how your argument might fit into
         this type.

2/17     Library Workday: Meet in Room 292
         PAPER #1 DUE

*[Topics of that day's class meeting]*

*[Notice of due date for paper draft]*

*[Notice of reading assignments to complete]*

*[Notice of quiz]*

*[Notice of final due date for paper]*

---

*Source:* Jennifer Gessner, Community College of Denver.

Low self-esteem and fear can stall your motivation. Here are some ideas about how to overcome these roadblocks and keep moving ahead.

## Build Self-Esteem

When people have faith in themselves, their self-esteem fuels their motivation to succeed. Belief, though, is only half the game. The other half is the action and effort that help you feel that you have earned your self-esteem, as basketball coach Rick Pitino explains: "Self-esteem is directly linked to deserving success. If you have established a great work ethic and have begun the discipline that is inherent with that, you will automatically begin to feel better about yourself."[10]

Although thinking positively sets the tone for success, taking action gets you there. In order to get moving in a positive direction, create personal guidelines that support your success—for example, "I turn in assignments on deadline." Then, follow up your guideline with the action you've promised to take—in this case, always turning in your assignments on time.

## Face Your Fears

Everyone experiences fear. Anything unknown—starting college, meeting new people, encountering new challenges—can be frightening. The following steps will help you work through fear with courage and reignite your motivation to succeed:

1. *Acknowledge fears.* Naming your fear begins to lessen its hold on you. Be specific.

2. *Examine fears.* Sometimes one fear hides a larger one. Do you fear a test, or the fact that if you pass it you will have to take a tougher class next?

3. *Develop and implement a plan.* Come up with ways to overcome your fear, and put them to work. For example, if reading a play by William Shakespeare intimidates you, you might ask an instructor for advice, rent a film adaptation, or listen to an audio version on your iPod.

# Practice Academic Integrity

Having academic integrity means valuing education and learning over grades. Academic integrity promotes learning and ensures a quality education based on *ethics* (your sense of what is right to do) and hard work. Read your school's code of honor, or academic integrity policy, in your student handbook. When you enrolled, you agreed to abide by it.

## What Academic Integrity Is

The Center for Academic Integrity, part of the Kenan Institute for Ethics at Duke University, defines academic integrity as a commitment to five fundamental values:[11]

- *Honesty.* Honesty defines the pursuit of knowledge and implies a search for truth in your classwork, papers and lab reports, and teamwork with other students.

**Successful Intelligence Connections Online**

Listen to author Sarah Kravits describe how to use analytical, creative, and practical intelligence to build and sustain motivation.

Go to the *Keys to Success* Companion Website at www.prenhall.com/carter to listen or download as a podcast.

SELF-ESTEEM
Belief in one's value as a person that builds as you achieve your goals.

ACADEMIC INTEGRITY
Following a code of moral values, prizing honesty and fairness in all aspects of academic life—classes, assignments, tests, papers, projects, and relationships with students and faculty.

- *Trust.* Trust means being true to your word. Mutual trust—between instructor and student, as well as among students—makes possible the exchange of ideas that is essential for learning.
- *Fairness.* Instructors must create a fair academic environment where students are judged against clear standards and in which procedures are well defined.
- *Respect.* In a respectful academic environment, both students and instructors accept and honor a wide range of opinions, even if the opinions are contrary to core beliefs.
- *Responsibility.* You are responsible for making choices that will provide you with the best education—choices that reflect fairness and honesty.

Unfortunately, the principles of academic integrity are frequently violated on college campuses. In a recent survey, three of four college students admitted to cheating at least once during their undergraduate careers.[12] Violations of academic integrity—turning in previously submitted work, using unauthorized devices during an exam, providing unethical aid to another student, or downloading passages or whole papers from the Internet—aren't worth the price. Consequences of violations vary from school to school and include participation in academic integrity seminars, grade reduction or course failure, suspension, or expulsion.

### Why Academic Integrity Is Worth It

Choosing to act with integrity has the following positive effects:

- *Increased self-esteem.* Self-esteem is tied to respectful and honorable action.
- *Acquired knowledge.* Honest work is more likely to result in knowledge that lasts.
- *Effective behavioral patterns.* When you play fair now, you set a positive pattern.
- *Mutual respect.* Respecting the work of others will encourage others to respect your work.

The risk to students who violate standards of integrity is growing because cheating is now easier to discover. Make a commitment to uphold the highest standards of academic integrity. See chapter 8 for more specifics on avoiding plagiarism when you write and the *Get Focused!* segment on page 275 for a personal inquiry into your own academic ethics.

## Learn from Failure and Celebrate Success

Even the most successful people make mistakes and experience failures. In fact, failure is one of the greatest teachers. Failure provides an opportunity to realize what you didn't know so that you can improve.

## Learning from Failure

Learning from your failures and mistakes involves careful thinking.

**Analyze what happened.** For example, imagine that after a long night of studying for a chemistry test, you forgot to complete an American history paper due the next day. Your focus on the test caused you to overlook other tasks. Now you may face a lower grade on your paper if you turn it in late, plus you may be inclined to rush it and turn in a product that isn't as good as it could be.

**Come up with creative ways to improve the situation and change for the future.** In the present, you can request an appointment with the instructor to discuss the paper. For the future, you can make a commitment to note deadlines in a bright color in your planner and to check due dates more often.

**Put your plan into action.** Do what you have decided to do—and keep an eye on how it is working. Talk with the instructor and see if you can hand in your paper late. If you decide to be better about noting deadlines, in the future you might work backwards from your paper due date, setting dates for individual tasks related to the paper and planning to have it done two days before it is due in order to have time for last-minute corrections.

Sometimes, however, you can't get motivated to turn things around. Here are some ways to boost your outlook when failure gets you down:

- Believe you are a capable person. Focus on your strengths and know you can try again.

- Share your disappointment with others. Blow off steam and exchange creative ideas that can help you learn from what happened.

- Look on the bright side. At worst, you got a lower grade because your paper was late. At best, you learned lessons that will help you avoid the same mistake in the future.

Your value as a human being does not diminish when you make a mistake. People who can manage failure demonstrate to themselves and others that they have the courage to take risks and learn. Employers often value risk takers more than people who always play it safe.

## Celebrating Success

Take a moment to acknowledge what you accomplish, whether it is a good grade, a job offer, or any personal victory. Let your success fuel your confidence that you can do it again. Don't forget to reward yourself when you succeed. Take the kind of break you like best—see a movie, socialize with some friends, read a book for fun, declare a no-work day. Enjoy what college has to offer outside of the classroom.

Finally, being a motivated, responsible, ethical, and committed student is no easy feat. Don't hesitate to reach out for support throughout your college experience.

# Assess Yourself as a Creative Thinker

For each statement, circle the number that feels right to you, from 1 for "not at all true for me" to 5 for "very true for me."

| | | |
|---|---|---|
| 1. | I tend to question rules and regulations. | 1 2 3 4 5 |
| 2. | I see myself as "unique," "full of ideas," "innovative." | 1 2 3 4 5 |
| 3. | When working on a problem in a group setting, I generate a lot of ideas. | 1 2 3 4 5 |
| 4. | I am energized when I have a brand-new experience. | 1 2 3 4 5 |
| 5. | If you say something is too risky, I'm ready to give it a shot. | 1 2 3 4 5 |
| 6. | I often wonder if there is a different way to do or see something. | 1 2 3 4 5 |
| 7. | Too much routine in my work or schedule drains my energy. | 1 2 3 4 5 |
| 8. | I tend to see connections among ideas that others do not. | 1 2 3 4 5 |
| 9. | I feel comfortable allowing myself to make mistakes as I test out ideas. | 1 2 3 4 5 |
| 10. | I'm willing to champion an idea even when others disagree with me. | 1 2 3 4 5 |

Total your answers here: _____

If your total ranges from 38–50, you consider your creative thinking skills to be *strong*.

If your total ranges from 24–37, you consider your creative thinking skills to be *average*.

If your total ranges from 10–23, you consider your creative thinking skills to be *weak*.

*Remember that you can improve your creative thinking skill with focus and practice.*

# How Can You Work Effectively with Others?

A century ago it was possible to live an entire lifetime surrounded only by people from your own culture. Not so today. American society consists of people from a multitude of countries and cultural backgrounds. In fact, in the 2000 census, American citizens described themselves in terms of 63 different racial categories, compared with only 5 in 1990.[13] Cable television, the Internet, and the global marketplace add to our growing cultural awareness, linking people from all over the world in ways that were unimaginable less than a decade ago.

Your success at school and at work will depend on your ability to cooperate with diverse people in a team setting. Valuing diversity and knowing how to work in groups are two keys to developing this ability.

## Value Diversity

What does *diversity* mean?

**Diversity means differences among people.** On an interpersonal level, diversity refers to the differences between ourselves and others, between the groups we belong to and the groups we are not part of. Differences in gender, skin color, ethnicity and national origin, age, physical characteristics and abilities, and sexual orientation are most obvious in this level of diversity. Differences in cultural and religious beliefs and practices, education, socioeconomic status, family background, and marital and parental status are less visible but no less significant in how they define people and affect relationships.

In college you are likely to meet classmates and instructors who reflect America's growing diversity, including people in the following demographic groups:

- Biracial or multiracial individuals
- People from families with more than one religious tradition
- Non-native English speakers who may have emigrated from outside the United States
- People older than "traditional" 18- to 22-year-old students
- Persons living with various kinds of disabilities
- Persons practicing different lifestyles—often expressed in the way they dress, their interests, their sexual orientation, or their leisure activities

Being able to appreciate and adjust to differences among people is crucial to your success at school and prepares you for success in life. Former University of Michigan student Fiona Rose describes the benefits of a positive approach to diversity this way:

> My years at U-M have been enhanced by relationships with men and women from all cultures, classes, races, and ethnicities. Such interactions are essential to an education. While courses teach us the history and academic value of diversity, friendships prepare us to survive and

thrive in our global community. Good institutions consider not only what a potential student will gain from classes and course work, but what he or she will bring to the campus community.[14]

**Diversity refers to the differences within people.** Another layer of diversity lies within each person. Among the factors that define this layer are personality traits, learning style, strengths and weaknesses, and natural talents and interests. No one else has been or will ever be exactly like you.

Chapter 9 will go into more detail about diversity and communication. Other chapters will focus on less visible aspects of diversity: In chapter 3, you will gain a greater understanding of your own and others' different ways of learning, and in chapter 4 you will explore differences in analytical, creative, and practical abilities.

## Develop Emotional and Social Intelligence

EMOTIONAL
INTELLIGENCE
The ability to perceive, assess, and manage one's own emotions as well as understand the emotions of others.

SOCIAL
INTELLIGENCE
Having an understanding of the complexity of social interaction and using that understanding to manage relationships effectively.

Successful relationships in a diverse world depend on competencies that go beyond intellectual and career skills. All relationships depend on what psychologist Daniel Goleman calls emotional intelligence and social intelligence.

### Emotional Intelligence

Your emotional intelligence quotient (EQ) is a set of competencies that involves knowing yourself, mastering your feelings, and understanding how to manage those feelings when interacting with others.[15] Goleman divides these competencies into two categories (see Key 1.4):[16]

- *Personal competence:* How you manage yourself—your self-awareness, self-regulation, and motivation
- *Social competence:* How you handle relationships with others, including awareness of the needs and feelings of others and ability to encourage others to do things

### Social Intelligence

When someone close to you is happy, sad, or fearful, you probably tend to experience some of the same feelings out of concern or friendship. New research shows that the human brain is hardwired to connect with other brains around it. On an MRI brain scan, the area of your friend's brain that lights up during an emotional experience also lights up in your brain as you "share" the emotion. Your nervous system has what are called "mirror neurons" that mimic an observed emotion, allowing you to "participate" in the feeling even though you did not originate it. These capacities of your nervous system are involved in social intelligence.

Goleman defines *social intelligence* as a combination of two key categories: "social awareness, what we sense about others—and social facility, what we then do with that awareness" (see Key 1.5).[17]

- *Social awareness* ranges from just sensing other peoples' emotions on a basic level to actively working to understand how other people feel. It also includes knowledge of how the social world works (with different understandings for different settings). Active, attuned listening is a key component.

**KEY 1.4** Become more emotionally intelligent by developing these qualities.

| PERSONAL COMPETENCE | SOCIAL COMPETENCE |
|---|---|
| **Self-Awareness** | **Social Awareness** |
| • I know my emotions and how they affect me.<br>• I understand my strengths and my limits.<br>• I am confident in my abilities.<br>• I am open to improvement. | • I sense the feelings and perspectives of others.<br>• I help others improve themselves.<br>• I know how to relate to people from different cultures.<br>• I can sense how to serve the needs of others. |
| **Self-Management** | **Social Skills** |
| • I can control my emotions and impulses.<br>• I can delay gratification when there is something more important to be gained.<br>• I am trustworthy.<br>• I can adapt to change and new ideas.<br>• I persist toward my goals despite obstacles. | • I know how to work in a team.<br>• I can inspire people to act.<br>• I understand how to lead a group.<br>• I know how to persuade people.<br>• I can make positive change happen. |

*Source:* Based on Daniel Goleman, *Working with Emotional Intelligence*, New York: Bantam Books, 1998, pp. 26–27.

- *Social facility* is the active and most practical component, where you put your social awareness to work to achieve a goal. It involves smooth nonverbal interaction, presenting yourself in ways appropriate to individual situations, actively shaping the course of social interactions, and acting on your sense of what others need.

Emotional and social intelligence influence your ability to communicate and maneuver in social environments and achieve your goals. You will see more about these topics in chapter 4, chapter 11, and throughout the text.

## Know How to Work with Others in Groups

A real-world application of diversity in action is likely to occur in the study group setting. Students taking the same course may form a study group that meets one or more times a week or right before exams. Instructors sometimes initiate student study groups, commonly for math or science courses, known as *peer-assisted study sessions* or *supplemental instruction.*

Don't wait until crunch time to benefit from studying with others. As you begin to get to know students in your classes, start now to exchange phone numbers and e-mails, form groups, and schedule meetings. When you study with one or more people, you will gain benefits like these:

- *Shared and solidified knowledge.* When students share their knowledge with one another in a group, the effort takes less time and energy than

KEY 1.5

# Become more socially intelligent through awareness and action.

| Social Awareness | Social Facility |
|---|---|
| I sense nonverbal signals about how others are feeling. | My nonverbal body language is appropriate to the situation and communicates what I am feeling. |
| I listen fully and tune in carefully to others. | Considering what I hear and sense from others, I present myself verbally and physically in ways that make a desired impression. |
| I make an effort to understand what others feel, think, and intend. | I put my understanding of others to work by using tact and self-control to shape the outcome of my interactions. |
| I have a sense of how the social world works, how people interact with one another. | I use my sense of the social world to note when people need support and to help them in appropriate and needed ways. |

*Source:* Based on Daniel Goleman, *Social Intelligence: The New Science of Human Relationships*, New York: Bantam Books, 2006, p. 84.

when students learn all of the material alone. Furthermore, when you discuss concepts or teach them to others, you solidify what you know and strengthen your critical thinking.

- *Increased motivation.* Knowing that you are accountable to others and that they will see your level of work and preparation, you may be more motivated to work hard.

- *Increased teamwork ability.* The more you understand the dynamics of working with a group and the more experience you have with teamwork, the more your interpersonal skills will grow.

- *Increased awareness and understanding of diversity.* Teams gain strength from the intellectual diversity of their members. When you work with others, you are bound to come up with ideas and solutions you never would have thought of on your own.

## Strategies for Study Group Success

Every study group is unique. The way a group operates depends on members' personalities, the subject you study, the location of the group, and the size of the

Having a sense of how to relate to others—in other words, drawing on your social intelligence—promotes positive and productive relationships on campus.

group. No matter what your particular group's situation, though, a few general strategies apply.

**Set long-term and short-term goals.** At your first meeting, determine what the group wants to accomplish. At the start of each meeting, have one person compile a list of questions to address.

**Determine a regular schedule and leadership rotation.** Determine what your group needs and what the members' schedules can handle. Try to meet weekly or, at the least, every other week. Rotating the leadership among members willing to lead helps all members take ownership of the results.

**Create study materials for one another and help one another learn.** Give each group member the task of finding a piece of information to compile, photocopy, and review for the other group members. Have group members teach pieces of information, make up quizzes for each other, or go through flash cards together.

**Share the workload and pool your note-taking resources.** The most important factor is a willingness to work, not knowlege level. Compare notes with group members and fill in information you don't have. Try different note-taking styles (see chapter 6 for a discussion of note taking).

**Know how to be an effective leader.** As a leader, you need a broad perspective that allows you to envision how different aspects of a project will come together. You must define projects, assign work, and set schedules. You also set meeting and project agendas, focus the group, keep people moving ahead, set a positive tone, and evaluate results.

**Know how to be an effective participant.** Participants are "part owners" of the team process with a responsibility for, and a stake in, the outcome. Let people know your ideas and your opinions about decisions. Be organized and willing to discuss. Fulfill the tasks you promise to do.

As you think about your tools and how you plan to use them to achieve your goals, you may be a bit uneasy about the road ahead and its inevitable stumbling blocks. You can give yourself the best possible chance to succeed if you remind yourself of the connection between your work in school and your ability to achieve goals in your life beyond graduation.

# How Can the Things You Learn Now Promote Life Success?

In his book *Techno Trends—24 Technologies That Will Revolutionize Our Lives*, futurist Daniel Burns describes a tomorrow that is linked to continuing education: "The future belongs to those who are capable of being retrained again and again," he says. "Think of it as periodically upgrading your human assets throughout your career. . . . Humans are infinitely upgradeable, but it does require an investment" in lifelong learning.[18]

The vast majority of Americans see lifelong learning as important in their own lives. In a survey of workers aged 18 to 24, conducted by the AFL-CIO, the country's leading labor union, 85% of respondents viewed education and

# get practical!

# Assess Yourself as a Practical Thinker

For each statement, circle the number that feels right to you, from 1 for "not at all true for me" to 5 for "very true for me."

1. I can find a way around any obstacle.     1 2 3 4 5

2. I see myself as a "doer," the "go-to" person; I "make things happen."     1 2 3 4 5

3. When working on a problem in a group setting, I like to figure out who will do what and when it should be done.     1 2 3 4 5

4. Because I learn well from experience, I don't tend to repeat a mistake.     1 2 3 4 5

5. I finish what I start and don't leave loose ends hanging.     1 2 3 4 5

6. I pay attention to my emotions in academic and social situations to see if they help or hurt me as I move toward a goal.     1 2 3 4 5

7. I can sense how people feel, and can use that knowledge to interact with others effectively in order to achieve a goal.     1 2 3 4 5

8. I manage my time effectively.     1 2 3 4 5

9. I find ways to adjust to the teaching styles of my instructors and the communication styles of my peers.     1 2 3 4 5

10. When involved in a problem-solving process, I can shift gears as needed.     1 2 3 4 5

Total your answers here: _____

If your total ranges from 38–50, you consider your practical thinking skills to be *strong*.

If your total ranges from 24–37, you consider your practical thinking skills to be *average*.

If your total ranges from 10–23, you consider your practical thinking skills to be *weak*.

*Remember that you can improve your practical thinking skill with focus and practice.*

training as the nation's top economic priority, and 9 out of 10 believed that the key to career advancement is ongoing education and training.[19]

In other words, you will need to continue to learn and grow in order to succeed. As a college student, you are making sacrifices—including a significant investment of time and money as well as a dramatic lifestyle change—to achieve success throughout your life. You are building the analytical, creative, and practical intelligence you need to cope with a changing world:

- *Knowledge in nearly every field is doubling every two to three years.* That means that if you stop learning, for even a few years, your knowledge base will be inadequate to keep up with the changes in your career.

- *Technology is changing how you live and work.* The Internet and technology will shape communications and improve knowledge and productivity during the next 20 years—and will require continual learning.

- *The global economy is moving from a product and service base to a knowledge and talent base.* Jobs of the past are being replaced by knowledge-based jobs, in the United States and abroad, that ask workers to think critically to come up with solutions.

- *Workers are changing jobs and careers more frequently.* The National Research Bureau reports that currently the average employee changes jobs every three to four years, and it is estimated that a 22-year-old college graduate in the year 2000 will have an average of eight employers in his or her first 10 years in the workplace.[20] Every time you decide to start a new career, you need new knowledge and skills.

All of these signs point to the need to become (lifelong learners). Through successful intelligence, you will maintain the kind of flexibility that will enable you to adapt to the demands of the global marketplace. If you analyze what is happening, come up with creative approaches for handling it, and make a practical plan to put your ideas into motion, you can stay on track toward your goals. Or, you may decide to shift direction toward a new goal that never occurred to you before the change. Facing change means taking risks.

**LIFELONG LEARNERS**
Individuals who continue to build knowledge and skills as a mechanism for improving their lives and careers.

# Successful Intelligence Wrap-Up

You have the power to engage your successful intelligence to pursue goals that are most important to you. Although college presents challenges and risks to everyone, persistent and motivated learners can manage them effectively. Here's how you have built skills in chapter 1:

## Analytical

By completing the three self-assessments, you analyzed where you are now in analytical, creative, and practical intelligence. At the beginning and end of the chapter, you explored how learning—in college and throughout life—can promote success. In learning about the theory of successful intelligence, you considered how it can enable you to reach important goals.

### Creative

Reading about the global marketplace may have inspired new ideas of what you want out of college. Thinking about the three parts of successful intelligence helped to provide a new perspective of your potential as a student. Exploring strategies about learning from failure, working with others in a team, and facing fears may have helped you see connections among these topics that you didn't see before.

### Practical

You examined specific practical actions that are the building blocks of college success: how to work with academic integrity, fulfill day-to-day academic responsibilities, stay motivated, and learn from failure. You also investigated emotional and social intelligence, two highly practical skills that allow you to work effectively with others. Finally, you considered specific, practical actions to take when working in a project team or study group.

# *Egyszer volt budán kutyavásár*

## *(edge-zehr volt bu-darn ku-tcho-vah-shahr)*

This unusual Hungarian phrase, translated literally, means "There was a dog-market in Buda only once." In modern English, you would interpret this to be a favorable opportunity that comes along only once—something that you should grasp with both hands, lest you regret not taking advantage of it later.[21]

For you, this opportunity has arrived. Make the most of all your college has to offer, and gather learning skills that you will use throughout your life. By taking the initiative to use your time well, you can build the successful intelligence that will help you realize your dreams.

"There is no elevator to success. You have to take the stairs."

UNKNOWN

  KEYS TO SUCCESS

# SUCCESSFUL INTELLIGENCE

*Think, Create, Apply*

**Activate yourself.** Robert Sternberg found that successfully intelligent people, despite differences in thinking and personal goals, have 20 particular characteristics in common. He calls these characteristics *self-activators*—things that get you moving and keep you going.[22]

**Step 1. Think it through:** *Analyze where you are now.* Use this self-assessment to see how developed you perceive your self-activators to be *right now*.

| 1 | 2 | 3 | 4 | 5 |
|---|---|---|---|---|
| Not at All Like Me | Somewhat Unlike Me | Not Sure | Somewhat Like Me | Definitely Like Me |

Please circle the number that best represents your answer:

1. I motivate myself well.                                        1 2 3 4 5
2. I can control my impulses.                                     1 2 3 4 5
3. I know when to persevere and when to change gears.            1 2 3 4 5
4. I make the most of what I do well.                            1 2 3 4 5
5. I can successfully translate my ideas into action.           1 2 3 4 5
6. I can focus effectively on my goal.                           1 2 3 4 5
7. I complete tasks and have good follow-through.               1 2 3 4 5
8. I initiate action—I move people and projects ahead.         1 2 3 4 5
9. I have the courage to risk failure.                          1 2 3 4 5
10. I avoid procrastination.                                     1 2 3 4 5
11. I accept responsibility when I make a mistake.              1 2 3 4 5
12. I don't waste time feeling sorry for myself.                1 2 3 4 5

13. I independently take responsibility for tasks.              1 2 3 4 5

14. I work hard to overcome personal difficulties.              1 2 3 4 5

15. I create an environment that helps me to concentrate
    on my goals.                                                1 2 3 4 5

16. I don't take on too much work or too little.                1 2 3 4 5

17. I can delay gratification in order to receive the benefits. 1 2 3 4 5

18. I can see both the big picture and the details in
    a situation.                                                1 2 3 4 5

19. I am able to maintain confidence in myself.                 1 2 3 4 5

20. I can balance my analytical, creative, and practical
    thinking skills.                                            1 2 3 4 5

**Step 2. Think out of the box:** *Brainstorm over time.* Looking at the self-assessment, choose five self-activators that you most want to develop throughout the term. Then, pretend you are an instructor recommending yourself for a scholarship or a job. Write yourself a short e-mail about how strong you are in the areas of those five self-activators. Save the e-mail as a reminder of what you would like such a person to be able to truly say about you.

**Step 3. Make it happen:** *Prepare yourself for action.* Let this self-assessment direct your decisions about how you approach the material in this course. If you wish to procrastinate less, for example, pay special attention to the time-management information in chapter 2. To jump-start your focus, look at the self-assessment again and circle or highlight the five self-activators that you most want to concentrate on at this point.

In the last chapter of this book you will revisit this self-assessment and get more specific about actions you have taken, and plan to take, to promote personal growth.

# TEAMWORK

## *Create Solutions Together*

**Motivators.** Gather in a group of three to five. Together, brainstorm motivation blockers—situations or things that most often kill your motivation to succeed in school. When you have as many problems as you have group members, each person should choose one problem and write it at the top of a blank sheet of paper.

Look at the motivation blocker on your page. Under it, write one practical idea you have about how to overcome it. When everyone is finished, pass the pages to the person on the left. Then write an idea about the new blocker at the top of the page you've received. If you can't think of anything, pass the page as is. Continue this way until your page comes back to you. Then discuss the ideas as a group, analyzing which ideas might work better than others. Add other ideas to the lists if you think of them.

The last step: On your own, keeping in mind your group discussion, list three specific actions that you commit to taking in order to keep motivation high when the going gets rough.

1. _____

2. _____

3. _____

# WRITING

## Journal and Put Skills to Work

*Record your thoughts on a separate piece of paper, in a journal, or on a computer file.*

**Journal entry: Reasons for college.** Think about why you are here. Why did you decide to attend college, and what do you want out of the experience? What sacrifices—in terms of time, hard work, finances—are you willing to make in your quest for success?

**Real-life writing: Initial impressions.** Although you have not been in school for long, you already have some sense of your instructors, their style, and how classes are likely to proceed. Compare and contrast your initial impressions of two of your instructors and the courses they teach. Discuss teaching style, course expectations, degree of difficulty, how the classroom is run, and any other factor that is significant to you. Finally, note any changes you think you should make—in your in-class or study approach—based on these impressions.

# PERSONAL PORTFOLIO

## Prepare for Career Success

*This is the first of 12 portfolio assignments you will complete, one for each chapter. By the end of the term, you will have built skills that promote success in pursuing any career as you compile a portfolio of documents that will help you achieve career goals.*

*Type your work and store the documents electronically in one file folder. Use loose paper for assignments that ask you to draw or make collages.*

**Setting career goals.** Whether you have a current career, have held a few different jobs, or have not yet entered the workplace, college is an ideal time to take stock of your career goals. The earlier in your college education that you consider career goals, the more you can take advantage of how college can help prepare you for work, in both job-specific and general ways. Having a strong vision of where you wish to go will also be a powerful motivator as you face some of the inevitable challenges of the next few years.

Take some time to think about your working life. Spend 15 minutes brainstorming everything that you wish you could be, do, have, or experience in your career 10 years from now—the skills you want to have, money you want to earn, benefits, experiences, travel, anything you can think of. List your wishes, draw them, depict them using cutouts from magazines, or combine these ideas—whatever you like best.

Now, look at your list. To discover how your wishes relate to one another, group them in order of priority. Label three computer pages or three pieces of paper Priority 1, Priority 2, and Priority 3. Write each wish where it fits, with Priority 1 being the most important, Priority 2 the second most important, and Priority 3 the third.

Look at your priority lists. What do they tell you about what is most important to you? What wishes are you ready to work toward right now? Circle or highlight the three highest-priority wishes (they will most likely appear on your Priority 1 page). Write down the trade-offs you may have to make today to make these wishes come true. Don't let yourself off the hook—be realistic and direct. You may want to look back at these materials at the end of the term to see what changes may have taken place in your priorities.

## Suggested Readings

Friedman, Thomas L. *The World Is Flat: A Brief History of the Twenty-first Century.* New York: Farrar, Straus & Giroux, 2006.

Jeffers, Susan. *Feel the Fear . . . and Do It Anyway.* New York: Ballantine Books, 2006.

Kadar, Andrew. *College Life 102: The No-Bull Guide to a Great Freshman Year.* Lincoln, NE: iUniverse, 2006.

Newport, Cal. *How to Win at College: Surprising Secrets for Success from the Country's Top Students.* New York: Broadway Books, 2005.

Simon, Linda. *New Beginnings: A Reference Guide for Adult Learners*, 3rd ed. Upper Saddle River, NJ: Prentice Hall, 2005.

Sternberg, Robert. *Successful Intelligence: How Practical and Creative Intelligence Determine Success in Life.* New York: Plume, 1997.

Students Helping Students. *Navigating Your Freshman Year: How to Make the Leap to College Life.* New York: Penguin, 2005.

Tyler, Suzette. *Been There, Should've Done That II: More Tips for Making the Most of College.* Lansing, MI: Front Porch Press, 2001.

## Internet and Podcast Resources

The Center for Academic Integrity: www.academicintegrity.org

Motivation on the Run podcasts: http://podcasts.yahoo.com/series?s=ed9231d7be13524016aeb51d5f40e2d1

NPR, "For Workers, 'The World Is Flat,'" April 14, 2005, broadcast of *Fresh Air from WHYY*: www.npr.org/templates/story/story.php?storyId=4600258

Student.Com—The Student Center: www.student.com

StudentNow—College Life, Fun, & Resources: www.studentnow.com

Prentice Hall Student Success SuperSite: www.prenhall.com/success

Success Stories: www.prenhall.com/success/Stories/index.html

Check your college Web site for podcasts produced by your school.

# Endnotes

[1] Thomas Friedman, *The World Is Flat*, New York: Farrar, Straus & Giroux, 2006, p. 8.

[2] Robert J. Sternberg, *Successful Intelligence: How Practical and Creative Intelligence Determine Success in Life*, New York: Plume, 1997, p. 11.

[3] Lawrence F. Lowery, *"The Biological Basis of Thinking and Learning,"* 1998, Full Option Science System, University of California at Berkeley (http://lhsfoss.org/newsletters/archive/pdfs/FOSS_BBTL.pdf).

[4] Carol Dweck, *Mindset: The New Psychology of Success*, New York: Random House, 2006, p. 22.

[5] Sternberg, *Successful Intelligence*, p. 12.

[6] Ibid., p. 127.

[7] Ibid., pp. 127–128.

[8] "Are the Classes Really That Much Harder Than High School?" New Mexico State University, June 1999 (https://www.nmsu.edu/aggieland/students/faq_classes.html).

[9] From student essay submitted by the First Year Experience students of Patty Parma, Palo Alto College, San Antonio, Texas, January 2004.

[10] Rick Pitino, *Success Is a Choice*, New York: Broadway Books, 1997, p. 40.

[11] *The Fundamental Values of Academic Integrity*, Center for Academic Integrity, Kenan Institute for Ethics, Duke University, October 1999 (www.academicintegrity.org/fundamental.asp).

[12] From "Facts About Plagiarism," 2007, Plagiarism.org (www.plagiarism.org/facts.html).

[13] "For 7 Million, One Census Race Category Wasn't Enough," *New York Times*, March 13, 2001, pp. A1, A14.

[14] Media Watch, *Diversity Digest*, Fall 1997 (www.diversityweb.org/Digest/F97/mediawatch.html#top).

[15] Daniel Goleman, *Emotional Intelligence: Why It Can Matter More Than IQ*, New York: Bantam Books, 1995.

[16] Daniel Goleman, *Working with Emotional Intelligence*, New York: Bantam Books, 1998, pp. 26–27.

[17] Quote and material for the following section are from Daniel Goleman, *Social Intelligence: The New Science of Human Relationships*, New York: Bantam Books, 2006, pp. 84–97.

[18] Cited in Colin Rise and Malcolm J. Nicholl, *Accelerated Learning for the 21st Century*, New York: Dell, 1997, pp. 5–6.

[19] Study cited in Susan Rosenblum, "Young Workers Name Lifelong Learning as Top Need for Economy of Future," *Nation's Cities Weekly*, September 6, 1999, p. 1.

[20] Jay Palmer, "Marry Me a Little," *Barron's*, July 24, 2000, p. 25.

[21] Christopher J. Moore, *In Other Words: A Language Lover's Guide to the Most Intriguing Words Around the World*, New York: Walker, 2004, p. 43.

[22] List and descriptions based on Sternberg, *Successful Intelligence*, pp. 251–269.

**VALUES, GOALS, AND TIME**

*Managing Yourself*

2

*"Successfully intelligent people are well aware of the penalties for procrastination. They schedule their time so that the important things get done—and done well."*

ROBERT STERNBERG

**T**his chapter divides the indispensable skill of self-management into three parts: using values to guide your goal setting, working through a process to achieve goals, and managing time in a way that propels you toward your goals and helps you manage stress. It also provides ideas about how to think through the important goal of choosing a major or concentration. Your ability to manage yourself will help you cope with what you encounter, achieve your goals, and build skills that fuel your success now and in the future.

*In this chapter you explore answers to the following questions:*

| Analytical | Creative | Practical |
|---|---|---|
| • Examining values<br>• Analyzing how you manage time<br>• Considering what goals are most important to you | • Developing ideas for how to reach a goal<br>• Creating ways to avoid procrastination<br>• Brainstorming what majors interest you | • How to set effective goals<br>• How to achieve a goal<br>• How to manage a schedule |

# Why Is It Important to Know What You Value?

VALUES

Principles or qualitites that you consider important.

You make life choices—what to do, what to believe, what to buy, how to act—based on your personal values. Your choice to pursue a degree, for example, reflects that you value the personal and professional growth that come from a college education. Being on time for your classes shows that you value punctuality. Paying bills regularly and on time shows that you value financial stability.

Values play a key role in your drive to achieve important goals, because they help you to do the following:

- *Understand what you want out of life.* Your most meaningful goals should reflect what you value most.
- *Build "rules for life."* Your values form the foundation for your decisions and behavior. You will return repeatedly to them for guidance, especially in unfamiliar territory.
- *Find people who inspire you.* Spending time with people who share similar values will help you clarify how you want to live and find support for your goals.

Your value system is complex, built piece by piece over time. Many forces affect your values—family, friends, culture, media, school, work, neighborhood, religious beliefs, world events. No matter how powerful these external influences may be, however, it is your decision whether or not to adopt a value. Making this decision involves answering questions like the following to evaluate whether a given value is right for you:

- Where did the value come from?
- What other different values could I consider?

# REAL QUESTIONS

## How can I choose a major that is right for me?

I've just started college and my school requires that all students choose a major right away, as entering freshmen. I know this is a very important decision because it could chart the direction of the rest of my life, so I want to make sure I find what's right for me.

I've always loved being outdoors, reading, and learning other languages—and I think I would make a great teacher, but I want to do more than just teach. I see myself going toward humanitarian aid or international affairs, and then later going back to school to get an advanced degree and become a professor some day. What kind of major should I look for that will make me a marketable candidate for a fulfilling and challenging career?

Courtney Mellblom
California Polytechnic
State University
San Luis Obispo,
California

# PRACTICAL ANSWERS

Antoine Pickett
Resident Engineer,
Federal Aviation
Administration
Aurora Air Traffic
Control Center,
Aurora, Illinois

## Explore the possibilities carefully and follow your heart.

Many college freshmen ask this type of question. It is not an easy decision to make at such a young age. Fortunately, you seem to have a sense of what direction you want to move in. Although many people go for the quick or big bucks, the most marketable candidate for a job is one who shows a great interest and desire in what they have studied. If you follow your heart in your studies you will not go wrong.

First, I suggest that you find out more about courses that could help you explore your interest in the international arena. In fact, you could consider a major that would allow you to focus on your humanitarian interests, such as international affairs or international relations. Becoming proficient in a foreign language would also tend to make you more marketable.

Second, work backwards. Examine potential careers in the area of international affairs, talk to people who have international experience, and from there try to gain work or intern experience while you are in college to see if it truly interests you. Your proactive research should inform your decision about what major to choose.

If your eventual goal is to become a college professor, many colleges require graduate and doctoral work but do not require a teaching certificate. Later, if you decide you don't want to become a professor, you can still pursue a certificate. Your experience in the working world will make you a better teacher. As someone once said, "The error of youth is to believe that intelligence is a substitute for experience, while the error of age is to believe that experience is a substitute for intelligence." Any experience you gain will help you learn and grow.

---

- What might happen as a result of adopting this value?
- Have I made a personal commitment to this choice? Have I told others about it?
- Do my life goals and day-to-day actions reflect this value?

Your values often shift to fit new circumstances as you grow. For example, a student who benefits from the support of friends and family while recovering from an auto accident may place greater value on relationships than he did before.

## How Values Affect Your Educational Experience

The fact that you are here in college means that you value education. Making education a priority is a practical choice that will help you do the following:

- *Keep going when the going gets tough.* "Success takes much hard work and dedication," says a student at Palo Alto College. "Since I have a hard time with writing, and I can't understand algebra, I've made a commitment to write in a journal every day and attend math tutoring at least three times a week."[1]

- *Choose your major and a career direction.* If you've always been an environmentalist, then you may choose to specialize in environmental science. If you feel fulfilled when you help people, then you might consider a career in social work.

- *Choose friends and activities that enrich your life.* Having friends who share your desire to succeed in school will increase your motivation and reduce your stress. Joining organizations whose activities reflect your values will broaden your educational experience.

- *Choose what you want to get out of school.* What kinds of skills and knowledge do you wish to build? Are you focused on building the foundation for a successful career? Your values will help you determine what you are willing to do to achieve academic goals.

## Values and Cultural Diversity

At college, you may meet people who seem different in unexpected ways. Unfamiliar attitudes and behaviors are rooted in unique cultures. A *culture* is a unique set of values, behaviors, tastes, knowledge, attitudes, and habits shared by a specific group of people.

Cultural misunderstandings can interfere with relationships. As someone who accepts and appreciates diversity, your goal is to develop cultural competence.[2] Chapter 9 will go into more detail about how to be a culturally competent communicator.

CULTURAL COMPETENCE

*The ability to understand and appreciate differences and to respond to people of all cultures in a way that values their worth, respects their beliefs and practices, and builds communication and relationships.*

As you continue to read *Keys to Success*, think of the wisdom of cultural diversity consultant Helen Turnbull on turning differences into strengths:

We must suspend our judgment. We should not judge others negatively because they are indirect, or their accents aren't clear, or their tone of voice is tentative, or they avoid eye contact. We must learn patience and suspend judgment long enough to realize these differences don't make one of us right and the other wrong. They simply mean that we approach communication from a different frame of reference and, many times, a different value system.[3]

Although clarifying your values will help you choose your educational path, goal-setting and goal-achievement skills will turn values into tools that help you travel that path to the end.

# Explore Your Values

Rate each of the values in the list on a scale from 1 to 5, with 1 being least important to you and 5 being most important.

_____ Knowing yourself
_____ Being liked by others
_____ Reading
_____ Self-improvement
_____ Taking risks
_____ Time to yourself
_____ Improving physical/mental health
_____ Time for fun/relaxation
_____ Lifelong learning
_____ Leadership and teamwork skills
_____ Staying fit through exercise
_____ Competing and winning

_____ Getting a good job
_____ Pursuing an education
_____ Spiritual/religious life
_____ Making a lot of money
_____ Good relationships with family
_____ Community involvement
_____ Creative/artistic pursuits
_____ Helping others
_____ Keeping up with the news
_____ Being organized
_____ Financial stability
_____ Other (write below)
_____

Write your top three values here:

1. _____

2. _____

3. _____

Now connect your values to educational goals. (*Example:* A student who values helping others chooses to study nursing.) Choose one top value that is a factor in an educational choice you have made. Explain the choice and how the value is involved:

_____

_____

Name an area of study that you think would help you live according to this value:

_____

# How Do You Set and Achieve Goals?

**GOAL**

An end toward which effort is directed; an aim or intention.

When you identify something that you want, you set a **goal.** Achieving goals, whether they are short term or long term, involves the careful formulation and execution of a goal-achievement plan. Think of this plan as a map that defines your route to destinations nearby and far away.

## Set Long-Term Goals

Start by setting *long-term goals*—objectives that you want to achieve in the next six months, year, or more. As a student, your long-term goals may include earning a degree or certificate and starting a career.

Some long-term goals have an open-ended time frame. This is especially the case with goals that involve creative expression, which depend on the time and freedom to consider different paths. For example, if your goal is to become the best jazz trombonist you can be, you will work at it over your entire life and use different methods to improve your technique. Other goals, such as completing the general education requirements at your school, have a shorter scope, a more definite end, and often fewer options for getting from A to Z.

Writing out a long-term goal statement can help you clarify the goal. Here's one example of a goal that would take forethought and years to reach:

> My goal is to build a business in which I, as a family doctor, create opportunities to expose young people in my community to the medical field. In this business, I will reach students through presentations, summer internships, and mentoring.

© Paul Murphy—Fotolia.com

For a student two years away from college graduation who is pursuing this long-term goal, here is a supporting set of one-year long-term goals:

> Design courses for the year to make sure I am on track for premed course completion. Find medical practices in the area that could serve as a model for my business. Research medical schools for application next year.

Just as this set of goals is tailored to one student's personality, abilities, and values, your goals should reflect your uniqueness. To determine your long-term goals, think about what you think is important to accomplish while you are in school and after you graduate. Here are some linkages between personal values and professional goals:

- **Values:** Health and fitness, helping others

  **Goal:** To work for a company that produces organic foods

- **Values:** Independence, financial success

  **Goal:** To obtain a degree in business and start a company

Basing your long-term goals on your values increases your motivation to succeed. The more your goals focus on what is most important to you, the greater your drive to reach them.

## Set Short-Term Goals

*Short-term goals* are smaller steps that move you toward a long-term goal. Lasting as short as an hour or as long as a few months, these goals help you manage broader aspirations as they narrow your focus and encourage progress. If you had a long-term goal of graduating with a degree in nursing, for example, you may want to accomplish the following short-term goals in the next six months:

- I will learn the names, locations, and functions of every human bone and muscle.
- I will work with a study group to understand the musculoskeletal system.

These goals can be broken down into even smaller parts, such as the following one-month goals:

- I will work with on-screen tutorials of the musculoskeletal system until I understand and memorize the material.
- I will spend three hours a week with my study partners.

© VisualField—Fotolia.com

In addition to monthly goals, you may have short-term goals that extend for a week, a day, or even a couple of hours in a given day. To support your monthlong goal of regularly meeting with your study partners, you may wish to set the following short-term goals:

- *By the end of today:* Call study partners to ask them about when they might be able to meet
- *One week from now:* Have scheduled each of our weekly meetings this month
- *Two weeks from now:* Have had our first meeting
- *Three weeks from now:* Type and distribute notes from first meeting; have second meeting

Your motivation is at its peak when you begin to move toward a goal and when you are about to achieve that goal. For that reason, try to pay special attention to goals that fall in the middle—for example, one-month or one-term goals on the way to a yearlong goal. If you work hard to stay motivated through the whole journey, you will have a better result.

As you consider your long- and short-term goals, notice how all of your goals are linked to one another. As Key 2.1 shows, your long-term goals establish a context for the short-term goals. In turn, your short-term goals make the long-term goals seem clearer and more reachable.

At any given time, you will be working toward goals of varying importance. Setting priorities helps you decide where and when to focus your energy and time.

## Prioritize Goals

When you (prioritize,) you evaluate everything you are working toward, decide which goals are most important, and plan how to achieve them. Prioritizing helps you avoid impulsive decisions that waste energy and time. What should you consider as you prioritize?

**PRIORITIZE**
To arrange or deal with in order of importance.

- *Your values.* Think about what you value to establish your top goals—for example, graduating in four years or developing a strong network of personal contacts.
- *Your personal situation.* Are you going to school and working part-time? Are you taking three classes or five classes? Are you a parent with

Goals reinforce one another.

| | | | |
|---|---|---|---|
| **LONG-TERM** | | Earn a degree | |
| **YEARLONG** | Declare major | | Pass classes |
| **SEMESTER** | Explore career areas | Work with study groups | Be in class and on time |
| **ONE MONTH** | Meet with academic advisor | Plan group meetings | Cut down on late-night socializing |
| **THIS WEEK** | Call advisor to set up appointment | Call friends from class about getting a group together | Study weeknights and go out on Friday nights |

young children? Are you an athlete on a sports team? Every individual situation requires unique priorities and scheduling.

- *Your time commitments.* Hours of your day may already be committed to class, team practices, a part-time job, or sleep. Your challenge is to make sure these commitments reflect what you value and to establish priorities for the remaining hours. As you will see later in the chapter, setting clear priorities will help you manage your time and accomplish more.

## Work to Achieve Goals

Being practical will help you achieve your goals. Remember, the more specific your plans, the more likely you are to fulfill them.

- *Define your goal-setting strategy: How do you plan to reach your goal?* Brainstorm different paths that might get you there. Choose one; then map out its steps and strategies. Focus on specific behaviors and events that are under your control and that are measurable.

- *Set a timetable: When do you want to accomplish your goal?* Set a realistic time line that includes specific deadlines for each step and strategy you have defined. Charting your progress will help you stay on track.

- *Be accountable for your progress: What safeguards will keep you on track?* Define a personal reporting or buddy system that makes accountability a priority.

- *Get unstuck: What will you do if you hit a roadblock?* Define two ways to get help with your efforts if you run into trouble. Be ready to pursue more creative ideas if those don't work.

# Map Out
## a Personal Goal

Working backwards can help you find an interesting path toward an important goal.

Name one important personal goal you have for this year:

_____

Now imagine that you have achieved your goal and an impressed friend asks you to describe how you did it. Write three important steps you took first:

1. _____

2. _____

3. _____

Briefly describe how you followed the rest of the plan:

_____

_____

_____

Finally, tell your friend what positive results have come from achieving your goal:

_____

_____

You just created a potential plan. Consider putting it—or a plan similar to it—to work. As you begin, let the image of the success you created in this exercise motivate and inspire you.

# How Can You Begin
## to Explore Majors?

MAJOR (OR CONCENTRATION) An academic subject area chosen as a field of specialization, requiring a specific course of study.

At some point near the completion of your general education requirements, you will be asked to declare a **major or concentration** (for the sake of simplicity, the term *major* will appear throughout the rest of the text). Although you likely have plenty of time to make this decision, start early to narrow down possibilities so you can match your talents, skills, and dreams with a concrete curriculum. Choosing a major is one of the most important decisions you'll make in college because your major largely determines the courses you will take, what you will learn, and with whom you will spend school time. Your major may also influence your future career.

Thinking practically, exploring your course emphasis early on can save you time and money. Because many of the courses that fulfill requirements in one major may not count toward another, changing your major might mean that you stay in college longer and spend additional money on courses, especially if you make the change in your junior or senior year. Having a sense of what you do or do not want to specialize in will make your course selection more efficient.

With what you know about setting and achieving goals, envision declaring a major as a long-term goal made up of the multiple steps (short-term goals) that follow. Start the process now even if, as is true of many students, you don't yet know what you want to study.

## Short-Term Goal #1: Use Self-Assessments to Identify Interests and Talents

When you identify your interests and talents and choose a major that focuses on them, you are likely to have a positive attitude and perform at your highest level. You may still be figuring out what inspires you, or you may have sensed a career direction since you were young. This was the case with University of Illinois student Brian DeGraff, whose interests were mechanical:

> I am amazed by how things work. The way a car can turn a tank of greasy, smelly, toxic liquid into my ride to school. People always say stop and smell the roses, but I'd rather stop and wonder why the roses smell. It was this passion that drove me to want to be an engineer.[4]

To pinpoint the areas that spark your interest, consider the following questions:

- What are my favorite courses? What do these courses have in common?
- What subjects interest me when I read?
- What activities do I look forward to?
- Am I a "natural" in any academic or skill area?
- What do people say I do well?
- How do I learn most effectively? (see chapter 3)

## Short-Term Goal #2: Explore Academic Options

Next, find out about the academic choices available at your school.

**Learn what's possible.** Consult your college catalog for guidelines on declaring (and changing) your major. Find answers to these questions:

- When do I have to declare a major? (Generally this is required at the end of the second year for four-year programs, or earlier for associate or certificate programs.)

- What are my options in majoring? (You may consider double majors, minors, *interdisciplinary majors* incorporating more than one discipline and designed with the help of an advisor.)
- What majors are offered at my school?

If a major looks interesting, explore it further by answering these questions:

- What minimum grade point average (GPA), if any, does the department require before it will accept me as a major?
- What GPA must I maintain in the courses included in the major?
- What preparatory courses (prerequisites) are required?
- What courses will I be required to take and in what sequence? How many credits do I need to graduate in the major?
- Should I consider a minor in this academic area? (A minor has fewer requirements than a major. Many students choose a minor suited for a career. For example, a sociology major who wants to work in an inner-city hospital might consider a minor in Spanish.)

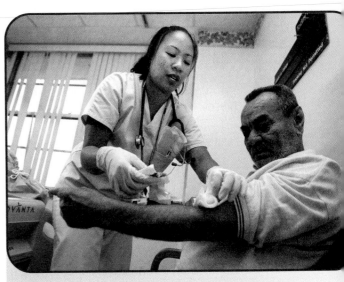

Exploring career-related interests early on can help you find a major that will support your career goals. Students interested in nursing might consider majoring in one of the sciences.

**Talk to people who can help.** Early on, begin discussing your major with your advisor; he or she can help you evaluate different options. You also may want to ask students who are a year or two ahead of you to describe their experiences with the courses, the workload, and the instructors.

**Visit the department.** When considering a major, analyze your comfort with the academic department as well as with the material. Ask the department secretary for information, sit in on a class, and consider asking an instructor in the department for an appointment. When Ashiana Esmail decided to major in Ethnic Studies at the University of California at Berkeley, she did so in part because she felt that working with a close-knit department "was better than an A+" in helping to build academic momentum.[5]

## Short-Term Goal #3: Establish Your Academic Schedule

Map out your time frame. How many years do you plan to study as an undergraduate or graduate student? Do you plan to attend graduate school? If so, do you plan to go there directly after graduation or take time off? From there, get more specific about scheduling.

**Set timing for short-term goals.** Work with your academic advisor to pinpoint when to accomplish the short-term goals that lead to graduation. What are the deadlines for completing core requirements or declaring a major? Although you won't need to plan out your entire course load right now, drafting a tentative (curriculum)—both within and outside your major—can help clarify where you are heading. Remember, you are not expected to do this alone. Your academic advisor is there to help you succeed.

**Identify dates connected to your goal fulfillment.** Pay attention to academic dates (you will find an academic calendar in each year's college catalog and on the college's Web site). Such dates include registration dates, final date to declare a major, final date to drop a course, and so forth. Plan ahead so you don't miss a deadline.

## Be Flexible as You Come to a Decision

Flexibility is essential when defining any important goal. Many students change their minds as they consider majors; some declare a major and then change it one or more times before finding a good fit. Once you have considered a change carefully, act on it right away by informing your advisor, completing required paperwork, and redesigning your schedule to reflect your choice.

Through this process, you will often be thinking about how well you are using your time. In fact, being able to achieve any significant goal is directly linked to effective time management.

# How Can You Effectively Manage Your Time?

Although everyone has the same 24 hours every day, on some days you may feel like you have hours to spare, while on others the clock becomes your worst enemy. Thinking about time before you act empowers you to make smart choices. Consider each day as a jigsaw puzzle: You have the pieces in a pile, and your task is to form a picture of how you want your day to look.

Successful time management starts with identifying your time-related needs and preferences. This self-knowledge sets the stage for building and managing your schedule, avoiding procrastination, and being flexible in the face of change. Finally, understanding the connection between time and stress will help you keep stress levels under control.

### Identify Your Time-Related Needs and Preferences

Body rhythms and habits affect how each person deals with time. Some people are night owls; others function best in the morning. Some people are chronically late; others get everything done with time to spare. Being aware of factors like these will help you create a schedule that maximizes your strengths and cuts down on stress. If you are a morning person, for example, look for sections of required courses that meet early in the day. If you work best at night, schedule most of your study time at a library that stays open late.

Take the following steps to identify your time-related needs and preferences:

**Create a personal time "profile."** Ask yourself these questions: At what time of day do I have the most energy? The least energy? Do I tend to be early, on time, or late? Do I focus well for long stretches or need regular breaks? Your answers will help you find your best schedule.

**Evaluate the effects of your profile.** Which of your time-related habits and preferences will have a positive impact on your success at school? Which are likely to cause problems?

**Establish the schedule preferences that suit your profile best.** Make a list of these preferences—or even map out an ideal schedule as a way of illustrating them. For example, one student's preference list might read: "Classes bunched together on Mondays, Wednesdays, and Fridays. Tuesdays and Thursdays free for studying and research. Study time primarily during the day."

Next, build a schedule that takes this information into account. Your goal should be to maximize your strengths and compensate for your weaker time-management areas.

**Successful Intelligence Connections Online**

Listen to author Sarah Kravits describe how to use analytical, creative, and practical intelligence to define your personal time profile.

Go to the *Keys to Success* Companion Website at www.prenhall.com/carter to listen or download as a podcast.

## Build a Schedule

Schedules help you gain control of your life in two ways: They provide segments of time for goal-related tasks and they remind you of tasks, events, due dates, responsibilities, and deadlines.

### Use a Planner

A planner is a tool for managing your time. Use it to keep track of events and commitments, schedule goal-related tasks, and rank tasks according to priority. Time-management expert Paul Timm says that "rule number one in a thoughtful planning process is: Use some form of a planner where you can write things down."[6]

There are two types of planners. One is a book or notebook where you can note commitments. If you write detailed daily plans, look for the kind that devotes a page to each day. If you prefer to see more days at a glance, try the kind that shows a week's schedule on a two-page spread. Some planners contain sections for monthly and yearly goals.

© Iryna Petrenko—
Fotolia.com

The other option is an electronic planner or personal digital assistant (PDA) such as a Palm Pilot, BlackBerry, or Sidekick. Basic PDA functions allow you to schedule days and weeks, note due dates, make to-do lists, perform mathematical calculations, and create and store an address book. You can also transfer information to and from a computer.

Though electronic planners are handy and have a large data capacity, they cost more than the paper versions, and their small size means they can be easily lost. Analyze your preferences and options, and decide which tool you are most likely to use every day. A blank notebook, used conscientiously, may work as well for some people as a top-of-the-line PDA.

## Keep Track of Events and Commitments

Your planner is designed to help you schedule and remember events and commitments. A quick look at your notations will remind you when items are approaching. Your class syllabus is also a tool for keeping track of reading and homework assignments and test dates (see the sample syllabus on page 14).

Putting your schedule in writing will help you think ahead to prepare for crunch times. For example, if you see that you have three tests and a presentation coming up all in one week, you may have to rearrange your schedule during the preceding week to create extra study time.

Among the events and commitments worth noting in your planner are the following:

- Test and quiz dates; due dates for papers, projects, and presentations
- Details of your academic schedule, including term and holiday breaks
- Club and organizational meetings
- Personal items—medical appointments, due dates for bills, birthdays, social events
- Milestones toward a goal, such as due dates for sections of a project

It's important to include class prep time—reading and studying, writing and working on assignments and projects—in the planner. According to one reasonable formula, you should schedule at least two hours of preparation for every hour of class—that is, if you take 15 credits, you should study about 30 hours a week, making your total classroom and preparation time 45 hours.

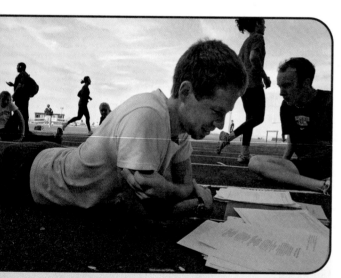

Getting adequate study time means thinking creatively about when and where to study. This student takes time to get some work done between races at a track meet.

Surveys have shown, however, that most students study 15 or fewer hours per week, and some study even less—often not enough to master the material. As a freshman at Boston College, William Imbriale had priorities other than course work. "I got a D on my first philosophy paper," said William. "That woke me up, big time." When a professor helped him plan his time more effectively, William increased his study time and received an A- on the final paper.[7]

Working students have to fit study time in where they can. Lisa Marie Webb, a University of Utah student, prepares for class while commuting to and from her job. Athletes, too, have to work hard to fit everything in. "I get up at 6:30, go to study hall from 7:30 to 9, have class from 9:30 to 1:15, then have practice at 2," said Ohio State defensive back A. J. Hawk.[8] Situations like these demand creative time management and attention to your schedule.

## Schedule Tasks and Activities That Support Your Goals

Linking day-to-day events in your planner to your broader goals will give meaning to your efforts, bring order to your schedule, and keep you motivated. Planning study time for an economics test, for example, will mean more to you if you link the hours you spend to your goal of being accepted into business school. Here is how a student might translate his goal of entering business school into action steps over a year's time:

- *This year:* Complete enough courses to meet curriculum requirements for business school and maintain class standing.
- *This term:* Complete my economics class with a B average or higher.
- *This month:* Set up economics study group schedule to coincide with quizzes and tests.
- *This week:* Meet with study group; go over material for Friday's test.
- *Today:* Go over chapter 3 in econ text.

The student can then arrange his time to move him in the direction of his goal. He schedules activities that support his short-term goal of doing well on the test and writes them in his planner as shown in the example below. Achieving his overarching long-term goal of doing well in a course he needs for business school is the source of his motivation.

| Monday | Tuesday | Wednesday | Thursday | Friday | Saturday | Sunday |
|---|---|---|---|---|---|---|
| 9 AM: Economics class Talk with study group members to schedule meeting. | 3–5 PM: Study econ chapter 3. | 9 AM: Economics class Drop by instructor's office hours to ask question about test | 6 PM: Go over chapter 3 7–9 PM: Study group meeting. | 9 AM: Economics class—Test 3:30 PM: Meet w/advisor to discuss GMAT and other business school requirements | Sleep in— schedule some down time | 5 PM: Go over quiz questions with study partner |

Before each week begins, remind yourself of your long-term goals and what you can accomplish over the next seven days to move you closer to them. Key 2.2 shows parts of a daily schedule and a weekly schedule.

## Indicate Priority Levels

Just as your goals have varying degrees of importance, so too do your daily and weekly tasks. Prioritizing these items helps you to identify your most important tasks so you can focus the bulk of your energy and time on them. It also helps you plan when in your day to get things done. Because many top-priority items (classes, work) occur at designated times, prioritizing helps you lock in these activities and schedule less urgent items around them.

Indicate level of importance using three different categories. You can identify these categories with any code that makes sense to you—some people use numbers, some use letters (A, B, C), and some use different-colored pens. The three categories are as follows:

- *Priority 1* items are the most crucial. They may include attending class, completing school assignments, working at a job, picking up a child from day care, and paying bills. Enter Priority 1 items on your planner first, before scheduling anything else.

**Monday, March 14**

| TIME | TASKS | PRIORITY |
|---|---|---|
| 6:00 A.M. | | |
| 7:00 | | |
| 8:00 | Up at 8am — finish homew | |
| 9:00 | | |
| 10:00 | Business Administration | |
| 11:00 | Renew driver's license @ D | |
| 12:00 P.M. | | |
| 1:00 | Lunch | |
| 2:00 | Writing Seminar (peer editi | |
| 3:00 | ↓ | |
| 4:00 | check on Ms. Schwartz's of | |
| 5:00 | 5:30 work out | |
| 6:00 | ↳→6:30 | |
| 7:00 | Dinner | |
| 8:00 | Read two chapters for | |
| 9:00 | Business Admin. | |
| 10:00 | ↓ | |
| 11:00 | | |
| 12:00 | | |

**Monday, March 28**

| | TASKS | | PRIORITY |
|---|---|---|---|
| 8 | | Call: Mike Blair | 1 |
| 9 | BIO 212 | Financial Aid Office | 2 |
| 10 | | EMS 262 *Paramedic | 3 |
| 11 | CHEM 203 | role-play* | 4 |
| 12 | | | 5 |
| Evening | 6pm yoga class | | |

**Tuesday, March 29**

| | TASKS | | PRIORITY |
|---|---|---|---|
| 8 | Finish reading assignment! | Work @ library | 1 |
| 9 | | | 2 |
| 10 | ENG 112 | (study for quiz) | 3 |
| 11 | ↓ | | 4 |
| 12 | | | 5 |
| Evening | | ↓ until 7pm | |

**Wednesday, March 30**

| | TASKS | | PRIORITY |
|---|---|---|---|
| 8 | | Meet w/advisor | 1 |
| 9 | BIO 212 | | 2 |
| 10 | | EMS 262 | 3 |
| 11 | CHEM 203 *Quiz | | 4 |
| 12 | | Pick up photos | 5 |
| Evening | 6pm Dinner w/study group | | |

- *Priority 2* items are important but more flexible parts of your routine. Examples include library study time, completing an assignment for a school club, and working out. Schedule these around Priority 1 items.

- *Priority 3* items are least important—the "it would be nice if I could get to that" items. Examples include phoning a friend, downloading a dozen new songs onto your iPod, and cleaning out a closet. Many people don't enter Priority 3 tasks in their planners until they know they have time for them. Others keep a separate list of these tasks so that when they have free time they can choose what they want to accomplish.

## Use Scheduling Techniques

The following strategies will help you turn your scheduling activities into tools that move you closer to your goals:

**Plan regularly.** Set aside a regular time each day, and perhaps a longer time at the end of each week, to plan out your schedule. Being methodical about scheduling will help you reduce stress and save the hassle that might result if you forget something important. Your planner can help you only if you use it—so keep it with you and check it throughout the day.

**Make and use to-do lists.** Use a to-do list to record the things you want to accomplish on a given day or week. Write your to-do items on a separate piece of paper so you can set priorities. Then transfer the items you plan to accomplish each day to open time periods in your planner. To-do lists are critical time-management tools for exam week and major projects. They will help you rank your responsibilities so that you get things done in order of importance.

**Post monthly and yearly calendars at home.** Keeping track of your major commitments on a monthly wall calendar will give you the overview you need to focus on responsibilities and upcoming events. Key 2.3 shows a monthly calendar. If you live with family or friends, create a group calendar to stay aware of each other's plans and avoid scheduling conflicts.

**Avoid time traps.** Try to stay away from situations that eat up time unnecessarily. Say no graciously if you don't have time for a project; curb excess social time; declare your cell phone off-limits when you study, delegate chores. Rein in the time you spend surfing the Internet and instant-messaging with friends, because these activities can eat up hours before you know it.

**Schedule down time.** Leisure time is more than just a nice break—it's essential to your health and success. Even a half-hour of down time a day will

### KEY 2.3  Keep track of your time with a monthly calendar.

## MARCH

| SUNDAY | MONDAY | TUESDAY | WEDNESDAY | THURSDAY | FRIDAY | SATURDAY |
|---|---|---|---|---|---|---|
| | **1** WORK | **2** Turn in English paper topic | **3** Dentist 2pm | **4** WORK | **5** | **6** |
| **7** Frank's birthday | **8** Psych Test 9am WORK | **9** | **10** 6:30 pm Meeting @ Student Ctr. | **11** WORK | **12** | **13** Dinner @ Ryan's |
| **14** | **15** English paper due WORK | **16** Western Civ paper—Library research | **17** | **18** Library 6 pm WORK | **19** Western Civ makeup class | **20** |
| **21** | **22** WORK | **23** 2 pm meeting, psych group project | **24** Start running program: 2 miles | **25** WORK | **26** Run 2 miles | **27** |
| **28** Run 3 miles | **29** WORK | **30** Western Civ paper due | **31** Run 2 miles | | | |

refresh you and improve your productivity when you get back on task. Fill the time with whatever relaxes you—reading, watching television, chatting online, playing a game or sport, walking, writing, or just doing nothing.

PROCRASTINATION

The act of putting off a task until another time.

## Fight Procrastination

It's human, and common for busy students, to leave difficult or undesirable tasks until later. If taken to the extreme, however, procrastination can develop into a habit that causes serious problems, often because a procrastinator may not think through the consequences of putting something off.

This excerpt from the Study Skills Library at California Polytechnic State University at San Luis Obispo illustrates how procrastination can quickly turn into a destructive pattern:

The procrastinator is often remarkably optimistic about his ability to complete a task on a tight deadline. . . . For example, he may estimate that a paper will take only five days to write; he has fifteen days; there is

## get practical!

### Make a To-Do List

Reduce stress by accomplishing practical goals. Make a to-do list for what you have to do on your busiest day this week. Include all the tasks and events you know about, including attending class and study time, and the activities you would like to do (working out at the gym, watching your favorite TV show) if you have extra time. Then prioritize your list using the coding system of your choice.

Date: _____

1. _____     7. _____

2. _____     8. _____

3. _____     9. _____

4. _____     10. _____

5. _____     11. _____

6. _____     12. _____

After examining this list, record your daily schedule in your planner (if you have a busy day, you may want to list Priority 3 items separately to complete if time permits). At the end of the day, evaluate this system. Did the list help you to manage your time and tasks effectively? If you liked it, use this exercise as a guide for using to-do lists regularly.

plenty of time, no need to start. Lulled by a false sense of security, time passes. At some point, he crosses over an imaginary starting time and suddenly realizes, "Oh no! I am not in control! There isn't enough time!"

At this point, considerable effort is directed toward completing the task, and work progresses. This sudden spurt of energy is the source of the erroneous feeling that "I work well only under pressure." Actually, at this point you are making progress only because you haven't any choice. . . . Progress is being made, but you have lost your freedom.

Barely completed in time, the paper may actually earn a fairly good grade; whereupon the student experiences mixed feelings: pride of accomplishment (sort of), scorn for the professor who cannot recognize substandard work, and guilt for getting an undeserved grade. But the net result is *reinforcement*: The procrastinator is rewarded positively for his poor behavior ("Look what a decent grade I got after all!"). As a result, the counterproductive behavior is repeated time and time again.[9]

Among the reasons people procrastinate are the following:

- *Perfectionism.* According to Jane B. Burka and Lenora M. Yuen, authors of *Procrastination: Why You Do It, What to Do About It*, habitual procrastinators often gauge their self-worth solely by their ability to achieve. In other words, "an outstanding performance means an outstanding person; a mediocre performance means a mediocre person."[10] To the perfectionist procrastinator, not trying at all is better than an attempt that falls short of perfection.

- *Fear of limitations.* Some people procrastinate in order to avoid the truth about what they can achieve. "As long as you procrastinate, you never have to confront the real limits of your ability, whatever those limits are,"[11] say Burka and Yuen. If you procrastinate and fail, you can blame the failure on waiting too long, not on any personal shortcoming.

- *Being unsure of the next step.* If you get stuck and don't know what to do, sometimes it seems easier to procrastinate than to make the leap to the next level of your goal.

- *Facing an overwhelming task.* Some big projects create immobilizing fear. If a person facing such a task fears failure, she may procrastinate in order to avoid confronting the fear.

Although it can bring relief in the short term, avoiding tasks almost always causes problems, such as a buildup of responsibilities and less time to complete them, work that is not up to par, the disappointment of others who are depending on your work, and stress brought on by the weight of the unfinished tasks. The following strategies can help you avoid procrastination and the problems associated with it:

- *Analyze the effects.* What may happen if you continue to put off a responsibility? Chances are you will benefit more in the long term from facing the task head-on.

- *Set reasonable goals.* Unreasonable goals can intimidate and immobilize you. Set manageable goals and allow enough time to complete them.

- *Break tasks into smaller parts.* If you concentrate on achieving one small step at a time, setting time limits for each step, the task may become less burdensome.

- *Get started whether or not you "feel like it."* The motivation techniques from chapter 1 might help you take the first step. Once you start, you may find it easier to continue.
- *Ask for help.* Once you identify what's holding you up, see who can help you face the task. Another person may come up with an innovative way to get you moving.
- *Don't expect perfection.* People learn by starting at the beginning, making mistakes, and learning from those mistakes. It's better to try your best than to do nothing at all.
- *Reward yourself.* Find ways to boost your confidence when you accomplish a particular task. Remind yourself—with a break, a movie, some kind of treat—that you are making progress.

## Be Flexible

Change is a part of life. No matter how well you think ahead and plan your time, sudden changes—ranging from a room change for a class to a medical emergency—can upend your plans. However, you have some control over how you handle your circumstances. Your ability to evaluate situations, come up with creative options, and put practical plans to work will help you manage changes.

Small changes—for instance, the need to work an hour overtime at your after-school job, or a meeting that runs late—can result in priority shifts that jumble your schedule. For changes that occur frequently, think through a backup plan ahead of time. For surprises, the best you can do is to keep an open mind about possibilities and rely on your internal and external resources.

When change involves serious problems—your car breaks down and you have no way to get to school, or you fail a class and have to consider summer school—use problem-solving skills to help you through (see chapter 4). There are resources available at your college to help you throughout this process. Your academic advisor, counselor, dean, financial aid advisor, and instructors may have ideas and assistance.

## Manage Stress by Managing Time

STRESS

*Physical or mental strain or tension produced in reaction to pressure.*

If you are feeling more (stress) in your everyday life as a student, you are not alone. Stress levels among college students have increased dramatically.[12] Stress factors for college students include being in a new environment, facing increased work and difficult decisions, and juggling school, work, and personal responsibilities.

Dealing with the stress of college life is, and will continue to be, one of your biggest challenges. But here's some good news: *Every time-management strategy you have read in this chapter contributes to your ability to cope with stress.* Remember that stress refers to how you react to pressure. When you create and follow a schedule that gets you places on time and helps you take care of tasks and responsibilities, you reduce pressure. Less pressure, less stress.

Analyze, and adjust if necessary, the relationship between stress and your time-management habits. For example, if you're a night person with early classes and are consistently stressed about waking up in time, use strategies such as going to bed earlier a few nights a week, napping in the afternoon, exercising briefly before class to boost energy, or exploring how to schedule later classes next term. Reduce anxiety by thinking before you act.

Following are some practical strategies for coping with stress through time management. You will find more detail on stress in chapter 10.

**Be realistic about time commitments.** For example, many students attempting to combine work and school find that they have to trim one or the other to reduce stress and promote success. Overloaded students often fall behind and experience high stress levels that can lead to dropping out. Determine what is reasonable for you; you may find that taking longer to graduate is a viable option if you need to work while in school.

**Put sleep and down time on your schedule.** Sleep-deprived bodies and minds have a harder time handling pressure effectively. Figure out how much sleep you need and do your best to get it. When you pull an all-nighter, make sure you play catch-up over the days that follow. Also, with time for relaxation in whatever form you choose, your mind will be better able to manage stress.

**Actively manage your schedule.** The most detailed datebook page or PDA entry can't help you unless you look at it. Get in the habit of checking at regular intervals throughout the day. Also, try not to put off tasks. If you can get it done ahead of time, get it done.

**Focus on one assignment at a time.** Stress is at its worst when you have five pressing assignments in five different classes all due in the next week. Focus on one at a time, completing it to the best of your ability as quickly as you can, then move to the next and the next until you're through.

**Check things off.** Use a physical action to indicate that you have completed a task—check off the item, delete it from your PDA task list, crumple up the Post-it Note. A physical act can relieve stress and highlight the confidence that comes from getting something done.

Sometimes stress freezes you in place and blocks you from finding answers. At those times, remember that taking even a small step is a stress-management strategy because it begins to move you ahead.

## Successful Intelligence Wrap-Up

Self-management is about making well-examined choices—and you are the manager who does the choosing. Think intelligently about what you value, what goals are important to you, and how to best manage your time. Here's how you have built skills in chapter 2:

### Analytical

In the *Get Analytical* exercise, you explored what you value and how your values inform educational goals. As you read the section on goals, you broke down the goal-setting process into its step-by-step parts. While exploring the topic of time management, you thought about who you are as a time manager and how that affects your scheduling and procrastination habits.

## Creative

With the *Get Creative* exercise to motivate you, you came up with ideas about how to pursue an important personal goal. What you read about majors may have inspired new ideas about what you want to major in or how to construct your major. Exploring the importance of flexibility in time management showed you the key role of creativity in the face of change.

## Practical

You explored the practical action of mapping out and pursuing goals step-by-step, and considered how this process applies to declaring a major. In the section on time management, you examined practical strategies for getting in control of your schedule, and created a to-do list tailored to an upcoming busy day in the *Get Practical* exercise. At the end of the chapter, you gathered practical, time-related techniques for managing the stress that all students encounter.

# *paseo*
## *(pass-eh-o)*

This Spanish word refers to an activity that traditionally takes place in Spanish towns in the time of evening after the afternoon *siesta*, or rest. At this late afternoon hour, families often dress up and enjoy a *paseo*—a walk outdoors in the town, to be seen and to socialize.[13]

The relaxed pace of traditional life in many European countries holds a lesson for the overscheduled, harried student. Like many other students, you may feel like you just can't afford to take a break when there is so much to do. However, you also might not be able to afford the negative effects of the stress that results when you *don't* take a break. When you manage your time effectively, you will be able to make time for relaxation, which is critical for stress reduction. So find your version of the *paseo*—a walk on the campus, a coffee shop visit, a game of soccer—and make it part of your life.

"Goals are dreams with deadlines."

DIANA SCHARF HUNT

# SUCCESSFUL INTELLIGENCE

*Think, Create, Apply*

Make your first term count. Campus resources, clubs, student activity groups, and other organizations can enrich your college experience. To benefit from what your school has to offer, set a goal to get involved sooner rather than later.

**Step 1. Think it through:** *Analyze your college self.* Making connections with people and groups in college starts with understanding who you are as a student, both alone and in relation to your school's student body. On a separate sheet of paper, describe your particular circumstances, opinions, and needs in a short paragraph, using questions like these to think through your description:

- How would you describe yourself in terms of culture, ethnicity, gender, age, and lifestyle?
- How would you describe your student status—traditional or returning, full- or part-time?
- How long are you planning to be in your current college? Is it likely that you will transfer?
- What family and work obligations do you have?
- What is your current living situation?
- What do you feel are your biggest challenges in college?
- What do you like to study, and why does it interest you?

**Step 2. Think out of the box:** *Brainstorm your ideal extracurriculars.* On a second piece of paper, write ideas about how you want to spend your time outside of class. To inspire creative ideas, try using one or more of the following questions as a starting point:

- If you had no fear, what horizon-broadening experience would you sign up for?
- When you were in elementary school, what were your favorite activities? Which activities might translate into current interests and pursuits?

- What kinds of organizations, activities, groups, experiences, or people make you think, "Wow, I want to do that"?
- Think about the people that bring out the best in you. What do you like to do with them? What kinds of things are they involved with?

**Step 3. Make it happen:** *Take practical steps toward the activities you like.* First, look in your student handbook at the resources and organizations your school offers. These may include some or all of the following:

| | |
|---|---|
| Academic centers (reading, writing, etc.) | On-campus work opportunities |
| Academic organizations | Disabled student groups |
| Adult education center | Religious organizations |
| Arts clubs (music, drama, dance, etc.) | School publications |
| | School TV/radio stations |
| Fraternities/sororities | Sports clubs |
| International student groups | Student associations |
| Minority student groups | Student government |
| | Volunteer groups |

Taking your analysis of yourself and your creative ideas into consideration, use the left-hand column on the grid that follows to list the three offices or organizations you most want to check out this term. Then—through your school publications and/or a little legwork—fill in the grid, answering the questions shown across the top for each item. The last column requires action—fill it in when you have made contact with each office or organization. Finally, if you wish to become more involved after your initial contact, go for it.

| Office or Organization | Location | Hours, or times of meetings | What it offers | Phone number or e-mail | Initial contact— date and what happened |
|---|---|---|---|---|---|
| | | | | | |
| | | | | | |
| | | | | | |
| | | | | | |
| | | | | | |

# TEAMWORK

## Create Solutions Together

**Multiple paths to a goal.** In a group of three or four, brainstorm important academic goals that can reasonably be accomplished in the course of one year in college. Write your ideas on a piece of paper. From that list, pick out one goal to explore together.

Each group member takes two minutes alone to think about this goal in terms of the first goal-achievement step on page 40—defining a strategy. In other words, answer the question "How would I do it?" Each person writes down all the paths he or she can think of.

The group then gathers and everyone shares their strategies. The group evaluates strategies and chooses one that seems effective. Finally, as a group, brainstorm the rest of the goal-achievement process, based on the chosen strategy or path:

- **Set a timetable.** When do you plan to reach your goal? Discuss different time frames and how each might change the path.

- **Be accountable.** What safeguards will keep you on track? Talk about different ways to make sure you are moving ahead consistently.

- **Get unstuck.** What will you do if you hit a roadblock? Brainstorm the roadblocks that could get in the way of this particular goal. For each, come up with ways to overcome the obstacle.

At the end of the process, you should have a wealth of ideas for how to approach one particular academic goal—and an appreciation for how many paths you could take in order to get there.

# WRITING

## Journal and Put Skills to Work

*Use the tables here to record data. Answer questions and write additional thoughts on a separate piece of paper, in a journal, or on a computer file.*

**Journal entry: Discover how you spend your time.** In the table on the following page, estimate the total time you think you spend per week on each listed activity. Then, add the hours. If your number is over 168 (the number of hours in a week), rethink your estimates and recalculate so that the total equals 168.

Now, spend a week recording exactly how you spend your time. The chart on pages 59–60 has blocks showing half-hour increments. As you go through the week, write in what you do each hour, indicating when you started and when you stopped. Don't forget activities that don't feel like "activities"—such as sleeping, relaxing, or watching TV. Finally, be sure to record your *actual* activities instead of how you want or think you should have spent your time. There are no wrong answers.

After a week, go through your filled-in chart and add up how many hours you spent on the activities for which you previously estimated your

| Activity | Estimated Time Spent | Activity | Estimated Time Spent |
|---|---|---|---|
| Class | | Chores and personal business | |
| Work | | Friends and important relationships | |
| Studying | | Communication time (phone, computer) | |
| Sleeping | | Leisure/entertainment | |
| Eating | | Spiritual life | |
| Family time/child care | | Other | |
| Commuting/traveling | | **TOTAL** | |

hours. Tally the hours in the boxes in the table on page 61 using straight tally marks; round off to half hours and use a short tally mark for each half hour. In the third column, total the hours for each activity. Leave the "Ideal Time in Hours" column blank for now.

Add the totals in the third column to find your grand total. Compare your grand total to your estimated grand total; compare your actual activity hour totals to your estimated activity hour totals. Use a separate sheet of paper to answer the following questions:

• What matches and what doesn't? Describe the most interesting similarities and differences.

• Where do you waste the most time? What do you think that is costing you?

Now evaluate what kinds of changes might improve your ability to achieve goals. Analyze what you do daily, weekly, and monthly. Go back to the table on page 61 and fill in the "Ideal Time in Hours" column. Consider the difference between actual hours and ideal hours. Ask yourself questions:

• On what activities do you think you should spend more or less time?

• What are you willing to do to change, and why?

Finally, write a short paragraph describing two key time-management changes in detail. Describe what goal you are aiming for, and map out how you plan to put the changes into action.

**Real-life writing: Examine two areas of academic specialty.** Use your course catalog to identify two academic areas that look interesting. Write a short report comparing and contrasting the majors or concentrations in these areas, being sure to note GPA requirements, number of courses, relevance to career areas, campus locations of departments, "feel" of the departments, other requirements, and any other relevant characteristics. Conclude your report with observations about how this comparison and evaluation process has refined your thinking.

| Monday | | Tuesday | | Wednesday | | Thursday | |
|---|---|---|---|---|---|---|---|
| **TIME** | **ACTIVITY** | **TIME** | **ACTIVITY** | **TIME** | **ACTIVITY** | **TIME** | **ACTIVITY** |
| 6:00 A.M. | | 6:00 A.M. | | 6:00 A.M. | | 6:00 A.M. | |
| 6:30 A.M. | | 6:30 A.M. | | 6:30 A.M. | | 6:30 A.M. | |
| 7:00 A.M. | | 7:00 A.M. | | 7:00 A.M. | | 7:00 A.M. | |
| 7:30 A.M. | | 7:30 A.M. | | 7:30 A.M. | | 7:30 A.M. | |
| 8:00 A.M. | | 8:00 A.M. | | 8:00 A.M. | | 8:00 A.M. | |
| 8:30 A.M. | | 8:30 A.M. | | 8:30 A.M. | | 8:30 A.M. | |
| 9:00 A.M. | | 9:00 A.M. | | 9:00 A.M. | | 9:00 A.M. | |
| 9:30 A.M. | | 9:30 A.M. | | 9:30 A.M. | | 9:30 A.M. | |
| 10:00 A.M. | | 10:00 A.M. | | 10:00 A.M. | | 10:00 A.M. | |
| 10:30 A.M. | | 10:30 A.M. | | 10:30 A.M. | | 10:30 A.M. | |
| 11:00 A.M. | | 11:00 A.M. | | 11:00 A.M. | | 11:00 A.M. | |
| 11:30 A.M. | | 11:30 A.M. | | 11:30 A.M. | | 11:30 A.M. | |
| 12:00 P.M. | | 12:00 P.M. | | 12:00 P.M. | | 12:00 P.M. | |
| 12:30 P.M. | | 12:30 P.M. | | 12:30 P.M. | | 12:30 P.M. | |
| 1:00 P.M. | | 1:00 P.M. | | 1:00 P.M. | | 1:00 P.M. | |
| 1:30 P.M. | | 1:30 P.M. | | 1:30 P.M. | | 1:30 P.M. | |
| 2:00 P.M. | | 2:00 P.M. | | 2:00 P.M. | | 2:00 P.M. | |
| 2:30 P.M. | | 2:30 P.M. | | 2:30 P.M. | | 2:30 P.M. | |
| 3:00 P.M. | | 3:00 P.M. | | 3:00 P.M. | | 3:00 P.M. | |
| 3:30 P.M. | | 3:30 P.M. | | 3:30 P.M. | | 3:30 P.M. | |
| 4:00 P.M. | | 4:00 P.M. | | 4:00 P.M. | | 4:00 P.M. | |
| 4:30 P.M. | | 4:30 P.M. | | 4:30 P.M. | | 4:30 P.M. | |
| 5:00 P.M. | | 5:00 P.M. | | 5:00 P.M. | | 5:00 P.M. | |
| 5:30 P.M. | | 5:30 P.M. | | 5:30 P.M. | | 5:30 P.M. | |
| 6:00 P.M. | | 6:00 P.M. | | 6:00 P.M. | | 6:00 P.M. | |
| 6:30 P.M. | | 6:30 P.M. | | 6:30 P.M. | | 6:30 P.M. | |
| 7:00 P.M. | | 7:00 P.M. | | 7:00 P.M. | | 7:00 P.M. | |
| 7:30 P.M. | | 7:30 P.M. | | 7:30 P.M. | | 7:30 P.M. | |
| 8:00 P.M. | | 8:00 P.M. | | 8:00 P.M. | | 8:00 P.M. | |
| 8:30 P.M. | | 8:30 P.M. | | 8:30 P.M. | | 8:30 P.M. | |
| 9:00 P.M. | | 9:00 P.M. | | 9:00 P.M. | | 9:00 P.M. | |
| 9:30 P.M. | | 9:30 P.M. | | 9:30 P.M. | | 9:30 P.M. | |
| 10:00 P.M. | | 10:00 P.M. | | 10:00 P.M. | | 10:00 P.M. | |
| 10:30 P.M. | | 10:30 P.M. | | 10:30 P.M. | | 10:30 P.M. | |
| 11:00 P.M. | | 11:00 P.M. | | 11:00 P.M. | | 11:00 P.M. | |
| 11:30 P.M. | | 11:30 P.M. | | 11:30 P.M. | | 11:30 P.M. | |
| 12–6 A.M. | | 12–6 A.M. | | 12–6 A.M. | | 12–6 A.M. | |

| Friday | | Saturday | | Sunday | | Notes |
|---|---|---|---|---|---|---|
| TIME | ACTIVITY | TIME | ACTIVITY | TIME | ACTIVITY | |
| 6:00 A.M. | | 6:00 A.M. | | 6:00 A.M. | | |
| 6:30 A.M. | | 6:30 A.M. | | 6:30 A.M. | | |
| 7:00 A.M. | | 7:00 A.M. | | 7:00 A.M. | | |
| 7:30 A.M. | | 7:30 A.M. | | 7:30 A.M. | | |
| 8:00 A.M. | | 8:00 A.M. | | 8:00 A.M. | | |
| 8:30 A.M. | | 8:30 A.M. | | 8:30 A.M. | | |
| 9:00 A.M. | | 9:00 A.M. | | 9:00 A.M. | | |
| 9:30 A.M. | | 9:30 A.M. | | 9:30 A.M. | | |
| 10:00 A.M. | | 10:00 A.M. | | 10:00 A.M. | | |
| 10:30 A.M. | | 10:30 A.M. | | 10:30 A.M. | | |
| 11:00 A.M. | | 11:00 A.M. | | 11:00 A.M. | | |
| 11:30 A.M. | | 11:30 A.M. | | 11:30 A.M. | | |
| 12:00 P.M. | | 12:00 P.M. | | 12:00 P.M. | | |
| 12:30 P.M. | | 12:30 P.M. | | 12:30 P.M. | | |
| 1:00 P.M. | | 1:00 P.M. | | 1:00 P.M. | | |
| 1:30 P.M. | | 1:30 P.M. | | 1:30 P.M. | | |
| 2:00 P.M. | | 2:00 P.M. | | 2:00 P.M. | | |
| 2:30 P.M. | | 2:30 P.M. | | 2:30 P.M. | | |
| 3:00 P.M. | | 3:00 P.M. | | 3:00 P.M. | | |
| 3:30 P.M. | | 3:30 P.M. | | 3:30 P.M. | | |
| 4:00 P.M. | | 4:00 P.M. | | 4:00 P.M. | | |
| 4:30 P.M. | | 4:30 P.M. | | 4:30 P.M. | | |
| 5:00 P.M. | | 5:00 P.M. | | 5:00 P.M. | | |
| 5:30 P.M. | | 5:30 P.M. | | 5:30 P.M. | | |
| 6:00 P.M. | | 6:00 P.M. | | 6:00 P.M. | | |
| 6:30 P.M. | | 6:30 P.M. | | 6:30 P.M. | | |
| 7:00 P.M. | | 7:00 P.M. | | 7:00 P.M. | | |
| 7:30 P.M. | | 7:30 P.M. | | 7:30 P.M. | | |
| 8:00 P.M. | | 8:00 P.M. | | 8:00 P.M. | | |
| 8:30 P.M. | | 8:30 P.M. | | 8:30 P.M. | | |
| 9:00 P.M. | | 9:00 P.M. | | 9:00 P.M. | | |
| 9:30 P.M. | | 9:30 P.M. | | 9:30 P.M. | | |
| 10:00 P.M. | | 10:00 P.M. | | 10:00 P.M. | | |
| 10:30 P.M. | | 10:30 P.M. | | 10:30 P.M. | | |
| 11:00 P.M. | | 11:00 P.M. | | 11:00 P.M. | | |
| 11:30 P.M. | | 11:30 P.M. | | 11:30 P.M. | | |
| 12–6 A.M. | | 12–6 A.M. | | 12–6 A.M. | | |

| Activity | Time Tallied Over One-Week Period | Total Time in Hours | Ideal Time in Hours |
|---|---|---|---|
| *Example:* Class | IHT IHT IHT Ii | 16.5 | |
| Class | | | |
| Work | | | |
| Studying | | | |
| Sleeping | | | |
| Eating | | | |
| Family time/child care | | | |
| Commuting/traveling | | | |
| Chores and personal business | | | |
| Friends and important relationships | | | |
| Telephone time | | | |
| Leisure/entertainment | | | |
| Spiritual life | | | |
| Other | | | |

# PERSONAL PORTFOLIO

## *Prepare for Career Success*

*Complete the following in your electronic portfolio or on separate sheets of paper.*

Knowledge, skills, and attitudes. No matter what career goals you ultimately pursue, certain knowledge, skills, and attitudes are useful in any career area. Consider this list of what employers look for in people they hire:

Acceptance

Critical thinking

Leadership

Communication

Flexibility

Positive attitude

Continual learning

Goal setting

Teamwork

Creativity

Integrity

Choose and circle three of these that you want to focus on developing this year.

Map out a plan for your progress by indicating a series of smaller goals that will lead you toward developing these skills. For example:

**Skill: Teamwork**

**Long-term goal:** To be comfortable and effective working with others

> **Short-term goal:** I will join, or form, a study group for my economics class.
>
> **Short-term goal:** I will participate in a short-term volunteering opportunity for which I am required to work in a team with others.
>
> **Short-term goal:** When looking into courses with my advisor, I will consider teamwork opportunities (small group work, small seminar courses) as one of my criteria.

## Suggested Readings

Allen, David. *Getting Things Done: The Art of Stress-Free Productivity.* New York: Penguin, 2003.

Burka, Jane B., and Lenora M. Yuen. *Procrastination.* Reading, MA: Perseus Books, 1990.

Charlesworth, Edward A., and Ronald G. Nathan. *Stress Management: A Comprehensive Guide to Wellness.* New York: Ballantine Books, 2004.

College Board. *The College Board Book of Majors,* 2nd ed. New York: Author, 2006.

Covey, Stephen. *The Seven Habits of Highly Effective People.* New York: Simon & Schuster, 2004.

Emmett, Rita. *The Procrastinator's Handbook: Mastering the Art of Doing It Now.* New York: Walker, 2000.

Fogg, Neeta, Paul Harrington, and Thomas Harrington. *The College Majors Handbook with Real Career Paths and Payoffs: The Actual Jobs, Earnings, and Trends for Graduates of 60 College Majors.* Indianapolis: Jist Works, 2004.

Gleeson, Kerry. *The Personal Efficiency Program: How to Get Organized to Do More Work in Less Time,* 2nd ed. New York: Wiley, 2000.

Hallowell, Edward M. *Crazy Busy: Overstretched, Overbooked, and About to Snap! Strategies for Handling Your Fast-Paced Life.* New York: Ballantine Books, 2007.

Phifer, Paul. *College Majors and Careers: A Resource Guide for Effective Life Planning,* 4th ed. Chicago: Ferguson, 2003.

Sapadin, Linda, and Jack Maguire. *Beat Procrastination and Make the Grade: The Six Styles of Procrastination and How Students Can Overcome Them.* New York: Penguin, 1999.

Simon, Sydney B. *In Search of Values: 31 Strategies for Finding Out What Really Matters Most to You.* New York: Warner Books, 1993.

Timm, Paul R. *Successful Self-Management, Revised Edition: Increasing Your Personal Effectiveness.* Los Altos, CA: Crisp Publications, 1993.

# Internet and Podcast Resources

About.com—Stress Management (resources, including a variety of self-assessments): **http://stress.about.com/**

Mind Tools—Time Management: **http://mindtools .com/pages/main/newMN_HTE.htm**

Time Management Secrets with Ruth Klein podcasts: **http://odeo.com/audio/633014/view**

Top Achievement (goal-setting and self-improvement resources): **www.topachievement.com**

Troubled With (help with stress management and personal issues): **www.troubledwith.com**

Riley Guide—Values Inventories (self-assessment resources): **www.rileyguide.com/assess .html#values**

"Stress Cops" episodes on Podcast.net: **www.podcast.net/show/22377**

Prentice Hall Student Success SuperSite: **www.prenhall.com/success**

Look to your college Web site for school-specific information on declaring a major.

# Endnotes

[1]Student essay submitted by the First Year Experience students of Patty Parma, Palo Alto College, San Antonio, Texas, January 2004.

[2]Mark A. King, Anthony Sims, and David Osher, "How Is Cultural Competence Integrated in Education?" March 2007, Center for Effective Collaboration and Practice (http://cecp.air.org/ cultural/Q_integrated.htm#def).

[3]Cited in Louis E. Boone and David L. Kurtz, *Contemporary Business Communication*, Upper Saddle River, NJ: Prentice Hall, 1994, p. 643.

[4]Students Speak: Excerpts from *Your Educational Experience Essays,* University of Illinois, October 2, 2001 (http://ae3_cen_uiuc_edu/stessay/ StudentsSpeak; no longer available).

[5]Cited in Terry Strathman, "What Do Students Want?" April 15, 2002, L & S Colloquium on Undergraduate Education (http://ls.berkeley.edu/?q=about-college/ l-s-divisions/undergraduate-division/ colloquium-undergraduate-education/ april-2002).

[6]Paul Timm, *Successful Self-Management: A Psychologically Sound Approach to Personal Effectiveness*, Los Altos, CA: Crisp Publications, 1987, pp. 22–41.

[7]Jeffrey R. Young, "'Homework? What Homework?' Students Seem to Be Spending Less Time Studying Than They Used To," *Chronicle of Higher Education*, December 6, 2002 (http://chronicle .com/weekly/v49/i15/15a03501.htm).

[8]Welch Suggs, "How Gears Turn at a Sports Factory: Running Ohio State's $79-Million Athletics Program Is a Major Endeavor, with Huge Payoffs and Costs," *Chronicle of Higher Education*, November 29, 2002 (http://chronicle.com/ weekly/v49/i14/14a03201.htm).

[9]William E. Sydnor, "Procrastination," from the California Polytechnic State University Study Skills Library (www.sas.calpoly.edu/asc/ssl/ procrastination.html). Based on *Overcoming Procrastination* by Albert Ellis. Used with permission.

[10]Jane B. Burka and Lenora M. Yuen, *Procrastination. Why You Do It, What to Do About It*, Reading, MA: Perseus Books, 1983, pp. 21–22.

[11]Ibid.

[12]Jodi Wilgoren, "Survey Shows High Stress Levels in College Freshmen," *New York Times*, January 23, 2000, p. NA.

[13]Christopher J. Moore, *In Other Words: A Language Lover's Guide to the Most Intriguing Words Around the World*, New York: Walker, 2004, pp. 36–37.

**LEARNING HOW YOU LEARN**

*Making the Most of Your Abilities*

*"Successfully intelligent people figure out their strengths and their weaknesses, and then find ways to capitalize on their strengths—make the most of what they do well—and to correct for or remedy their weaknesses—find ways around what they don't do well, or make themselves good enough to get by."*

ROBERT STERNBERG

As a college student, you invest valuable resources—time, effort, and money—in your education. How well you learn—in other words, your return on your investment—depends in part on how well you understand yourself as a learner and maximize your potential for positive change and growth. This chapter focuses first on self-assessments—tools that will help you to dive into an exploration of your learning strengths and challenges and to identify who you are as a social being as you interact with people. You will use this information to make practical decisions about how you work and what you choose to study.

*In this chapter you explore answers to the following questions:*

- Why explore who you are as a learner? 66
- What tools can help you assess how you learn and interact with others? 69
- How can you use your self-knowledge? 75
- How can you identify and manage learning disabilities? 85
- Successful Intelligence Wrap-Up 88

**Analytical**

- Analyzing your eight multiple intelligences
- Investigating how you relate to others
- Evaluating how useful you find particular strategies

**Creative**

- Creating new ways to develop your abilities
- Envisioning career ideas based on how you learn
- Developing a new vision of yourself as a learner

**Practical**

- How to choose and use your best study strategies
- How to adjust to an instructor's teaching style
- How to manage a learning disability

# Why Explore Who You Are as a Learner?

People have particular ideas about themselves that often come from family members, friends, and experiences. Maybe your mother thinks you are "the funny one," or "the quiet one." School experiences may have resulted in a label of "thinker," "slacker," "go-getter," or "shy." However, you probably have *not* thought about yourself as a learner. Most students, even those who do well in the areas traditionally valued by schools (verbal and mathematical skills), conclude that "this high (or low) GPA is who I am. I am intelligent (or not)." More often than not, decisions stretching throughout a lifetime are made based on that self-assessment.

## Your Unique Intelligence Can Change and Develop

Each person in the world is unique, with an individual blend of characteristics that define everything from how you look to your health to your ability to take on physical and mental challenges. Each person also has a particular way in which the mind receives and processes information. However, even when instructors are aware of these learning differences, it is impossible for them to tailor a classroom presentation to 15, 40, or 300 unique learners.

Everyone is also born with particular levels of ability and potential in different areas. For example, there are "natural" musicians who can play any-thing they hear, and champion chess players who can anticipate an opponent's moves. Those natural abilities, plus effort and environmental influences, combine to create a recipe for the achievement level a person can attain.

## How can I maximize what I do well?

How can I make the most of my strengths in a course if the professor doesn't use teaching methods that I can relate to? For example, I'm an artist and I tend to connect with information visually. I tend to rely on written notes, maps, and diagrams to absorb information. When I have professors who only lecture, I find it very hard to listen and take notes at the same time—but I need the notes to look at later for studying. How can I deal with this situation?

Cheryl Whitley
Florida Community College
at Jacksonville

# PRACTICAL ANSWERS

Darren Love
Midwestern University
Phoenix, Arizona

### Use what you do well to adapt to what challenges you.

I know firsthand that it takes time and some training to adapt to a different teaching style than you're used to. When I began college, I was mostly a visual learner, and I quickly learned that I had to either adapt to different styles or be left behind. I became more flexible with practice as I tried new study techniques. As the years passed, I discovered I could adjust to whatever format I encountered in the classroom, including lecture and group-based learning.

Try using techniques in an area of strength to compensate for an area of weakness. I know that you are a visual learner (strength) but most of your courses are lecture-based (weakness). Using visually focused techniques will help you adjust to lectures and ultimately integrate the two styles. First, ask your professor if you can videotape or audiotape the lectures so that you will always have the lecture material. Second, when you write your notes, fold your paper in half. On one side, write the notes in pencil or one color of pen; then, when you go home, complement the partial notes that you took earlier by consulting your text and writing text notes in pen (if you used pencil) or a different color of pen (if you used pen) on the other side of the paper. Third, use the audio or videotape of the lecture and convert the material to something that is more visual, such as charts, graphs, or a picture. Fourth, try writing your notes in shorthand, using your visual strength to convert words to symbols or pictures to represent the professor's words.

Now I am in grad school, where one course is often taught by several professors, each with a different style of lecturing. I am adapting once again, accenting my strengths in visual and interpersonal learning to manage the challenges I face in lecture-based classrooms. Over time, as you emphasize your strength, the confidence you build will help you face styles less natural to you.

Picture a bag of a variety of rubber bands. Some are thick, some are thin; some are long, some are short. *But all of them can stretch.* A small rubber band, stretched out, can reach the length of a larger one that lies unstretched. In other words, with effort and focus, you can grow to some extent whatever raw material you have at the start. *To reach your individual potential is your most worthy goal, and the most you can ask of yourself.*

When people adhere to the idea of unchangeable intelligence, they tend to lock themselves into a level of performance consistent with the labels pinned on them, as Sternberg did in his early education. If you believe that

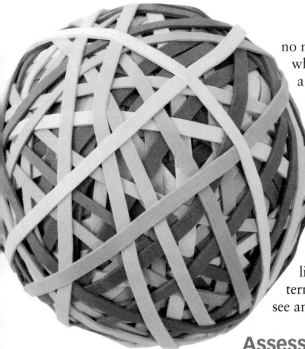

© Jaimie Duplass—Fotolia.com

no matter what you do, you can never learn to write well, why try to write? If, however, you believe you can become a strong writer with effort and practice, you are likely to strive to improve. Studies of the brain, showing that humans of any age are able to build new neuropathways and thereby learn new ideas and skills, support Sternberg's theory that intelligence can change over time.[1]

Set aside the notion that your intelligence has a "fixed" level as you continue through this chapter, through college, and into your life after college. Work instead to understand your strengths—to define the characteristics of your rubber band and stretch it to the limit. And, as you work with others, work to see them in terms of their potential, doing what you can to help them see and stretch their own rubber bands.

## Assessments Can Help You Learn About Yourself

Whereas a test seeks to identify a level of performance, an assessment, as professor and psychologist Howard Gardner puts it, is "the obtaining of information about a person's skills and potentials . . . providing useful feedback to the person."[2] You can think of an assessment as an exploration that, if honest, will reliably produce interesting and helpful information.

POTENTIALS

Abilities that may be developed.

With the information you gain from the two assessments you will take in this chapter—*Multiple Pathways to Learning* and the *Personality Spectrum*—you will learn more about what your strengths and weaknesses are, leading you to the ability to maximize those strengths and compensate for those weaknesses as a successfully intelligent learner. For example, if math gives you trouble, you can draw diagrams of math problems if you have strength in visual-spatial intelligence or talk out problems with a study partner if you have strength in interpersonal intelligence. (You will learn about these intelligences and other characteristics later in the chapter.)

INTELLIGENCE

As defined by Howard Gardner, an ability to solve problems or create products that are of value in a culture.

Understanding yourself as a learner will also help you to see and appreciate how people differ. In a study group or classroom, each person is taking in the material in a unique way. You can use what you know about how others approach learning to improve communication and teamwork.

## Self-Knowledge Is an Important, Lifelong Goal

Self-knowledge is a key to personal power. There is much about yourself, your surroundings, and your experiences that you cannot control. However, with self-knowledge, you *can* work toward controlling how you respond to circumstances as you and your environment change, making adjustments that will help you cope and grow. Because you and your circumstances will change throughout your life, self-knowledge is a lifelong quest.

What role do assessments play in this quest for self-knowledge? Any assessment is simply a snapshot, a look at who you are at a given moment. There are no "right" answers, no "best" set of scores. Use these assessments to help you look at the present—and plan for the future—by asking questions: "Who am I right now?" "How does this compare with who I want to be?"

As you continue through the chapter and complete the assessments, beware of seeing them as definitive answers to the question of who you are. Compare the process of responding to the assessment questions to the experience of trying on new eyeglasses to correct blurred vision. The glasses will not create new paths and possibilities, but they will help you see more clearly the ones that exist today.

# What Tools Can Help You Assess How You Learn and Interact with Others?

This chapter presents two assessments designed to help you get a closer look at your learning capacities and favored modes of interaction with others. The first—*Multiple Pathways to Learning*—focuses on eight areas of potential, and is based on Howard Gardner's Multiple Intelligences theory. The second—the *Personality Spectrum*—is based on the Myers-Briggs Type Indicator® (MBTI) and helps you evaluate how you react to people and situations.

Following each assessment is information about the typical traits of each intelligence or personality spectrum dimension. As you will see from your scores, you have abilities in all areas, though some are more developed than others.

## Assess Your Multiple Intelligences with *Multiple Pathways to Learning*

In 1983, Howard Gardner changed the way people perceive intelligence and learning with his Multiple Intelligences theory. Like Robert Sternberg, Gardner had developed the belief that the traditional view of intelligence—based on mathematical, logical, and verbal measurements comprising an "intelligence quotient" or IQ—did not comprehensively reflect the spectrum of human ability. Whereas Sternberg focused on the spectrum of actions that help people achieve important goals, Gardner honed in on the idea that humans possess a number of different areas of natural ability and potential:

> I believe that we should . . . look . . . at more naturalistic sources of information about how peoples around the world develop skills important to their way of life. Think, for example, of sailors in the South Seas, who find their way around hundreds, or even thousands, of islands by looking at the constellations of stars in the sky, feeling the way a boat passes over the water, and noticing a few scattered landmarks. A word for intelligence in a society of these sailors would probably refer to that kind of navigational ability.[3]

### The Theory of Multiple Intelligences

Gardner's reading and research in biology, neuropsychology, and other disciplines led him to believe that there are eight unique "intelligences," or areas of ability. These include the areas traditionally associated with the term *intelligence*—logic and verbal skills—but go beyond, to encompass a

Each intelligence is linked to specific abilities.

| INTELLIGENCE | DESCRIPTION | HIGH-ACHIEVING EXAMPLE |
|---|---|---|
| **Verbal-Linguistic** | Ability to communicate through language; listening, reading, writing, speaking | Playwright William Shakespeare |
| **Logical-Mathematical** | Ability to understand logical reasoning and problem solving; math, science, patterns, sequences | Microsoft founder Bill Gates |
| **Bodily-Kinesthetic** | Ability to use the physical body skillfully and to take in knowledge through bodily sensation; coordination, working with hands | Ice skating champion Michelle Kwan |
| **Visual-Spatial** | Ability to understand spatial relationships and to perceive and create images; visual art, graphic design, charts and maps | Architect Frank Gehry |
| **Interpersonal** | Ability to relate to others, noticing their moods, motivations, and feelings; social activity, cooperative learning, teamwork | Telejournalist Oprah Winfrey |
| **Intrapersonal** | Ability to understand one's own behavior and feelings; self-awareness, independence, time spent alone | The Dalai Lama |
| **Musical** | Ability to comprehend and create meaningful sound; sensitivity to music and musical patterns | Singer and musician Alicia Keys |
| **Naturalist** | Ability to identify, distinguish, categorize, and classify species or items, often incorporating high interest in elements of the natural environment | Conservationist Steve Irwin |

wide range of potentials of the human brain. Note that these intelligences almost never function in isolation. Gardner emphasizes that, with few exceptions, "intelligences always work in concert," and adults will almost always use several of them for any significant role or task.[4]

Look at Key 3.1 for descriptions of each intelligence. To further illustrate the intelligences, the table lists examples of people who have unusually high levels of ability in each intelligence. Although few people will have the verbal-linguistic intelligence of William Shakespeare or the interpersonal intelligence of Oprah Winfrey, everyone has some level of ability in each intelligence. Your goal is to identify what your levels are and to work your strongest intelligences to your advantage.

Gardner defines *an intelligence* as "a biophysical potential to process information that can be activated in a cultural setting to solve problems or create products that are of value in a culture."[5] Restated more simply, an intelligence is an ability that is valued by a group of people for what it can produce. As Tibetan mountain natives prize the bodily-kinesthetic ability of a top-notch Himalayan mountain guide, so the Detroit auto manufacturing community appreciates the visual-spatial talents of a master car designer. Different cultures and situations need different abilities.

This definition takes the concept of intelligence beyond what a standard IQ test can measure. Is a sailor who can navigate a boat thousands of miles based on star position, weather, and landmarks less "intelligent" than a top-rated lawyer? Is a social worker highly skilled in negotiation less "intelligent" than a mathematician? Gardner would answer no, that each person in these examples produces something that his or her culture values. Although the culture of the South Seas values the navigational ability exhibited by the sailor, the culture of a law office values the detail-oriented, well-researched opinions that the lawyer can produce.

## Your Own Eight Intelligences

You have your own personal "map" of abilities, which is a combination of what you are born with and what you work to develop. Gardner believes that all people possess some capacity in each of the eight intelligences, and that every person has developed some intelligences more fully than others. When you find a task or subject easy, you are probably using a more fully developed intelligence. When you have trouble, you may be using a less developed intelligence.[6]

Furthermore, Gardner believes your levels of development in the eight intelligences can grow or recede throughout your life, depending on your efforts and experiences. Although you will not become a world-class pianist if you have limited musical ability, for example, you still can grow what you have with focus and work. Conversely, even a highly talented musician will lose ability without practice. This reflects how the brain grows with learning and slows without it.

The *Multiple Pathways to Learning* assessment helps you determine the levels to which your eight intelligences are developed. Key 3.2, immediately following the assessment, describes specific skills associated with the eight intelligences. Finally, the *Multiple Intelligence Strategies* grids in chapters 5 through 11 will demonstrate how to apply your learning styles knowledge to key college success skills and to specific areas of study.

# MULTIPLE PATHWAYS TO LEARNING

Each intelligence has a set of numbered statements. Consider each statement on its own. Then, on a scale from 1 (lowest) to 4 (highest), rate how closely it matches who you are right now and write that number on the line next to the statement. Finally, total each set of six questions.

| rarely | sometimes | usually | always |
|---|---|---|---|
| 1 | 2 | 3 | 4 |

1. _____ I enjoy physical activities.
2. _____ I am uncomfortable sitting still.
3. _____ I prefer to learn through doing.
4. _____ When sitting I move my legs or hands.
5. _____ I enjoy working with my hands.
6. _____ I like to pace when I'm thinking or studying.

_____ TOTAL for BODILY–KINESTHETIC

1. _____ I enjoy telling stories.
2. _____ I like to write.
3. _____ I like to read.
4. _____ I express myself clearly.
5. _____ I am good at negotiating.
6. _____ I like to discuss topics that interest me.

_____ TOTAL for VERBAL–LINGUISTIC

1. _____ I use maps easily.
2. _____ I draw pictures/diagrams when explaining ideas.
3. _____ I can assemble items easily from diagrams.
4. _____ I enjoy drawing or photography.
5. _____ I do not like to read long paragraphs.
6. _____ I prefer a drawn map over written directions.

_____ TOTAL for VISUAL–SPATIAL

1. _____ I like math in school.
2. _____ I like science.
3. _____ I problem-solve well.
4. _____ I question how things work.
5. _____ I enjoy planning or designing something new.
6. _____ I am able to fix things.

_____ TOTAL for LOGICAL–MATHEMATICAL

1. _____ I listen to music.
2. _____ I move my fingers or feet when I hear music.
3. _____ I have good rhythm.
4. _____ I like to sing along with music.
5. _____ People have said I have musical talent.
6. _____ I like to express my ideas through music.

_____ TOTAL for MUSICAL

1. _____ I need quiet time to think.
2. _____ I think about issues before I want to talk.
3. _____ I am interested in self-improvement.
4. _____ I understand my thoughts and feelings.
5. _____ I know what I want out of life.
6. _____ I prefer to work on projects alone.

_____ TOTAL for INTRAPERSONAL

1. _____ I like doing a project with other people.
2. _____ People come to me to help settle conflicts.
3. _____ I like to spend time with friends.
4. _____ I am good at understanding people.
5. _____ I am good at making people feel comfortable.
6. _____ I enjoy helping others.

_____ TOTAL for INTERPERSONAL

1. _____ I like to think about how things, ideas, or people fit into categories.
2. _____ I enjoy studying plants, animals, or oceans.
3. _____ I tend to see how things relate to, or are distinct from, one another.
4. _____ I think about having a career in the natural sciences.
5. _____ As a child I often played with bugs and leaves.
6. _____ I like to investigate the natural world around me.

_____ TOTAL for NATURALISTIC

*Source:* Developed by Joyce Bishop, Ph.D., Golden West College, Huntington Beach, CA. Based on Howard Gardner, *Frames of Mind: The Theory of Multiple Intelligences.* New York: HarperCollins, 1993.[7]

# SCORING GRID FOR MULTIPLE PATHWAYS TO LEARNING

For each intelligence, shade the box in the row that corresponds with the range where your score falls. For example, if you scored 17 in Bodily–Kinesthetic intelligence, you would shade the middle box in that row; if you scored a 13 in Visual–Spatial, you would shade the last box in that row. When you have shaded one box for each row, you will see a "map" of your range of development at a glance.

A score of 20–24 indicates a high level of development in that particular type of intelligence, 14–19 a moderate level, and below 14 an underdeveloped intelligence.

| | 20-24 (Highly Developed) | 14-19 (Moderately Developed) | Below 14 (Underdeveloped) |
|---|---|---|---|
| Bodily–Kinesthetic | | | |
| Visual–Spatial | | | |
| Verbal–Linguistic | | | |
| Logical–Mathematical | | | |
| Musical | | | |
| Interpersonal | | | |
| Intrapersonal | | | |
| Naturalistic | | | |

**KEY 3.2** Particular abilities and skills are associated with each intelligence.

### Verbal-Linguistic

- Analyzing own use of language
- Remembering terms easily
- Explaining, teaching, learning, using humor
- Understanding syntax and word meaning
- Using writing or speech to convince someone to do or believe something

### Musical-Rhythmic

- Sensing tonal qualities
- Creating/enjoying rhythms, melodies
- Being sensitive to sounds and rhythms
- Using an understanding of musical patterns to hear music
- Understanding the symbols and structure of music

### Logical-Mathematical

- Recognizing abstract patterns
- Using facts to support an idea, and generating ideas based on evidence
- Discerning relationships and connections
- Performing complex calculations
- Reasoning scientifically (formulating and testing a hypothesis)

### Visual-Spatial

- Perceiving and forming objects accurately
- Recognizing relationships between objects
- Representing something graphically
- Manipulating images
- Finding one's way in space

### Bodily-Kinesthetic

- Strong mind–body connection
- Controlling and coordinating body movement
- Improving body functions
- Expanding body awareness to all senses
- Using the body to create products or express emotion

### Intrapersonal

- Accessing one's internal emotions
- Understanding feelings and using them to guide behavior
- Evaluating own thinking
- Understanding self in relation to others
- Forming a comprehensive self-concept

### Interpersonal

- Seeing things from others' perspectives
- Noticing moods, intentions, and temperaments of others
- Cooperating within a group
- Communicating verbally and nonverbally
- Creating and maintaining relationships

### Naturalistic
- Ability to categorize something as a member of a group or species
- Ability to distinguish items in a group from one another
- Understanding of relationships among natural organisms
- Appreciation of the delicate balance in nature
- Deep comfort with, and respect for, the natural world

*Source:* Adapted from David Lazear, *Seven Pathways of Learning,* Tucson: Zephyr, 1994.

# Assess Your Style of Interaction with the *Personality Spectrum*

The multiple intelligences assessment focuses on your potential in areas of ability. In contrast, personality assessments help you understand how you respond to the world around you, including people, work, and school. They also can help guide you as you explore majors and careers.

The concept of dividing human beings into four basic personality types goes as far back as Aristotle and Hippocrates, ancient Greek philosophers. Psychologist and philosopher Carl Jung, working in the early half of the 20th century, got more specific about personality typology. He defined the following:[8]

- *An individual's preferred "world."* Jung said that *extroverts* tend to prefer the outside world of people and activities, while *introverts* tend to prefer the inner world of thoughts, feelings, and fantasies.

- *Different ways of dealing with the world, or "functions."* Jung said that we all have them, but in different proportions. He laid out four: *sensing* (learning through what your senses take in), *thinking* (evaluating information rationally), *intuiting* (learning through an instinct that comes from many integrated sources of information), and *feeling* (evaluating information through emotional response).

Katharine Briggs and her daughter, Isabel Briggs Myers, developed an assessment based on Jung's typology. They constructed three dimensions from his work—Extrovert/Introvert, Sensing/Intuiting, and Thinking/Feeling—and added one more dimension, Judging/Perceiving. This Myers-Briggs Type Indicator® or MBTI, is one of the most widely used personality inventories in the world. People completing the MBTI will find that they fall into one of 16 possible types (each a unique combination of the four dimensions).

David Keirsey and Marilyn Bates combined the Myers-Briggs types into four temperaments, and developed a corresponding assessment called the Keirsey Sorter. The *Personality Spectrum* assessment in this chapter is based on the Keirsey Sorter as well as on the MBTI. It adapts and simplifies the material into four personality types—Thinker, Organizer, Giver, and Adventurer—and was developed by Dr. Joyce Bishop, one of the authors of *Keys to Success*.

Like the assessments on which it is based, the *Personality Spectrum* assessment helps you identify the kinds of interactions that are most, and least, comfortable for you. As with multiple intelligences, personality results may change over time in reaction to new experiences, effort, and practice. Key 3.3, on page 78, shows skills that are characteristic of each personality type.

*TYPOLOGY*

*A systematic classification or study of types.*

# PERSONALITY SPECTRUM

**STEP 1.** Rank-order all four responses to each question from most like you (4) to least like you (1) so that for each question you use the numbers 1, 2, 3, and 4 one time each. Place numbers in the boxes next to the responses.

**4** most like me    **3** more like me    **2** less like me    **1** least like me

1. I like instructors who
   - a. ☐ tell me exactly what is expected of me.
   - b. ☐ make learning active and exciting.
   - c. ☐ maintain a safe and supportive classroom.
   - d. ☐ challenge me to think at higher levels.

2. I learn best when the material is
   - a. ☐ well organized.
   - b. ☐ something I can do hands-on.
   - c. ☐ about understanding and improving the human condition.
   - d. ☐ intellectually challenging.

3. A high priority in my life is to
   - a. ☐ keep my commitments.
   - b. ☐ experience as much of life as possible.
   - c. ☐ make a difference in the lives of others.
   - d. ☐ understand how things work.

4. Other people think of me as
   - a. ☐ dependable and loyal.
   - b. ☐ dynamic and creative.
   - c. ☐ caring and honest.
   - d. ☐ intelligent and inventive.

5. When I experience stress I would most likely
   - a. ☐ do something to help me feel more in control of my life.
   - b. ☐ do something physical and daring.
   - c. ☐ talk with a friend.
   - d. ☐ go off by myself and think about my situation.

6. I would probably not be close friends with someone who is
   - a. ☐ irresponsible.
   - b. ☐ unwilling to try new things.
   - c. ☐ selfish and unkind to others.
   - d. ☐ an illogical thinker.

7. My vacations could be described as
   - a. ☐ traditional.
   - b. ☐ adventuresome.
   - c. ☐ pleasing to others.
   - d. ☐ a new learning experience.

8. One word that best describes me is
   - a. ☐ sensible.
   - b. ☐ spontaneous.
   - c. ☐ giving.
   - d. ☐ analytical.

**STEP 2.** Add up the total points for each letter.

TOTAL FOR   **a.** ☐ Organizer    **b.** ☐ Adventurer    **c.** ☐ Giver    **d.** ☐ Thinker

**STEP 3.** Plot these numbers on the brain diagram on page 77.

# SCORING DIAGRAM FOR PERSONALITY SPECTRUM

Write your scores from page 76 in the four squares just outside the brain diagram—Thinker score at top left, Giver score at top right, Organizer score at bottom left, and Adventurer score at bottom right.

Each square has a line of numbers that go from the square to the center of the diagram. For each of your four scores, place a dot on the appropriate number in the line near that square. For example, if you scored 15 in the Giver spectrum, you would place a dot between the 14 and 16 in the upper right-hand line of numbers. If you scored a 26 in the Organizer spectrum, you would place a dot on the 26 in the lower left-hand line of numbers.

Connect the four dots to make a four-sided shape. If you like, shade the four sections inside the shape using four different colors.

## THINKER

Technical
Scientific
Mathematical
Dispassionate
Rational
Analytical
Logical
Problem Solving
Theoretical
Intellectual
Objective
Quantitative
Explicit
Realistic
Literal
Precise
Formal

## GIVER

Interpersonal
Emotional
Caring
Sociable
Giving
Spiritual
Musical
Romantic
Feeling
Peacemaker
Trusting
Adaptable
Passionate
Harmonious
Idealistic
Talkative
Honest

## ORGANIZER

Tactical
Planning
Detailed
Practical
Confident
Predictable
Controlled
Dependable
Systematic
Sequential
Structured
Administrative
Procedural
Organized
Conservative
Safekeeping
Disciplined

## ADVENTURER

Active
Visual
Risking
Original
Artistic
Spatial
Skillful
Impulsive
Metaphoric
Experimental
Divergent
Fast-paced
Simultaneous
Competitive
Imaginative
Open-minded
Adventuresome

For the Personality Spectrum,
26–36 indicates a strong tendency in that dimension,
14–25 a moderate tendency,
and below 14 a minimal tendency.

*Source for brain diagram: Understanding Psychology,* 3rd ed. by Morris, © 1996.
Adapted by permission of Prentice-Hall, Inc., Upper Saddle River, NJ.

**KEY 3.3** Particular abilities and skills are associated with each Personality Spectrum dimension.

Thinker

© Tracy Martinez—Fotolia.com

- Solving problems
- Developing models and systems
- Analytical and abstract thinking
- Exploring ideas and potentials
- Ingenuity
- Going beyond established boundaries
- Global thinking—seeking universal truth

Organizer

© mckryak—Fotolia.com

- Responsibility, reliability
- Operating successfully within social structures
- Sense of history, culture, and dignity
- Neatness and organization
- Loyalty
- Orientation to detail
- Comprehensive follow-through on tasks
- Efficiency
- Helping others

Giver

© James Steidl—Fotolia.com

- Honesty, authenticity
- Successful, close relationships
- Making a difference in the world
- Cultivating potential of self and others
- Negotiation; promoting peace
- Openness
- Helping others

Adventure

© Howard Sandler—Fotolia.com

- High ability in a variety of fields
- Courage and daring
- Hands-on problem solving
- Living in the present
- Spontaneity and action
- Ability to negotiate
- Nontraditional style
- Flexibility
- Zest for life

*Source:* © 2001, Joyce Bishop, in *Keys to Success*, 3rd ed., Upper Saddle River, NJ: Pearson Prentice Hall, 2001.

# How Can You Use Your Self-Knowledge?

Now that you've completed your assessments, how can you apply what you learned about yourself to promote success? Generally, self-knowledge helps you make choices that maximize your strengths and manage your weaknesses. For example, when you understand your stronger intelligences, you can choose—and, most importantly, actively *use*—study strategies that will help you learn more, remember better, and use your knowledge more successfully. Acting on these choices is what counts the most.

In completing the *Multiple Pathways to Learning* and the *Personality Spectrum* assessments, you have explored your levels of potential in eight abilities as well as how you tend to interact with others. By combining this information, you get a clearer picture of who you are. This section of the chapter focuses on how you can use this new picture to choose effective strategies inside the classroom, during study time, and in the workplace, giving examples from both assessments.

## Classroom Benefits

Instructors have a range of teaching styles, reflecting their learning strengths and preferred styles of interaction. How you prefer to learn may work well with some instructors and be a mismatch with others. After several class meetings, you should be able to assess an instructor's teaching styles (see Key 3.4). Then you can use what you know about your most effective ways to learn to creatively get the most out of any instructor's teaching style.

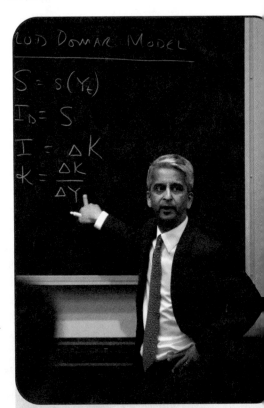

Although presentation styles vary, the standard lecture is still the norm in most classrooms. For this reason, the traditional college classroom is generally a happy home for the verbal or logical learner and the Thinker and the Organizer. However, many students learn best when interacting with other students more than a traditional lecture allows. What can you do when your preferences don't match up with how your instructor teaches? Here are three suggestions:

- *Play to your strengths.* For example, a musical learner with an instructor who delivers material in a random way might record lecture highlights digitally and listen to them on an MP3 player as a study tool. Likewise, a Giver taking a straight lecture course with no student-to-student contact might be motivated by meeting with a study group to go over the details and fill in factual gaps.

- *Work to strengthen weaker areas.* While a visual learner is reviewing notes from a structured lecture course, he could use logical-mathematical strategies such as outlining notes or thinking about cause-and-effect relationships within the material. An Organizer, studying for a test from notes delivered by an instructor with a random presentation, could find ways to organize the material (for example, by creating notes in a table format).

The lecture format is most common in the college classroom. Students who find it challenging can make the most of a lecture-based course using strategies that suit their strenghts.

- *Ask your instructor for additional help.* If you are having trouble with course work, take the initiative to communicate with your instructor

**KEY 3.4** Instructors often prefer one or more teaching styles.

| TEACHING STYLE | WHAT TO EXPECT IN CLASS |
|---|---|
| **Lecture, verbal focus** | Instructor speaks to the class for the entire period, with little class interaction. Lesson is taught primarily through words, either spoken or written on the board, overhead projector, handouts, or text. |
| **Lecture with group discussion** | Instructor presents material but encourages class discussion. |
| **Small groups** | Instructor presents material and then breaks class into small groups for discussion or project work. |
| **Visual focus** | Instructor uses visual elements such as PowerPoint slides, diagrams, photographs, drawings, transparencies, and videos. |
| **Logical presentation** | Instructor organizes material in a logical sequence, such as by steps, time, or importance. |
| **Random presentation** | Instructor tackles topics in no particular order, and may jump around a lot or digress. |
| **Conceptual presentation** | Instructor spends the majority of time on the big picture, focusing on abstract concepts and umbrella ideas. |
| **Detailed presentation** | Instructor spends the majority of time, after introducing ideas, on the details and facts that underlie them. |
| **Experience-based presentation** | Instructor uses demonstrations, experiments, props, and class activities to show key points. |

through e-mail or during office hours. This is especially important in large lectures where you are anonymous unless you speak up. A visual learner, for example, might ask the instructor to recommend graphs, figures, or videos that illustrate the lecture.

No instructor can give each of a diverse group of learners exactly what each one needs. The flexibility that helps you manage how you adjust to instructors' teaching styles is a tool for career and life success. Just as you can't hand-pick your instructors, you will rarely, if ever, be able to choose your work colleagues or their work styles. When there are many different instructors teaching sections of a course, ask other students about the instructors' teaching styles and how the courses are structured.

## Study Benefits

First, when you can, use what you know about yourself to choose study techniques that capitalize on your strengths. For example, if you tend to learn successfully from a linear, logical presentation, you can look for order (for example, a *chronology*—information organized sequentially according to event dates—or a problem-and-solution structure) as you review notes. If you are strong in interpersonal intelligence, you can try to work in study groups whenever possible.

# Get Analytical, Creative, Practical!

## Maximize Your Classroom Experience

Consider first what you know about yourself as a learner. Then, reflect on your instructors' teaching styles this term. Analyze which instructors mesh well with how you learn, and which don't. Make notes here about the situation that you think is the most challenging.

Course: _____ Instructor style: _____

Your analysis of the problem: _____

_____

Next, brainstorm at least three ideas about actions you can take to improve the situation:

1. _____

2. _____

3. _____

Finally, choose one action and put it to practical use. Briefly note what happened: Were there improvements as a result? _____

_____

_____

When you are faced with a task or topic that challenges your weaknesses, use strategies that may boost your ability in those areas. An Adventurer who does *not* respond well to linear information, for example, has two choices when faced with logical presentations. She can apply her strengths to the material—for example, she might find a hands-on approach. Or she can focus on developing study skills that work well for Thinker-dominant learners.

When you study with others, an understanding of diverse learning styles will help you assign tasks effectively and learn more comprehensively, as these suggestions show:

- An Interpersonal learner could take the lead in teaching material to others.
- An Organizer could coordinate the group schedule.
- A Naturalistic learner might organize facts into categories that solidify concepts.

Key 3.5 shows study strategies that suit each intelligence, and Key 3.6 shows study strategies that suit each Personality Spectrum dimension.

KEY 3.5 Particular study techniques maximize each intelligence.

**Verbal-Linguistic**
- Reading text; highlighting selectively
- Using a computer to retype and summarize notes
- Outlining chapters
- Teaching someone else
- Reciting information or writing scripts/debates

**Musical-Rhythmic**
- Creating rhythms out of words
- Beating out rhythms with hand or stick while reciting concepts
- Writing songs/raps that help you learn concepts
- Writing out study material to fit into a wordless tune you have on a CD or MP3 player; chanting or singing the material to the tune as you listen
- Taking music breaks

**Logical-Mathematical**
- Organizing material logically; if it suits the topic, using a spreadsheet program
- Explaining material sequentially to someone
- Developing systems and finding patterns
- Writing outlines
- Analyzing and evaluating information

**Visual-Spatial**
- Developing graphic organizers for new material
- Drawing mind maps and think links
- Using a computer to develop charts and tables
- Using color in notes to organize
- Linking material in your mind with items or places that you can visualize (method of loci)

**Bodily-Kinesthetic**
- Moving while you learn; pacing and reciting
- Using tangible items as memory devices
- Rewriting or retyping notes to engage "muscle memory"
- Designing and playing games to learn material
- Acting out scripts of material

**Intrapersonal**
- Reflecting on personal meaning of information
- Visualizing information
- Keeping a journal
- Studying in quiet areas
- Imagining essays or experiments before beginning

**Interpersonal**
- Studying in a group
- As you study, discussing information over the phone or sending instant messages
- Using flash cards with others
- Teaching someone else the material
- Making time to discuss assignments and tests with your instructor

**Naturalistic**
- Breaking down information into categories
- Looking for ways that items fit or dont fit together
- Looking for relationships among ideas, events, facts
- Studying in a natural setting if it helps you to focus
- Forming study groups of people with similar interests

*Source:* Adapted from David Lazear, *Seven Pathways of Learning,* Tucson: Zephyr, 1994.

**KEY 3.6** Particular study techniques maximize each Personality Spectrum dimension.

## Thinker

© Tracy Martinez—Fotolia.com

- Finding time to reflect independently on new information
- Learning through problem solving
- Designing new ways of approaching issues
- Converting material into logical charts, flow diagrams, and outlines
- Trying to minimize repetitive tasks
- Looking for opportunities to work independently

## Organizer

© mckryak—Fotolia.com

- Defining tasks in concrete terms so that you know what is required
- Looking for a well-structured study environment
- Requesting feedback from instructors and classmates via e-mail or phone
- Using a planner or PDA to schedule tasks and dates
- Organizing material by rewriting and summarizing class and/or text notes
- Using flash cards
- Highlighting materials and notes carefully

## Giver

© James Steidl—Fotolia.com

- Studying with others in person, on the phone, or using instant messages
- Teaching material to others
- Seeking out tasks, groups, and subjects that involve helping people
- Expressing thoughts and feelings clearly and honestly
- Prioritizing your most important academic relationships

## Adventurer

© Howard Sandler—Fotolia.com

- Looking for environments/courses that encourage nontraditional approaches
- Finding hands-on ways to learn
- Seeking instructors and students whom you find stimulating
- Using or developing games and puzzles to help memorize terms
- Fighting boredom by asking to do something extra or performing a task in a more active way

Because you have some level of ability in each area, and because there will be times that you need to boost your ability in a weaker area, you may find useful suggestions under any of the headings. Try different techniques, analyze how effective they are, and use what works best for you.

## Workplace Benefits

The self-knowledge you build throughout this chapter has practical application on the job and for career planning. A self-aware employee or job candidate can expect many benefits.

### Better Performance and Teamwork

Knowing how you learn and interact with others will help you work more effectively. When you understand your strengths, you can find ways to use them on the job more readily. For tasks that require you to use less developed skills, you will be more able to find ways to compensate, such as seeking help. In addition, you will be better able to find ways to work with others effectively. For example, if you are a Giver you might enjoy helping new hires adjust to the people and environment. Or a team leader assigning tasks to an intrapersonal team member might offer the chance to take material home to think about before a meeting.

### Better Career Planning

Exploring ways to use your strengths in school will help you make better choices about what internships, jobs, or careers will suit you. For instance, Cody Patterson's love of math and strong interpersonal intelligence guided him toward jobs and school activities that helped inform his career goals:

A family joke around the Patterson household centers on the roots of eldest son Cody's love affair with mathematics. Like any young child, the story goes, Cody would grow impatient when forced to wait in line in a public place. In an attempt to distract her fidgeting son, his mother, Janalyn, would dig in her purse for her pocket calculator. Once in his hands, the calculator's blinking electronic numerals would mesmerize young Cody, and the wait was soon forgotten. . . . Patterson, 21, laughed as he recalled the hours spent punching buttons on that little gadget. "A lot of guys grew up with G.I. Joes and action figures," he said with a smile. "I grew up with calculators."

Whether or not his mother's calculator did indeed encourage a life dedicated to mathematical pursuits, there is no doubt that Patterson was born with a gift for numbers. He worked as a teaching assistant for an upper-level analysis course, a "math problem" writer formath competitions, a help session leader for advanced math courses, and has served as a Math Camp counselor and vice president of the Pi Mu Epsilon math honor society.

This biology researcher engages her naturalistic intelligence and strength in the Thinker dimension on a daily basis as she studies the sensory organs of alligators and crocodiles.

"I'd like to be a college teacher and help students like me who have had opportunities to hit the big time," Patterson said, "and find some other students who are trying to find their place in academics, get them interested in math, and make believers out of them."[9]

For most college students, internships and majors are more immediate steps on the road to a career. A strength in one or more intelligences might lead you to particular internships and majors that may make sense for you. Key 3.7 shows some possibilities for majors and internships that link to the eight intelligences. This list is by no means complete; rather, it represents only a fraction of the available opportunities. Use what you see here to inspire thought and spur investigation. See Key 11.6 on page 363, in the section on careers in chapter 11, for ideas about how intelligences may link to particular careers.

Although all students have areas of strength and weakness, some challenges are more significant and are diagnosed as learning disabilities. These merit specific attention. Focused assistance can help students who have learning disabilities to manage their conditions and excel in school.

# How Can You Identify and Manage Learning Disabilities?

Some learning disabilities cause reading problems, some create difficulties in math, some create issues that arise when working with others, and some make it difficult for students to process the language they hear. The following will help you understand learning disabilities and, should you be diagnosed with one, give you the tools to manage your situation.

## Identifying a Learning Disability

The National Center for Learning Disabilities (NCLD) defines learning disabilities as follows:[10]

© Dimitrije Tanaskovic—Fotolia.com

- They are neurological disorders that interfere with one's ability to store, process, and produce information.

- They do *not* include mental retardation, autism, behavioral disorders, impaired vision, hearing loss, or other physical disabilities.

- They do *not* include attention deficit disorder and attention deficit hyperactivity disorder, although these problems may accompany learning disabilities.[11]

- They often run in families and are lifelong, although people with learning disabilities can use specific strategies to manage and even overcome areas of weakness.

- Persons with a disability must be diagnosed by professionals in order to receive federally funded aid.

KEY 3.7  Multiple intelligences may open doors to majors and internships.

| Multiple intelligence | Consider majoring in . . . | Think about an internship at a . . |
|---|---|---|
| Bodily-Kinesthetic | Massage or Physical Therapy<br>Kinesiology<br>Construction Engineering<br>Sports Medicine<br>Dance or Theater | Sports physician's office<br>Physical or massage therapy center<br>Construction company<br>Dance studio or theater company<br>Athletic club |
| Intrapersonal | Psychology<br>Finance<br>Computer Science<br>Biology<br>Philosophy | Accounting firm<br>Biology lab<br>Pharmaceutical company<br>Publishing house<br>Computer or Internet company |
| Interpersonal | Education<br>Public Relations<br>Nursing<br>Business<br>Hotel/Restaurant Management | Hotel or restaurant<br>Social service agency<br>Public relations firm<br>Human Resources department<br>Charter school |
| Naturalistic | Geology<br>Zoology<br>Atmospheric Sciences<br>Agriculture<br>Environmental Law | Museum<br>National park<br>Environmental law firm<br>Zoo<br>Geological research firm |
| Musical | Music<br>Music Theory<br>Voice<br>Composition<br>Performing Arts | Performance hall<br>Radio station<br>Record label or recording studio<br>Children's music camp<br>Orchestra or opera company |
| Logical-Mathematical | Math<br>Physics<br>Economics<br>Banking/Finance<br>Computer Science | Law firm<br>Consulting firm<br>Bank<br>Information technology company<br>Research lab |
| Verbal-Linguistic | Communications<br>Marketing<br>English/Literature<br>Journalism<br>Foreign Languages | Newspaper or magazine<br>PR/marketing firm<br>Ad agency<br>Publishing house<br>Network TV affiliate |
| Visual-Spatial | Architecture<br>Visual Arts<br>Multimedia Design<br>Photography<br>Art History | Photo or art studio<br>Multimedia design firm<br>Architecture firm<br>Interior design firm<br>Art gallery |

How can you determine if you should be evaluated for a learning disability? According to the NCLD, persistent problems in any of the following areas may indicate a learning disability:[12]

- Reading or reading comprehension
- Math calculations, understanding language and concepts
- Social skills or interpreting social cues
- Following a schedule, being on time, meeting deadlines
- Reading or following maps
- Balancing a checkbook
- Following directions, especially on multistep tasks
- Writing, sentence structure, spelling, and organizing written work

Details on specific learning disabilities appear in Key 3.8. For an evaluation, contact your school's learning center or student health center for a referral to a licensed professional.

## Managing a Learning Disability

If you are diagnosed with a learning disability, there are steps you can take to help you manage it and maximize your ability to learn and succeed:

**Be informed about your disability.** Search the library and the Internet—try NCLD at www.ncld.org or LD Online at www.ldonline.org (other

**KEY 3.8** What different learning disabilities are and how to recognize them

| DISABILITY OR CONDITION | WHAT ARE THE SIGNS? |
|---|---|
| **Dyslexia and related reading disorders** | Problems with reading (spelling, word sequencing, comprehension) and processing (translating written language to thought or the reverse) |
| **Dyscalculia (developmental arithmetic disorders)** | Difficulties in recognizing numbers and symbols, memorizing facts, understanding abstract math concepts, and applying math to life skills (time management, handling money) |
| **Developmental writing disorders** | Difficulties in composing sentences, organizing a writing assignment, or translating thoughts coherently to the page |
| **Handwriting disorders (dysgraphia)** | Disorder characterized by writing disabilities, including distorted or incorrect language, inappropriately sized and spaced letters, or wrong or misspelled words |
| **Speech and language disorders** | Problems with producing speech sounds, using spoken language to communicate, and/or understanding what others say |
| **LD-related social issues** | Problems in recognizing facial or vocal cues from others, controlling verbal and physical impulsivity, and respecting others' personal space |
| **LD-related organizational issues** | Difficulties in scheduling and in organizing personal, academic, and work-related materials |

*Source:* "LD Basis," 2006, LD Online (www.ldonline.org/ldbasics).

© Andres Rodriguez—Fotolia.com

Web sites are listed at the end of the chapter). Or call NCLD at 1-888-575-7373. You may have received an individualized education program (IEP) in high school. This is a document describing your disability and recommended strategies.

**Seek assistance from your school.** Speak with your advisor about getting a referral to the counselor, who can help you get specific accommodations in your classes. Services mandated by law for students who are learning disabled include the following:

- Extended time on tests
- Note-taking assistance (for example, having a fellow student take notes for you)
- Assistive technology devices (MP3 players, tape recorders, laptop computers)
- Modified assignments
- Alternative assessments and test formats

Other services that may be offered include tutoring, study skills assistance, and counseling.

**Be a dedicated student.** Be on time and attend class. Read assignments before class. Sit where you can focus. Review notes soon after class. Spend extra time on assignments. Ask for help.

**Build a positive attitude.** See your accomplishments in light of how far you have come. Rely on people who support you. Know that the help you receive will give you the best possible chance to learn and grow.

# Successful Intelligence Wrap-Up

Think back to chapter 1, and to Robert Sternberg's definition of successful intelligence—"the kind of intelligence used to achieve important goals." Knowing who you are and how you learn are keys to determining what will work best for you as you pursue goals that are important to you. Here's how you have built skills in chapter 3:

## Analytical

With the *Multiple Pathways to Learning* self-assessment, you analyzed your levels of ability in the Multiple Intelligences. With the *Personality Spectrum* self-assessment, you examined how you relate to people and the world around you. In the *Maximize Your Classroom Experience* exercise, you examined how your instructors' teaching styles relate to how you learn.

## Creative

As you read about multiple intelligences and the personality spectrum, you may have developed new ideas about your abilities and talents and how you relate to others. In the *Maximize Your Classroom Experience* exercise, you brainstormed ideas about how to improve a situation where how you learn doesn't match up well with how an instructor teaches. Reading Key 3.7 about how intelligences relate to majors and internships may have inspired thoughts about your major and job plans.

## Practical

In the *Maximize Your Classroom Experience* exercise, you put an action to practical use in trying to improve your experience in a classroom where you have trouble with the teaching style. Reading Keys 3.5 and 3.6 gave you practical study strategies relating to each intelligence and Personality Spectrum dimension. Reading the material on learning disabilities offered practical ways to address and manage any learning disability that you have.

# *Oruko lonro ni*

## *(o-roo-ko lon-ro nee)*

In the language of the Yoruba, an ethnic group living primarily in Nigeria and other West African countries, *oruko lonro ni* translates as "names affect behavior." This belief, common among the Yoruba people, refers to the idea that people live up to the names given to them by others or even chosen by themselves.[13] As Robert Sternberg learned when he found himself living up to his "lackluster" label as an elementary school student, names and labels have enormous power.

As you think about how you learn, use this idea to understand, and rise above, the confines of the names and labels that you give yourself or that others give you. Use the Multiple Intelligences theory and the Personality Spectrum dimensions as tools to learn more, not boxes into which to fit yourself. Work to clearly see your unique learning strengths and challenges and understand your potential for change.

". . . no two selves, no two consciousnesses, no two minds are exactly alike. Each of us is therefore situated to make a unique contribution to the world."

HOWARD GARDNER, PSYCHOLOGIST AND EDUCATOR

# PERSONAL TRIUMPH CASE STUDY

## OVERCOMING A LEARNING DISABILITY

DR. JOYCE BISHOP, PROFESSOR OF PSYCHOLOGY,
GOLDEN WEST COLLEGE, HUNTINGTON BEACH, CALIFORINIA

*Dr. Bishop, the creator of the assessments in this chapter, has a passion for learning that was inspired by her ordeal as a college student with a learning disability. As it did with her, knowing who you are as a learner can help you surmount the obstacles that come your way. Read the account; then answer the questions on page 91.*

 I have difficulty understanding words I hear, which made listening to lectures in college very hard. No one would know I had this difficulty because I learned how to compensate for it. In fact, I didn't know it myself until years after I graduated. It is a learning disability in the area of auditory discrimination.

College was confusing for me. I did well in some classes and felt totally lost in others. The hardest were the lecture-based classes. When I wasn't familiar with the information or the words, I couldn't make sense of what I was hearing.

If I read the material ahead of time, I could make visual pictures in my mind that would help me absorb the material. I could also look up words and research concepts I didn't understand. Then the lectures made more sense.

I read lips and facial expressions well, so I did well in small classes where I could consistently see the teacher's face. The disadvantage for me in small classes was that, because I heard voices around me as much as I heard the speaker, I had trouble blocking the extra noise. In an attempt to make lecture classes easier to understand, I would drag a tape recorder to class so that I could play back the lecture a number of times later. I found, however, that it didn't really help when I re-listened to the tapes. After that, I bargained with my classmates to borrow their notes in exchange for typing their term papers. Typing is bodily-kinesthetic and helped me to internalize what I was learning.

What helped me get by in college was that I am strong in logical-mathematical intelligence. School is primarily taught in the verbal-linguistic and logical-mathematical learning styles. I am also a strong visual learner. Science classes were easiest for me because they are more visual. I switched from sociology to biology my freshman year; it was easier for me to remember the visual biology material as opposed to the more verbal liberal arts classes. Without my commitment to my education and my will to succeed, I probably would not have graduated.

Twelve years after graduating, I pursued my master's in public health. Part of why I waited so long was that I needed to heal from the trauma of my own learning process. My graduate classes were much more hands-on, but there was still a great deal of reading. One day my eye doctor expressed concern about the stress my schoolwork was causing my eyes and suggested that I get tested for a learning problem. He sent me to a center that usually tests small children for learning disabilities. The person giving the test said words and I was to spell out the words with blocks. I couldn't get some of the words right. I would consistently confuse or mistake words with close sounds. It was determined that I processed language on a fourth-grade level, a condition that has not changed in my adult life.

"How far did you go through school?" asked the therapist conducting the test.

"How far do you think I went?" I asked.

After thinking for a moment, she answered, "The tenth grade." I shared that I was just completing my master's degree. Her eyes got big and she said, "You work really hard in school, don't you?"

At that moment my head flooded with memories of report cards saying "doesn't pay attention in class" and "isn't working up to potential." I started to cry. An explanation for what had brought years of pain and struggle had finally come to the surface.

Now that I know what the problem is, I use strategies that allow me to deal with the way I learn. This is why I am so passionate about the power of knowing how you learn. We all have our strengths and weaknesses; the way we work to manage those weaknesses while maximizing our strengths makes all the difference.

## SUCCESSFUL INTELLIGENCE

*Think, Create, Apply*

**Learn from the experiences of others.** Look back to Joyce Bishop's Personal Triumph on page 90. After you've read her story, relate her experience to your own life by completing the following on a separate sheet of paper or on a computer file:

**Step 1. Think it through:** *Analyze your experience and compare it to Joyce's.* What is a consistent challenge for you as a student, and how does this relate to Joyce's experience? How might this be explained by what you know about how you learn?

**Step 2. Think out of the box:** *Imagine ways of advising.* You are an advisor to a student identical to yourself. Be a harsh advisor—how would you criticize your performance as a student? Then be a wise advisor, focused on tapping into information about intelligences and the Personality Spectrum dimensions—how would you identify challenges and suggest ways to handle them?

**Step 3. Make it happen:** *Head off your own challenges with practical strategies.* You have named a consistent challenge—and you have imagined what you would say as your own advisor. Now identify steps that will help you face your challenge (choosing particular courses, meeting with an advisor or instructor who can give you ideas, approaching work in particular ways).

## TEAMWORK

*Create Solutions Together*

**Ideas about personality types.** Divide into groups according to the four types of the *Personality Spectrum* assessment—Thinker-dominant students in one group, Organizer-dominant students in another, Giver-dominant students in a third, and Adventurer-dominant students in the fourth. If you have scored the same in more than one of these types, join whatever group is smaller. With your group, brainstorm the following lists for your type:

1. The strengths of this type
2. The struggles, or things that cause stress, for this type
3. Career areas that tend to suit this type
4. Career areas that are a challenge for this type
5. Challenges for this type in relating to the other three Personality Spectrum types

If there is time, each group can present this information to the entire class; this will boost understanding and acceptance of diverse ways of relating to information and people.

# WRITING

## *Journal and Put Skills to Work*

*Record your thoughts on a separate piece of paper, in a journal, or on a computer file.*

**Journal entry: Connect your strengths.** Look at the characteristics and study strategies for both your strongest multiple intelligence and your strongest Personality Spectrum dimension. How do these two areas of strength relate to one another? How do they differ? Discuss how you can reconcile the different study strategies.

**Real-life writing: Link how you learn to course work and career.** First, write a summary of yourself as a learner in a paragraph or two, taking into account your results from the assessments in this chapter. Next, schedule a meeting with an advisor at your school's career center. Give the advisor an overview of how you learn from your summary. Ask for advice about what kinds of academic areas and careers might suit your characteristics, and take notes. Finally, choose one possible academic and career area from your discussion, and summarize in writing why it would make sense for you to explore it further.

# PERSONAL PORTFOLIO

## *Prepare for Career Success*

*Complete the following on separate sheets of paper or electronically (if you can use a graphics program).*

**Self-portrait.** Because self-knowledge helps you to make the best choices about your future, a self-portrait is an important step in your career exploration. Use this exercise to synthesize everything you have been exploring about yourself into one comprehensive "self-portrait." Design your portrait in "think link" style, using words and visual shapes to describe your dominant multiple intelligences, Personality Spectrum dimensions, values, abilities and interests, personal characteristics, and anything else that you have discovered through self-exploration.

A think link is a visual construction of related ideas, similar to a map or web, which represents your thought process. Ideas are written inside geometric shapes, often boxes or circles, and related ideas and facts are attached to those ideas by lines that connect the shapes (see the note-taking section in chapter 6 for more about think links).

If you want to use the style shown in the example in Key 3.9, create a "wheel" of ideas coming off your central shape. Then, spreading out from each of those ideas (interests, values, and so forth), draw lines connecting

**KEY 3.9**   One example of a self-portrait.

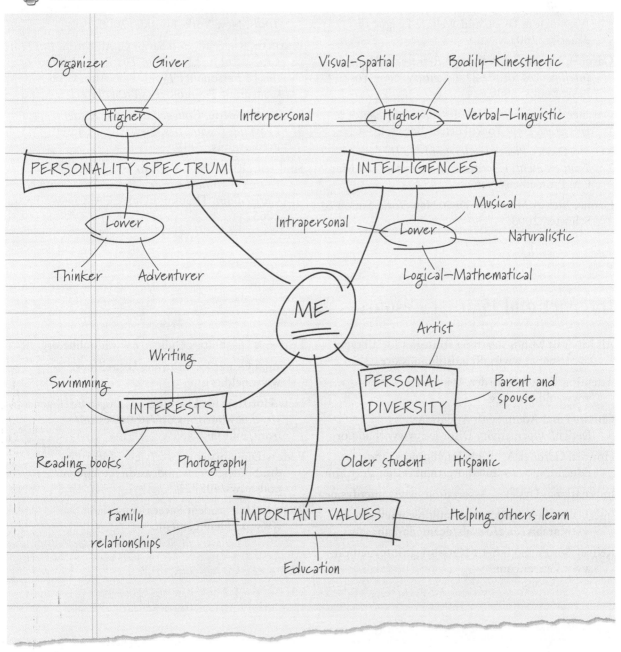

the thoughts that go along with that idea. Connected to "Interests," for example, might be "singing," "stock market," and "history."

You don't have to use the wheel image, however. You might want to design a treelike think link, a line of boxes with connecting thoughts, or anything else you like. Let your design reflect who you are, just as what you write does. You may want to look back at it at the end of the term to see how you have changed and grown from the self-image you have today.

## Suggested Readings

Cobb, Joyanne. *Learning How to Learn: A Guide for Getting into College with a Learning Disability, Staying in, and Staying Sane.* Washington, DC: Child Welfare League of America, 2001.

Gardner, Howard. *Intelligence Reframed: Multiple Intelligences for the 21st Century.* New York: Basic Books, 2000.

Gardner, Howard. *Multiple Intelligences: New Horizons.* New York: Perseus Books, 2006.

Keirsey, David. *Please Understand Me II: Temperament, Character, Intelligence.* Del Mar, CA: Prometheus Nemesis, 1998.

Levine, Mel. *A Mind at a Time.* New York: Simon & Schuster, 2003.

Mooney, Jonathan, and David Cole. *Learning Outside the Lines: Two Ivy League Students with Learning Disabilities and ADHD Give You the Tools.* New York: Fireside, 2000.

Pearman, Roger R., and Sarah C. Albritton. *I'm Not Crazy, I'm Just Not You: The Real Meaning of the 16 Personality Types.* Palo Alto, CA: Consulting Psychologists Press, 1997.

Sclafani, Annette. *College Guide for Students with Learning Disabilities.* New York: Laurel Publications, 2003.

Smilstein, Rita. *We're Born to Learn: Using the Brain's Natural Learning Process to Create New Curriculum.* Thousand Oaks, CA: Corwin Press, 2005.

## Internet and Podcast Resources

All Kinds of Minds (learning strategies for all types of learners): **www.allkindsofminds.org**

Attention Deficit Disorder Association: **www.add.org**

Children and Adults with Attention Deficit/Hyperactivity Disorder: **www.chadd.org**

Howard Gardner, Multiple Intelligences, and Education: **www.infed.org/thinkers/gardner.htm**

International Dyslexia Association: **www.interdys.org**

Internet Archive (podcast on multiple intelligences): **www.archive.org/details/dcampdaraabrams**

Keirsey Sorter and other Myers-Briggs information: **www.keirsey.com**

Learning Disabilities Online: **www.ldonline.org**

National Center for Learning Disabilities: **www.ncld.org**

New Horizons for Learning—Multiple Intelligences: **www.newhorizons.org/strategies/mi/front_mi.htm**

PodcastDirectory.com (overview of learning disabilities): **www.podcastdirectory.com/podshows/407721**

Prentice Hall Student Success SuperSite: **www.prenhall.com/success**

# Endnotes

[1]One such study is K. Warner Schaie, "The Seattle Longitudinal Studies of Adult Intelligence," in *Essential Papers on the Psychology of Aging,* M. Powell Lawton and Timothy A. Salthouse, eds., New York: New York University Press, 1998, pp. 263–271. Also available online: (www.memory-key.com/Seniors/longitudinal_study.htm).

[2]Howard Gardner, *Multiple Intelligence: New Horizons,* New York: Basic Books, 2006, p. 180.

[3]Howard Gardner, *Multiple Intelligences: The Theory in Practice,* New York: HarperCollins, 1993, pp. 5–49.

[4]Gardner, *Multiple Intelligence: New Horizons,* p. 8.

[5]Howard Gardner, *Intelligence Reframed: Multiple Intelligences for the 21st Century,* New York: Basic Books, 2000, pp. 33–34.

[6]Gardner, *Multiple Intelligences: The Theory in Practice,* p. 7.

[7]Developed by Joyce Bishop, Ph.D., Golden West College, Huntington Beach, CA. Based on Howard Gardner, *Frames of Mind: The Theory of Multiple Intelligences,* New York: HarperCollins, 1993.

[8]C. George Boeree, "Personality Theories: Carl Jung," 2006 (http://webspace.ship.edu/cgboer/jung.html).

[9]Kara Bounds Socol, "Cody Patterson '03: Math Student Benefits from Private Gifts," n.d., Texas A&M Foundation, Impact of Giving (http://giving.tamu.edu/content/impactofgiving/studentstories/studentget.php?get=6).

[10]"LD at a Glance," 2007, National Center for Learning Disabilities. (www.ncld.org/index.php?option=content&task=view&id=448).

[11]National Center for Learning Disabilities, "Adult Learning Disabilities: A Learning Disability Isn't Something You Outgrow—It's Something You Learn to Master" (pamphlet), New York: National Center for Learning Disabilities.

[12]*LD Advocates Guide,* n.d., National Center for Learning Disabilities (www.ncld.org/index.php?option=content&task=view&id=291).

[13]Christopher J. Moore, *In Other Words: A Language Lover's Guide to the Most Intriguing Words Around the World,* New York: Walker, 2004, p. 78.

# Prepare with a Study Plan and Schedule

Because some instructors may schedule exams early and often in the term, begin now to develop strategies for test success. The material in this segment is designed to help you organize yourself and manage time efficiently as you prepare for exams. When you reach chapter 7, "Test Taking: Showing What You Know," you will study test taking in depth, including test preparation, test anxiety, general test-taking strategies, strategies for handling different types of test questions, and learning from test mistakes.

## Decide on a Study Plan

Start your test preparation by deciding what you will study. Go through your notes, texts, related primary sources, and handouts, and set aside materials you don't need. Then prioritize the remaining materials. Your goal is to focus on information that is most likely to be on the exam. Use the test-preparation tips on pages 236–239 in chapter 7 and the material on studying your text in chapter 5 to boost your effectiveness as you prepare.

## Create a Study Schedule and Checklist

Next, use the time-management and goal-setting skills from chapter 2 to prepare a schedule. Consider all of the relevant factors—your study materials, the number of days until the test, and the time you can study each day. If you establish your schedule ahead of time and write it in a planner, you are more likely to follow it.

A comprehensive checklist like the one on the facing page will help you organize and stay on track as you prepare. Use a checklist to assign specific tasks to particular study times and sessions. That way, not only do you know when you have time to study, but you also have defined goals for each study session.

## Decide How Well These Techniques Work for You

Now put these studying and scheduling techniques into action by using them every time you prepare for an exam. Make extra copies of the checklist so that they're ready to fill out as soon as an exam is announced.

# Prepare for a Test

Complete the following checklist for each exam to define your study goals, get organized, and stay on track:

Course: _____ Instructor: _____

Date, time, and place of test: _____

Type of test (Is it a midterm or a minor quiz?): _____

What instructor said about the test, including types of test questions, test length, and how much the test counts toward your final grade:

_____

_____

Topics to be covered on the test, in order of importance (information should also come from your instructor):

1. _____

2. _____

3. _____

4. _____

5. _____

Study schedule, including materials you plan to study (texts, class notes, homework problems, and so forth) and dates you plan to complete each:

**Material**                                                           **Completion Date**

1. _____     _____

2. _____     _____

3. _____     _____

4. _____     _____

5. _____     _____

Materials you are expected to bring to the test (textbook, sourcebook, calculator, etc.):

_____

_____

_____

Special study arrangements (such as planning study group meeting, asking the instructor for special help, getting outside tutoring):

_____

_____

_____

Life-management issues (such as rearranging work hours):

_____

_____

_____

*Source:* Adapted from Ron Fry, *"Ace" Any Test,* 3rd ed., Franklin Lakes, NJ: Career Press, 1996, pp. 123–124.

After you use these strategies one or more times, answer the following questions:

- How did this approach help you organize your time before an exam?

  _____

  _____

  _____

  _____

- How did this approach help you organize your study material so that you remembered to cover every topic?

  _____

  _____

  _____

  _____

- Can you think of ways to change the checklist to improve you test-prep efficiency? If you can, list the ways here and incorporate them into the checklist.

  _____

  _____

  _____

  _____

Chapter 4
*Critical, Creative, and Practical Thinking: Solving Problems and Making Decisions*

Chapter 5
*Reading and Studying: Focusing on Content*

Chapter 6
*Listening, Note Taking, and Memory: Taking In, Recording, and Remembering Information*

Chapter 7
*Test Taking: Showing What You Know*

Chapter 8
*Researching and Writing: Gathering and Communicating Ideas*

Get Focused!
*Time and Math Tests*

PART

II

# Developing Academic Skills

# CRITICAL, CREATIVE, AND PRACTICAL THINKING

*Solving Problems and Making Decisions*

> *"Successfully intelligent people define problems correctly and thereby solve those problems that really confront them, rather than extraneous ones. . . . [They] carefully formulate strategies for problem solving. In particular, they focus on long-range planning rather than rushing in and then later having to rethink their strategies."*

ROBERT STERNBERG

**T**o serve you successfully, your education must do more than fill your head with facts and figures: It must also give you the tools to work through problems and decisions. These tools take the form of analytical, creative, and practical thinking skills and are at the heart of *successful intelligence*.

This chapter will help you build your ability to analyze information, come up with creative ideas, and put a practical plan into action. As you build these skills, you will become a better problem solver and decision maker, moving ever more effectively toward your goals.

*In this chapter you explore answers to the following questions:*

- What does it mean to think with successful intelligence?  102
- How can you improve your analytical thinking skills?  105
- How can you improve your creative thinking skills?  110
- How can you improve your practical thinking skills?  114
- How can you use successful intelligence to solve problems and make decisions? 120

## Chapter 4's
### Successful Intelligence Skills

**Analytical**

- Evaluating fact, opinion, assumptions, and perspectives
- Analyzing whether examples support ideas
- Evaluating potential and actual solutions and choices

**Creative**

- Brainstorming
- Taking risks and promoting a creative environment
- Developing potential solutions and choices

**Practical**

- How to identify problems and decisions
- How to use a plan to work through problems and decisions
- How to adapt to your environment and learn from experience

# What Does It Mean to Think with Successful Intelligence?

Some tasks primarily engage one thinking skill at a time. You might use analytical thinking (also known as *critical thinking*) to complete a quiz, creative thinking to write a poem, or practical thinking to get errands done on a busy day. However, when you need to solve a problem or make a decision, combining your analytical, creative, and practical thinking skills gives you the greatest chance of moving forward successfully.[1] These three skills give you myriad ways to connect to material in school and out (see Key 4.1).

## Successfully Intelligent Thinking Means Asking and Answering Questions

What is thinking? According to experts, it is what happens when you ask questions and move toward the answers.[2] "To think through or rethink anything," says Dr. Richard Paul, director of research at the Center for Critical Thinking, "one must ask questions that stimulate our thought. Questions define tasks, express problems, and delineate issues. . . . Only students who have questions are really thinking and learning."[3]

As you answer questions, you transform raw data into information that you can use to achieve goals. A *Wall Street Journal* article titled "The Best Innovations Are Those That Come from Smart Questions" relays the story of a cell biology student, William Hunter, whose professor told him that "the difference between good science and great science is the quality of the

### How can I succeed in college if I don't test well?

My grades were good in high school, and I was also involved in extracurricular activities such as the freshman mentor program and tae kwon do (I am a black belt and instructor). My family and my teachers always told me that I will do well in college.

But I am not so sure. I have a hard time with multiple-choice tests and I did not do well on the SAT and ACT. I worry that maybe I am just not smart enough, even though I can express myself well in essays and conversation. How can I do better on these tests, and how can I make the most of what I already do well?

Parisa Malekzadeh
University of Arizona
Major: Undeclared

## PRACTICAL ANSWERS

Benjamin E. Victorica,
MD Professor Emeritus,
Pediatric Cardiology
University of Florida

### Strive to improve your skills, and know that your other strengths will lead you to success.

To accomplish goals, one must remain focused on the objectives and maintain perseverance. You have already demonstrated that you can focus and persevere by your academic performance and level of expertise in tae kwon do. These qualities will prove more important to your success than test scores.

I had a similar experience with multiple-choice testing. At the time of my medical education in Argentina, all my tests were oral. In order to continue my postgraduate education in this country, I had to pass the ECFMG examination, which is almost entirely multiple-choice. Since I knew the medical material, I learned how to properly answer multiple-choice questions by reviewing and taking sample tests. The majority of my wrong answers occurred because I was quickly glancing at the questions instead of reading carefully. With more focus, I passed the test and was able to continue my training.

My success as a physician has come from combining analytical work (analyzing the key signs and symptoms of a condition and correlating them to clinical and laboratory findings) with creativity (thinking through situations comprehensively) and practical ability (discussing the diagnosis with the patient, applying the appropriate treatment, and monitoring the results). Work hard to improve testing and analytical skills, but value and build your practical and creative skills just as much, knowing that the combination will help you reach your goals.

questions posed."[4] Now a physician, Dr. Hunter asks questions about new ways to use drugs. His questions have led to the promotion of a revolutionary product—a drug-coated mesh used to strengthen vessels in limbs that are threatened by late-stage arterial disease. Through seeking answers to probing questions, Dr. Hunter reached a significant goal.[5]

You use questions in order to analyze ("How bad is my money situation?"), come up with creative ideas ("How can I earn more money?"), and apply practical solutions ("Who do I talk to about getting a job on campus?"). Later in the chapter, in the sections on analytical, creative, and

## Successful intelligence helps you achieve goals in any discipline.

| DISCIPLINE | ANALYTICAL THINKING | CREATIVE THINKING | PRACTICAL THINKING |
|---|---|---|---|
| **Behavioral Science** | Comparing one theory of child development with another | Devising a new theory of child development | Applying child development theories to help parents and teachers understand and deal with children more effectively |
| **Literature** | Examining the development of the main character in a novel | Writing alternative endings to the novel | Using the experience of the main character to better understand and manage one's own life situations |
| **History** | Considering similarities and differences between World War I and World War II | Imagining yourself as a German citizen dealing with economic depression after WWI | Seeing what WWI and WWII lessons can be applied to current Middle East conflicts |
| **Sports** | Taking a close look at the opposing team's strategy on the soccer field | Coming up with innovative ways to move the ball downfield | Using tactics to hide your strategy from an opposing team—or a competing company |

*Source:* Adapted from Robert J. Sternberg, *Successful Intelligence,* New York: Plume, 1996, p. 149.

practical thinking, you will find examples of the kinds of questions that drive each skill.

Like any aspect of thinking, questioning is usually not a straightforward process. Sometimes the answer doesn't come right away. Often the answer leads to more—and more specific—questions. Patience is key in your exploration as you search for results.

## Successfully Intelligent Thinking Requires Purpose and Drive

In order to ask useful questions, you need to know *why* you are questioning. A general question can be your starting point for defining your purpose: "What am I trying to accomplish, and why?" As you continue your thought process, you will find more specific purposes that help you generate questions along the way.

Knowing your purpose helps you with one of the most important tools you need in order to activate your thinking powers: The *drive* to think. "Critical-thinking skills are different from critical-thinking dispositions, or a willingness to deploy these skills," says cognitive psychologist D. Alan Bensley of Frostburg State University in Maryland. In other words, having the skills isn't enough—you also have to want to use them. Skilled thinkers not motivated to use their thinking skills are likely to make decisions in ways similar to those who don't have the skills to deploy.[6]

The bottom line is that the three skills, or aspects, of successful intelligence are useful to you only if you activate them. As Sternberg says, "It is more important to know when and how to use these aspects of successful intelligence than just to have them."[7] If you know and understand your purpose, you are more likely to be willing to use your skills.

Begin by exploring the analytical thinking skills that you'll need to solve problems and make decisions effectively.

# How Can You Improve Your Analytical Thinking Skills?

*Analytical thinking* is the process of gathering information, analyzing it in different ways, and evaluating it for the purposes of gaining understanding, solving a problem, or making a decision. The first step in analytical thinking is to define your purpose by asking what you want to analyze, and why. Then you gather the necessary information, analyze and clarify the ideas, and evaluate what you've found. Throughout the process, you will formulate new questions that may take you in unforeseen directions or even change your purpose.

## Gather Information

Information is the raw material for thinking. Choosing what to gather requires analyzing how much information you need, how much time to spend gathering it, and whether it is relevant. Say, for instance, that you have to write a paper on one aspect of the media (TV, radio, Internet) and its influence on a particular group. If you gathered every available resource on the topic, the course would be over long before you got to the writing stage.

Here's how you might use analysis to effectively gather information for that paper:

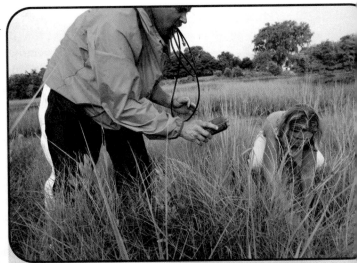

You will rarely use just one aspect of successful intelligence at a time. This instructor and student are gathering data (analytical intelligence) as they work hands-on with terrapins in a bayside marsh (practical intelligence).

- Reviewing the assignment, you learn that the paper should be approximately 10 pages and describe at least three significant points of influence.

- At the library and online, you find thousands of articles on the topic. After an hour, you decide to focus your paper on how the Internet influences young teens (ages 13–15).

- You get an overview from six comprehensive articles that lead you to three in-depth sources.

In this way you achieve a subgoal—a selection of useful materials—on the way to your larger goal of writing a well-crafted paper.

# Analyze and Clarify Information

Once you've gathered the information, the next step is to analyze it to determine whether the information is reliable and useful in helping you answer your questions.

## Break Information into Parts

When analyzing information, you break information into parts and examine the parts so that you can see how they relate to each other and to information you already know. The following strategies help you break down information into pieces and set aside what is unclear, unrelated, or unimportant, resulting in a deeper and more reliable understanding:

**Separate the ideas.** If you are reading about how teens aged 13–15 use the Internet, you might discuss method of access, popular Web sites, and how they interact via instant message or blogs.

**Compare and contrast.** Look at how things are similar to, or different from, each other. You might explore how different young teen subgroups (boys versus girls, for example) have different purposes for setting up pages on sites such as Facebook or MySpace.

**Examine cause and effect.** Look at the possible reasons why something happened (possible causes) and its consequences (effects, both positive and negative). You might examine the effect that Internet use has on how young teens spend their time outside of school.

An important caution: Analyze carefully to seek out *true causes*—some apparent causes may not be actual causes (often called *false causes*). For example, changes in this group since the Internet became popular may have been the result of a number of different factors, including increased or decreased parental and school pressure and the impact of other media such as film and television.

**Look for themes, patterns, and categories.** Note connections that form as you look at how bits of information relate to one another. For example, you might see patterns of Internet use that link young teens from particular cultures or areas of the country together into categories.

Once the ideas are broken down, you can examine whether examples support ideas, separate fact from opinion, consider perspective, and investigate hidden assumptions.

## Examine Whether Examples Support Ideas

When you encounter an idea or claim, examine how it is supported with examples or *evidence* (facts, expert opinion, research findings, personal experience, and so on). How useful an idea is to your work may depend on whether, or how well, it is backed up with solid evidence or made concrete with examples. Be critical of the information you gather; don't take it at face value.

© David Davis—Fotolia.com

For example, a blog written by a 12-year-old may make statements about what kids do on the Internet. The word of one person, who may or may not be telling the truth, is not adequate support. On the other hand, a study of kids' technology use by the Department of Commerce under the provisions of the Children's Internet Protection Act may be more reliable. Whenever you see an (argument) in written materials, you use questioning to judge the quality of the evidence, whether it supports the central idea, and whether examples and ideas connect logically.

*ARGUMENT*
*A set of connected ideas, supported by examples, made by a writer to prove or disprove a point.*

Finding credible, reliable information with which to answer questions and come up with ideas enables you to separate fact from opinion.

## Distinguish Fact from Opinion

A *statement of fact* is information presented as objectively real and verifiable ("The Internet is a research tool"). In contrast, a *statement of opinion* is a belief, conclusion, or judgment that is inherently difficult, and sometimes impossible, to verify ("The Internet is always the best and most reliable research tool"). When you critically evaluate materials that you read, looking carefully at whether an argument is based on fact or opinion will help you determine how reliable it is. Key 4.2 defines important characteristics of fact and opinion.

Even though facts may seem more solid, you can also make use of opinions if you determine that they are backed up with facts. However, it is important to examine opinions for their underlying perspectives and assumptions.

### KEY 4.2   Examine how fact and opinion differ.

| Facts include statements that . . . | Opinions include statements that . . . |
|---|---|
| . . . *deal with actual people, places, objects, or events.* Example: "In 2002, the European Union introduced the physical coins and banknotes of a new currency—the euro—that was designed to be used by its member nations." | . . . *show evaluation.* Any statement of value indicates an opinion. Words such as *bad, good, pointless,* and *beneficial* indicate value judgments. Example: "The use of the euro has been beneficial to all the states of the European Union." |
| . . . *use concrete words or measurable statistics.* Example: "The charity event raised $50,862." | . . . *use abstract words.* Hard-to-define words like *misery* or *success* usually indicate a personal opinion. Example: "The charity event was a smashing success." |
| . . . *describe current events in exact terms.* Example: "Mr. Barrett's course has 378 students enrolled this semester." | . . . *predict future events.* Statements about future occurrences are often opinions. Example: "Mr. Barrett's course is going to set a new enrollment record this year." |
| . . . *avoid emotional words and focus on the verifiable.* Example: "Citing dissatisfaction with the instruction, 7 out of the 25 students in that class withdrew in September." | . . . *use emotional words.* Emotions are unverifiable. Words such as *delightful* or *miserable* express an opinion. Example: "That class is a miserable experience." |
| . . . *avoid absolutes.* Example: "Some students need to have a job while in school." | . . .*use absolutes.* Absolute *qualifiers,* such as *all, none, never,* and *always,* often express an opinion. Example: "All students need to have a job while in school." |

*Source:* Adapted from Ben E. Johnson, *Stirring Up Thinking,* New York: Houghton Mifflin, 1998, pp. 268–270.

## Examine Perspectives and Assumptions

A perspective can be broad, such as a generally optimistic or pessimistic view of life. Or it can be more focused, such as an attitude about whether students should commute or live on campus.

Perspectives are associated with assumptions. For example, the perspective that there are many successful ways to handle the issue of media exposure leads to assumptions such as "Parents can control children's exposure to the Internet" and "Children can access the Internet without being exposed to inappropriate content." Having a particular experience with children and the Internet can build or reinforce a perspective.

Assumptions often hide within questions and statements, blocking you from considering information in different ways. Take this classic puzzler as an example: "Which came first, the chicken or the egg?" Thinking about this question, most people assume that the egg is a chicken egg. If you think past that assumption and come up with a new idea—such as, the egg is a dinosaur egg—then the obvious answer is that the egg came first!

Examining perspectives and assumptions enables you to judge whether material is reliable and free of bias, what particular perspective and intent the author may have, and what assumptions underlie the material. It also helps you identify whether your own perspectives and assumptions are clouding your judgment.

**Perspectives and assumptions in information.** Perspectives and assumptions permeate nearly everything you read. Being able to separate them from the facts will help you identify bias and evaluate information effectively. For example, the conclusions in two articles on Internet advertising may differ if one appears on the Web site of a company that advertises on the Internet and one appears in a publication that wants the Internet to be an advertising-free zone. Another example: A historical Revolutionary War document that originated in the colonies may assume that the rebellion against the British was entirely justified and leave out information to the contrary.

**Personal perspectives and assumptions.** Your perspective affects how accurately you view information. A student who thinks that the death penalty is wrong, for example, may have a hard time analyzing arguments that defend it, or when researching may focus on materials that support his perspective. Try to set aside perspectives and assumptions when you analyze information. "Anticipate your reactions and prejudices and then consciously resist their influence," says Colby Glass, professor of information research and philosophy at Palo Alto College.[8]

There's an added benefit to opening yourself to new perspectives: It will give you more information to work with as you encounter life's problems. Come to the classroom ready to hear and read new ideas, think about their merits, and make informed decisions about what you believe. Says Sternberg: "We need to . . . see issues from a variety of viewpoints and, especially, to see how other people and other cultures view issues and problems facing the world."[9]

## Evaluate Information

You've gathered and analyzed your information. You examined its components, its evidence, its validity, its perspective, and any underlying

**PERSPECTIVE**

A characteristic way of thinking about people, situations, events, and ideas.

**ASSUMPTION**

A judgment, generalization, or bias influenced by experience and values.

**BIAS**

A preference or inclination, especially one that prevents evenhanded judgment.

assumptions. Now, based on an examination of evidence and careful analysis, you *evaluate* whether an idea or piece of information is important or unimportant, applicable or trivial, strong or weak, and why. You then set aside what is not useful and use the rest to form an opinion, possible solution, or decision.

In preparing your paper on young teens and the Internet, for example, you gathered pertinent information, came up with an idea you wanted to write about, researched information and materials, and analyzed how your research applied to your position. You then drafted your paper, presenting what you learned in an organized, persuasive way.

See Key 4.3 for some questions you can ask to build and use analytical thinking skills.

 **KEY 4.3**

## Ask questions like these in order to analyze.

| **To gather information, ask:** | • What kinds of information do I need to meet my goal?<br>• What information is available? Where and when can I get to it?<br>• Of the sources I found, which ones will best help me achieve my goal? |
|---|---|
| **To analyze, ask:** | • What are the parts of this information?<br>• What is similar to this information? What is different?<br>• What are the reasons for this? Why did this happen?<br>• What ideas, themes, or conclusions emerge from this material?<br>• How would you categorize this information? |
| **To see if evidence or examples support an idea, ask:** | • Does the evidence make sense?<br>• How do the examples support the idea/claim?<br>• Are there examples that might disprove the idea/claim? |
| **To distinguish fact from opinion, ask:** | • Do the words in this information signal fact or opinion?<br>• What is the source of this information? Is the source reliable?<br>• If this is an opinion, is it supported by facts? |
| **To examine perspectives and assumptions, ask:** | • What perspectives might the author have, and what may be emphasized or deemphasized as a result?<br>• What assumptions might lie behind this statement or material?<br>• How could I prove, or disprove, an assumption?<br>• How might my perspective affect the way I see this material? |
| **To evaluate, ask:** | • What information will support what I'm trying to prove or accomplish?<br>• Is this information true or false, and why?<br>• How important is this information? |

*Source:* Adapted from "Questions That Probe Reasons and Evidence" (www-ed.fnal.gov/trc/tutorial/taxonomy.html), based on Richard Paul, *Critical Thinking: How to Prepare Students for a Rapidly Changing World,* Santa Rosa, CA: Center for Critical Thinking, 1993; and from Barbara Fowler, "Bloom's Taxonomy and Critical Thinking," 1996, Longview Community College (http://mcckc.edu/longview/ctac/blooms.htm).

# Analyze a Statement

Consider this statement; then analyze it by answering the questions that follow.

*"The Internet is the best place to find information about any topic."*

Is this statement fact or opinion? Why?

_____

_____

What examples can you think of that support or negate this statement?

_____

_____

What perspectives are guiding this statement?

_____

_____

What assumptions underlie the statement? Pose a problem: What negative effects might result from accepting these assumptions and therefore agreeing with the statement?

_____

_____

As a result of your critical thinking, what is your evaluation of this statement?

_____

_____

_____

Pursuing your goals, in school and in the workplace, requires not just analyzing information but also thinking creatively about how to use what you've learned from your analysis.

## How Can You Improve Your Creative Thinking Skills?

What is creativity?

- Some researchers define *creativity* as combining existing elements in an innovative way to create a new purpose or result (using a weak adhesive to mark pages in a book, a 3M scientist created Post-it Notes).

- Others see creativity as the ability to generate new ideas from looking at how things are related (noting what ladybugs eat inspired organic farmers to bring them in to consume crop-destroying aphids).[10]

- Still others, including Sternberg, define it as the ability to make unusual connections—to view information in quirky ways that bring about unique results.

To think creatively is to generate new ideas that may bring change. Here's an example of how creativity can work in the classroom: Working with study group partners, Smith College junior Meghan E. Taugher devised a solar-powered battery for a laptop for their class on electrical circuits:

> We took the professor's laptop, put all the parts together, and sat outside watching it with a little device to see how much power it was saving. When it fully charged the battery, it was one of those times I felt that what I was learning was true, because I was putting it to use in real life.[11]

Meghan's experience led her to generate an idea of a new major and career—engineering.

Even though some people seem to have more or better ideas than others, creative thinking is a skill that can be developed. Creativity expert Roger von Oech highlights mental flexibility. "Like race-car drivers who shift in and out of different gears depending on where they are on the course," he says, you can enhance creativity by learning to "shift in and out of different types of thinking depending on the needs of the situation at hand."[12]

The following actions will help you make those shifts and build your ability to think creatively. Because ideas often pop up randomly, get in the habit of writing them down as they arise. Keep a pen and paper by your bed, your PDA in your pocket, a notepad in your car, or a tape recorder in your backpack so that you can grab ideas before they fade.

## Brainstorm

Brainstorming is also referred to as *divergent thinking:* You start with a question and then let your mind diverge—go in many different directions—in search of solutions. Brainstorming is *deliberate* creative thinking. When you brainstorm, try to generate ideas without thinking about how useful they are; evaluate their quality later. Brainstorming works well in groups because group members can become inspired by, and make creative use of, one another's ideas.[13]

One way to inspire ideas when brainstorming is to think of similar situations—in other words, to make *analogies* (comparisons based on a resemblance of things otherwise unlike). For example, Velcro is a product of analogy: When imagining how two pieces of fabric could stick to each other, the inventor thought of the similar situation of a burr sticking to clothing.

When you are brainstorming ideas, don't get hooked on finding the one right answer. Questions may have many "right answers"—or many answers

*[Handwritten margin note:] BRAINSTORMING Letting your mind free-associate to come up with different ideas or answers.*

that have degrees of usefulness. The more possibilities you generate, the better your chance of finding the best one. Also, don't stop the process when you think you have the best answer—keep going until you are out of steam. You never know what may come up in those last gasps of creative energy.[14]

## Take a New and Different Look

If no one ever questioned established opinion, people would still think the sun revolved around the earth. Here are some ways to change how you look at a situation or problem:

**Challenge assumptions.** In the late 1960s, conventional wisdom said that school provided education and television provided entertainment. Jim Henson, a pioneer in children's television, asked, "Why can't we use TV to educate young children?" From that question, the characters of Sesame Street, and eventually a host of other educational programs, were born.

**Shift your perspective.** Try on new perspectives by asking others for their views, reading about new ways to approach situations, or deliberately going with the opposite of your first instinct.[15] Then use those perspectives to inspire creativity. For a political science course, for example, craft a position paper for a senatorial candidate. For a fun example of how looking at something in a new way can unearth a totally different idea, look at the perception puzzles in Key 4.4.

**Ask "what if" questions.** Set up hypothetical environments in which new ideas can grow—for example, "What if I had unlimited money or time?" The founders of Seeds of Peace, faced with generations of conflict in the Middle East, asked: What if Israeli and Palestinian teens met at a summer camp in Maine so that the next generation has greater understanding and

 **KEY 4.4** Use perception puzzles to experience a shift in perspective.

There are two possibilities for each image. What do you see? (See page 133 for answers.)

*Source of middle puzzle:* "Sara Nadar" illustration from *Mind Sights* by Roger Shepard. Copyright © 1990 by Roger Shepard. Reprinted by permission of Henry Holt and Company, LLC.

respect? And what if follow-up programs and reunions are set up to cement friendships so that relationships change the politics of the Middle East? Based on the ideas that came up, they created an organization that helps teenagers from the Middle East develop leadership and communication skills.

## Set the Stage for Creativity

Use these strategies to give yourself the best possible chance at generating creative ideas:

**Choose, or create, environments that free your mind.** Find places that energize you. Play music that moves you. Seek out people who inspire you.[16]

**Be curious.** Try something new and different: Take a course outside of your major, listen to a new genre of music, read a book on an unfamiliar topic. Try something you don't think you would like in order to see if you had misjudged your reaction. Seeking out new experiences will broaden your knowledge, giving you more raw materials with which to build creative ideas.[17]

**Give yourself time to "sit" with a question.** American society values speed, so much so that we equate being "quick" with being smart.[18] In fact, however, creative ideas often come when you give your brain permission to "leave the job" for a while.[19] Take breaks when figuring out a problem—get some exercise, nap, talk with a friend, work on something else, do something fun.

## Take Risks

Creative breakthroughs can come from sensible risk taking.

**Fly in the face of convention.** Entrepreneur Michael Dell turned tradition on its ear when he took a "tell me what you want and I will build it for you" approach to computer marketing instead of a "build it and they will buy it" approach. The possibility of failure did not stop him from risking money, time, energy, and reputation to achieve a truly unique and creative goal.

**Let mistakes be okay.** Open yourself to the learning that comes from not being afraid to mess up. When a pharmaceutical company failed to develop a particular treatment for multiple sclerosis, the CEO said, "You have to celebrate the failures. If you send the message that the only road to career success is experiments that work, people won't ask risky questions, or get any dramatically new answers."[20]

As with analytical thinking, asking questions powers creative thinking. See Key 4.5 for examples of the kinds of questions you can ask to get your creative juices flowing.

Creativity connects analytical and practical thinking. When you generate ideas, solutions, or choices, you need to think analytically to evaluate their quality. Then, you need to think practically about how to make the best solution or choice happen.

**KEY 4.5** Ask questions like these in order to jump-start creative thinking.

| | |
|---|---|
| **To brainstorm, ask:** | • What do I want to accomplish?<br>• What are the craziest ideas I can think of?<br>• What are 10 ways that I can reach my goal?<br>• What ideas have worked before, and how can I apply them? |
| **To shift your perspective, ask:** | • How has this always been done—and what would be a different way?<br>• How can I approach this task or situation from a new angle?<br>• How would someone else do this or view this?<br>• What if . . . ? |
| **To set the stage for creativity, ask:** | • Where, and with whom, do I feel relaxed and inspired?<br>• What music helps me think out of the box?<br>• When in the day or night am I most likely to experience a flow of creative ideas?<br>• What do I think would be new and interesting to try, to see, to read? |
| **To take risks, ask:** | • What is the conventional way of doing this? What would be a totally different way?<br>• What would be a risky approach to this problem or question?<br>• What is the worst that can happen if I take this risk? What is the best?<br>• What have I learned from this mistake? |

# How Can You Improve Your Practical Thinking Skills?

You've analyzed a situation. You've brainstormed ideas. Now, with your practical skill, you make things happen and learn from your actions.

Practical thinking does incorporate "common sense" or "street smarts" but has a broader reach. When you take practical action, you figure out how to adapt to your environment, or shape or change your environment to adapt to you, in order to pursue important goals. Think again about the successfully intelligent boy in the story in chapter 1: He quickly sized up his environment (bear and slower boy) and adapted (got ready to run) in order to pursue his goal (to escape becoming the bear's dinner).

Here is another example: Your goal is to pass your required freshman composition course. You are a visual learner. To achieve your goal, you can use the instructor's PowerPoints or other visual media to enhance your learning (adapt to your environment) or enroll in an Internet course that is primarily visual (change your environment to adapt to you)—or both.

## Why Practical Thinking Is Important

Although the traditional classroom tends to focus on analytical thinking, real-world problems and decisions require you to move beyond analysis

## Activate Your Creative Powers

First, think about the past month; then, list three creative acts you performed.

1. In order to study, I _____
2. In my personal life, I _____
3. At work or in the classroom, I _____

Now think of a problem or situation that is on your mind. Brainstorm one new idea for how to deal with it.

_____

_____

Write down a second idea—but focus on the risk-taking aspect of creativity. What would be a risky way to handle the situation? How do you hope it would pay off?

_____

_____

Finally, sit with the question—then write down one more idea *only* after you have been away from this page for at least 24 hours.

_____

_____

Keep these in mind. You may want to use one soon!

alone. Your success in a sociology class, for example, usually is not just a product of your academic work—it may depend in part on adapting to your instructor's style or personality as well. Similarly, the way you solve a personal financial dilemma has a more significant impact on your life than how you work through a problem in an accounting course.

Furthermore, academic knowledge on its own isn't enough to bring you success in the workplace. You need to be able to actively apply what you know to problems and decisions that come up periodically. For example, while students majoring in elementary education may successfully quote child development facts on an exam, it won't mean much to their career success unless they can adapt to the classroom by evaluating and addressing real children's needs. Successfully solving real-world problems demands a practical approach.[21]

The accomplishments of David Hosei, a finance and entrepreneurship major at Indiana University, show how practical thinking helps you bridge the gap between being a successful student and achieving real-world success. Pursuing a goal to help others, Hosei formed HELP (Help Educate Lots of People), a nonprofit organization, to teach peers about money management. In addition, he organizes an annual fund-raiser—the IU Battle of the Bands—to raise money for Jill's House, a refuge for families seeking cancer treatments at a local medical center.[22] Achieving any important goal requires you to put practical skill into play.

## Through Experience You Acquire Emotional and Social Intelligence

You gain much of your ability to think practically from personal experience, rather than from formal lessons.[23] What you learn from experience answers "how" questions—how to talk, how to behave, how to proceed.[24] For example, after completing several papers for a course, you may learn what your instructor expects and deliver it. Following a couple of conflicts with a partner, you may learn how to avoid sore spots when the conversation heats up. See Key 4.6 for ways in which this kind of knowledge can be shown in "if-then" statements.

Experience teaches you how to "navigate" personal emotions and social interactions. The emotional and social intelligence you gain as a result of life experiences are essential tools for achieving personal and professional goals (see chapter 11 for a discussion of how emotional and social intelligence contribute to workplace success).

- *Emotional intelligence.* As you learned in chapter 1, *emotional intelligence* is defined by psychologist Daniel Goleman as the ability to

**KEY 4.6**  Here is one way to map out what you learn from experience.

Goal: You want to talk to the soccer coach about your status on the team.

IF the team has had a good practice and IF you've played well during the scrimmage and IF the coach isn't rushing off somewhere, THEN grab a moment with him right after practice ends.

IF the team is having a tough time and IF you've been sidelined and IF the coach is in a rush and stressed, THEN drop in on his office hours tomorrow.

perceive, assess, and manage one's own emotions and understand the emotions of others. This ability helps you to notice what emotions arise in others in reaction to what you say or do, make choices about how to respond to those emotions, and assess what results from your choices. This sequence results in a greater ability to choose appropriate practical actions in future situations.

- *Social intelligence.* The concept of *social intelligence,* also introduced in chapter 1, involves understanding social interactions and using that understanding to maximize your relationships. If you pay attention to how things work in social situations at school, at home, and at work, experience can provide continual practical lessons about which actions to take.

Look closely at what happens among the social players as well as within your emotional landscape, and consider what will promote success. Say, for example, that you receive a disappointing grade on a paper, and you are angry about it. An emotionally and socially intelligent response involves these practical actions:

- Cooling off before you schedule a meeting with the instructor
- Calmly making your point at the meeting
- Listening carefully to what your instructor says in response
- Politely requesting what is possible (a rewrite, for example)

Social intelligence skills, such as sensing what others feel and making a desired impression through what you say verbally and nonverbally, will help you make the most out of your interactions with instructors.

With this course of action, you maximize the likelihood that your instructor will be receptive and helpful (social intelligence), and you maximize your ability to manage your own emotions and use them effectively to work toward your goal (emotional intelligence).

## Practical Thinking Means Action

Action is an extension of practical thinking. Basic student success strategies that promote action—staying motivated, making the most of your strengths, learning from failure, managing time, taking the initiative to seek help from instructors and advisors, and believing in yourself—will keep you moving toward your goals.[25]

The key to making practical knowledge work is to use what you discover, assuring that you will not have to learn the same lessons over and over again. As Sternberg says, "What matters most is not how much experience you have had but rather how much you have profited from it—in other words, how well you apply what you have learned."[26]

See Key 4.7 for some questions you can ask in order to apply practical thinking to your problems and decisions.

## Ask questions like these to activate practical thinking.

| **To learn from experience, ask:** | • What worked well, or not so well, about my approach? My timing? My tone? My wording?<br>• What did others like or not like about what I did?<br>• What did I learn from that experience, conversation, event?<br>• How would I change things if I had to do it over again?<br>• What do I know I would do again? |
|---|---|
| **To apply what you learn, ask:** | • What have I learned that would work here?<br>• What have I seen others do, or heard about from them, that would be helpful here?<br>• What does this situation have in common with past situations I've been involved in?<br>• What has worked in similar situations in the past? |
| **To boost your ability to take action, ask:** | • How can I get motivated and remove limitations?<br>• How can I, in this situation, make the most of what I do well?<br>• If I fail, what can I learn from it?<br>• What steps will get me to my goal, and what trade-offs are involved?<br>• How can I manage my time more effectively? |

get practical!

# Take a Practical Approach to Building Successful Intelligence Skills

Use the wheel on the facing page to get a big-picture look at how you perceive your skills in all three aspects of successful intelligence. In the appropriate sections of the circle, write your self-assessment scores from *Get Analytical* (page 12), *Get Creative* (page 18), and *Get Practical* (page 24) in chapter 1. Then, in each of the three areas of the wheel, draw a curved line approximately at the level of the number of your score and fill in the wedge below that line. Look at what the wheel says about how balanced you perceive your three aspects of successful intelligence to be. If it were a real wheel, would it roll?

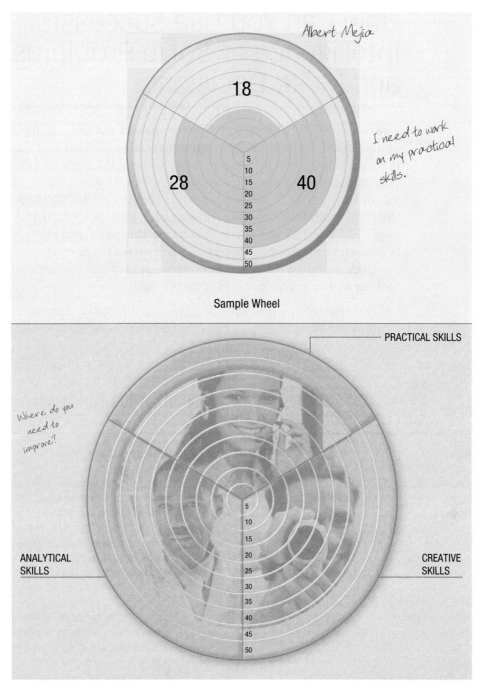

*Albert Mejia*

**18**

**28**    **40**

5
10
15
20
25
30
35
40
45
50

*I need to work on my practical skills.*

Sample Wheel

PRACTICAL SKILLS

*Where do you need to improve?*

5
10
15
20
25
30
35
40
45
50

ANALYTICAL
SKILLS

CREATIVE
SKILLS

*Source:* Based on "The Wheel of Life" model developed by the Coaches Training Institute. © Co-Active Space 2000.

Based on looking at your wheel, in which area do you most want to build strength?

_____

Write down two practical actions you can take that will improve your skills in that area. For example, someone who wants to be more creative could take a course focused on creativity; someone who wants to be more practical could work on paying attention to social cues; someone who wants to be more analytical could decide to analyze one newspaper article every week.

_____

_____

# How Can You Use Successful Intelligence to Solve Problems and Make Decisions?

The best problem solvers and decision makers put their analytical, creative, and practical thinking skills together to solve problems and make decisions. Problem solving and decision making follow similar paths, both requiring you to identify and analyze a situation, generate possibilities, choose one, follow through on it, and evaluate its success. Key 4.8 gives an overview of the path, indicating how you think at each step. Keys 4.10 and 4.11 on pages 123 and 125 will show how to use this path, and provide a visual organizer, to map out problems and decisions effectively.

Understanding the differences between problem solving and decision making will help you know how to proceed:

- Problem solving generally requires more focus on coming up with possible solutions. In contrast, when you face a decision, your choices are often determined.

 **KEY 4.8** Solve problems and make decisions using successful intelligence.

| PROBLEM SOLVING | THINKING SKILL | DECISION MAKING |
|---|---|---|
| Define the problem—recognize that something needs to change, identify what's happening, look for true causes. | STEP 1 DEFINE | Define the decision—identify your goal (your need) and then construct a decision that will help you get it. |
| Analyze the problem—gather information, break it down into pieces, verify facts, look at perspectives and assumptions, evaluate information. | STEP 2 ANALYZE | Examine needs and motives—consider the layers of needs carefully, and be honest about what you really want. |
| Generate possible solutions—use creative strategies to think of ways you could address the causes of this problem. | STEP 3 CREATE | Name and/or generate different options—use creative questions to come up with choices that would fulfill your needs. |
| Evaluate solutions—look carefully at potential pros and cons of each, and choose what seems best. | STEP 4 ANALYZE (EVALUATE) | Evaluate options—look carefully at potential pros and cons of each, and choose what seems best. |
| Put the solution to work—persevere, focus on results, and believe in yourself as you go for your goal. | STEP 5 TAKE PRACTICAL ACTION | Act on your decision—go down the path and use practical strategies to stay on target. |
| Evaluate how well the solution worked—look at the effects of what you did. | STEP 6 ANALYZE (REEVALUATE) | Evaluate the success of your decision—look at whether it accomplished what you had hoped. |
| In the future, apply what you've learned—use this solution, or a better one, when a similar situation comes up again. | STEP 7 TAKE PRACTICAL ACTION | In the future, apply what you've learned—make this choice, or a better one, when a similar decision comes up again. |

- A problem exists when a situation has negative effects, and problem solving aims to remove or counteract those effects. In contrast, decision making aims to fulfill a need.

See Key 4.9 for some examples. Remember, too, that whereas all problem solving involves decision making, only some decision making requires you to solve a problem.

## Solving a Problem

Use these strategies as you move through the problem-solving process outlined in Key 4.8.

**Use probing questions to define problems.** Focus on causes. If you are not happy in a class, for example, you could ask questions like these:

- What do I think about when I feel unhappy?
- Do my feelings involve my instructor? My classmates? School in general?
- Is the subject matter difficult? The volume of work too much?

Chances are that how you answer one or more of these questions may lead to a clear definition—and ultimately to the right solution.

**Analyze carefully.** Gather information for a comprehensive examination. Consider how the problem is similar to, or different from, other problems. Clarify facts. Note your own perspective, and ask others for theirs. Make sure your assumptions are not clouding your analysis.

**Generate possible solutions based on causes, not effects.** Addressing a cause provides a lasting solution, whereas "fixing" an effect cannot. Say, for example, that your shoulder hurts when you use your computer. Getting a friend to massage it is a helpful but temporary solution, because the pain returns whenever you go back to work. Changing the height of your keyboard and mouse is a better idea, because it eliminates the cause of your pain.

KEY 4.9

### Examine how problems and decisions differ.

| Situation | You have a problem if . . . | You need to make a decision if . . . |
| --- | --- | --- |
| **Planning summer activities** | Your low GPA means you need to attend summer school—and you've already accepted a summer job. | You've been accepted into two summer abroad internship programs. |
| **Declaring a major** | It's time to declare, but you don't have all the prerequisites for the major you want. | There are three majors that appeal to you and you qualify for them all. |
| **Handling communications with instructors** | You are having trouble following the lecture style of a particular instructor. | Your psychology survey course has seven sections taught by different instructors; you have to choose one. |

**Evaluate your solution and let it lead to future action.** Look at how things went and ask yourself what worked that you would do again, and what didn't work that you would avoid or change in the future.

What happens if you don't work through a problem comprehensively? Take, for example, a student having an issue with an instructor. The student may get into an argument with the instructor, stop showing up to class, or take a quick-and-dirty approach to assignments. All of these choices have negative consequences. Now look at how the student might work through this problem using analytical, creative, and practical thinking skills. Key 4.10 shows how his effort can pay off.

## Making a Decision

As you use the steps in Key 4.8 to make a decision, remember these strategies:

**Look at the given options—then try to think of more.** Some decisions have a given set of options. For example, your school may allow you to major, double major, or major and minor. However, you may be able to brainstorm with an advisor to come up with more options, such as an interdisciplinary major. As with problem solving, consider similar situations you've been in or heard about, what decisions were made, and what resulted from those decisions.

**Think about how your decision affects others.** What you choose might have an impact on friends, family, and others around you. Your conclusions about that impact may affect what decision you ultimately make.

**Gather perspectives.** Talk with others who have made similar decisions. There are more ways of doing things than one brain can possibly imagine on its own.

**Look at the long-term effects.** As with problem solving, a final evaluation is crucial. For important decisions, do a short-term evaluation and another evaluation after a period of time. Examine whether your decision has sent you down a path that has continued to bring positive effects or whether you should rethink your choice.

**Consider all of the factors.** Psychologists who study decision making realize that many random factors influence the choices people make. For example, you may choose a major, not because you love the subject, but because you think your parents will approve of it. The goal is to make well-considered decisions despite factors that may derail your thinking.

What happens when you make important decisions too quickly? Consider the student trying to decide whether to transfer schools. If she makes her decision based on a reason that ultimately is not the most important one for her (for example, a boyfriend or close friends go to the other school), she may regret her choice later. Key 4.11 shows how she worked through the analytical, creative, and practical parts of the process.

KEY 4.10 Working through a problem
relating to an instructor.

| DEFINE PROBLEM HERE: | ANALYZE THE PROBLEM |
|---|---|
| I don't like my Freshman Composition instructor | We have different views and personality types— I don't feel respected or heard. I'm not interested in being there and my grades are suffering from my lack of motivation. |

*Use boxes below to list possible solutions:*

| POTENTIAL POSITIVE EFFECTS | SOLUTION #1 | POTENTIAL NEGATIVE EFFECTS |
|---|---|---|
| *List for each solution:* Don't have to deal with that instructor Less stress | Drop the course | *List for each solution:* Grade gets entered on my transcript I'll have to take the course eventually; it's required for my major |
| Getting credit for the course Feeling like I've honored a commitment | **SOLUTION #2** Put up with it until the end of the semester | Stress every time I'm there Lowered motivation Probably not such a good final grade |
| A chance to express myself Could get good advice An opportunity to ask direct questions of the instructor | **SOLUTION #3** Schedule meetings with advisor and instructor | Have to face instructor one-on-one Might just make things worse |

*Now choose the solution you think is best—circle it and make it happen.*

| ACTUAL POSITIVE EFFECTS | PRACTICAL ACTION | ACTUAL NEGATIVE EFFECTS |
|---|---|---|
| *List for chosen solution:* Got some helpful advice from advisor Talking in person with the instructor actually promoted a fairly honest discussion I won't have to take the course again | I scheduled and attended meetings with both advisor and instructor, and opted to stick with the course. | *List for chosen solution:* The discussion was difficult and sometimes tense I still don't know how much learning I'll retain from this course |

**FINAL EVALUATION: Was it a good or bad solution?**

The solution has improved things. I'll finish the course, and even though the instructor and I aren't the best of friends, we have a mutual understanding now. I feel more respected and more willing to put my time into the course.

*Source:* Based on heuristic created by Frank T. Lyman Jr. and George Eley, 1985.

**KEY 4.11** Making a decision about whether to transfer schools.

| DEFINE THE DECISION | EXAMINE NEEDS AND MOTIVES |
|---|---|
| Whether or not to transfer schools | I attend a small private college. My father has changed jobs and can no longer afford my tuition. My goal is to become a physical therapist, so I need a school with a full physical therapy program. My family needs to cut costs. I need to transfer credits. |

*Use boxes below to list possible choices:*

| POTENTIAL POSITIVE EFFECTS | CHOICE #1 | POTENTIAL NEGATIVE EFFECTS |
|---|---|---|
| *List for each solution:* | Continue at the current college | *List for each solution:* |
| No need to adjust to a new place or new people | | Need to finance most of my tuition and costs on my own |
| Ability to continue course work as planned | | Difficult to find time for a job |
| | | Might not qualify for aid |

| | CHOICE #2 | |
|---|---|---|
| Opportunity to connect with some high school friends | Transfer to a state college | Need to earn some money or get financial aid |
| Cheaper tuition and room costs | | Physical therapy program is small and not very strong |
| Credits will transfer | | |

| | CHOICE #3 | |
|---|---|---|
| Many physical therapy courses available | Transfer to the community college | No personal contacts there that I know of |
| School is close so I could live at home and save room costs | | Less independence if I live at home |
| Reasonable tuition; credits will transfer | | No bachelor's degree available |

*Now choose the one you think is best—circle it and make it happen.*

| ACTUAL POSITIVE EFFECTS | PRACTICAL ACTION | ACTUAL NEGATIVE EFFECTS |
|---|---|---|
| *List for chosen solution:* | Go to community college for two years; then transfer to a four-year school to get a B.A. and complete physical therapy course work. | *List for chosen solution:* |
| Money saved | | Loss of some independence |
| Opportunity to spend time on studies rather than on working to earn tuition money | | Less contact with friends |
| Availability of classes I need | | |

| FINAL EVALUATION: Was it a good or bad choice? |
|---|
| I'm satisfied with the decision. It can be hard being at home at times, but my parents are adjusting to my independence and I'm trying to respect their concerns. With fewer social distractions, I'm really getting my work done. Plus the financial aspect of the decision is ideal. |

*Source:* Based on heuristic created by Frank T. Lyman Jr. and George Eley, 1985.

## Keeping Your Balance

No one has equal strengths in analytical, creative, and practical thinking. Successfully intelligent thinkers are able to analyze their abilities, come up with creative ideas about how to maximize their strengths and build their weaknesses, and put them to use with practical action. Staying as balanced as possible requires that you do the following:

- Use what you've learned in this chapter and the rest of the text to maximize your analytical, creative, and practical abilities.

- Reflect on what you do well, and focus on strengthening weaker skills.

- Combine all three thinking skills to accomplish your goals, knowing when and how to apply your analytical, creative, and practical abilities.

- Believe in your skills as a thinker.

"Successfully intelligent people," says Sternberg, "defy negative expectations, even when these expectations arise from low scores on IQ or similar tests. They do not let other people's assessments stop them from achieving their goals. They find their path and then pursue it, realizing that there will be obstacles along the way and that surmounting these obstacles is part of the challenge."[27] Let the obstacles come, as they will for everyone, in all aspects of life. You can face and overcome them with the power of your successfully intelligent thinking.

## Successful Intelligence Wrap-Up

With the power of successful intelligence, you can identify your most significant goals, devise ways to pursue them, and most importantly, take concrete actions to attain them. In addition, you can move beyond a fixed view of your intelligence. Here's how you have built skills in chapter 4:

## Analytical

You explored the steps and parts of analytical thinking in the section on analytical thinking skills, including crucial topics such as fact vs. opinion, perspective, and how examples support an idea. In the *Get Analytical* exercise, you honed your skills by analyzing a statement. At the end of the chapter, you considered how to use your analytical skills to evaluate potential ideas and choices in the problem-solving and decision-making processes.

## Creative

You developed a detailed understanding of creative thinking as you read the section on creative thinking skills. You learned of some creativity-boosting strategies and probably thought of more. In the *Get Creative* exercise, you brainstormed creative acts as well as new ideas about how to deal with a problem. In the section on problem solving and decision making, you explored ways to brainstorm solutions and choices.

## Practical

You broadened your concept of practical thinking as you read the section on practical thinking skills, including developing more specific ideas of how to apply your emotional and social intelligence. In the *Get Practical* exercise, you built a picture of how you see your successful intelligence and generated practical ideas about how to improve. When reading about problem solving and decision making, you explored practical ways to put solutions and choices to work.

# *kunnskaping*
## *(kun-skahp-ping)*

This Norwegian word is a creative combination of *kunnskap* (meaning "knowledge") and *verdiskaping* (meaning "value creation"). It translates loosely as "knowledging," which can be read as developing knowledge and meaning that are of use in school and work.[28] In the global marketplace described by Thomas Friedman (see chapter 1), knowledge as a tool and product is more important than ever before.

Think of this concept as you use your analytical, creative, and practical thinking skills to solve problems, make decisions, innovate, and question. Successful intelligence enables you to put knowledge to work as you strive toward your goals. It also empowers you to be creative, in much the same way that some clever Norwegian was when he or she coined *kunnskaping* and made it part of the language.

"I am enough of an artist to draw freely upon my imagination. Imagination is more important than knowledge. Knowledge is limited. Imagination encircles the world."

ALBERT EINSTEIN, MATHEMATICIAN AND SCIENTIST

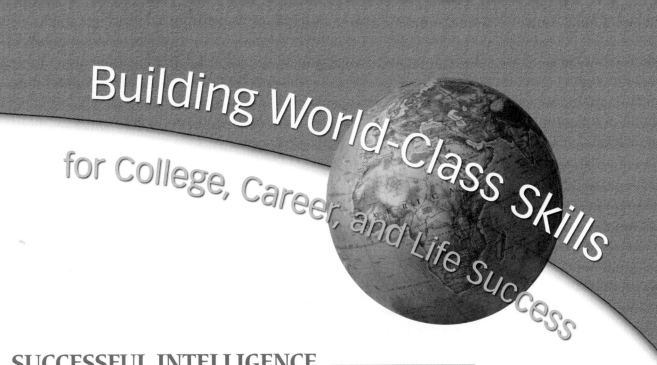

## SUCCESSFUL INTELLIGENCE
### *Think, Create, Apply*

Make an important decision. Put the decision-making process to work on something that matters to you. You will apply your analytical, creative, and practical thinking skills. Use a separate sheet of paper for steps 2, 3, and 5.

**Step 1. Analyze:** *Define the decision.* Write an important long-term goal that you have, and define the decision that will help you fulfill it. Example: "My goal is to become a nurse. My decision: What to specialize in."

**Step 2. Analyze:** *Examine needs and concerns.* What are your needs, and how do your values come into play? What is most needed in the health market, and how can you fulfill that need? What roadblocks might be involved? List everything you come up with. For example, the prospective nurse might list needs like these: "I need to feel that I'm helping people. I intend to help with the shortage of perinatal or geriatric nurses. I need to make a good living."

**Step 3. Be creative:** *Generate options.* Ask questions to imagine what's possible. Where might you work? What might be the schedule and pace? Who might work with you? What would you see, smell, and hear on your job? What would you do every day? List, too, all of the options you know of. The prospective nurse, for example, might list perinatal surgery, neonatal intensive care unit, geriatric nursing in a hospital or in a retirement community, and so forth.

**Step 4. Analyze:** *Evaluate options.* Think about how well your options will fulfill your needs. For two of your options, write potential positive and negative effects (pros and cons) of each.

Option 1:

_____

Potential pros:

_____

Potential cons:

_____

Option 2:

_____

Potential pros:

_____

Potential cons:

_____

**Step 5. Get practical: *Imagine acting on your decision.*** Describe one practical course of action, based on your thinking so far, that you might follow. List the specific steps you would take. For example, the prospective nurse might list actions that help him determine what type of nursing suits him best, such as interning, summer jobs, academic goals, and talking to working nurses.

An additional practical action is to go where the job is and talk to people. The prospective nurse might go to a hospital, a clinic, and a health center at a retirement community. Get a feel for what the job is like day-to-day so that can be part of your decision.

# TEAMWORK

## *Create Solutions Together*

Powerful group problem solving. On a 3-by-5 card or a plain sheet of paper, each student in the class writes a school-related problem—this could be a fear, a challenge, a sticky situation, or a roadblock. Students hand these in without names. The instructor writes the list on the board.

Divide into groups of two to four. Each group chooses one problem to work on (try not to have two groups working on the same problem). Use the problem-solving flowchart (Key 4.12) on page 129 to fill in your work.

**Analyze: *Define and examine the problem.*** As a group, look at the negative effects and state your problem specifically. Write down the causes and examine them to see what's happening. Gather information from all group members, verify facts, and go beyond assumptions.

**Create: *Generate possible solutions.*** From the most likely causes of the problem, derive possible solutions. Record all the ideas that group members offer. After 10 minutes or so, each group member should choose one possible solution to evaluate independently.

**Analyze: *Evaluate each solution.*** In thinking independently through the assigned solution, each group member should (1) weigh the positive and negative effects, (2) consider similar problems, and (3) describe how the solution affects the causes of the problem. Will your solution work?

**Get practical: *Choose a solution.*** Group members then come together, share observations and recommendations, and then take a vote: Which solution is the best? You may have a tie or may want to combine two different solutions. Try to find the solution that works for most of the group. Then, together, come up with a plan for how you would put your solution to work.

  KEYS TO SUCCESS

# Work through a problem using this flowchart.

| DEFINE PROBLEM HERE: | ANALYZE THE PROBLEM |
|---|---|

*Use boxes below to list possible solutions:*

| POTENTIAL POSITIVE EFFECTS | SOLUTION #1 | POTENTIAL NEGATIVE EFFECTS |
|---|---|---|
| *List for each solution:* | | *List for each solution:* |

**SOLUTION #2**

**SOLUTION #3**

*Now choose the solution you think is best—circle it and make it happen.*

| ACTUAL POSITIVE EFFECTS | PRACTICAL ACTION | ACTUAL NEGATIVE EFFECTS |
|---|---|---|
| *List for chosen solution:* | | *List for chosen solution:* |

**FINAL EVALUATION: Was it a good or bad solution?**

*Source:* Based on heuristic created by Frank T. Lyman Jr. and George Eley, 1985.

# WRITING

## Journal and Put Skills to Work

*Record your thoughts on a separate piece of paper, in a journal, or on a computer file.*

**Journal entry: Make a wiser choice.** Think about a decision you made that you wish you had handled differently. Describe the decision and its consequences. Then, describe what you would do if you could approach the decision again, applying your analytical, creative, and practical skills to reach a more effective outcome.

**Real-life writing: Address a problem.** Think about a problem that you are currently experiencing in school—it could be difficulty with a course, a scheduling nightmare, or perhaps a conflict with a classmate. Write a letter—to an advisor, instructor, friend, medical professional, or anyone else who may logically help—that would solicit input on your problem. Be specific about what you want and how the person to whom you are writing can help you. After you finish, you may want to consider sending your letter via mail or e-mail. Carefully assess the potential effects that your letter may have—and if you determine that it is likely to help more than harm, send it only after having someone you trust review it for you.

# PERSONAL PORTFOLIO

## Prepare for Career Success

**Generating ideas for internships.** Pursuing internships is part of a comprehensive career decision-making process. It's a practical way to get experience, learn what you like and don't like, and make valuable connections. Even if you intern in a career area that you don't ultimately pursue, you build skills that are useful in any career.

First, use personal contacts to gather information about career fields. List three people here:

*People whom I want to interview about their fields/professions, and why:*

1. _____    *Field:* _____

*Because:* _____

2. _____    *Field:* _____

*Because:* _____

3. _____    *Field:* _____

*Because:* _____

_____

_____

Talk to the people you have listed, and take notes.

Next, look up each of these fields in the *Occupational Outlook Handbook* published by the U.S. Department of Labor (available at the library, or online at http://stats.bls.gov/oco/home.htm). To get a better idea of whether you would want to intern in these fields, read OOH categories for each—such as Nature of the Work, Training, Working Conditions, Advancement, Job Outlook, Earnings, and so on. Take notes and compare the fields based on what you've learned.

Finally, consult someone in your school's career office about local companies that offer internships. Get specific information about internship job descriptions, timing (during the term, summer), and whether there is any pay involved.

Analyze what you have learned from your reading, your interviews, and the career office information. Write here in what field or fields you would like to intern and why, and describe what practical action you plan to take to secure an internship within the next two years:

_____

_____

_____

_____

_____

## Suggested Readings

Cameron, Julia, with Mark Bryan. *The Artist's Way: A Spiritual Path to Higher Creativity*, 10th ed. New York: Putnam, 2002.

deBono, Edward. *Lateral Thinking: Creativity Step by Step*. New York: Perennial Library, 1990.

Goleman, Daniel. *Emotional Intelligence: Why It Can Matter More Than IQ, 10th Anniversary Edition*. New York: Bantam Books, 2006.

Goleman, Daniel. *Social Intelligence: The New Science of Social Relationships*. New York: Bantam Books, 2006.

Moscovich, Ivan. *1000 Playthinks*. New York: Workman, 2001.

Noone, Donald J. *Creative Problem Solving*. New York: Barron's, 1998.

SARK. *Make Your Creative Dreams Real: A Plan for Procrastinators, Perfectionists, Busy People, and People Who Would Rather Sleep All Day*. New York: Fireside, 2004.

von Oech, Roger. *A Kick in the Seat of the Pants*. New York: Harper & Row, 1986.

von Oech, Roger. *A Whack on the Side of the Head*. New York: Warner Books, 1998.

## Internet and Podcast Resources

Creativity at Work (resources for workplace creativity): **www.creativityatwork.com**

Creativity for Life (tips and strategies for creativity): **www.creativityforlife.com**

Free Management Library—Problem Solving: **www.managementhelp.org/prsn_prd/prob_slv.htm**

"Get Creative" podcast from Podcast Alley, on the topic of problem solving and creativity: **www.podcastalley.com/search.php?searchterm=problem+solving**

"LSAT Logic in Everyday Life" podcasts on thinking, from the *Princeton Review*: **www.princetonreview.com/podcasts/lsat.asp**

Mind Tools—Decision Making Techniques:
**www.mindtools.com/pages/main/newMN_TED.htm**

Roger von Oech's Creative Think Web site:
**www.creativethink.com**

Prentice Hall Student Success Supersite:
**www.prenhall.com/success**

## Endnotes

[1] Matt Thomas, "What Is Higher-Order Thinking and Critical/Creative/Constructive Thinking?" n.d., Center for Studies in Higher-Order Literacy (http://a-s.clayton.edu/tparks/What%20is%20Higher%20Order%20Thinking.doc).

[2] Vincent Ruggiero, *The Art of Thinking*, 2001, quoted in "Critical Thinking," Oregon State University (http://success.oregonstate.edu/criticalthinking.html).

[3] From "The Role of Socratic Questioning in Thinking, Teaching, and Learning," n.d., The Critical Thinking Community, Foundation for Critical Thinking (www.criticalthinking.org/page.cfm?PageID=522&CategoryID=71), based on Richard W. Paul, Douglas Martin, and Ken Adamson, *Critical Thinking Handbook: High School*, 1989, Foundation for Critical Thinking.

[4] "The Best Innovations Are Those That Come from Smart Questions," *Wall Street Journal*, April 12, 2004, p. B1.

[5] Angiotech Pharmaceuticals, "Angiotech Submits Application for European Regulatory Approval for Its Vascular Wrap Product," news release, November 16, 2006 (www.angiotech.com/news/press-releases/?id=709).

[6] Sharon Begley, "Critical Thinking: Part Skill, Part Mindset and Totally Up to You," *Wall Street Journal*, October 20, 2006, p. B1.

[7] Robert J. Sternberg, *Successful Intelligence*, New York: Plume, 1996, p. 128.

[8] Colby Glass, "Strategies for Critical Thinking," March 1999 (www.criticalthink.info/Phil1301/ctstrategies.htm).

[9] Sternberg, *Successful Intelligence*, p. 49.

[10] Charles Cave, "Definitions of Creativity," August 1999 (http://members.optusnet.com.au/~charles57/Creative/Basics/definitions.htm).

[11] Elizabeth F. Farrell, "Engineering a Warmer Welcome for Female Students: The Discipline Tries to Stress Its Social Relevance, an Important Factor for Many Women," *Chronicle of Higher Education*, February 22, 2002 (http://chronicle.com/weekly/v48/i24/24a03101.htm).

[12] Roger von Oech, *A Kick in the Seat of the Pants*, New York: Harper & Row, 1986, pp. 5–21.

[13] Dennis Coon, *Introduction to Psychology: Exploration and Application*, 6th ed., St. Paul: West, 1992, p. 295.

[14] Roger von Oech, *A Whack on the Side of the Head*, New York: Warner Books, 1990, pp. 11–168.

[15] J. R. Hayes, *Cognitive Psychology: Thinking and Creating*, Homewood, IL: Dorsey, 1978.

[16] Sternberg, *Successful Intelligence*, p. 219.

[17] Adapted from T. Z. Tardif and R. J. Sternberg, "What Do We Know About Creativity?" in *The Nature of Creativity*, R. J. Sternberg, ed., London: Cambridge University Press, 1988.

[18] Sternberg, *Successful Intelligence*, p. 212

[19] Hayes, *Cognitive Psychology.*

[20] "The Best Innovations," p. B1.

[21] Sternberg, *Successful Intelligence*, pp. 229–230.

[22] "Amazing Student, David Hosei—Entrepreneur with a Heart," 2003 Indiana University (http://excellence.indiana.edu/hosei; no longer available).

[23] Sternberg, *Succesful Intelligence*, p. 236.

[24]Robert J. Sternberg and Elena L. Grigorenko, "Practical Intelligence and the Principal," Yale University: Publication Series No. 2, 2001, p. 5.

[25]Sternberg, *Successful Intelligence*, pp. 251–269.

[26]Ibid., p. 241.

[27]Ibid., p. 128.

[28]Christopher J. Moore, *In Other Words: A Language Lover's Guide to the Most Intriguing Words Around the World*, New York: Walker, 2004, p. 61.

**Answers to perception puzzles on page 112**

First puzzle: A duck or a rabbit

Second puzzle: A face or a musician

Third puzzle: Lines or the letter E

*"Successful intelligence is most effective when it balances all three of its analytical, creative, and practical aspects. It is more important to know when and how to use these aspects of successful intelligence than just to have them."*

ROBERT J. STERNBERG

**Y**our ability to read—and to understand, analyze, and use what you read—is the cornerstone of college learning. Taking a step-by-step approach to reading linked to analytical, creative, and practical thinking techniques will help you master content, whether you are getting ahead of the game with a stack of summer reading or staying up late studying for finals. This chapter introduces strategies to increase your efficiency and depth of understanding so that every hour you spend reading will be more valuable.

*In this chapter you explore answers to the following questions:*

- What will improve your reading comprehension? 136
- How can SQ3R help you master content? 147
- How can you respond critically to what you read? 156
- How do you customize your text with highlighting and notes? 157
- *Successful Intelligence Wrap-Up 163*

## Analytical

- Identifying steps to improve comprehension
- Mastering SQ3R
- Building vocabulary by mastering roots, prefixes, and suffixes
- Critically evaluating reading passages

## Creative

- Creating an environment that encourages concentration
- Adapting SQ3R to your unique studying needs
- Using colors and notations to highlight text and take text notes

## Practical

- How to study word parts to build vocabulary
- How to make SQ3R a personal tool
- How to put highlighting and note-taking systems into action

# What Will Improve Your Reading Comprehension?

Reading is an analytical process that requires you, the reader, to make meaning from written words. You do this by connecting what you know to what you read. Your understanding is affected by your familiarity with a subject, your cultural background and life experiences, and the way you interpret words and phrases.

Because these factors are different for every person, your reading experiences are uniquely your own. If, for example, your family owns a hardware store where you worked during summers, you will read a retailing chapter in a business text from the perspective of your work in the store. While you are comparing text concepts to your family's business practices, your classmates may be reading for basic ideas and vocabulary.

Improving your reading comprehension is especially important in college because assignments are generally longer, more difficult, and require a lot of independent work. In addition, what you learn from introductory-level texts is the foundation for your understanding in advanced courses. When you struggle through and master concepts that you considered impossible the first time you read them, you'll be proud of your ability to overcome obstacles instead of giving up. This pride will motivate you every time you read.

## How can I improve my reading and studying despite my learning disabilities?

In elementary school I needed extra help with reading. By high school, I was having a hard time keeping up, and a test showed I had dyslexia. Study assistance helped, but I attended high school for an extra year to improve my record.

I learn best by hearing, seeing, and doing all at once. If I just hear something, it doesn't sink in. I keep hanging in there though. Eventually, when I have a career, I would like to help others. I can see myself being on the lookout for early signs of disabilities like mine. What suggestions do you have that will help me cope with my learning disabilities?

Darrin Estepp
Ohio State University,
Columbus, Ohio

# PRACTICAL ANSWERS

Morgan Paar
Graduate Student,
Academy of Art College
San Francisco, California

*One thing I learned in college is that there is more than one way to succeed, even when I had trouble keeping up with the reading.*

First, I attended every single class without exception. Second, if I got behind in my note taking (and I often did), I would borrow a friend's notes and rewrite mine, combining the two versions. Third, I made friends with my teachers, and they would help me during their office hours.

One incident showed me that anything is possible. A friend worked for a newspaper and asked me to write a story. I laughed—I said I could barely spell my name, never mind write an article. I labored through it; my friend loved the writing (despite my "creative grammar"), and it appeared as a two-part story in the travel section. I have since had 17 articles published.

It never gets easy—but one route to success is to do something you love. I write travel stories because I love traveling and sharing stories. I am now a filmmaker, and I am studying film in graduate school so I can someday teach it. Darrin, you already know the skills you need to achieve your goals, though maybe they are deep in your subconscious mind. I was 27 years old before I knew what I really wanted to do. Just keep following your passions, never give up, figure out what you need to do to achieve your goals, and know that there is more than one path to your destination.

## Set Your Expectations

On any given day, you may be faced with reading assignments like this:

- A 10-page textbook chapter on the history of South African apartheid (world history)
- An original research study on the relationship between sleep deprivation and the development of memory problems (psychology)
- The first three chapters in John Steinbeck's classic novel, *The Grapes of Wrath* (American literature)
- A technical manual on the design of computer antivirus programs (computer science, software design)

# See the Movie— Read the Book

Movies from *Gone With the Wind* to *The Devil Wears Prada* are based on popular books. The Mid-Continent Public Library (www.mcpl.lib.mo.us/readers/movies/year.cfm) compiles a yearly list of movies made from books. Search this list, choose a movie you would like to see (or see again), and then watch it on video. List the name of the movie here:

_____

On a separate sheet or computer file, jot down your thoughts about the plot and characters and describe your reaction. Hold on to these thoughts for later.

During a school break, when you have time to read for pleasure, *read the book* on which the movie is based and write a similar page of reflections.

Then compare what you thought of the movie version to what you thought of the book. List three major differences here:

1. _____
2. _____
3. _____

Describe what you gained from reading the book that you *did not* get from watching the movie.

_____

_____

Based on this experience, are you likely to make the movie–book connection again? Why or why not?

_____

_____

How might you use another work as a starting point for your own creative effort?

_____

_____

_____

This material is rigorous by anyone's standards. You can help yourself handle it by setting higher expectations—*know at the start that you will read more than you ever did in high school*—and by challenging yourself to handle more complex ideas.

To get through it all—and master what you read—you need a systematic approach that taps into your analytic and practical thinking skills. Without one, you may face problems similar to those of a student at a large northeastern university, who explains:

> I did not get off to a great start because I had never really learned to study this enormous amount of material in a systematic way. I tended to do one subject for a big span of time and then neglect it for a week. Then I moved on to another subject, and forgot about that for a week. So there was no continuity within each course. That had a lot to do with it. Finally I figured it out. This year, I'm pushing myself to spend a little bit of time every day on each subject.[1]

## Take an Active Approach to Difficult Texts

Because college texts are generally written to challenge the intellect, even those that are well written may be tough going, especially when you encounter new concepts and terms. This is often the case when assignments are from *primary sources*—original documents, including academic journal articles and scientific studies—rather than from *secondary sources*—other writers' interpretations of these documents.

The following strategies will help you take an active, positive approach to reading difficult material:

**Think positively.** Instead of telling yourself that you cannot understand, think positively. Tell yourself: *I can learn this material. I am a good reader. I can succeed.*

**Have an open mind.** Be careful not to prejudge assignments as impossible or boring or a waste of time and energy before you begin.

**Look for order and meaning in seemingly chaotic reading materials.** Use SQ3R and the critical reading strategies introduced later in this chapter to discover patterns and connections.

**Don't expect to master material on the first pass.** Instead, create a multistep plan: On your first reading, your goal is to gain an overview of key concepts and interrelationships. On subsequent readings, you grasp ideas and relate them to what you already know. By your last reading, you master concepts and details and can apply the material to problems.

**Know that some texts require extra work and concentration.** If new material doesn't click, scan background material—including the text you used last term—for information that will help you understand. Set a goal to make your way through the material, whatever it takes. *If you want to learn, you will.*

**Define unclear concepts and words.** Use your practical intelligence as you consult resources—instructors, study group partners, tutors, and reference materials—for help. Build a library of texts in your major and minor areas of study and refer to them when needed, and bookmark helpful Web sites.

**Ask yourself questions.** Put on your analytical thinking cap as you engage in an internal question-and-answer session before reading a chapter. Look at the chapter headings and think about what the material means and why it is being presented in this way. Write down your thoughts. Then read the chapter summary to see if your questions are answered. (Questioning is at the heart of the SQ3R study system that you will learn later in this chapter.)

**Be honest with yourself.** Ask yourself: Do I understand what I just read? Are ideas and supporting evidence clear? Am I able to explain the material to someone else?

## Choose the Right Setting

Find the right place and time to focus on your reading:

**Select the right company (or no company at all).** If you prefer to read alone, find an out-of-the-way spot at the library. Even if you don't mind activity nearby, try to minimize distractions.

**Select the right location.** Many students study at a desk or in a comfortable chair. Still others like to spread out papers on the floor. Be careful about studying in bed—some students tend to fall asleep.

**Select a time when you are alert and focused.** Eventually, you will associate certain times with focused reading. Pay attention to your natural body rhythms and study when your energy is high. While night owls are productive when everyone else is sleeping, morning people have a hard time working during late-night sessions. Knowing yourself is a key to emotional intelligence.

Students with young children face the additional challenge of keeping their family busy while they work. Key 5.1 explores some ways that parents or others caring for children can maximize their study efforts.

## Learn to Concentrate

CONCENTRATION

*The act of applying all your mental energy and focus to your academic work.*

When you focus your attention on one thing and one thing only, you are engaged in the act of concentration. Following are active learning methods for remaining focused as you study. Many involve tapping your emotional and social intelligence.

**Be intensely involved.** Tell yourself that what you are doing is important and needs your full attention—no matter what is going on around you. It might help to place a purpose statement at the top of your desk. For example: "I'm concentrating on the U.S. Constitution because it is the basis for our laws and because it will be on Friday's exam."

**Banish extraneous thoughts onto paper.** Don't let unrelated thoughts block your efforts. When such thoughts come up, write them down and deal with them later. Keeping a monthly calendar of classes, appointments, and events will help you stay organized.

**Deal with internal distractions.** Internal distractions—for example, personal worries or even hunger—can get in the way of work. Taking a break to deal with what's bothering you (a sign of emotional intelligence) will make you more efficient. Physical exercise may relax and focus you; studying while listening to music may relieve stress; and a snack break will reduce hunger.

## Use these techniques to manage children while studying.

### KEEP THEM UP-TO-DATE ON YOUR SCHEDULE

Let them know when you have a big test or project due and when you are under less pressure, and what they can expect of you in each case.

### EXPLAIN WHAT YOUR EDUCATION ENTAILS

Tell them how it will improve your life and theirs. This applies, of course, to older children who can understand the situation and compare it with their own schooling.

### FIND HELP

Ask a relative or friend to watch your children or arrange for a child to visit a friend. Consider trading baby-sitting hours with another parent, hiring a sitter to come to your home, or using a day care center.

### KEEP THEM ACTIVE WHILE YOU STUDY

Give them games, books, or toys. If there are special activities that you like to limit, such as watching videos or TV, save them for your study time.

### STUDY ON THE PHONE

You might be able to have a study session with a fellow student over the phone while your child is sleeping or playing quietly.

### OFFSET STUDY TIME WITH FAMILY TIME AND REWARDS

Children may let you get your work done if they have something to look forward to, such as a movie night or a trip for ice cream.

### SPECIAL NOTES FOR INFANTS

Study at night if your baby goes to sleep early, or in the morning if your baby sleeps late.

Study during nap times if you aren't too tired yourself.

Lay your notes out and recite information to the baby. The baby will appreciate the attention, and you will get work done.

Put baby in a safe and fun place while you study, such as a playpen, motorized swing, or jumping seat.

**Compartmentalize your life.** Social invitations may be easier to resist if you have a policy of separating study time from play time. Tell yourself: "I will be able to go out with my friends on Saturday because I'm finishing this assignment on Friday so I won't have to work over the weekend."

**Analyze your environment to see if it helps or hurts concentration.** Think about your last study session. How long did you *try to* concentrate and how long did you *actually* concentrate? If you spent more than 10% of

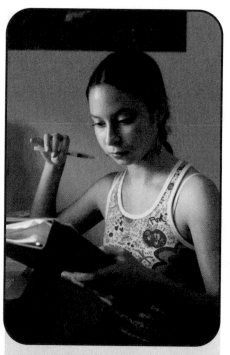

Different people respond better to some reading environments than to others. This student chose to live in a substance-free dormitory and prefers to study in her room.

your time blocking out distractions (people, things going on around you), try another location.

**Don't let technology distract you.** Don't Web-surf, e-mail, instant-message, or download songs onto your iPod while you are trying to read. Get into the habit of turning off your cell phone, and check voice mail and text messages only after you finish your work.

**Structure your study session so you know the time you will spend and the material you will study.** No one can concentrate for unlimited periods, so set realistic goals and a specific plan for dividing your time. Tell yourself: "I'm going to answer these 15 questions and then eat lunch with my friends for 45 minutes."

**Plan a reward.** Make sure you have something to look forward to, because you deserve it!

The strongest motivation to concentrate comes from within—not from the fear of failing a test or disappointing a teacher. When you see the connection between what you study and your short- and long-term goals, you will be better able to focus, to remember, to learn, and to apply.

## Become Emotionally Involved

You are more likely to remember material that evokes an emotional response than material that does not affect you, as student success expert Eric Jensen explains:

> The stronger you feel about something you read the more likely you are to remember it and make sense out of it. The good thing about this is that it works both ways; hating something or disagreeing with something works just as well as liking something or strongly agreeing with it.[2]

This is easy to do with controversial material, but how do you surround normally "dry" text chapters with emotions? These suggestions might help:

- Stop and think about your reaction to ideas, to the author's point of view and writing style, to chapter features and text design, and even to the chapter order.

- Discuss specific points with classmates, and have a heated discussion when you disagree. This will also help you understand the material.

- Think through the implications of a concept when it is applied in the real world.

## Define Your Reading Purpose

When you define your purpose, you ask yourself *why* you are reading particular material. One way to do this is by completing this sentence: "In reading this material, I intend to define/learn/answer/achieve . . ." *Write down your goal before you begin and look at it whenever you lose focus or get bogged down in details.* With a clear purpose, you can decide how much time and effort to expend on various assignments. This is particularly important in college where you may be overwhelmed by assignments unless you prioritize. Later in this chapter, you will find suggestions for prioritizing the readings on your plate.

## Purpose Determines Reading Strategy

Following are four reading purposes. You may have one or more for any "reading event."

- *Purpose 1: Read for understanding.* Here you read to comprehend concepts and details. Details help explain or support general concepts, and concepts provide a framework for details.

- *Purpose 2: Read to evaluate analytically.* Analytical evaluation requires that you approach material with an open mind as you examine causes and effects, evaluate ideas, and ask questions that test arguments and assumptions. Analytical reading brings a level of understanding that goes beyond basic information recall (see pages 156–157 for more on this topic).

- *Purpose 3: Read for practical application.* Here you gather usable information to apply to a specific goal. When you read an instruction booklet for new software or a lab manual for chemistry, your goal is to learn how to do or use something. Reading and action usually go hand in hand.

- *Purpose 4: Read for pleasure.* Some materials you read for entertainment, such as *Sports Illustrated* magazine or a mystery or romance novel.

Use your class syllabus to help define your purpose for each assignment. If, for example, you know that the topic of inflation will be discussed in your next economics class, read the assigned chapter, targeting what your instructor will expect you to know and do with the material. He may expect you to master definitions, economic models, causes and consequences, government intervention strategies, and historical examples—and be able to apply your knowledge to economic problems. In this case, depending on what your instructor expects, you may have three reading purposes—understanding, critical evaluation, and practical application. If you are confused about your purpose, e-mail your instructor for clarification. He is likely to be impressed with your motivation to stay on top of your assignments.

## Spend Enough Time

You'll need more than good intentions to finish assignments on schedule. You'll have to put in hours of work every day. One formula for success is this: *For every hour you spend in the classroom each week, spend at least two hours preparing for the class.* For example, if you are carrying a course load of 15 credit hours, you should spend 30 hours a week studying outside of class. Students who fall far short of this goal are likely to have trouble keeping up. Check your syllabus for the dates reading assignments are due, and give yourself enough time to complete them. (The syllabus on page 14 specifies reading assignments and due dates.)

## Use Special Strategies With Math and Science Texts

Math and science readings present unique challenges to many students. Try some of the following analytical, creative, and practical thinking techniques to succeed:

- *Interact with the material critically as you go.* Math and science texts are problem-and-solution based. Keep a pad nearby to solve problems and take notes. Draw sketches to help visualize material. Try not to move on until you understand the example and how it relates to the central ideas. Write down questions for your instructor or classmates.

- *Note formulas.* Make sure you understand the principle behind every formula—why it works—before memorizing it.

- *Use memory techniques.* Science textbooks are packed with specialized vocabulary. To learn these new words, use mnemonic devices, flash cards, and rehearsing aloud or silently (for more on memory techniques, see chapter 6). Selective highlighting and summarizing your readings in table format will also help.

## Develop Strategies to Manage Learning Disabilities

Students with reading-related learning disabilities may need to engage their practical thinking skills and emotional and social intelligence to manage reading assignments. Roxanne Ruzic of the Center for Applied Special Technology explored the strategies used by two LD students at an urban college in the Northeast:

- Danielle received an A in her Art History survey course, in part because she chose some courses with heavy reading requirements and some with light requirements. This allowed her to complete all her assignments on time. In addition, she frequently sought instructors' advice about what they wanted her to learn from assigned texts and used tutors whenever she needed extra help.

- Chloe received an A in her Introduction to Psychology course, in part because she met twice weekly with a tutor who helped her prioritize reading assignments and keep on top of her work. She also learned to tailor the amount of time she spent on different text sections to the importance of the material on upcoming tests. Finally, when she felt comfortable with text concepts, she read them quickly or skipped them entirely, but when she had trouble with the material, she did extra reading or sought help.[3]

If you have a learning disability, think of these students as you investigate the services your college offers through reading centers and tutoring programs. Remember: *The ability to succeed is often linked to the willingness to ask for help.* (See chapter 3 for more on learning disabilities and support services.)

# Expand Your Vocabulary

As reading materials become more complex, your vocabulary influences how much you comprehend—and how readily you do it. Use the following techniques to learn unfamiliar words as you encounter them.

## Analyze Word Parts

If you understand part of a word, you often can figure out the entire word. This is true because many English words combine Greek and Latin prefixes, roots, and suffixes. *Prefixes* are word parts that are added to the beginning of a root. The root is the central part or basis of a word around which prefixes and/or suffixes are added to produce different words. *Suffixes* are added to the end of the root.

ROOT
The central part or basis of a word around which prefixes and suffixes can be added to produce different words.

Key 5.2 contains just a few of the prefixes, roots, and suffixes you will encounter as you read. Taking the time to memorize these verbal building blocks will help you grow your vocabulary. (Keep in mind that although prefixes, roots, and suffixes are reliable tools, they do not always apply to words with complex origins.)

## Use a Dictionary

When reading a textbook, the first "dictionary" to search is the end-of-book glossary that explains technical words and concepts. Those definitions are usually limited to the meanings used in the text.

Standard dictionaries provide broader information such as word origin, pronunciation, part of speech, synonyms, antonyms, and multiple meanings. Buy a standard dictionary, keep it nearby, and consult it to learn unfamiliar words. You may even want to invest in an electronic handheld dictionary or, if you prefer an online version, investigate Web sites like Dictionary.com (http://dictionary.reference.com). The following suggestions will help you make the most of your dictionary:

**Read every meaning, not just the first.** Think critically about which meaning suits the context of the word in question, and choose the one that makes the most sense to you.

**Say the word out loud—then write it down to make sure you can spell it.** Check your pronunciation against the dictionary symbols as you say each word, or listen to the pronunciation on a handheld electronic or online dictionary. (Merriam-Webster Online, at http://merriamwebster.com, has a pronunciation feature.) Speaking and writing new words will boost recall.

**Restate the definition in your own words.** When you can do this with ease, you know that you understand the meaning and are not merely parroting a dictionary definition.

**Try to use the word in conversation in the next 24 hours.** Not only does this demonstrate that you know how the word is used, but it also aids memorization.

## Learn Specialized Vocabulary

As you learn a subject, you will encounter specialized, unfamiliar vocabulary (see Key 5.3 for examples from four college texts). Even if you

## Build your vocabulary with common prefixes, roots, and suffixes.

| PREFIX | PRIMARY MEANING | EXAMPLE |
|---|---|---|
| a, ab | from | abstain, avert |
| ad, af, at | to | adhere, affix, attain |
| con, cor, com | with, together | convene, correlate, compare |
| di | apart | divert, divorce |
| il | not | illegal, illegible |
| ir | not | irresponsible |
| post | after | postpone, postpartum |
| pro | before | prologue |
| sub, sup | under | subordinate, suppose |
| **ROOT** | **PRIMARY MEANING** | **EXAMPLE** |
| -logue | to speak | dialogue |
| -com | fill | incomplete |
| -strict | bind | restriction |
| -cept | take | receptacle |
| -chron | time | synchronize |
| -ann | year | biannual |
| -sper | hope | desperate |
| -clam | cry out | proclamation |
| -voc | speak, talk | convocation |
| **SUFFIX** | **PRIMARY MEANING** | **EXAMPLE** |
| -able | able | recyclable |
| -arium | place for | aquarium, solarium |
| -cule | very small | molecule |
| -ist | one who | pianist |
| -meter | measure | thermometer |
| -ness | state of | carelessness |
| -sis | condition of | hypnosis |
| -y | inclined to | sleepy |

feel like you are diving into a foreign language, know that continual exposure will lead to mastery.

Apply a basic vocabulary-building approach to learn these terms. Understand words in the context of the chapter; then turn to the glossary for a review, record definitions in your notes, create vocabulary flash cards, use terms in your own sentences, and more. Instead of rushing through unfamiliar words, look them up, ask other students about them, and relate them to what you already know.

**KEY 5.3** Every text includes specialized vocabulary.

| BIOLOGY TEXT | CRIMINAL JUSTICE TEXT | PSYCHOLOGY TEXT | BUSINESS TEXT |
|---|---|---|---|
| actin | biometrics | experimental method | double-entry accounting |
| chaparral | detainee | great person theory | leverage |
| exoskeleton | habitual offender | homeostasis | relationship marketing |
| gravitropism | RICO statute | trichromats | strategic alliance |
| prophase | writ of habeas corpus | vestibular senses | Uniform Commercial Code (UCC) |

Your instructors will test you on your ability to define and use course-specific vocabulary, so make sure you understand terms well enough to define them correctly on short-answer tests and to use them on essay exams.

## Use Memory Aids to Ensure Recall

Most students find that their most important vocabulary-building tool is the simple but very practical flash card. Your efforts will pay off if you study several cards a day and push yourself to use your new words in conversation and writing. Memorization tools, including mnemonic devices and flash cards, are discussed in chapter 6.

# How Can SQ3R Help You Master Content?

SQ3R stands for *Survey, Question, Read, Recite,* and *Review.* Developed more than 60 years ago by Francis Robinson, the technique is still used today because it works.[4]

As you move through the stages of SQ3R, you will skim and scan your text. Skimming refers to the rapid reading of such chapter elements as section introductions and conclusions, boldfaced or italicized terms, pictures and charts, and summaries. The goal of skimming is a quick construction of the main ideas. In contrast, scanning involves a careful search for specific information. You might use scanning during the SQ3R review phase to locate particular facts.

Approach SQ3R as a *flexible framework* on which to build your study method. When you bring your personal learning styles and study preferences to the system, it will work better than if you follow it rigidly. For example, you and another classmate may focus on elements in a different order when you survey, write different types of questions, or favor different sets of

SKIMMING

*Rapid, superficial reading of material to determine central ideas and main elements.*

SCANNING

*Reading material in an investigative way to search for specific information.*

review strategies. Explore different strategies, evaluate what works, and then make the system your own. (Note that SQ3R is not appropriate for literature.)

## Survey

*Surveying*, the first stage in SQ3R, is the process of previewing, or pre-reading, a book before you study it. Compare it to looking at a map before starting a road trip; determining the route and stops along the way in advance will save time and trouble while you travel.

Most textbooks include elements that provide a big-picture overview of the main ideas and themes. You need the big picture to make sense of the thousands of information nuggets contained in the text and to learn the order of topics and the amount of space allotted to each.

### Front Matter

Skim the *table of contents* for the chapter titles, the main chapter topics, and the order in which they will be covered, as well as special features. Then skim the *preface,* which is a note from the author that tells you what the book will cover and its point of view. For example, the preface for the American history text *Out of Many* states that it highlights "the experiences of diverse communities of Americans in the unfolding story of our country."[5] This tells you that cultural diversity is a central theme.

### Chapter Elements

Generally, every chapter includes structural elements that highlight important content:

- Chapter title, which establishes the topic and often the author's perspective
- Chapter introduction, outline, list of objectives, or list of key topics
- First, second, and third level headings
- Information in the margins including definitions, quotes, questions, and exercises
- Tables, charts, photographs, and captions that express important concepts
- Side-bar boxed features that are connected to text-wide themes
- Particular styles or arrangements of type (**boldface,** *italics,* <u>underlining,</u> larger fonts, bullet points, boxed text) that call attention to vocabulary or concepts
- An end-of-chapter summary that reviews chapter content
- Review questions and exercises that help you analyze and master content

In Key 5.4, a typical page from the college textbook *Psychology: An Introduction* by Charles G. Morris and Albert A. Maisto, how many elements do you recognize? How do these elements help you grasp the subject even before reading it?[6]

Various survey elements are included on this text page.

**Classical (or Pavlovian) conditioning** The type of learning in which a response naturally elicited by one stimulus comes to be elicited by a different, formerly neutral stimulus.

**Unconditioned stimulus (US)** A stimulus that invariably causes an organism to respond in a specific way.

**Unconditioned response (UR)** A response that takes place in an organism whenever an unconditioned stimulus occurs.

**Conditioned stimulus (CS)** An originally neutral stimulus that is paired with an unconditioned stimulus and eventually produces the desired response in an organism when presented alone.

**Conditioned response (CR)** After conditioning, the response an organism produces when only a conditioned stimulus is presented.

you are experiencing insight. When you imitate the steps of professional dancers you saw last night on television, you are demonstrating observational learning. Like conditioning, cognitive learning is one of our survival strategies. Through cognitive processes, we learn which events are safe and which are dangerous without having to experience those events directly. Cognitive learning also gives us access to the wisdom of people who lived hundreds of years ago, and it will give people living hundreds of years from now some insight into our experiences and way of life.

Our discussion begins with *classical conditioning*. This simple kind of learning serves as a convenient starting point for examining what learning is and how it can be observed.

## Classical Conditioning

*How did Pavlov's discovery of classical conditioning help to shed light on learning?*

Ivan Pavlov (1849–1936), a Russian physiologist who was studying digestive processes, discovered classical conditioning almost by accident. Because animals salivate when food is placed in their mouths, Pavlov inserted tubes into the salivary glands of dogs to measure how much saliva they produced when they were given food. He noticed, however, that the dogs salivated before the food was in their mouths: The mere sight of food made them drool. In fact, they even drooled at the sound of the experimenter's footsteps. This aroused Pavlov's curiosity. What was making the dogs salivate even before they had the food in their mouths? How had they learned to salivate in response to the sound of the experimenter's approach?

To answer these questions, Pavlov set out to teach the dogs to salivate when food was not present. He devised an experiment in which he sounded a bell just before the food was brought into the room. A ringing bell does not usually make a dog's mouth water but, after hearing the bell many times just before getting fed, Pavlov's dogs began to salivate as soon as the bell rang. It was as if they had learned that the bell signaled the appearance of food, and their mouths watered on cue even if no food followed. The dogs had been conditioned to salivate in response to a new stimulus—the bell—that would not normally have prompted that response (Pavlov, 1927). Figure 5–1, shows one of Pavlov's procedures in which the bell has been replaced by a touch to the dog's leg just before food is given.

### Elements of Classical Conditioning

Generally speaking, **classical (or Pavlovian) conditioning** involves pairing an *involuntary* response (for example, salivation) that is usually evoked by one stimulus with a different, formerly neutral stimulus (such as a bell or a touch on the leg). Pavlov's experiment illustrates the four basic elements of classical conditioning. The first is an **unconditioned stimulus (US)**, such as food, which invariably prompts a certain reaction—salivation, in this case. That reaction—the **unconditioned response (UR)**—is the second element and always results from the unconditioned stimulus: Whenever the dog is given food (US), its mouth waters (UR). The third element is the neutral stimulus—the ringing bell—which is called the **conditioned stimulus (CS)**. At first, the conditioned stimulus is said to be "neutral" with respect to the desired response (salivation), because dogs do not salivate at the sound of a bell unless they have been conditioned to react in this way by repeatedly presenting the CS and US together. Frequent pairing of the CS and US produces the fourth element in the classical conditioning process: the **conditioned response (CR)**. The conditioned response is the behavior that the animal has learned in response to the conditioned stimulus. Usually, the unconditioned response and the conditioned

*Source: Psychology: An Introduction, 12th ed. By Morris/Maisto, © 2005. Reprinted by permission of Pearson/Prentice Hall, Upper Saddle River, NJ.*

## Back Matter

Some texts include a *glossary* that defines text terms, an *index* to help you locate topics, and a *bibliography* that lists additional readings.

Practice will improve your surveying skills. So start now with this text or another you are currently using.

- Skim the front matter, including the table of contents and preface. What does this material tell you about the theme? About the book's approach and point of view?

  _____

  _____

  _____

- Are there unexpected topics listed in the table of contents? Are there topics you expected to see that are missing?

  _____

  _____

- Now look at a typical chapter. List the devices that organize the structure and content of the material.

  _____

  _____

- After skimming the chapter, what do you know about the material? What elements helped you skim quickly?

  _____

  _____

- Finally, skim the back matter. What elements can you identify?

  _____

  _____

- How do you plan to use each of the elements you identified in your text survey when you begin studying?

  _____

  _____

# Question

Your next step is to *ask questions* about your assignment. This process leads you to discover knowledge on your own, which is the essence of critical thinking (see chapter 4). As you pose questions and discover the answers in your text, you teach yourself the material.

## Step 1: Ask Yourself What You Know About the Topic

Before you begin reading, summarize in writing what you already know about the topic, if anything. As you perform this task, you delve into your knowledge base, preparing yourself to apply what you know to new material.

Thinking about your current knowledge is especially important in your major, where the concepts you learn in one course prepare you for subsequent courses. For example, while your first business course may introduce the broad concept of marketing research, an upper- level marketing course may explore how marketing research analyzes consumer behavior according to age, education, income and economic status, and attitudes. Learning this advanced material depends on understanding the basics.

## Step 2: Write Questions Linked to Chapter Headings

Next, examine the chapter headings and, on a separate page or in the text margins, write questions linked to them. For an assignment without headings, divide the material into logical sections, and then develop questions based on what you think is the main idea of each section.

Key 5.5 shows how this works. The column on the left contains primary- and secondary-level headings from a section of *Out of Many*. The column on the right rephrases these headings in question form.

KEY 5.5    Create questions from headings.

| HEADING | QUESTION |
| --- | --- |
| The Meaning of Freedom | What did freedom mean for both slaves and citizens in the United States? |
| Moving About | Where did African Americans go after they were freed from slavery? |
| The African American Family | How did freedom change the structure of the African American family? |
| African American Churches and Schools | What effect did freedom have on the formation of African American churches and schools? |
| Land and Labor after Slavery | How was land farmed and maintained after slaves were freed? |
| The Origins of African American Politics | How did the end of slavery bring about the beginning of African American political life? |

There is no "correct" set of questions. Given the same headings, you could create different questions. Your goal is to engage the material as you begin to think critically about it.

## Use Bloom's Taxonomy to Formulate Questions

Educational psychologist Benjamin Bloom developed Bloom's taxonomy because he believed that not all questions are created equal and that the greatest learning results from rigorous inquiry.[7] While some questions ask for a simple recall, said Bloom, others ask for higher levels of thinking. Key 5.6 shows the six levels of questions identified by Bloom: knowledge, understanding, application, analysis, synthesis, and evaluation. It also identifies verbs that are associated with each level. As you read, using these verbs to formulate specific questions will help you learn. Recognizing these verbs on essay tests will help you answer effectively.

 **KEY 5.6** **Use Bloom's taxonomy to formulate questions at different cognitive levels.**

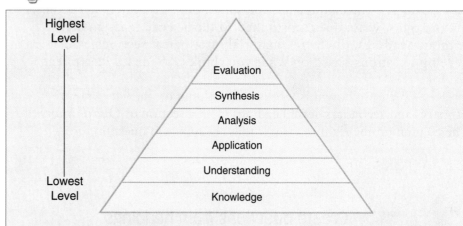

Highest Level

Evaluation
Synthesis
Analysis
Application
Understanding
Knowledge

Lowest Level

**Verbs That Indicate Each Level**

1. *Knowledge:* average, define, duplicate, label, list, memorize, name, order, recognize, relate, recall, repeat, reproduce, state.
2. *Understanding:* classify, describe, discuss, explain, express, identity, indicate, locate, recognize, report, restate, review, select, translate.
3. *Application:* apply, choose, demonstrate, dramatize, employ, illustrate, interpret, operate, practice, schedule, sketch, solve, use, write.
4. *Analysis:* analyze, appraise, calculate, categorize, compare, contrast, criticize, differentiate, discriminate, distinguish, examine, experiment, question, test.
5. *Synthesis:* arrange, assemble, collect, compose, construct, create, design, develop, formulate, manage, organize, plan, prepare, propose, set up, write.
6. *Evaluation:* appraise, argue, assess, attach, choose, compare, defend, estimate, judge, predict, rate, score, select, support, value, evaluate.

# Read

Your text survey and questions give you a starting point for *reading*, the first R in SQ3R. Retaining what you read requires an active approach, as follows:

- *Focus on the key points of your survey.* Pay special attention to points raised in headings, in italics and boldface type, in chapter objectives, and in the summary.

- *Focus on your Q-stage questions.* Read the material with the purpose of answering each question. Write down or highlight ideas and examples that relate to your questions.

- *Mark up your text and take text notes.* Write notes in the margins or on separate paper, circle critical ideas, or highlight key points to focus on what's important. These cues will help you study for exams. Text-marking and note-taking techniques will be examined later in the chapter.

- *Create text tabs.* Place plastic index tabs or adhesive notes at the start of different chapters so you can flip back and forth with ease.

## Find the Main Idea

Understanding what you read depends on your ability to recognize *main ideas* and link other ideas to them. Here are places you are likely to find these core ideas:

- In a topic sentence at the beginning of the paragraph, stating the topic of the paragraph and what about that topic the author wants to communicate, followed by support

- At the end of the paragraph, following supporting details that lead up to it

- Buried in the middle of the paragraph, sandwiched between supporting details

- In a compilation of ideas from various sentences, each of which contains a critical element, leaving it up to you to piece together these elements to find the main idea

When the main idea of a passage is unclear, use a three-step approach to decide what it is:[8]

1. *Search for the topic of the paragraph.* The topic of the paragraph is not the same as the main idea. Rather, it is the broad subject being discussed—for example, Apple CEO Steve Jobs, hate crimes on campus, or binge drinking on campus.

2. *Identify the aspect of the topic that is the paragraph's focus.* If the general topic is Steve Jobs, the author may focus on any of thousands of aspects of that topic, such as his cofounding of Apple Computer in 1976, his role in the Pixar computer animation company, or his role in the development of the iPod portable music player.

3. *Find what the author wants you to know about that specific aspect; this is the main idea.* The main idea of a paragraph dealing with Jobs's role in the development of the iPod may be this:

   > In his role as CEO of Apple, Steve Jobs oversaw the creation of the iPod portable music player, which changed the way the world listens to and purchases music.

## Prioritize Your Reading Assignments

Ask yourself what is important and what you have to remember. According to Adam Robinson, cofounder of the *Princeton Review,* successful students can tell the difference between information worthy of study, information they should know in a general way, and information they should ignore. Says Robinson: "The only way you can effectively absorb the relevant information is to ignore the irrelevant information. . . . Trying to digest and understand all the information in a textbook is . . . an excellent way to become quickly and hopelessly confused."[9]

The following questions will help you determine if text material is important enough to study in depth:

- Is the material stressed in headings, charts, tables, captions, key terms, and definitions? In mid-chapter and end-of-chapter exercises? In the chapter introduction and summary? (Surveying before reading will help you answer these questions.)

- Is the material a definition, a crucial concept, an example, an explanation of a variety or type, a critical relationship or comparison?

- Does it spark questions and reactions as you read?

- Does it surprise or confuse you?

- Did your instructor stress the material in class? Does your assignment ask you to focus on something specific?

When trying to figure out what to study and what to skim, ask yourself whether your instructor would expect you to know the material. If you are unsure and if the topic is not on your syllabus, e-mail your instructor and ask for clarification.

## Recite

Once you finish reading a topic, stop and answer the questions you raised in the Q stage of SQ3R. *Even if you have already done this during the reading phase, do it again now—with the purpose of learning and committing the material to memory.*

You may decide to *recite* each answer aloud, silently speak the answers to yourself, "teach" the answers to another person, or write your ideas and answers in note form. Whatever recitation method you choose, make sure you know how ideas connect to one another and to the general concept being discussed.

*Writing is the most effective way to learn new material.* Using your own words to explain new concepts gives you immediate feedback: When you can do it effectively, you know the material. When you can't, you still need to work with the text or a study partner. Whatever you do, don't get discouraged. Just go back and search for what you missed.

Writing comprehensive responses at this stage can save time later. As you respond to your Q-stage questions, you can compare what you write to the text and make adjustments. Your responses then become a study tool for review.

Keep your learning styles in mind when you explore different strategies (see chapter 3). For example, an intrapersonal learner may prefer writing, while an interpersonal learner may choose to recite answers aloud to a classmate. A logical-mathematical learner may benefit from organizing material into detailed outlines or charts, while a musical learner might want to chant information aloud to a rhythm.

When do you stop to recite? Waiting for the end of a chapter is too late; stopping at the end of a paragraph is too soon. The best plan is to recite at the end of each text section, right before a new text heading. Repeat the question-read-recite cycle until you complete the chapter.

If you find yourself fumbling for thoughts, you have not mastered the ideas. Reread the section that's giving you trouble until you know it cold.

## Review

*Reviewing*, both immediately and periodically in the days and weeks after you read, will help you learn and memorize material. If you close the book after reading it once, chances are that you will forget almost everything—which is why students who read material for the first time right before a test often do poorly. *Reviewing is your key to learning.*

Reviewing the same material over time will also help you identify knowledge gaps. It's natural to forget material between study sessions, especially if it's confusing or complex. When you come back after a break, you can focus on your deficits.

Here are some reviewing techniques. Try them all, and use the ones that work best:

- Reread your notes. Then summarize them from memory.

- Review and summarize in writing the text sections you highlighted or bracketed. Try to condense the material so that you can focus on key ideas.

- Answer the end-of-chapter review, discussion, and application questions.

- Reread the preface, headings, tables, and summary.

- Recite important concepts to yourself, or record and play them back on a tape player.

- Listen to audio recordings of your text and other reading materials on your MP3 player.

- Make flash cards with a word or concept on one side and a definition, examples, or other related information on the other. Test yourself.

- Quiz yourself, using the questions you raised in the Q stage. If you can't answer a question, scan the text for the answer.

- Discuss the concepts with a classmate or in a study group. Use each other's Q-stage questions to help one another learn.

- Finally, ask your instructor for help with difficult material. Define exactly what you want to discuss and then schedule a meeting during office hours or e-mail your questions.

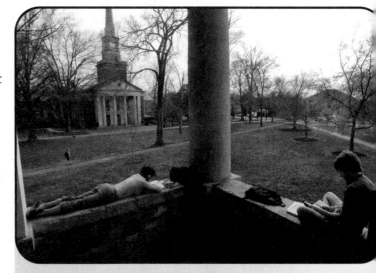

Reviewing material with a classmate nearby can give you the opportunity to discuss and clarify ideas together.

## Use SQ3R to become an active reader and learn new concepts.

| STAGE OF SQ3R | DESCRIPTION |
|---|---|
| Survey | Pre-reading a book before studying it—involves skimming and scanning as you examine the front matter, chapter elements, and back matter for clues about text content and organization. |
| Question | Developing questions linked to chapter headings and to what you already know about the topic. Questioning engages your critical thinking skills. |
| Read | Reading the material to answer the questions formulated in the Q stage and find main ideas. You can take notes as you read or highlight key ideas and information in your text. |
| Recite | Recitation involves answering—perhaps for a second time—your Q-stage questions. You may decide to recite the answers aloud or silently to yourself, teach them to a study partner, or record them in writing. |
| Review | Using various techniques to learn the material before an exam. Become actively involved with the material through summarizing notes, answering study questions, writing outlines or think links, reciting concepts, using flash cards, thinking critically, and so on. |

All this effort takes time, but the potential payoff is huge if you're motivated to work hard. Although at times it may be tempting to photocopy a classmate's text notes instead of reading and taking your own notes, you will learn only if you do the work yourself.

Refreshing your knowledge is easier and faster than learning the first time. Make a review schedule—for example, every three days—and stick to it until you're sure of your knowledge. Use different reviewing techniques as you work toward mastery.

Key 5.7 summarizes how SQ3R turns you into an active reader.

# How Can You Respond Critically to What You Read?

Think of the reading process as an archaeological dig. The first step is to excavate a site and uncover the artifacts. The second step is to investigate your findings, evaluate meaning, and derive knowledge from your discoveries. Critical reading is comparable to this crucial second step.

Critical reading, like critical thinking, taps your analytical intelligence (see chapter 4). Instead of simply *accepting* what you read, seek *understanding* by questioning material as you move from idea to idea. The best critical readers question every statement for accuracy, relevance, and logic.

## Use Knowledge of Fact and Opinion to Evaluate Arguments

Critical readers evaluate arguments to determine whether they are accurate and logical. In this context, the word *argument* refers to a persuasive case—a set of connected ideas supported by examples—that a writer makes to prove or disprove a point.

It's easy—and common—to accept or reject an argument outright, according to whether it fits with your point of view. If you ask questions, however, you can determine the argument's validity and understand it in greater depth. Evaluating an argument involves looking at these factors:

- The quality of the (evidence)
- Whether the evidence fits the concept
- The logical connections

When quality evidence combines with tight logic, the argument is solid.

**What is the quality of the evidence?** Ask the following questions to evaluate the evidence:

- What is the source?
- Is the source reliable and free of bias?
- Who wrote this and with what intent?
- What assumptions underlie this material?
- Is the argument based on opinion?
- How does the evidence compare with evidence from other sources?

**How well does the evidence support the idea?** Ask these questions to determine whether the evidence fits the concept:

- Is there enough evidence to support the central idea?
- Do examples and ideas logically connect to one another?
- Is the evidence convincing? Do the examples build a strong case?
- What different and perhaps opposing arguments seem just as valid?

Approach every argument with healthy skepticism. Have an open mind in order to assess whether you are convinced or have serious questions.

In addition to the foregoing critical reading strategies, transforming your textbook into a valuable work tool through highlighting and notes will help you make the most of study time as you set the stage for review.

# How Do You Customize Your Text with Highlighting and Notes?

Textbooks are designed and written with students in mind, but they are not customized to meet your unique reading and studying needs. It is up to you to do that for yourself through text highlighting and notes. Your goal is to transform your texts into very personal study tools.

## How to Highlight a Text

*Highlighting* involves the use of special markers or regular pens or pencils to flag important passages. When used correctly, highlighting is an essential study technique. The following techniques will help you make highlighting a learning tool:

- *Develop a highlighting system and stick to it.* For example, use your creative intelligence to decide if you will use different colored markers for different elements, brackets for long passages, or pencil underlining. Make a key that identifies each notation.

- *Consider using a regular pencil or pen instead of a highlighter pen.* The copy will be cleaner and look less like a coloring book than a textbook.

- *Read an entire paragraph before you begin to highlight, and don't start until you have a sense of what is important.* Only then put pencil or highlighter to paper as you pick out key terms, phrases, and ideas.

- *Avoid overmarking.* A phrase or two in any paragraph is usually enough. Enclose long passages with brackets rather than marking every line. Avoid underlining entire sentences, when possible. The less color the better.

- *Highlight supporting evidence.* Mark examples that explain important ideas.

Although these techniques will help you highlight effectively, they won't help you learn the material and, ironically, they may actually obstruct learning as you diligently add color to the page. Experts agree that you will not learn what you highlight unless you *interact* with the material through surveying, questioning, reciting, and review. Without this interaction, all you are doing is marking your book.

## How to Take Text Notes

When you combine highlighting with marginal notes or text flags, you remind yourself what a particular passage is about and why you consider it important. This combination customizes your text, which helps you study for exams. Going a step further by taking a full set of text notes is an excellent way to commit material to memory.

As you will also see in chapter 6, note taking on texts and in class is critical because material is cumulative—that is, what you learn today builds on what you learned yesterday and the day before since the beginning of the term.

### Taking Marginal Notes

Here are some tips for taking marginal notes right on the pages of your text:

- Use pencil so you can erase comments or questions that are answered as you read.

- Write your Q questions from SQ3R in the margins right next to text headings.

- Mark critical sections with marginal notations such as "def." for definition, "e.g." for helpful example, or "concept" for an important concept.

- Write notes at the bottom of the page connecting the text to what you learned in class or in research. You can also attach adhesive notes with your comments.

Key 5.8 shows how to underline effectively and take marginal notes in an introduction to business textbook that introduces the concept of target marketing and market segmentation.

Your customized text will be uniquely yours; no one else will highlight or take text notes as you do because no one else has your knowledge, learning style, or study techniques. Because text customization is so important to learning, you may find it hard to use previously owned texts that are heavily highlighted or filled with marginal notations. Even if the prior owner was a good student, he or she is not you—and that fact alone will affect your ability to master content.

## Creating Full-Text Summaries

Taking a full set of notes on assigned readings helps you learn as you summarize main ideas in your own words. Taking notes makes you an active participant as you think about how material fits into what you already know and how to capture key points.

To construct a summary, focus on the main ideas and examples that support them. Don't include your own ideas or evaluations at this point. Your summary should simply condense the material, making it easier to focus on concepts and interrelationships when you review.

Here are suggestions for creating effective full-text summaries:

- Try to use your own words, because repeating the author's words may mean parroting concepts you do not understand. When studying a technical subject with precise definitions, you may have little choice but to use text wording.

- Try to make your notes, simple, clear, and brief. Include what you need to understand about the topic, while eliminating less important details.

- Consider outlining the text so you can see how ideas relate to one another.

- Before you write, identify the main idea of a passage.

- Once that idea ends and another begins, begin taking notes from memory, using your own words. Go back into the text, as needed, to cull information that you didn't get on first reading.

- Take notes on tables, charts, photographs, and captions; these visual presentations may contain information presented nowhere else in the text.

- Use shorthand symbols to write quickly (see chapter 6).

- Create notes in visual form:
  ○ Construct your own charts, tables, and diagrams to depict written concepts.

Underlining and taking marginal notes help you master content.

Chapter 10: Understanding Marketing Processes and Consumer Behavior          **297**

*How does target marketing and market segmentation help companies sell product?*

### ■ TARGET MARKETING AND MARKET SEGMENTATION

Marketers have long known that products cannot be all things to all people. Buyers have different tastes, goals, lifestyles, and so on. The emergence of the marketing concept and the recognition of consumer needs and wants led marketers to think in terms of **target markets**—groups of people with similar wants and needs. <u>Selecting target markets is usually the first step in the marketing strategy.</u>

Target marketing requires **market segmentation**—dividing a market into categories of customer types or "segments." <u>Once they have identified segments, companies may adopt a variety of strategies.</u> Some <u>firms market products to more</u> than one <u>segment. General Motors</u> *(www.gm.com)*, for example, offers compact cars, vans, trucks, luxury cars, and sports cars with various features and at various price levels. GM's strategy is to provide an automobile for nearly every segment of the market.

In contrast, <u>some businesses offer a narrower range of products</u>, each aimed toward a specific segment. Note that segmentation is a strategy for analyzing consumers, not products. The process of fixing, adapting, and communicating the nature of the product itself is called *product positioning*.

*Definitions*

**target market**
Group of people that has similar wants and needs and that can be expected to show interest in the same products

← *GM eg*

**market segmentation**
Process of dividing a market into categories of customer types

*GM makes cars for diff. market segments*

*How do companies identify market segments?*

### Identifying Market Segments

By definition, <u>members of a market segment</u> must <u>share some common traits that affect</u> their <u>purchasing decisions.</u> In identifying segments, researchers look at several different influences on consumer behavior. Three of the most important are *geographic, demographic,* and *psychographic variables.*

*What effect does geography have on segmentation strategies?*

**Geographic Variables** Many buying decisions are affected by the places people call home. The heavy rainfall in Washington State, for instance, means that people there buy more umbrellas than people in the Sun Belt. Urban residents don't need agricultural equipment, and sailboats sell better along the coasts than on the Great Plains. **Geographic variables** are the geographical units, from countries to neighborhoods, that may be considered in a segmentation strategy.

<u>These patterns affect decisions about marketing mixes for a huge range of products.</u> For example, consider a plan to market down-filled parkas in rural Minnesota. Demand will be high and price competition intense. Local newspaper ads may be

*Buying decisions influenced by where people live*

**geographic variables**
Geographical units that may be considered in developing a segmentation strategy

*— good eg —
selling parkas in Minnesota*

*Thought*
*Geographical variables change with the seasons*

*Source: Business Essentials,* 5th ed., by Ebert/Griffin, © 2005. Reprinted by permission of Pearson/Prentice Hall, Upper Saddle River, NJ.

○ Devise a color-coding system to indicate level of importance of different ideas, and then mark up your notes with these colors.

○ Devise symbols and numbers and use them consistently to indicate the level of importance of different ideas. Write these in different-colored pens.

# Mark Up a Page to Learn a Page

Below, the text material in Key 5.8 continues. Put your own pencil to paper as you highlight concepts and take marginal notes. Compare your efforts to those of your classmates to see how each of you approached the task and what you can learn from their methods.

effective, and the best retail location may be one that is easily reached from several small towns.

Although the marketability of some products is geographically sensitive, others enjoy nearly universal acceptance. Coke, for example, gets more than 70 percent of its sales from international markets. It is the market leader in Great Britain, China, Germany, Japan, Brazil, and Spain. Pepsi's international sales are about 15 percent of Coke's. In fact, Coke's chief competitor in most countries is some local soft drink, not Pepsi, which earns 78 percent of its income at home.

**demographic variables**
Characteristics of populations that may be considered in developing a segmentation strategy

**Demographic Variables** Demographic variables describe populations by identifying such traits as age, income, gender, ethnic background, marital status, race, religion, and social class. For example, several general consumption characteristics can be attributed to certain age groups (18–25, 26–35, 36–45, and so on). A marketer can, thus, divide markets into age groups. Table 10.1 lists some possible demographic breakdowns. Depending on the marketer's purpose, a segment can be a single classification (*aged 20–34*) or a combination of categories (*aged 20–34, married with children, earning* $25,000–$34,999). Foreign competitors, for example, are gaining market share in U.S. auto sales by appealing to young buyers (under age 30) with limited incomes (under $30,000). Whereas companies such as Hyundai (*www.hyundai.net*), Kia (*www.kia.com*), and Daewoo (*www.daewoous.com*) are winning entry-level customers with high quality and generous warranties, Volkswagen (*www.vw.com*) targets under-35 buyers with its entertainment-styled VW Jetta.[4]

**psychographic variables**
Consumer characteristics, such as lifestyles, opinions, interests, and attitudes, that may be considered in developing a segmentation strategy

**Psychographic Variables** Markets can also be segmented according to such **psychographic variables** as lifestyles, interests, and attitudes. Take, for example, Burberry (*www.burberry.com*), whose raincoats have been a symbol of British tradition since 1856. Burberry has repositioned itself as a global luxury brand, like Gucci (*www.gucci.com*) and Louis Vuitton (*www.vuitton.com*). The strategy, which recently resulted in a 31-percent sales increase, calls for attracting a different type of customer—the top-of-the-line, fashion-conscious individual—who shops at such stores as Neiman Marcus and Bergdorf Goodman.[5]

Psychographics are particularly important to marketers because, unlike demographics and geographics, they can be changed by marketing efforts. For example, Polish companies have overcome consumer resistance by promoting the safety and desirability of using credit rather than depending solely on cash. One product of changing attitudes is a booming economy and the emergence of a robust middle class.

**TABLE 10.1**
Demographic Variables

| | |
|---|---|
| **Age** | Under 5, 5–11, 12–19, 20–34, 35–49, 50–64, 65+ |
| **Education** | Grade school or less, some high school, graduated high school, some college, college degree, advanced degree |
| **Family life cycle** | Young single, young married without children, young married with children, older married with children under 18, older married without children under 18, older single, other |
| **Family size** | 1, 2–3, 4–5, 6+ |
| **Income** | Under $9,000, $9,000–$14,999, $15,000–$24,999, $25,000–$34,999, $35,000–$45,000, over $45,000 |
| **Nationality** | African, American, Asian, British, Eastern European, French, German, Irish, Italian, Latin American, Middle Eastern, Scandinavian |
| **Race** | Native American, Asian, Black, White |
| **Religion** | Buddhist, Catholic, Hindu, Jewish, Muslim, Protestant |
| **Sex** | Male, female |

# MULTIPLE INTELLIGENCE STRATEGIES

## FOR READING

**APPLY DIFFERENT INTELLIGENCES TO CONCEPTS IN SOCIOLOGY.**

| INTELLIGENCE | USE MI STRATEGIES *to become a better reader* | APPLY MI READING STRATEGIES *to learn about social groups for your introduction to sociology course* |
|---|---|---|
| Verbal-Linguistic | • Use the steps in SQ3R, focusing especially on writing Q-stage questions, summaries, and so on.<br>• Make marginal text notes as you read. | • Summarize in writing the technical differences among social groups, categories, and crowds.* |
| Logical-Mathematical | • Logically connect what you are reading with what you already know. Consider similarities, differences, and cause-and-effect relationships.<br>• Draw charts showing relationships and analyze trends. | • Create a table comparing and contrasting the characteristics of primary and secondary social groups. |
| Bodily-Kinesthetic | • Use text highlighting to take a hands-on approach to reading.<br>• Take a hands-on approach to learning experiments by trying to recreate them yourself. | • Create an experiment that might turn a crowd of strangers into a social group joined together by a common problem. |
| Visual-Spatial | • Make charts, diagrams, or think links illustrating difficult ideas you encounter as you read.<br>• Take note of photos, tables, and other visual aids in the text. | • Create a visual aid showing four primary mechanisms through which people with shared experiences, loyalties, and interests meet—for example, through school and business—and how initial contacts may lead to deep social group relationships. |
| Interpersonal | • Discuss reading material and clarify concepts in a study group.<br>• Talk to people who know about the topic you are studying. | • Interview people who shared a difficult experience with a crowd of strangers—for example, people stuck in an elevator or train for an extended period—about how relationships changed as focus turned to a common problem. |
| Intrapersonal | • Apply concepts to your own life; think about how you would manage.<br>• Try to understand your personal strengths and weaknesses to lead a study group on the reading material. | • After reading about the nature of primary groups, think about the nature of your personal family relationships and the degree to which family members are your key support system. |
| Musical | • Recite text concepts to rhythms or write a song to depict them.<br>• Explore relevant musical links to the material. | • Listen to a rock concert that was performed in front of a live crowd. Then listen to the same music recorded in a studio. Think about performance differences that might link to the presence or absence of a crowd. |
| Naturalistic | • Tap into your ability to notice similarities and differences in objects and concepts by organizing reading materials into relevant groupings. | • Over the next few weeks, ask some close friends if you can have dinner with them and their families. After the visits, try to identify characteristics that all the families share. Create a chart to report your findings. |

*For information on social groups, see John J. Macionis, *Sociology,* 11th ed., Upper Saddle River, NJ: Prentice Hall, 2007.

# Successful Intelligence Wrap-Up

Reading and studying are the tools you will use over and over again to acquire information in your personal and community life and career. After college, you will be figuring out almost everything on your own—your 401(k) retirement plan, a new office-wide computer system, or even the fine print in a cell phone contract. Your reading success may depend on your ability to use successful intelligence. Here's how you have built skills in chapter 5:

## Analytical

You explored an analytical approach to reading comprehension, taking a close look at reading environment, reading purpose, and vocabulary. In the *Get Analytical* exercise, you used surveying skills to analyze the front matter and one chapter of a textbook. Within the section on critical reading, you examined how to consider fact and opinion, how arguments are supported, and perspectives in your approach to reading materials.

## Creative

In the *Get Creative* exercise, you generated ideas from reading a book and then seeing a movie made from the same story. Reading about concentration may have inspired ideas about how to create a reading environment that suits you best. When exploring the SQ3R reading method, you may have adopted different ideas about how to implement it into a blend that is uniquely your own.

## Practical

You discovered practical actions that can build your knowledge of roots, prefixes, and suffixes. You explored how emotional involvement can deepen your reading experience. You saw examples of how to put the practical steps of the SQ3R reading system into action. In the *Get Practical* exercise, you applied your knowledge of how to highlight and mark up text to a specific textbook page, solidifying your understanding of what strategies work best for you.

# *yokomeshi*
## *(yo-ko-meh-shi)*

Reading your college textbooks may feel at times like what this Japanese word literally means: "eating a meal sideways" (*meshi* means "boiled rice" and *yoko* means "horizontal"). The Japanese use this word to describe how difficult it is to learn a foreign language, since Japanese characters are vertical while most other world languages are horizontal. When the Japanese use this word to describe a difficult intellectual task, they force themselves to laugh at the image, which decompresses the stress.

If you feel overwhelmed by the new concepts and specialized vocuabulary in your readings, just think of the challenge of eating a meal sideways. Then take heart in the certainty that you are not alone in trying to figure out what things mean. You will succeed by taking as many deep breaths as you need, by keeping your sense of humor, and by committing yourself to using the strategies suggested in this chapter to meet new reading challenges.[10]

"Somewhere, something incredible is waiting to be known."

CARL SAGAN, ASTRONOMER

# Building World-Class Skills
## for College, Career, and Life Success

## SUCCESSFUL INTELLIGENCE
*Think, Create, Apply*

Studying a text page. The following page is from the chapter "Groups and Organizations" in the sixth edition of John J. Macionis's *Sociology*.[11] Apply SQ3R as you read the excerpt. Using what you learned in this chapter about study techniques, complete the questions that follow (some questions ask you to mark the page itself).

**Step 1. Think it through:** *Gather information and analyze it.* Skim the excerpt. Identify the headings on the page and the relationships among them. Mark primary-level headings with a #1, secondary headings with a #2, and tertiary (third-level) headings with a #3. Then analyze:

Which heading serves as an umbrella for the rest?

_____

What do the headings tell you about the content of the page?

_____

What are three concepts that seem important to remember?

1. _____
2. _____
3. _____

**Step 2. Think out of the box:** *Create useful study questions.* Based on the three concepts you pulled out, write three study questions that you can review with an instructor, a teaching assistant, or a fellow student:

1. _____
2. _____
3. _____

**Step 3. Make it happen:** *Read and remember.* Read the excerpt, putting SQ3R to work. Using a marker, highlight key phrases and sentences. Write

## SOCIAL GROUPS

Virtually everyone moves through life with a sense of belonging; this is the experience of group life. A **social group** refers to *two or more people who identify and interact with one another.* Human beings continually come together to form couples, families, circles of friends, neighborhoods, churches, businesses, clubs, and numerous large organizations. Whatever the form, groups encompass people with shared experiences, loyalties, and interests. In short, while maintaining their individuality, the members of social groups also think of themselves as a special "we."

### Groups, Categories, and Crowds

People often use the term "group" imprecisely. We now distinguish the group from the similar concepts of category and crowd.

**Category.** A *category* refers to people who have some status in common. Women, single fathers, military recruits, homeowners, and Roman Catholics are all examples of categories.

Why are categories not considered groups? Simply because, while the individuals involved are aware that they are not the only ones to hold that particular status, the vast majority are strangers to one another.

**Crowd.** A *crowd* refers to a temporary cluster of individuals who may or may not interact at all. Students sitting in a lecture hall do engage one another and share some common identity as college classmates; thus, such a crowd might be called a loosely formed group. By contrast, riders hurtling along on a subway train or

bathers enjoying a summer day at the beach pay little attention to one another and amount to an anonymous aggregate of people. In general, then, crowds are too transitory and impersonal to qualify as social groups.

The right circumstances, however, could turn a crowd into a group. People riding in a subway train that crashes under the city streets generally become keenly aware of their common plight and begin to help one another. Sometimes such extraordinary experiences become the basis for lasting relationships.

### Primary and Secondary Groups

Acquaintances commonly greet one another with a smile and the simple phrase, "Hi! How are you?" The response is usually a well scripted, "Just fine, thanks, how about you?" This answer, of course, is often more formal than truthful. In most cases, providing a detailed account of how you are *really* doing would prompt the other person to beat a hasty and awkward exit.

Sociologists classify social groups by measuring them against two ideal types based on members' genuine level of personal concern. This variation is the key to distinguishing *primary* from *secondary* groups.

According to Charles Horton Cooley (1864–1929), a **primary group** is a *small social group whose members share personal and enduring relationships.* Bound together by primary relationships, individuals in primary groups typically spend a great deal of time together, engage in a wide range of common activities, and feel that they know one another well. Although not without periodic conflict, members of primary groups display sincere concern for each other's welfare. The family is every society's most important primary group.

Cooley characterized these personal and tightly integrated groups as *primary* because they are among the first groups we experience in life. In addition, the family and early play groups also hold primary importance in the socialization process, shaping attitudes, behavior, and social identity.

---

*Source: Sociology,* 6th ed., by John J. Macionis, © 1997. Reprinted by permission of Pearson Education, Inc., Upper Sadde River, NJ.

short marginal notes to help you review the material later. After reading this page thoroughly, write a short summary paragraph:

_____

_____

_____

**Step 4. Tap your multiple intelligences:** *Use MI strategies to improve your reading.* The Multiple Intelligence Strategies table in this chapter (see page 162) encourages you to use different reading strategies to study the topic of social groups. Identify the strategies that work best for you and incorporate them into your studying routine.

# TEAMWORK

## Create Solutions Together

**Organizing a study group.** Organize a study group with three or four members of your class. At the group's first meeting do the following:

- **Set a specific goal**—to prepare for an upcoming test, for example—and create a weekly schedule. Write everything down and give everyone a copy.
- **Talk about the specific ways you will work together.** Discuss which of the following methods you want to try in the group: pooling your notes; teaching each other difficult concepts; making up, administering, and grading quizzes for each other; creating study flash cards; using SQ3R to review required readings. Set specific guidelines for how group members will be held accountable.

As an initial group exercise, try the following:

- **Review the study questions that you wrote for the** *Sociology* **excerpt in the previous exercise.** Each person should select one question to focus on while reading (no two people should have the same question). Group members should then reread the excerpt individually, thinking about their questions as they read and answering them in writing.
- **When you finish reading critically, gather as a group.** Each person should take a turn presenting the question, the response or answer that was derived through critical reading, and other thoughts. Other members may then add to the discussion. Continue until everyone presents a concept.

Over several weeks, evaluate the different methods as a group, singling out those that were most helpful. Then incorporate them into your ongoing study sessions.

# WRITING

## Journal and Put Skills to Work

*Record your thoughts on a separate piece of paper, in a journal, or on a computer file.*

**Journal entry: Reading challenges.** Which of the courses you are currently taking presents your most difficult reading challenge? What makes the reading tough—the type of material, the length of the assignments, the level of difficulty? Describe techniques you learned in this chapter that you will use to meet your reading challenge. Describe why you think they will help.

**Real-life writing: Asking for help.** Self-help plans often involve reaching out to others. Draft an e-mail to your instructor that describes the difficulties you are facing in the course you wrote about in the journal entry and that details the specific help you need in order to move to the next step.

To accomplish your goal while also coming across as a respectful, diligent student, make sure that your message is clear and accurate; that your grammar, spelling, and punctuation are correct; and that your tone is appropriate. (See Quick Start to College at the front of the book for guidelines for communicating with instructors.) Whether or not you send the e-mail is up to you. In either case, writing it will help you move forward in your reading improvement plan.

# PERSONAL PORTFOLIO

## *Prepare for Career Success*

*Complete the following in your electronic portfolio or on separate paper.*

**Reading skills on the job.** Excellent reading skills are a requirement for almost every 21st century job. Employers expect that you will read independently to master new skills and keep up with change. Whether it is in print or electronic form, on-the-job reading will challenge you as much—if not more—than college reading. For example, although taking sociology courses involves reading textbooks, journals, and case studies, actually working in the field requires that you keep on top of case reports, government regulations, court documents, and an unending stream of work-related e-mails.

Prepare yourself for what's ahead by honestly assessing your practical skills *right now*. Use the following list to rate your ability on a scale of 1 to 10, with 10 being the highest:

- Ability to concentrate, no matter the distractions
- Ability to use emotional triggers to learn and remember material
- Ability to define your reading purpose and use it to guide your focus and pace
- Ability to use specific vocabulary-building techniques to improve comprehension
- Ability to use every aspect of SQ3R to master content
- Ability to skim and scan
- Ability to use analytical thinking skills when reading
- Ability to use highlighting and notes to help you master content

For the two skill areas in which you rated yourself lowest, think about how you can improve. Make a problem-solving plan for each (you may want to use a flowchart like the one on page 130). Check your progress in one month and at the end of the term. Finally, write down the ways in which you anticipate using the reading skills you learned in this chapter in your chosen career.

# Suggested Readings

Armstrong, William H., and M. Willard Lampe II. *Barron's Pocket Guide to Study Tips: How to Study Effectively and Get Better Grades.* New York: Barron's, 2004.

Chesla, Elizabeth. *Reading Comprehension Success: In 20 Minutes a Day*, 2nd ed. Florence, KY: Thomson Delmar Learning, 2002.

Cutler, Wade E. *Triple Your Reading Speed*, 4th ed. New York: Pocket Books, 2003.

Labunski, Richard E. *The Educated Student: Getting the Most Out of Your College Years.* Versailles, KY: Marley and Beck, 2003.

Luckie, William R., Wood Smethurst, and Sarah Beth Huntley. *Study Power Workbook: Exercises in Study Skills to Improve Your Learning and Your Grades.* Cambridge, MA: Brookline Books, 1999.

Olsen, Amy E. *Active Vocabulary: General and Academic Words*, 3rd ed. New York: Longman, 2006.

Silver, Theodore. *The Princeton Review Study Smart: Hands-On, Nuts and Bolts Techniques for Earning Higher Grades.* New York: Villard Books, 1996.

# Internet and Podcast Resources

Academictips.org (study tips and links): **www.academictips.org**

College Tutor Study Guide: **www.amelox.com/study.htm**

HowToStudy.com (study advice with valuable links): **www.howtostudy.com**

Improve Your Study Skills (tips form SoYouWanna.com): **www.soyouwanna.com/site/syws/studyskills/studyskills.html**

Lesson Tutor—Good Study Habits: **www.lessontutor.com/studygeneralhome.html**

Merriam-Webster's Word of the Day (free word of the day in audio form available on the Internet or as podcasts): **www.merriam-webster.com/cgi-bin/mwwod.pl**

Princeton Review Vocab Minute (free vocabulary-building podcasts using songs to help you remember): **RobinR@Review.com**

Study Guides and Strategies: **www.studygs.net**

Taking College Courses: **www.math.usf.edu/~mccolm/Aclasses.html**

Prentice Hall Student Success SuperSite: **www.prenhall.com/success**

# Endnotes

[1] Richard J. Light, *Making the Most of College: Students Speak Their Minds,* Cambridge, MA: Harvard University Press, 2001, pp. 23–24. Copyright © 2001 by Richard J. Light. Reprinted by permission of the publisher.

[2] Eric Jensen, "*Student Success Secrets*," 5th ed., New York: Barron's, 2003, p. 88.

[3] Roxanne Ruzic, "Lessons for Everyone: How Students with Reading-Related Learning Disabilities Survive and Excel in College Courses with Heavy Reading Requirements," paper presented at the Annual Meeting of the American Educational Research Association, Seattle, April 13, 2001 (http://iod.unh.edu/EE/articles/lessons_for_everyone.html).

[4] Francis P. Robinson, *Effective Behavior,* New York: Harper & Row, 1941.

[5] John Mack Faragher, Mari Jo Buhle, Daniel Czitrom, and Susan H. Armitage, *Out of Many: A History of the American People*, 3rd ed., Upper Saddle River, NJ: Prentice Hall, p. xxxvii.

[6] Charles G. Morris and Albert A. Maisto, *Psychology: An Introduction,* 12th ed., Upper Saddle River, NJ: Pearson Prentice Hall, 2005, p. 186.

[7] Benjamin S. Bloom, *Taxonomy of Educational Objectives, Handbook I: The Cognitive Domain,* New York: McKay, 1956.

[8] Ophelia H. Hancock, *Reading Skills for College Students,* 5th ed., Upper Saddle River, NJ: Prentice Hall, 2001, pp. 54–59.

[9] Adam Robinson, *What Smart Students Know,* New York: Three Rivers Press, 1993, p. 82.

[10] Christopher J. Moore, *In Other Words: A Language Lover's Guide to the Most Intriguing Words Around the World,* New York: Walker, 2004, p. 87.

[11] John J. Macionis, *Sociology,* 6th ed., Upper Saddle River, NJ: Prentice Hall, 1997, p. 174.

# LISTENING, NOTE TAKING, AND MEMORY

*Taking In, Recording, and Remembering Information*

## 6

*"Successfully intelligent people find their path and then pursue it, realizing that there will be obstacles along the way and that surmounting these obstacles is part of their challenge."*

ROBERT J. STERNBERG

**C**ollege exposes you daily to all kinds of information—and your job as a student is to take it in, write it down, and keep what is important. This chapter shows you how to accomplish this by building your skills in the area of listening (taking in information), note-taking (recording what's important), and memory (remembering information). Each process engages your analytical, creative, and practical abilities and helps you build knowledge you can use.

*In this chapter you explore answers to the following questions:*

## Analytical

- Understanding the listening process and the challenge of good listening
- Evaluating the importance of class notes and different note-taking systems
- Analyzing the nature of memory and why memory strategies work

## Creative

- Constructing active listening strategies that help you learn
- Personalizing note-taking systems and strategies
- Thinking of and using mnemonic devices to boost recall

## Practical

- How to overcome distractions to listen actively
- How to use note-taking systems and shorthand and craft a master note set
- How to use mnemonics to learn

# How Can You Become a Better Listener?

LISTENING

A process that involves sensing, interpreting, evaluating, and reacting to spoken messages.

The act of hearing is not the same as the act of listening. *Hearing* refers to sensing spoken messages from their source. *Listening* involves a complex process of communication. Successful listening occurs when the listener understands the speaker's intended message. In school and at work, poor listening may cause communication breakdowns, while skilled listening promotes success. The good news is that listening is a teachable—and learnable—skill that engages analytical and practical abilities.

## Know the Stages of Listening

Listening is made up of four stages that build on one another: sensing, interpreting, evaluating, and reacting. These stages take the message from the speaker to the listener and back to the speaker (see Key 6.1), as follows:

- During the *sensation* stage (also known as *hearing*) your ears pick up sound waves and transmit them to the brain. For example, you are sitting in class and hear your instructor say, "The only opportunity to make up last week's test is Tuesday at 5 p.m."

- In the *interpretation* stage, you attach meaning to a message: You understand what is said and link it to what you already know. You relate this message to your knowledge of the test, whether you need to make it up, and what you are doing on Tuesday at 5:00.

# REAL QUESTIONS

## How can I improve my memory?

When I took a memory test in a psychology class, I discovered that my classmates and I are better at remembering a full definition to a word rather than reading the definition and remembering the word. We would have thought that it would be easier to recall a word than an entire definition, but that was not the case.

Sometimes I find memorization work difficult, even though I know I have the ability. For instance, I know I have the material written down in my notes, down to the exact page, but then on the test, I sometimes can't remember the answers.

I try to incorporate mnemonic devices as I study, but that doesn't always work. I know that rereading and repetition reinforce learning, but it's hard to devote enough time to retaining information for five classes. I've just been accepted to law school, and I'm concerned because law requires learning technical terms. Can you suggest ways for me to improve my memory?

Shyama Parikh
DePaul University
Chicago, Illinois

# PRACTICAL ANSWERS

Stephen Beck
Director, Learn-to-Learn Company
Winston-Salem,
North Carolina

## Understanding material will help you memorize and retain information.

Understanding what you study and grasping the way material is organized are crucial memory tools. The definitions exercise you took in your psychology class illustrates that you are more likely to remember a sentence of 30 words than a list of 15 random words because the sentence has meaning for you. Similarly, if a system of categorizing biology terms makes sense, you are more likely to understand and remember the terms. Mentally placing information in logical categories enhances recall, as do mnemonic devices.

Take the time to scope out the organization of a text or chapter before you start reading. Read the table of contents, preface, and chapter section and subsection titles. Look at chapter objectives and summaries. This overview will help you form meaningful connections and will set the stage for learning the details.

As you study, be an active participant by continually asking yourself whether information makes sense. If it doesn't, try to figure out why you're stuck—what strand of understanding is missing. To reinforce reading comprehension, pause at good stopping points and take notes from memory. Your notes are proof that you can recall and understand the material. How do you know if you have memorized a list? Write it down to find out exactly what you do and do not know.

This active pause-reflect-and-write technique is critical for learning new material.

- In the *evaluation* stage, you evaluate the message as it relates to your needs and values. If the message goes against your values or does not fulfill your needs, you may reject it, stop listening, or argue in your mind with the speaker. In this example, if you need to make up the test but have to work Tuesday at 5:00, you may evaluate the message in an unfavorable way.

**KEY 6.1**

The listening process moves messages along a listening loop.

SPEAKER DELIVERS MESSAGE TO LISTENER

| REACTION | EVALUATION | INTERPRETATION | SENSATION |
|---|---|---|---|
| Listener provides feedback to speaker through questions and comments | Listener judges message against personal needs and values | Listener attaches meaning to message | Listener hears message when ears pick up sound waves |

- The final stage of listening is a *reaction* to the message in the form of direct feedback. In a classroom, direct feedback often comes in the form of questions and comments. Your reaction, in this case, may be to ask the instructor if she can schedule another test time.

You will become a better listener by learning to recognize and manage listening challenges and becoming actively involved with the material.

## Manage Listening Challenges

Classic studies have shown that immediately after listening, students are likely to recall only half of what was said. This low retention rate is due, in part, to the following listening challenges.[1]

### Divided Attention and Distractions

Internal and external distractions often divide your attention. *Internal distractions* include anything from hunger to headache to personal worries. Something the speaker says may also trigger a recollection that may cause your mind to drift. In contrast, *external distractions* include factors outside yourself, such as noise and excessive heat or cold. They also involve sending and receiving text messages on your cell phone, instant-messaging friends, or surfing the Internet on your laptop.

Use practical strategies that tap your emotional and social intelligence to reduce distractions as they arise: Try your best to put your worries aside during class; sit near the front of the room; move away from chatting classmates; ban technology for social uses during class; get enough sleep to stay alert; and eat enough to avoid hunger.

### Listening Lapses

Your instructors are responsible for communicating information, but they cannot make you listen. That responsibility is in your hands. If you decide that a subject is too difficult or uninteresting, you may tune out and miss the foundation for what comes next. You may also fall into the trap of focusing on specific points and shutting out the rest of the message. If you experience a listening lapse, try to refocus quickly instead of worrying about what you missed. After class, look at a classmate's notes to fill in the gaps.

Preventing listening lapses starts with having the right attitude. Remind yourself that what your instructors say is valuable and that they often present material in class that is not in the text. If you work to take in the whole message, you will be able to read over your notes later, combine your class and text notes, and think critically about what is important.

## The Rush to Judgment

It is common for people to stop listening when they hear something they don't like. Their focus turns to their personal reactions and away from the message. Students who disagree during a lecture often spend valuable class time thinking about their reaction.

Judgments also involve reactions to the speakers themselves. If you do not like your instructors or have preconceived notions about their ideas or background, you may dismiss their message. Anyone whose words have ever been ignored because of race, ethnicity, gender, physical characteristics, or disability understands how prejudice interferes with listening. Although it is human nature to stop listening at times in reaction to a speaker or message, this tendency can get in the way of your education. Use your analytical intelligence to overcome the tendency to rush to judgment. It will make you more socially and emotionally competent.

## Partial Hearing Loss and Learning Disabilities

If you have a hearing loss, seek out special services, including tutoring and equipment, that can help you listen in class. For example, listening to a taped lecture at a higher-than-normal volume can help you hear things you missed. Ask your instructors if digitalized recordings are available, which you can download onto your computer or iPod. Meeting with your instructor outside of class to clarify your notes may also help, as will sitting near the front of the room.

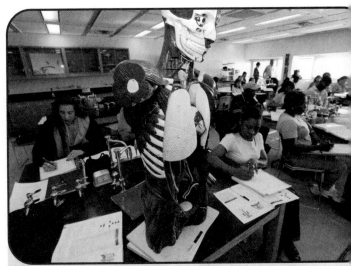

Other disabilities, such as attention deficit disorder (ADD) or a problem with processing spoken language, can add to listening difficulties. People with these problems may have trouble paying attention or understanding what they hear. If you have a disability that creates a listening challenge, seek help through the services available at your college.

Active listening means being in class and connecting with the material by taking notes and asking questions. These students benefit from a visual aid as they take notes in an anatomy class.

# Become an Active Listener

On the surface, listening seems like a passive activity: You sit back as someone else speaks. In reality, effective listening is an active process that involves the following factors:

## Be There

Being an active listener requires that you show up on time—preferably a few minutes before class begins. Instructors often make important announcements in the first few minutes and may also summarize the last lecture.

## Set Purposes for Listening

Before every class, use your analytical intelligence to establish what you want to achieve, such as understanding difficult concepts or mastering a task. Many instructors start a lecture with a statement of purpose, so listen carefully to their introductory words. Then write them at the top of your notes to help you focus.

Accomplishing your purpose requires that you read assignments before class and review your notes from the previous class. This preparation will set the stage for you to follow the lecture and will help you tell the difference between important and unimportant material. Without it, you may find yourself scrambling to take down every word.

Making your purpose for listening *personal* will motivate you to listen closely. As you prepare for class, ask yourself how the material relates to your academic goals. With the mind-set that what you hear will help *you*, you will be more able to make listening a top priority in class.

## Focus on Understanding

Rather than taking notes on everything, record information only when you can say to yourself, "I get it!" If you miss important material, leave holes in your notes and return later. Your instructor may repeat the point you missed, or another comment may help you piece it together.

## Ask Questions

Active listeners ask analytical questions to clarify their understanding and to associate new ideas with what they already know. Questions like "What is this part of?" or "How is it similar to yesterday's topic?" signal active involvement. Get into the habit of jotting down your questions and coming back to them during a discussion period so they don't interfere with listening.

*VERBAL SIGNPOSTS*
*Spoken words or phrases that call attention to information that follows.*

## Pay Attention to Verbal Signposts

Instructors' choice of words may tell you what they consider important and help you predict test questions. For example, an idea described as "new and exciting" or "classic" is more likely to be on a test than one described as "interesting." Verbal signposts—words or phrases that call attention to what comes next—help organize information, connect ideas, and indicate what is important and what is not (see Key 6.2). Use your practical intelligence to pay attention to these signals and to become more socially attuned.

KEY 6.2 Pay attention to verbal signposts.

| SIGNALS POINTING TO KEY CONCEPTS | SIGNALS OF SUPPORT |
|---|---|
| A key point to remember . . . | A perfect example, . . . |
| Point 1, point 2, etc. . . . | Specifically, . . . |
| The impact of this was . . . | For instance, . . . |
| The critical stages in the process are . . . | Similarly, . . . |

| SIGNALS POINTING TO DIFFERENCES | SIGNALS THAT SUMMARIZE |
|---|---|
| On the contrary, . . . | From this you have learned, . . . |
| On the other hand, . . . | In conclusion, . . . |
| In contrast, . . . | As a result, . . . |
| However, . . . | Finally, . . . |

## Expect the Unexpected

Active listening requires opening your mind to diverse points of view and to the heated classroom debates that may result. When the literature students in the following example listened actively, where the discussion led surprised them:

> The professor said she had attended a symposium where the author Ward Just said: "In my books, I always make sure readers know by about page 35 how each of the key characters earns their living. I just think this is critical to help each reader put all the characters in my writing in a context."
>
> My instructor then assigned two books for us to read. One was by Ward Just, and it was organized exactly as promised. The other was by a different writer, who . . . obviously couldn't care less whether readers ever learned how characters earned their living. Each of us was asked to come prepared to either agree or disagree with Mr. Just's idea. . . . It was clear the professor was hoping for some disagreement.
>
> Well, she got it. Three of us took the same position as Mr. Just. The other five strongly disagreed. And about a half-hour into the discussion, which was as spirited as we had all semester, one of the women said she couldn't help noticing that the three who shared Mr. Just's view just happened to be the three men in the class, while the five who disagreed happened to be the five women. "Does that imply anything?" she wondered. Which, as you can easily imagine, quickly led to an even more spirited discussion about how gender of both author and reader might influence the way we think about the structure of writing.[2]

Effective listening skills are the basis for effective note taking—an essential and powerful study tool.

**Successful Intelligence Connections Online**

Listen to author Sarah Kravits describe how to use analytical, creative, and practical intelligence to improve your listening skills.

Go to the *Keys to Success* Companion Website at www.prenhall.com/carter to listen or download as a podcast.

# GET ANALYTICAL!

## Discover Yourself as a Listener

Complete the following as you focus on your personal listening habits:

- Analyze how present you are as a listener. Are you easily distracted, or can you focus well? Do you prefer to listen or do you tend to talk?

  _____

  _____

- When you are listening, what tends to distract you?

  _____

  _____

- What happens to your listening skills when you become confused?

  _____

  _____

- How do you react when you strongly disagree with something your instructor says—when you are convinced that you are "right" and your instructor is "wrong"?

  _____

  _____

- Thinking about your answers and about your listening challenges, list two strategies from the chapter that will help you improve your listening skills:

  1. _____

  2. _____

# How Can You Make the Most of Class Notes?

Taking notes makes you an active class participant—even when you don't say a word—and provides you with study materials. What's on the line is nothing short of your academic success.

Class notes have two primary purposes: to serve as a record of what happened in class and to use for studying, alone and in combination with your text notes. Because it is virtually impossible to take notes on everything you hear, note taking encourages you to use your analytical intelligence to critically evaluate what is worth remembering.

## Note-Taking Systems

The most common note-taking systems are outlines, the Cornell system, and think links. Choose the system that you find most comfortable and that works best with course content. Be willing to change systems in different sitations.

### Take Notes in Outline Form

Outlines use a standard structure to show how ideas interrelate. *Formal outlines* indicate idea dominance and subordination with Roman numerals, uppercase and lowercase letters, and numbers. In contrast, *informal outlines* show the same associations but replace the formality with a system of consistent indenting and dashes (see Key 6.3). Many students find informal outlines easier for in-class note taking. Key 6.4 shows how the structure of an informal outline helps a student take notes on the topic of tropical rain forests. The Multiple Intelligence Strategies table in this chapter (see page 181) is designed to help harness different learning approaches for an earth science course. Specifically, the table will suggest different note-taking strategies you can use when you study the topic of tropical rain forests.

From time to time, an instructor may give you a guide, usually in outline form, to help you take notes in class. This outline, known as

**KEY 6.3** **Outlines show levels of importance as they link details to main ideas.**

| FORMAL OUTLINE | INFORMAL OUTLINE |
|---|---|
| TOPIC | TOPIC |
| I. First Main Idea | First Main Idea |
|   A. Major supporting fact |   —Major supporting fact |
|   B. Major supporting fact |   —Major supporting fact |
|     1. First reason or example |     —First reason or example |
|     2. Second reason or example |     —Second reason or example |
|       a. First supporting fact |       —First supporting fact |
|       b. Second supporting fact |       —Second supporting fact |
| II. Second Main Idea | Second Main Idea |
|   A. Major supporting fact |   —Major supporting fact |
|     1. First reason or example |     —First reason or example |
|     2. Second reason or example |     —Second reason or example |
|   B. Major supporting fact |   —Major supporting fact |

### KEY 6.4  An informal outline is excellent for taking class notes.

| |
|---|
| Tropical Rain Forests[3] |
| —What are tropical rain forests? |
| —Areas in South America and Africa, along the equator |
| —Average temperatures between 25° and 30° C (77°–86° F) |
| —Average annual rainfalls range between 250 to 400 centimeters (100 to 160 inches) |
| —Conditions combine to create the Earth's richest, most biodiverse ecosystem. |
| —A biodiverse ecosystem has a great number of organisms co-existing within a defined area. |
| —Examples of rain forest biodiversity |
| —2½ acres in the Amazon rain forest has 283 species of trees |
| —a 3-square-mile section of a Peruvian rain forest has more than 1,300 butterfly species and 600 bird species. |
| —Compare this biodiversity to what is found in the entire U.S. |
| —only 400 butterfly species and 700 bird species |
| —How are humans changing the rain forest? |
| —Humans have already destroyed about 40% of all rain forests. |
| —They are cutting down trees for lumber or clearing the land for ranching or agriculture. |
| —Biologist Edwin O. Wilson estimates that this destruction may lead to the extinction of 27,000 species. |
| —Rain forest removal is also linked to the increase in atmospheric carbon dioxide, which worsens the greenhouse effect. |
| —The greenhouse effect refers to process in which gases such as carbon dioxide trap the sun's energy in the Earth's atmosphere as heat, resulting in global warming. |
| —Recognition of the crisis is growing as are conservation efforts. |

*guided notes*, may be on the board, on an overhead projector, or on a handout that you receive at the beginning of class. Because guided notes are usually general and sketchy, they require that you fill in the details.

## Use the Cornell System

The *Cornell note-taking system*, also known as the *T-note system*, consists of three sections on ordinary notepaper:[4]

- Section 1, the largest section, is on the right. Record your notes here in whatever form you choose. Skip lines between topics so you can clearly see where a section begins and ends.

- Section 2, to the left of your notes, is the *cue column*. Leave it blank while you read or listen, and then fill it in later as you review. You might insert key words or comments that highlight ideas, clarify meaning, add examples, link ideas, or draw diagrams. Many students use this column to raise questions, which they answer when they study.

- Section 3, at the bottom of the page, is known as the *summary area*. Here you reduce your notes to critical points, a process that will help you learn the material. Use this section to provide an overview of what the notes say.

# MULTIPLE INTELLIGENCE STRATEGIES

## FOR NOTE TAKING

### APPLY DIFFERENT INTELLIGENCES TO TAKING NOTES IN EARTH SCIENCE.

| INTELLIGENCE | USE MI STRATEGIES *to become a better note taker* | APPLY MI NOTE-TAKING STRATEGIES *to the topic of tropical rain forests for an earth science course* |
|---|---|---|
| Verbal-Linguistic | • Rewrite your class notes in an alternate note-taking style to see connections more clearly.<br>• Combine class and text notes to get a complete picture. | • Rewrite and summarize your reading and lecture notes to understand the characteristics of tropical rain forests.[*] |
| Logical-Mathematical | • When combining notes into a master set, integrate the material into a logical sequence.<br>• Create tables that show relationships. | • Create a table comparing and contrasting the different species found in a typical rain forest. |
| Bodily-Kinesthetic | • Think of your notes as a crafts project that enables you to see "knowledge layers." Use colored pens to texture your notes.<br>• Study with your notes spread in sequence around you so that you can see knowledge building from left to right. | • Fill a tube with 160 inches of water (that's $13\frac{1}{3}$ feet!) to give you a physical sense of the annual rainfall in a rain forest. Or fill a bathtub with 10 inches of water and multiply by 16 to imagine rainfall totals. How would you react to living with so much rain? Take notes on your reaction. |
| Visual-Spatial | • Take notes using colored markers or pens.<br>• Rewrite lecture notes in think link format, focusing on the most important points. | • As part of your notes, create a chart that covers the types of vegetation that grow in a rain forest. Use a different colored marker for each plant species. |
| Interpersonal | • Try to schedule a study group right after a lecture to discuss class notes.<br>• Review class notes with a study buddy. Compare notes to see what the other missed. | • Interview someone you know who has visited a rain forest about what she saw, or interview a natural scientist at a museum about this environment. Use a different note-taking system for each person. |
| Intrapersonal | • Schedule some quiet time soon after a lecture to review and think about your notes.<br>• As you review your notes, decide whether you grasp the material or need help. | • Think about the conflict between economic modernization and the preservation of rain forests in underdeveloped areas. Include your thoughts in your notes. |
| Musical | • To improve recall, recite concepts in your notes to rhythms.<br>• Write a song that includes material from your class and text notes. Use the refrain to emphasize what is important. | • Use the Internet to find songs about the biodiversity of rain forests written by indigenous peoples who live in or near them. Then, use the song to remember key concepts. Take notes on what you find. |
| Naturalistic | • As you create a master note set, notice similarities and differences in concepts by organizing material into natural groupings. | • If possible, visit a museum of natural history with exhibits of rain forests. Try to see common characteristics that make vegetation and species thrive in this environment. Take notes on your observations. |

* For information on tropical rain forests, see Frederick Lutgens, Edward Tarbuck, and Dennis Tasa, *Foundations of Earth Science,* 5th ed., Upper Saddle River, NJ: Prentice Hall, 2008.

Create this note-taking structure before class begins. Picture an upside-down letter T as you follow these directions:

- Start with a sheet of 8½-by-11-inch lined paper. Label it with the date and lecture title.

- To create the cue column, draw a vertical line about 2½ inches from the left side of the paper. End the line about 2 inches from the bottom of the sheet.

- To create the summary area, start at the point where the vertical line ends (about 2 inches from the bottom of the page) and draw a horizontal line that spans the entire paper.

Key 6.5 shows how the Cornell system is used in a business course.

## Create a Think Link

A *think link*, also known as a *mind map* or *word web*, is a visual form of note taking that encourages flexible thinking. When you draw a think link, you use shapes and lines to link ideas with supporting details and examples. The visual design makes the connections easy to see, and shapes and pictures extend the material beyond words.

To create a think link, start by circling or boxing your topic in the middle of the paper. Next, draw a line from the topic and write the name of one major idea at the end of the line. Circle that idea. Then, jot down specific facts related to the idea, linking them to the idea with lines. Continue the process, connecting thoughts to one another with circles, lines, and words. Key 6.6, a think link on the sociological concept of stratification, follows this structure, just one of many possible designs.

Other examples of think link designs include stair steps showing connected ideas that build toward a conclusion, and a tree with trunk and roots as central concepts and branches as examples. Key 6.1 on page 184 shows another type of think link called a "jellyfish."

A think link may be difficult to construct in class, especially if your instructor talks quickly. If this is the case, transform your notes into think link format later when you review.

## Use Other Visual Strategies

Other strategies that help organize information are especially useful to visual learners, although they may be too involved to complete during class. Use them when taking text notes or combining class and text notes for review. These strategies include the following:

- **Time lines.** Use a time line to organize information into chronological order. Draw a vertical or horizontal line on the page and connect each item to the line, in order, noting the dates and basic event descriptions.

- **Tables.** Use the columns and rows of a table to organize information as you condense and summarize your class and text notes.

- **Hierarchy charts.** Charts showing an information hierarchy can help you visualize how pieces fit together. For example, you can use a hierarchy chart to show levels within a government bureaucracy or levels of scientific classification of animals and plants.

**KEY 6.5** The Cornell system has space for notes, comments, and a summary.

October 3, 200x, p. 1

UNDERLINE UNDERSTANDING EMPLOYEE MOTIVATION

| Why do some workers have a better attitude toward their work than others? | Purpose of motivational theories<br>—To explain role of human relations in motivating employee performance<br>—Theories translate into how managers actually treat workers |

2 specific theories

Some managers view workers as lazy; others view them as motivated and productive.

—Human resources model, developed by Douglas McGregor, shows that managers have radically different beliefs about motivation.
—Theory X holds that people are naturally irresponsible and uncooperative
—Theory Y holds that people are naturally responsible and self-motivated

Maslow's Hierarchy

self-actualization needs
(challenging job)
esteem needs
(job title)
social needs
(friends at work)
security needs
(health plan)
physiological needs
(pay)

—Maslow's Hierarchy of Needs says that people have needs in 5 different areas, which they attempt to satisfy in their work.
—Physiological need: need for survival, including food and shelter
—Security need: need for stability and protection
—Social need: need for friendship and companionship
—Esteem need: need for status and recognition
—Self-actualization need: need for self-fulfillment
Needs at lower levels must be met before a person tries to satisfy needs at higher levels.
—Developed by psychologist Abraham Maslow

Two motivational theories try to explain worker motivation. The human resources model includes Theory X and Theory Y. Maslow's Hierarchy of Needs suggests that people have needs in 5 different areas: physiological, security, social, esteem, and self-actualization.

## Note Taking Is a Three-Step Process

Taking good class notes requires practice—practice preparing, practice doing, and practice reviewing. Involved are a number of analytical and practical strategies.

## Prepare

Showing up for class on time with pad and pen in hand is only the beginning.

## Use a think link to connect ideas visually.

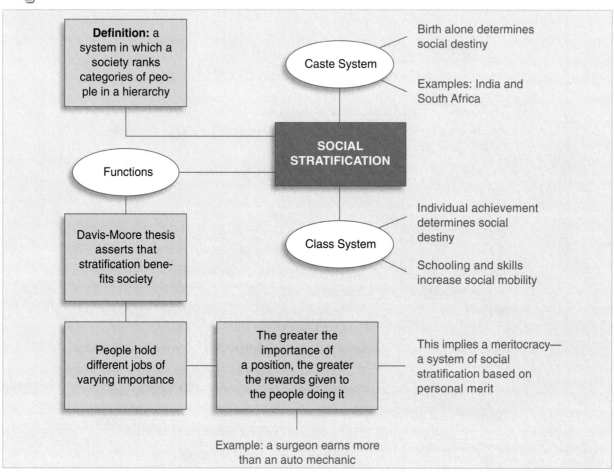

**Definition:** a system in which a society ranks categories of people in a hierarchy

**Caste System**

Birth alone determines social destiny

Examples: India and South Africa

**SOCIAL STRATIFICATION**

**Functions**

Davis-Moore thesis asserts that stratification benefits society

**Class System**

Individual achievement determines social destiny

Schooling and skills increase social mobility

People hold different jobs of varying importance

The greater the importance of a position, the greater the rewards given to the people doing it

This implies a meritocracy—a system of social stratification based on personal merit

Example: a surgeon earns more than an auto mechanic

**Preview your reading material.** *More than anything else you can do, reading assigned materials before class will give you the background to take effective notes.* Check your class syllabi daily to see when assignments are due, and then plan your reading time with these deadlines in mind. (The syllabus on page 14 shows when specific reading assignments are due.)

**Review what you know.** Taking 15 minutes before class to review your notes from the previous class and your reading assignment notes for that day will enable you to follow the lecture from the start. Without this preparation, you may find yourself flipping back in your notebook instead of listening to new information.

**Gather your supplies.** Use a separate notebook for each course, and start a new page for each class. If you use a three-ring binder, punch holes in handouts and insert them right after your notes for that day. If you use a laptop, open the file containing your class notes right away.

**Location, location, location.** Find a comfortable seat that is away from friends to minimize distractions. Be ready to write as soon as the instructor begins speaking.

**Choose the best note-taking system.** Use your emotional and social intelligence to select a system that will work best in each class. Take these factors into account when making your choices:

- *The instructor's style* (which will be clear after a few classes). In the same term, you may have one instructor who is organized and speaks slowly, another who jumps around and talks rapidly, and a third who digresses in response to questions. Be flexible enough to adapt your note taking to each situation.

- *The course material.* You may decide that an informal outline works best for a highly structured lecture and that a think link is right for a looser presentation. Try one note-taking system for several classes, then adjust if necessary.

- *Your learning style.* Choose strategies that make the most of your strengths and compensate for weaknesses. A visual-spatial learner might prefer think links or the Cornell system; a thinker type might be comfortable with outlines; an interpersonal learner might use the Cornell system and fill in the cue column in a study group. You might even find that one system is best in class and another in review sessions.

**Gather support.** In each class, set up a support system with one or two students so you can look at their notes after an absence.

## Record Information Effectively During Class

The following practical suggestions will help you record what is important in a format that you can review later:

- Date and identify each page. When you take several pages of notes, add an identifying letter or number to the date to keep track of page order: 11/27A, 11/27B, for example, or 11/27—1 of 2, 11/27—2 of 2. Indicate the lecture topic at the top so you can gather all your notes on that topic.

- If your instructor jumps from topic to topic during a single class, it may help to start a new page for each new topic.

- Record whatever your instructor emphasizes by paying attention to verbal and nonverbal cues (see Key 6.7).

- Write down all key terms and definitions.

- Try to capture explanations of difficult concepts by noting relevant examples, applications, and links to other material.

- Write down every question your instructor raises, since these questions may be on a test.

- Be organized, but not fussy. Remember that you can always improve your notes later.

- Write quickly but legibly, using shorthand and short phrases instead of full sentences.

*get practical!*

# Face a Note-Taking Challenge

In the spaces below, record how you will prepare to take notes in your most challenging course.

- Course name and date of class:

  _____

- List all the reading assignments you have to finish before your next class:

  _____

  _____

- Where will you sit in class to focus your attention and minimize distractions?

  _____

- Which note-taking system is best suited for the class and why?

  _____

  _____

- Write the phone numbers or e-mail addresses of two students whose notes you can look at if you miss a class:

  _____

  _____

- Leave blank spaces between points to make it easy see where one topic ends and another begins. (This suggestion does not apply if you are using a think link.)
- Draw pictures and diagrams to illustrate ideas.
- A consistent system will help you find information with minimal stresss. Use the same system to show importance—such as indenting, spacing, or underlining—on each page.
- If you have trouble understanding a concept, record as much as you can; then, leave space for an explanation, and flag the margin with a large question mark. After class, try to clarify your questions in the text or ask a classmate or your instructor for help.
- Consider that your class notes are part, but not all, of what you need to learn. As you will see later in this chapter, you will learn best when you combine your text and class notes into a comprehensive master set.

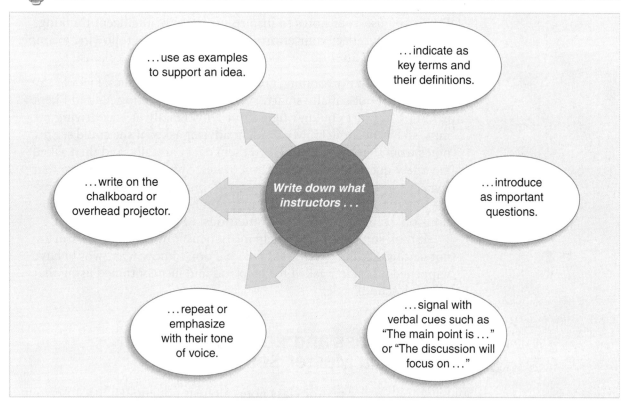

## Instructors signal important material in a variety of ways.

**Write down what instructors . . .**

...use as examples to support an idea.

...indicate as key terms and their definitions.

...write on the chalkboard or overhead projector.

...introduce as important questions.

...repeat or emphasize with their tone of voice.

...signal with verbal cues such as "The main point is . . ." or "The discussion will focus on . . ."

**Take notes during class discussions.** During discussion periods, one student may say something, then another, and finally the instructor may summarize or link the comments to make a point. Getting the most out of class discussions and recording critical points engages your ability to "read" others, which is the basis for social intelligence. Here are suggestions for recording what you need to know during these discussions:

- Listen carefully to everyone. Jot down relevant points and ignore points that seem tangential. If you're not sure, ask the instructor whether a student's statement is important.
- Listen for idea threads that weave through comments.
- Listen for ideas the instructor picks up on and for encouraging comments to students, such as "You make a great point," "I like your idea," and so on.
- Take notes when the instructor rephrases and clarifies a student's point.
- Try using a think link since discussions often take the form of brainstorming sessions. A think link will help you connect ideas that come at you from different perspectives.

## Review and Revise

By their very nature, class notes require revision. They may be incomplete in some places, confusing in others, and illegible in still others. That is why it is critical that you review and revise your notes as soon as possible after

LISTENING, NOTE TAKING, AND MEMORY **187**

class. This will enable you to fill in gaps while the material is fresh, to clarify sloppy handwriting, or to raise questions. Reviewing and revising your class notes prepares you for the vital step of combining class and text notes.

When you use your notes to inspire successfully intelligent thinking, your grades may reflect your efforts. The student in the following example learned this lesson after doing poorly on some tests. He explains:

> All four of us in my rooming group are taking economics. I would say we are all about equally smart. . . . Yet they are getting A's and I kept getting C's. I just couldn't figure out why. Finally, it was driving me nuts, so I went for help. My resident advisor asked if she could see my notes from that class. She looked them over carefully, and then asked me a few questions based on those notes. She helped me realize that I was great on "giving back the facts," but not so good at all at extending those facts to new situations. Yet here at college, all the questions on exams are about new situations. . . .
>
> It took someone here to help me refocus how I study. . . . I still am not getting A's, but at least solid B+'s. I don't know what would have happened if I hadn't asked for help and had just continued using that old high school style.[5]

## Combine Class and Reading Notes into a Master Set

Studying from either text or class notes alone is not enough, because your instructor may present material in class that is not in your text or may gloss over topics that your text covers in depth. The process of combining class and text notes enables you to see patterns and relationships among ideas, find examples for difficult concepts, and much more.

Follow these steps to combine your class and text notes into a master note set:

MASTER NOTE SET
The complete, integrated note set that contains both class and text notes.

**Step 1: Act quickly.** Combine your class and reading notes into a logical, comprehensive presentation while the material is fresh in your mind.

**Step 2: Focus on what's important by condensing to the essence.** Now, reduce your combined notes so they contain only key terms and concepts. (You are likely to find repetition in your notes, which will make it easy to reduce the material.) Tightening and summarizing forces you to critically evaluate which ideas are most important and to rewrite your notes with only this material. As you begin to study, move back and forth between the full set and the reduced set. Key 6.8 shows a comprehensive outline and a reduced key term outline of the same material.

**Step 3: Recite what you know.** As you approach exam time, use the terms in your bare-bones notes as cues for reciting what you know about a topic. Many students assume that they know concepts simply because they understand what they read. What they are actually demonstrating is a passive understanding that doesn't necessarily mean that they can re-create the material on an exam or apply it to problems. Make the process more active by reciting out loud during study sessions, writing your responses on paper, making flash cards, or working with a partner.

# Reducing a full set of notes into key term notes will help you master content.

**MASTER SET OF CLASS AND TEXT NOTES**

Different Views of Freedom and Equality in the American Democracy

I. U. S. democracy based on 5 core values: freedom and equality, order and stability, majority rule, protection of minority rights, and participation.

    A. U. S. would be a "perfect democracy" if it always upheld these values.

    B. U. S. is less than perfect; so it is called an "approaching democracy."

II. Freedom and Equality

    A. Historian Isaiah Berlin defines freedom as either positive or negative.

        1. Positive freedoms allow us to exercise rights under the Constitution, including right to vote.

        2. Negative freedoms safeguard us from government actions that restrict certain rights, such as the right to assemble. The 1st Amendment restricts government action by declaring that "Congress shall make no law . . ."

    B. The value of equality suggests that all people be treated equally, regardless of circumstance. Different views on what equality means and the implications for society.

        1. Equality of opportunity implies that everyone has the same chance to develop inborn talents.

            a. But life's circumstances—affected by factors like race and income—differ. This means that people start at different points and have different results. E.g., a poor, inner-city student will be less prepared for college than an affluent, suburban student.

            b. It is impossible to equalize opportunity for all Americans.

        2. Equality of result seeks to eliminate all forms of inequality, including economic differences, through wealth redistribution.

    C. Freedom and equality are in conflict, say text authors Berman and Murphy: "If your view of freedom is freedom from government intervention, then equality of any kind will be difficult to achieve. If government stays out of all citizen affairs, some people will become extremely wealthy, others will fall through the cracks, and economic inequality will multiply. On the other hand, if you wish to promote equality of result, then you will have to restrict some people's freedoms—the freedom to earn and retain an unlimited amount of money, for example."[6]

**KEY TERM OUTLINE OF THE SAME MATERIAL**

Different Views of Freedom and Equality in the American Democracy

I. America's 5 core values: freedom and equality, order and stability, majority rule, protection of minority rights, and participation.

    a. "Perfect democracy"

    b. "Approaching democracy"

II. Value #1—Freedom and equality

    a. Positive Freedoms and Negative Freedoms

    b. Different views of equality: equality of opportunity versus equality of result

    c. Conflict between freedom and equality centers on differing views of government's role

**Step 4: Use critical thinking.** Now toss around ideas in the following ways as you reflect on your combined notes—both the comprehensive and reduced sets:

- Brainstorm examples from other sources that illustrate central ideas. Write down new ideas or questions that come up as you review.

- Think of ideas from your readings or from class that support or clarify your notes.

- Consider what in your class notes differed from your reading notes and why.

- Apply concepts to problems at the end of text chapters, to problems posed in class, or to real-world situations.

**Step 5: Review and review again.** To ensure learning and prepare for exams, review your key word summary and critical thinking questions until you know every topic.

Try to vary your review methods, focusing on active involvement. Recite the material to yourself, have a Q&A session with a study partner, take a practice test. Another helpful technique is to summarize your notes in writing from memory after you review them. This will tell you whether you'll be able to recall the information on a test. You may even want to summarize as you read, then summarize from memory, and compare the two summaries.

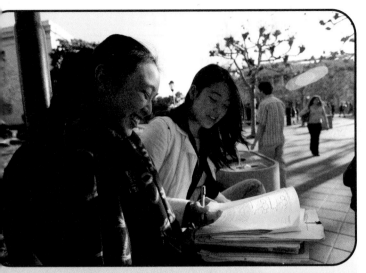

Reviewing notes with a classmate improves your memory and comprehension of the material. These students look over notes together between classes.

## How Can You Take Notes Faster?

SHORTHAND

A system of rapid handwriting that employs symbols, abbreviations, and shortened words to represent words and phrases.

Personal shorthand is a practical intelligence strategy that enables you to write faster. Because you are the only intended reader, you can misspell and abbreviate words in ways that only you understand. A risk of using shorthand is that you might forget what your writing means. To avoid this problem, review your notes shortly after class and spell out words that could be misinterpreted.

Another risk is forgetting to remove shorthand from work you hand in. This can happen when you use the same system for class notes as you do when talking to friends online. For example, when students take notes in text message "language," they may be so accustomed to omitting capitalization and punctuation, using acronyms, and replacing long words with incorrect contractions that they may forget to correct their final work.

The following suggestions will help you master shorthand. Many will be familiar and, in fact, you may already use them to speed up your e-mail and text and instant messaging.

1. Use standard abbreviations in place of complete words:

| | | | | |
|---|---|---|---|---|
| w/ | with | cf | compare, in comparison to |
| w/o | without | ff | following |
| → | means; resulting in | Q | question |
| ← | as a result of | p. | page |
| ↑ | increasing | * | most importantly |
| ↓ | decreasing | < | less than |
| ∴ | therefore | > | more than |
| ∵ or b/c | because | = | equals |
| ≈ | approximately | % | percent |
| + or & | and | △ | change |
| – | minus; negative | 2 | to; two; too |
| No. or # | number | vs | versus; against |
| i.e. | that is, | e.g. | for example |
| etc. | and so forth | c/o | care of |
| ng | no good | lb | pound |

2. Shorten words by removing vowels from the middle of words:

   prps = purpose
   lwyr = lawyer
   cmptr = computer

3. Substitute word beginnings for entire words:

   assoc = associate; association
   info = information
   subj = subject

4. Form plurals by adding *s* to shortened words:

   prblms = problems
   envlps = envelopes
   prntrs = printers

5. Make up your own symbols and use them consistently:

   b/4 = before
   4tn = fortune
   2thake = toothache

6. Use standard or informal abbreviations for proper nouns such as places, people, companies, scientific substances, events, and so on:

   DC = Washington, D.C.
   $H_2O$ = water
   Moz. = Wolfgang Amadeus Mozart

7. If you know that a word or phrase will be repeated, write it once, and then establish an abbreviation for the rest of your notes. For example, the first time your political science instructor mentions the *Iraq Study Group*, the 2006 bipartisan commission that issued recommendations to the president on the Iraq War, write the name in full. After that, use the initials *ISG*.

8. Write only what is essential. Include only the information nuggets you want to remember, even if your instructor says much more. Do this by paring down your writing. Say, for example, your instructor had this to say on the subject of hate crimes:

> After the terrorist attacks on September 11, 2001, law enforcement officials noted a dramatic shift in the nature of hate crimes. For the first time, replacing crimes motivated by race as the leading type of hate crime were crimes that targeted religious and ethnic groups and particularly Muslims. [7]

Your notes, which include some shorthand, might look something like this:

—After 9/11 HCs ▲ & focus targeted religious and ethnic groups, esp. Muslims.
—Reduction of HC based on race.

# How Can You Improve Your Memory?

Your accounting instructor is giving a test tomorrow on key taxation concepts. You feel confident because you spent hours last week memorizing your notes. Unfortunately, as you start the test, you can't answer half the questions, even though you studied the material. This is not surprising, because most forgetting occurs within minutes after memorization.

If forgetting is so common, why do some people have better memories than others? Some may have an inborn talent for remembering. More often, though, they succeed because they take an active approach and master techniques to improve recall.

## How Your Brain Remembers: Short-Term and Long-Term Memory

Memories are stored in three different "storage banks" in your brain. The first, called *sensory memory*, is an exact copy of what you see and hear and lasts for a second or less. Certain information is then selected from sensory memory and moved into short-term memory, a temporary information storehouse that maintains data for no more than 10 to 20 seconds. You are consciously aware of material in short-term memory. Unimportant information is quickly dumped. Important information is transferred to long-term memory—the mind's more permanent storehouse.

Targeting long-term memory will solidify learning the most. "Short-term—or working—memory is useful when we want to remember a phone number until we can dial or an e-mail address until we can type it into the computer," says biologist James Zull. "We use short-term memory for these

**SHORT-TERM MEMORY**
The brain's temporary information storehouse in which information remains for only a few seconds.

**LONG-TERM MEMORY**
The brain's permanent information storehouse from which information can be retrieved

momentary challenges, all the time, every day, but it is limited in capacity, tenacity, and time."[8] Zull explains that short-term memory holds only small amounts of information for brief periods and is unstable—a distraction can easily bump out information. As you learn new material, your goal is to anchor information in long-term memory.

## Memory Strategies Improve Recall

The following strategies will help improve your ability to remember what you learn.

### Have Purpose, Intention, and Emotional Connection

Why can you remember the lyrics to dozens of popular songs but not the functions of the pancreas? Perhaps this is because you *want* to remember the lyrics or you have an emotional tie to them. To achieve the same results at school, try to create the purpose and will to remember. This is often linked to being emotionally involved with the material.

For example, as a student in a city-planning course, it may be easier for you to remember the complex rules surrounding housing subsidies if you think about families who benefit from these programs. If someone you know lives in a city housing project, the personal connection will probably make recall even easier.

### Understand What You Memorize

If you are having trouble remembering something new, think about how the new idea fits into what you already know. A simple example: If you can't remember the meaning of the word *antebellum*, try to identify the word's root, prefix, or suffix. Knowing that the root *bellum* means "war" and the prefix *ante* means "before" will help you remember that *antebellum* means "before the war." If you take the additional step of searching the Internet for the term, you'll discover that the elegant plantation homes in the classic movie *Gone with the Wind* were built before the Civil War and are considered *antebellum architecture*.

This basic, practical principle applies to everything you study. Identify logical connections, and use these connections to aid learning. In a plant biology course, memorize plant families; in a history course, memorize events by linking them in a cause-and-effect chain.

### Use Critical Thinking

Critical thinking encourages you to associate new information with what you already know. Imagine that you have to remember information about the signing of the Treaty of Versailles, the agreement that ended World War I. You might use critical thinking—combined with some quick Internet research—in the following ways:

- Recall everything that you know about the topic.
- Think about how this event is similar to other events in history.
- Consider what is different and unique about this treaty in comparison with other treaties.

- Explore the causes that led up to this event, and look at the event's effects.
- From the general idea of treaties that ended wars, explore other examples of such treaties.

Critical exploration of this kind will make it easier for you to remember specific facts and overarching concepts.

## Recite, Rehearse, and Write

When you *recite* material, you repeat key concepts aloud, in your own words, to aid memorization. *Rehearsing* is similar to reciting but is done silently. *Writing* is reciting on paper. All three processes are practical tools that actively involve you in learning and remembering material. You will get the greatest benefit if you separate your learning into the following steps:

- As you read, focus on the points you want to remember. These are usually found in the topic sentences of paragraphs. Then recite, rehearse, or write down the ideas.
- Convert each main idea into a key word, phrase, or visual image—something that is easy to recall and that will set off a chain of memories that will bring you back to the original information. Write each key word or phrase on an index card.
- One by one, look at the key words on your cards and recite, rehearse, or write all the associated information you can recall. Check your recall against your original material.

These steps are part of the process for consolidating and summarizing your lecture and text notes as you study.

Reciting, rehearsing, and writing involve more than rereading material and parroting words out loud, in your head, or on paper. Because rereading does not necessarily require any involvement, you can reread without learning. However, you cannot help but think and learn as you convert text concepts into key points and rewrite important points as key words and phrases.

## Limit and Organize the Items You Are Processing

This involves three key activities:

- **Separate main points from unimportant details.** Highlight only the key points in your texts, and write notes in the margins about central ideas (see Key 5.8 on page 160.)
- **Divide material into manageable sections.** Generally, when material is short and easy to understand, studying it from start to finish improves recall. Divide longer material into logical sections, master each section, put all the sections together, and then test your memory of all the material.
- **Use organizational tools.** Rely on an outline or another organizational tool to connect ideas. These tools will show logical connections and expose gaps in understanding.

## Study During Short, Frequent Sessions

Research has shown that you can improve your chances of remembering material by learning it more than once. Spread your study sessions over time: A pattern of short sessions—say three 20-minute study sessions, followed by brief periods of rest—is more effective than continual studying with little or no rest. With this in mind, try studying during breaks in your schedule, and even consider using these time slots to study with classmates.

Sleep can actually aid memory because it reduces interference from new information. Because you can't always go to sleep immediately after studying for an exam, try postponing the study of other subjects until your exam is over. When studying for several tests at once, avoid studying two similar subjects back to back. Your memory is likely to be more accurate when you study history right after biology rather than chemistry after biology.

## Practice the Middle

When you are trying to learn something, you usually study some material first, attack other material in the middle of the session, and approach still other topics at the end. The weak link is likely to be the material you study midway. It pays to give this material special attention in the form of extra practice.

## Use Flash Cards

Flash cards are a great visual memory tool. They give you short, repeated review sessions that provide immediate feedback, and they are portable, which gives you the flexibility to use them wherever you go. Use the front of a 3-by-5-inch index card to write a word, idea, or phrase you want to learn. Use the back for a definition, explanation, and other key facts. Key 6.9 shows two flash cards used to study for a pychology exam.

Here are some suggestions for making the most of your flash cards:

- *Use the cards as a self-test.* As you go through them, divide them into two piles—the material you know and the material you are learning.

KEY 6.9

Flash cards help you memorize important facts.

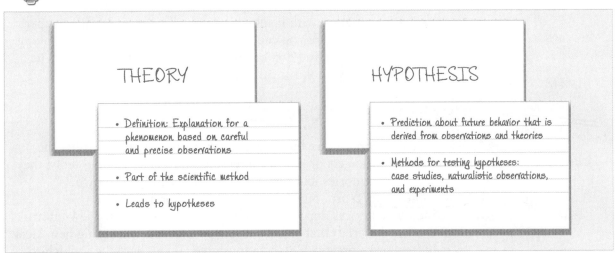

THEORY

- Definition: Explanation for a phenomenon based on careful and precise observations
- Part of the scientific method
- Leads to hypotheses

HYPOTHESIS

- Prediction about future behavior that is derived from observations and theories
- Methods for testing hypotheses: case studies, naturalistic observations, and experiments

- *Carry the cards with you and review them frequently.* You'll learn the most if you start using your flash cards early in the course, well ahead of exam time.

- *Shuffle the cards and learn the information in various orders.* This will help you avoid putting too much focus on some information and not enough on other.

- *Test yourself in both directions.* First, look at the terms and provide the definitions or explanations. Then turn the cards over and reverse the process.

- *Reduce the stack as you learn.* Eliminate cards when you are certain of your knowledge. Watching the pile get smaller is a reward that reinforces your motivation. As test time approaches, put all the cards together again for a final review.

### Use a Tape Recorder and MP3 Player

Questions on tape can work like audio flash cards. One method is to record short-answer study questions, leaving 10 to 15 seconds between questions for you to answer out loud. Recording the correct answer after the pause will give you immediate feedback. For example, part of a recording for a writing class might say, "Three elements that require analysis before writing are . . . (10–15 second pause). . . topic, audience, and purpose."

Pearson Education, the publisher of this and many of the other textbooks you will be using in college, developed VangoNotes to help you learn material through your MP3 player. Plug in your earphones to listen to chapter summaries and answer audio tests while walking between classes or shopping for food. Lindleigh Whetstone, a student at Tidewater Community College in Virginia, uses her iPod to learn Spanish when she is doing her laundry. "I get a lot more listening in than I did before," she says. She estimates that her listening/study time has grown from 30 minutes a week to about five hours a week.[9]

### Use the Information

In the days after you learn something new, use your analytical intelligence to use what you learned. Think about other contexts in which the information applies and link it to new problems. Then test your knowledge to make sure the material is in long-term memory. "Don't confuse recognizing information with being able to recall it," says learning expert Adam Robinson. "Be sure you can recall the information without looking at your notes for clues. And don't move on until you have created some sort of sense-memory hook for calling it back up when you need it."[10]

## Use Mnemonic Devices

MNEMONIC DEVICES
Memory techniques that use vivid associations to link new information with information you already know.

There are performers who build careers on the ability to remember the names of 100 strangers or repeat 30 ten-digit numbers. Undoubtedly, they have superior memories, but they also rely on techniques known as mnemonic devices (pronounced neh-*mahn*-ick) for assistance.

Mnemonic devices depend on vivid associations (relating new information to other material) that engage emotions. Instead of learning new facts by *rote* (repetitive practice), associations give you a "hook" on which to hang these facts for later retrieval. They are formed with the help of your creative intelligence.

There are different kinds of mnemonic devices, including visual images and associations and acronyms. Study how these devices work, then apply them to your own challenges. These devices take time and effort to create, and you'll need motivation to remember them. Because of this, it is smart to use mnemonic devices only when you really need them—for instance, to distinguish confusing concepts that consistently trip you up or to recall items in order.

## Create Visual Images and Associations

To remember that the Spanish artist Picasso painted *The Three Women*, you might imagine the women in a circle dancing to a Spanish song with a pig and a donkey (pig-asso). The most effective images involve bright colors, three dimensions, action scenes, inanimate objects with human traits, and humor. The more outlandish the image, the better.

## Use Visual Images to Remember Items in a List

Using the *mental walk* strategy, imagine yourself storing new ideas in familiar locations. Say, for example, that for your biology course you have to remember the major endocrine glands, starting in the brain and working downward through the body. To do this, think of your route to the library. You pass the campus theater, the science center, the bookstore, the cafeteria, the athletic center, and the social science building before reaching your destination. At each spot along the way, you "place" the concept you want to learn. You then link the concept with a similar-sounding word that brings to mind a vivid image (see Key 6.10):

- At the campus theater, you imagine bumping into actor Brad <u>Pitt</u>, who is holding <u>two</u> cell phones and has a <u>terri</u>ble cold (pituitary gland).
- At the science center, you visualize Mr. Universe with bulging <u>thighs</u>. When you are introduced, you learn that his name is <u>Roy</u> (thyroid gland).
- At the campus bookstore, you envision a second Mr. Universe with his <u>thighs</u> covered in <u>mus</u>tard (thymus gland).
- In the cafeteria, you see an <u>ad</u> for <u>Dean Al</u> for president (adrenal gland).
- At the athletic center, you visualize a student throwing a ball into a <u>pan</u> and <u>crea</u>tures applauding from the bleachers (pancreas).
- At the social science building, you imagine receiving a standing <u>ovation</u> (ovaries).
- And at the library, you visualize sitting at a table taking a <u>test</u> that is <u>easy</u> (testes).

## Create Acronyms

An (acronym) is a word formed from the first letters of a series of words created in order to help you remember the series. In history class, you can remember the Allies during World War II—Britain, America, and Russia— with the acronym *BAR*. This is an example of a *word acronym*, because the first letters of the items you want to remember spell a word. Keep in mind that the word or words spelled don't necessarily have to be real words.

> **ACRONYM**
>
> A word formed from the first letters of a series of words, created to help you recall the series.

# A mental walk mnemonic helps you remember items in a list.

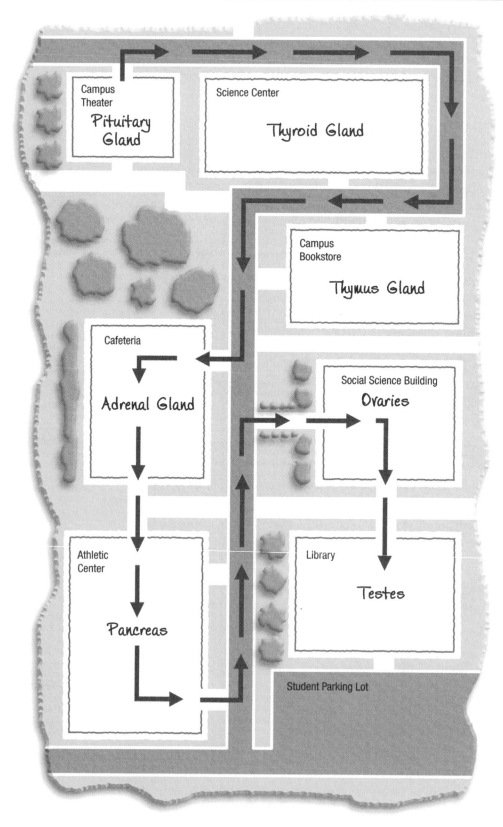

Other acronyms take the form of an entire sentence in which the first letter of each word in each sentence stands for the first letter of the memorized term. This is called a *list order acronym*. For example, music students use the phrase *Every Good Boy Does Fine* to remember the notes that correspond to the lines on the treble clef (E, G, B, D, and F).

You can create your own acronyms. For example, to remember the names of the first six U.S. presidents—Washington, Adams, Jefferson, Madison, Monroe, and Adams—you notice that the first letters of their last names read *W A J M M A*. To remember them, first you might insert an *e* after the *J* and create a short nonsense word: *wajemma*. Then, to make sure you don't forget the nonsense word, picture the six presidents sitting in a row and wearing pajamas.

## Use Songs or Rhymes

Some of the classic mnemonic devices are rhyming poems that tend to stick in your mind. One you may have heard is the rule about the order of *i* and *e* in spelling.

> I before E, except after C, or when sounded like "A" as in "neighbor" and "weigh." Four exceptions if you please: either, neither, seizure, seize.

Use your creativity to make up your own poems or songs, linking familiar tunes or rhymes with information you want to remember. Thinking back to the "wajemma" example, imagine that you want to remember the presidents' first names as well. You might set these names—George, John, Thomas, James, James, and John—to the tune of "Happy Birthday." Or, to extend the history theme, you might use the first musical phrase of "The Star-Spangled Banner."

Haverford College physics professor Walter Smith hosts a Web site— www.physicssongs.org—dedicated to helping students enjoy physics and learn essential concepts by putting them to music. Here, for example, is "The Gauss's Law Song," written by Professor Smith and Marian McKenzie and sung to the tune of "East Side, West Side."

*Inside, outside, count the lines to tell—*

*If the charge is inside, there will be net flux as well.*

*If the charge is outside, be careful and you'll see*

*The goings in and goings out are equal perfectly.*

*If you wish to know the field precise,*

*And the charge is symmetric,*

*you will find this law is nice—*

*Q upon a constant—eps'lon naught they say—*

*Equals closed surface integral of E dot n dA.*

© 2001 Walter Fox Smith [11]

Professor Smith's students credit musical mnemonics for helping them retain complex equations. Some students, like Katie Baratz, have been inspired to write their own songs. For her final class project she paired lyrics entitled "In My Mind, I've Got Physics Equations" with the James Taylor tune "Carolina in My Mind." [12]

# Craft Your Own Mnemonic

Create a mnemonic to help you remember some facts.

- Identify a group of connected facts that you have to memorize—for example, for political science, the names of every presidential candidate after World War II; for literature, the names of all the characters in Shakespeare's *Romeo and Juliet*. Write your choice here:

_____

_____

_____

_____

- Now create your own mnemonic to remember the grouping using any of the devices in this chapter. Write the mnemonic here and on additional paper if necessary.

_____

_____

_____

_____

_____

_____

_____

Improving your memory requires energy, time, and work. It also helps to master SQ3R, the textbook study technique that was introduced in chapter 5. By going through the steps in SQ3R and using the specific memory techniques described in this chapter, you will be able to learn more in less time—and remember what you learn long after exams are over. These techniques will be equally valuable when you start a career.

# Successful Intelligence Wrap-Up

Achieving competence in listening, note taking, and memorizing requires more than just analytical ability. When you use all three components of successful intelligence to find your own way to listen and take in information, record information that you will need in the future, and remember what you learn, you set yourself up for future academic success. Here's how you have built skills in chapter 6:

## Analytical

Within the material about listening, you examined the listening process and the challenges you face each step along the way, getting more specific in your analysis of your own listening skills with the *Get Analytical* exercise. You explored note-taking systems, considering what systems may work best for your particular classroom and study situations. Near the end of the chapter, you examined the nature of memory and the importance of memory challenges.

## Creative

Investigating different note-taking systems may have inspired new ideas about how to approach note taking in your courses. With what you learned about note taking, you are prepared to create self-styled methods that suit your personal preferences, the material you are working with, and your instructor's style. After you explored how mnemonic devices work, completing the *Get Creative* exercise gave you experience in crafting your own original mnemonic device.

## Practical

You compiled practical tools for listening actively in class, getting a sense of how to manage listening challenges. You explored how to use different note-taking systems in different situations, applying your knowledge to a specific note-taking challenge in the *Get Practical* exercise. You added practical techniques in personal shorthand and creating a master set of notes to your skills. You broadened your understanding of the ways in which experience solidifies memory.

# Lagom
## (lag-ohm)

In Swedish, the word *lagom* refers to the place between extremes, the spot that is neither too much nor too little, but just right. Many Swedish people aspire to this place in everything they do. They tend to seek stability yet remain open to what is new and different.

Think of the quest for *lagom* as you challenge yourself to improve your listening, note-taking, and memory skills. With *lagom* as your guide, you will appreciate that your goal is not perfection in any of these skills, but rather the ability to hear as much as you can, to take appropriate notes that will be the foundation for your studying, and to develop just the right number of memory strategies that will help you remember what is valuable. You can never hope to take in, record, and memorize every word that your instructor speaks—and that's okay. You are aiming for "just right."[13]

"Happiness does not come from doing easy work but from the afterglow of satisfaction that comes after the achievement of a difficult task that demanded our best."

THEODORE I. RUBIN, PSYCHIATRIST AND AUTHOR

# PERSONAL TRIUMPH CASE STUDY
## FROM HOMELESSNESS TO COLLEGE SUCCESS

VICTORIA GOUGH, STUDENT, GLENDALE COMMUNITY COLLEGE, GLENDALE, ARIZONA

*...otivation. Perseverance. Drive. Determination. Words ...e inadequate to describe Victoria Gough's journey ...om homelessness to college success—a journey fueled ... willpower, native intelligence, support from family, ...lief in herself, and practical learning methods. Read ...is account, then use separate paper or a computer file ... answer the questions on page 204.*

I grew up homeless in southern Illinois. I've lived in sheds, boxcars, and salvage yards—with my parents and without them. Sometimes I wouldn't eat for three days in a row. I attended school on and off starting in third grade, but never ...ent back after eighth. I never set foot inside a high ...chool. It may be hard to believe that people grow ...p this poor and isolated in the United States, but ...ey do.

For a short while I lived with my dad. When he re-...ed us, my brothers and sister and I left. My mom ...ld us we would have to go to a state home. When I ...efused, she convinced me to marry at 13, which I did. ...had three children in five years. I was able to let my ...ster live with me. We got odd jobs cleaning houses ...r people and working at restaurants. We rented a ...ailer, which was the nicest place I'd ever lived. Mean-...hile, I dreamed of going to school and longed to live ...a house and go to a grocery store. I took a giant step ...oward that goal when I got my high school equiva-...ency degree in 1993.

In 1994 I married again. My husband and I live near ...lendale Community College, and he encouraged me ...o enroll. I entered the admissions office shaking like a ...eaf. The administrators helped me register for reme-...ial classes to start with. In class I said as little as pos-...ible. I didn't know where to write my name on a paper ...r how to buy books at a bookstore. The first time I ...earned how to turn on a computer I cried.

My first instructor told me I should drop out before ...couldn't get my money back. I went back to my admission counselor, who put me in a different class with a wonderful instructor. I ate up the material. When I started getting 100% correct on my papers, I thought maybe the teachers considered me a sympathy case. When I received a letter telling me I made the national honor roll, I thought they made a mistake. Slowly, I'm starting to realize how capable I really am. My long-term goal is to be involved in some type of research in the medical field.

I study from six to eight hours every day, because I have so much catching up to do. Recently, an instructor nominated me for the Outstanding Achievement award on our campus. She said she never had a student sit through as many classes as I do. If the instructor lets me, I sit through the class twice. The first time I listen, and the second time I take notes.

I see students on my campus who quit school, and I have friends who say, "This is too hard." I think they're giving up too easily. If I don't understand something in class, I'll raise my hand. Sometimes I'll hear students in the back of the class say, "Someone make her shut up." It hurts my feelings a little, but I feel sadder for them than for myself. They don't seem to realize what a treasure education is. If I keep going, I'll be able to get my associate's degree in general studies the same time my granddaughter graduates from high school. What a great celebration that will be!

My personal mission is to help my other family members to break free of their grim existence and to expose the marginalized in our society to the outside world. No one in my family has ever graduated from high school, and I'm the first to enroll in college. All my children graduated from high school and went on to college. My son has a Ph.D., is a professor of sociology and criminology, and has written a book. I get goose bumps thinking about how far I've come and all the possibilities ahead of me. Learning is one of the greatest joys of my life.

Elie Sanon, the student artist who created this drawing, emigrated from Haiti at 8 years old. Two years later his mother died, and like Victoria he had enormous adjustments to face, dealing with his loss as well as with a new ...untry, a new language, and family financial pressures. He had shown artistic talent at an early age, and through encouragement from a mentor as well as his own determination, he was ultimately accepted to the prestigious Rhode Island School of Design where he is currently studying. For more of Elie's story, please visit www.prenhall.com/carter.

# Building World-Class Skills

## for College, Career, and Life Success

## SUCCESSFUL INTELLIGENCE

*Think, Create, Apply*

Learn from the experiences of others. Look back at Victoria Gough's Personal Triumph on page 203. Read her story, and then relate her experience to your own life by completing the following:

**Think it through: *Analyze your own motivation.***
How motivated are you to achieve your academic goals? What challenges have you overcome to get where you are today? From your memory of reaching important goals, what strategies will you use to make sure you complete your education? How does reading about Victoria affect your commitment to overcome obstacles in your life?

**Think out of the box: *Let others inspire ideas.*** Choose two people whom you respect. Put your listening skills to work: Spend a few minutes talking with each of them about the major obstacles they overcame to achieve success. Ask them for advice that will help ensure that you will stay in school and get a degree. From what you hear, begin brainstorming ideas about how to overcome obstacles that may stand in the way of graduation. Take notes throughout this listening process.

**Make it happen: *Put a practical plan together.*** Map out your action steps. Create a mnemonic device that will help you remember your plan. Envision your success as you put your plan into action.

## TEAMWORK

*Create Solutions Together*

Create a note-taking team. In your most demanding course, form a study group with two classmates. Ask everyone to gather together a week's worth of class notes so that you can review and compare the different versions. Focus on the following:

- Legibility (Can everyone read what is written?)
- Completeness (Did you all record the same information? If not, why not?)
- Organizational effectiveness (Does everyone get an idea of how ideas flow?)
- Value of the notes as a study aid (Will this help everyone remember the material?)

What did you learn? Use your insights to improve your personal note-taking skills.

# WRITING
## *Journal and Put Skills to Work*

*Record your thoughts on a separate piece of paper, in a journal, or on a computer file.*

**Journal entry: How people retain information.** How do you react to the following statement?

> We retain 10% of what we read, 20% of what we hear, 30% of what we see, 50% of what we hear and see, 70% of what we say, and 90% of what we say and do.

How can you use this insight to improve your ability to retain information? What will you do differently as a result of this insight?

**Real-life writing: Combining class and text notes.** Create a master set of notes for one course that combines one week's classes and reading assignments. Your goal is to summarize and connect all the important information covered during the period.

# PERSONAL PORTFOLIO
## *Prepare for Career Success*

**Learning more about career success.** Put your listening and note-taking skills to work as you investigate what brings success in the workplace. Choose a career area that interests you, and then interview two people in that area—one from an academic setting (such as an instructor or an academic advisor) and one from the working world (a person who is doing a job that interests you). Choose a setting where you can listen well and take effective notes.

Ask your interview subjects what they feel is the recipe for success in their career. You might ask specifically about curriculum (what courses are required for this area, and what courses are beneficial but not required), other preparation such as extracurricular activities and internships, qualities such as leadership and commitment, day-to-day attitudes, and anything else you are wondering about. Ask them also about the role that listening, note-taking, and memory skills play in career success. For example, if you are interviewing an account manager at an advertising agency, he might tell you that the ability to listen well, take accurate notes, and recall critical concepts is essential at client meetings. Practicing and perfecting these skills while listening to your instructors will help you in your career.

When you complete your interviews, create a report that lays out the "recipe for success." Keep in mind the skills and attitudes you wish to develop as you choose next term's courses and activities.

## Suggested Readings

Burley-Allen, Madelyn. *Listening: The Forgotten Skill: A Self-Teaching Guide*. New York: Wiley, 1995.

DePorter, Bobbi, and Mike Hernacki. *Quantum Notes: Whole-Brain Approaches to Note-Taking*. Chicago: Learning Forum, 2000.

Dunkel, Patricia A., Frank Pialorsi, and Joane Kozyrez. *Advanced Listening Comprehension: Developing Aural and Note-Taking Skills*, 3rd ed. Boston: Heinle & Heinle, 2004.

Higbee, Kenneth L. *Your Memory: How It Works and How to Improve It*. New York: Marlowe, 2001.

Lebauer, R. Susan. *Learn to Listen, Listen to Learn: Academic Listening and Note-Taking*. Upper Saddle River, NJ: Prentice Hall, 2000.

Levin, Leonard. *Easy Script Express: Unique Speed Writing Methods to Take Fast Notes and Dictation*. Chicago: Legend, 2000.

Lorayne, Harry. *Super Memory—Super Student: How to Raise Your Grades in 30 Days*. Boston: Little, Brown, 1990.

Lorayne, Harry. *The Memory Book: The Classic Guide to Improving Your Memory at Work, at School, and at Play*. New York: Ballantine Books, 1996.

Roberts, Billy. *Working Memory: Improving Your Memory for the Workplace*. London: Bridge Trade, 1999.

Roberts, Billy. *Educate Your Memory: Improvement Techniques for Students of All Ages*. London: Allison & Busby, 2000.

Zull, James. *The Art of Changing the Brain: Enriching the Practice of Teaching by Exploring the Biology of Learning*. Sterling, VA: Stylus, 2002.

## Internet and Podcast Resources

Coping.org—Tools for Coping with Life's Stressors—Improving Listening Skills: **www.coping.org/ dialogue/listen.htm**

Dyslexia at College—Taking Notes (tips on taking notes from books and at lectures): **www.dyslexia-college.com/notes.html**

ForgetKnot (a source for mnemonic devices): **http:// members.tripod.com/~ForgetKnot**

Kishwaukee College Learning Skills Center (helpful advice on listening skills): **www.kish.cc.il.us/**  **learning_skills_center/study_skills_help/ good_listening.shtml**

Merriam-Webster's Word of the Day (free word of the day in audio form available on the Internet or as podcasts): **www.merriam-webster.com/cgi-bin/ mwwod.pl**

Princeton Review Vocab Minute (free vocabulary-building podcasts using songs to help you remember): **RobinR@Review.com**

Prentice Hall Student Success Supersite: **www.prenhall.com/success**

## Endnotes

[1] Ralph G. Nichols, "Do We Know How to Listen? Practical Helps in a Modern Age," *Speech Teacher*, March 1961, pp. 118–124.

[2] Richard J. Light, *Making the Most of College: Students Speak Their Minds*, Cambridge, MA: Harvard University Press, 2001, pp. 48–49. Copyright © 2001 by Richard J. Light. Reprinted by permission of the publisher.

[3] Teresa Audesirk, Gerald Audesirk, and Bruce E. Byers, *Life on Earth*, 2nd ed. Upper Saddle River, NJ: Prentice Hall, 2000, pp. 660–662.

[4] System developed by Cornell professor Walter Pauk. See Walter Pauk, *How to Study in College*, 7th ed., Boston: Houghton Mifflin, 2001, pp. 236–241.

[5] Light, *Making the Most of College*, p. 38.

[6] Based on Larry Berman and Bruce Allen Murphy, *Approaching Democracy: Portfolio Edition,* Upper Saddle River, NJ: Pearson/Prentice Hall, 2005, pp. 6–8.

[7] Information from Frank Schmalleger, *Criminal Justice Today,* 8th ed., Upper Saddle River, NJ: Prentice Hall, 2005, p. 71.

[8] James Zull, *The Art of Changing the Brain: Enriching Teaching by Exploring the Biology of Learning,* Sterling, VA: Stylus, 2002.

[9] Cited in Madlen Read, "Growing Number of Students Use MP3 Players as a Study Tool," *Napa Valley Register,* February 7, 2007 (www. napavalleyregister.com/articles/2007/02/07/ business/local/doc45c9e13a31a47296818650.txt).

[10] Adam Robinson, *What Smart Students Know: Maximum Grades, Optimum Learning, Minimum Time,* New York: Three Rivers Press, 1993, p. 118.

[11] "The Gauss's Law Song," © 2001 Walter Fox Smith, Haverford College (www.haverford.edu/ physics-astro/songs/Gauss).

[12] Christopher Conkey "It's All Relative: Songs to Make Physics Easier," *Wall Street Journal,* March 17, 2005, p. B1.

[13] Christopher J. Moore, *In Other Words: A Language Lover's Guide to the Most Intriguing Words Around the World,* New York: Walker, 2004, p. 45.

**TEST TAKING**
*Showing What You Know*

*"Successfully intelligent people seek to perform in ways that not only are competent but distinguish them from ordinary performers. They realize that the gap between competence and excellence may be small but the greatest rewards, both internal and external, are for excellence."*

ROBERT J. STERNBERG

**W**hen you successfully show what you know on tests, you achieve educational goals and develop confidence. Exams also help you gauge your progress so that, when needed, you can ramp up your efforts. Most importantly, smart test preparation results in real learning that you take from course to course and into your career and life. As you will see in this chapter, test taking is about preparation, persistence, and strategy—all of which tap into your analytical, creative, and practical abilities. It is also about conquering fears, focusing on details, and learning from mistakes.

*In this chapter you explore answers to the following questions:*

## Chapter 7's
### Successful Intelligence Skills

### Analytical

- Matching test-preparation strategies with personal needs
- Identifying the nature of test anxiety
- Analyzing how to answer objective and subjective test questions
- Identifying patterns that cause you to make test errors

### Creative

- Constructing a new perspective of tests as helpful evaluative tools
- Developing a pretest to assess material mastery before an exam
- Creating an effective study schedule and regimen

### Practical

- How to attack objective test questions
- How to write a test essay
- How to evaluate and learn from test mistakes

# How Can Preparation Improve Test Performance?

You prepare for exams every day of the term. By attending class, staying on top of assignments, completing readings and projects, and participating in class discussions, you are actively learning and retaining what you need to know in order to do well on exams. This knowledge is the most important test-preparation tool you have.

The following additional measures will help you prepare as exams approach because they put your analytical, creative, and practical thinking skills into action.

## Identify Test Type and Material Covered

Before you begin studying, be practical as you find out as much as you can about the test, including the following:

- *Topics that will be covered:* Will the test cover everything since the term began, or will it be more limited?

# REAL QUESTIONS

## How can I combat test anxiety?

I am a Yu'pik Eskimo from a village on the Yukon River. Before attending college, I worked for six years as a clerk at the Native Corporation, a gas station and general store. When the manager passed away, the business offered to make me a manager. Even though I knew how to do the work, I didn't feel I was ready, so I decided to go to school for more training.

I felt like I was a success at work, but I don't feel successful as a student. College life is different from what I am accustomed to. The hardest part has been taking tests. I study hard, but then when the test begins, my mind goes blank. Sometimes I feel like quitting, but I also think that I will have more choices if I stick with it. How can I conquer my test anxiety?

Peter Changsak
Sheldon-Jackson College
Sitka, Alaska

# PRACTICAL ANSWERS

Tonjua Williams, M.Ed.
Associate Provost,
Health Programs
St. Petersburg College

## Preparation and a positive attitude will help you cope with test pressure.

Many students experience test anxiety, especially when they are new to college. Often, anxiety is a result of feeling uncomfortable in unfamiliar waters. That's why the first test in a class can be nerve-racking. Preparation is the best way to deal with nerves:

- Attend class regularly.
- Pay attention and take good notes.
- Join a study group.
- Spend two hours studying outside of class for every hour you spend in class and start studying early.
- Communicate with your instructor to make sure you understand course expectations; use your syllabus as a guide.
- Before the exam, get plenty of rest and eat a light breakfast or snack.

To calm yourself right before the exam, try the following:

- Close your eyes, take a deep breath, then review the test.
- Start with questions you are comfortable answering.
- Look for clues that will help you answer more difficult questions.

After the exam review what you did right and wrong to pinpoint areas you need to work on.

Test anxiety, believe it or not, can encourage you to rise to the occasion. The stress of an upcoming test can help you work hard so you are fully prepared. It is important to think of exams as opportunities to show off your knowledge. Changing your attitude and looking forward to the chance to demonstrate what you know will help you do your best work.

- *Material you will be tested on:* Will the test cover only what you learned in class and in the text, or will it also include outside readings? Will you be given material to work with—for example, will you be asked to analyze a poem?

- *Types of questions:* Will the questions be objective (multiple-choice, true/false, sentence-completion), subjective (essay), or a combination?

- *How the test will be graded:* Will partial credit be given for short-answer questions? Do you need to show problem-solving steps to get full credit? Are certain sections worth more than others?

Your instructors may answer many of these questions. They may tell you the question format and the topics that will be covered. They may also drop hints about possible questions, either directly ("I might ask a question on . . .") or more subtly ("One of my favorite theories is . . . "). Use your social intelligence to pick up as many clues as you can.

As you begin thinking about the test, remember that *not all tests are created equal*—a quiz is not as important as a midterm or final, although accumulated grades on small quizzes add up and can make a difference in your final grade. Plan and prioritize your study time and energy according to the value of the quiz or test. Your syllabus will tell you when quizzes and tests are scheduled throughout the term (see page 14 for a sample syllabus).

Here are other practical strategies for predicting what may be on a test. To prepare effectively, combine these with the strategies you learned throughout *Keys to Success*:

**Use SQ3R to identify what's important.** Often, the questions you ask yourself as you read assigned materials will be part of the test. Textbook study questions are also good candidates.

**Listen for clues at review sessions.** Many instructors offer review sessions before midterms and finals in order to answer last-minute questions. Bring your questions to these sessions and listen to the questions others ask. They may cover material you thought you knew, but actually need to review or learn more about.

**Make an appointment to see your instructor.** Spending a few minutes talking about the test one-on-one may clarify misunderstandings and help you focus on what to study.

**Talk to people who already took the course and look at comments on teacher evaluation Web sites.** Try to get a sense of test difficulty, whether tests focus primarily on assigned readings or class notes, what materials are usually covered, and the types of questions that are asked. If you learn that the instructor emphasizes specific facts, for example, use flash cards to drill. If she emphasizes a global overview, focus on big-picture concepts. Use your social intelligence to make others want to share information about their experiences.

**Examine old tests, if the instructor makes them available.** You may find old tests in class, online, or on reserve in the library. Old tests will help you answer questions like these:

- Do tests focus on examples and details, general ideas and themes, or a combination?
- Are the questions straightforward, or confusing and sometimes tricky?
- Will you be asked to apply principles to new situations and problems?

After taking the first exam in a course, you will have a better idea of what to expect.

# Create a Study Schedule and Checklist

Use the guidelines presented in the *Get Focused!* end-of-part section on page 97 to create a study plan and schedule. Make copies of the checklist on page 97 and complete it for every exam. It is an invaluable tool for organizing your pre-exam studying.

Studying for final exams, which usually take place the last week of the term, is a major commitment that requires careful time management. Your college may schedule study days (also called a "reading period") between the end of classes and the beginning of finals. Lasting from a day or two to several weeks, these days give you uninterrupted hours to prepare for exams and finish papers.

End-of-year studying often requires flexibility. For example, instead of working at the library during this period, some students at the University of Texas at Austin are often seen at Barton Springs, a spring-fed pool near campus. Anna Leeker and Jillian Adams chose this site to study biology because of the beautiful surroundings—and also because they had little choice. "We heard that the libraries are packed, and that students are waiting in line for tables," said Jillian. Both realize that they have to work to maintain their focus, no matter where they study.[1]

# Prepare Through Careful Review

A thorough review, using analytical and practical strategies like the following, will give you the best shot at remembering material:

**Use SQ3R.** This reading method provides an excellent structure for reviewing your reading materials (see pages 147–156).

**Actively review your combined class and text notes.** One of the best ways to review for an exam is to combine and condense your text and class notes (see chapter 6). Work with this combined note set to prepare for exams as follows:

- *As exam time nears, go through your key terms and concepts outline and recite everything you know about a topic.* Reading your notes is not enough. Learning takes place only if you express content in your own words and apply it to problems.

- *Use critical thinking to become actively involved.* Think about examples and ideas from outside readings and experiences that illustrate concepts, and ideas and opinions that take another point of view. Use what you know to solve problems.

- *Continue to actively review until you demonstrate a solid knowledge of every topic.* Involve yourself with the material by taking a practice test, doing a Q&A with a study partner, and answering your SQ3R questions in writing one more time. Don't stop until you are sure you can apply concepts to new material.

# Take a Pretest

Use end-of-chapter text questions to create your own pretest. If your course doesn't have an assigned text, develop questions from your notes and assigned outside readings. Old homework problems will also help target areas that need work. Choose questions that are likely to be covered, then answer them under test-like conditions—in a quiet place, with no books or notes (unless the exam is open book), and with a clock to tell you when to quit.

The same test-preparation skills you learn in college will help you do well on standardized tests for graduate school. Sharon Smith describes how students in her preparatory program used practice tests and other techniques to help boost their scores on the Medical College Admission Test (MCAT). They "started with un-timed practices in order to work on accuracy, and timed practices were incorporated as the term progressed. Everyone tried to finish the tests/passages in the allotted time, and, at the end of each practice session, go over answer choices to understand why they are correct or incorrect." During the spring term they were "given mock exams, and it was important to treat the mock MCAT as if it were the real exam. This gave the best assessment of performance on test day."[2]

## Write Your Own Test

Check your syllabi for the courses you are taking now, and find the test that is coming up first. Use the tips in this chapter to predict the material that will be covered on this test, the types of questions that will be asked (multiple-choice, essay, and so forth), and the nature of the questions (a broad overview of the material or specific details).

Then be creative. Your goal is to write questions that your instructor is likely to ask—interesting questions that tap what you have learned and make you think about the material in different ways. Go through the following steps:

1. Write the questions you come up with on a separate sheet of paper.

2. Use what you created as a pretest. Set up test-like conditions—a quiet, timed environment—and see how you do.

3. Evaluate your pretest answers against your notes and the text. How did you do?

_____

_____

4. Finally, after you take the actual exam, evaluate whether you think this exercise improved your performance. Would you use this technique again? Why or why not?

_____

_____

## Prepare Physically

Most tests ask you to work at your best under pressure, so try to get a good night's sleep before the exam. Sleep improves your ability to remember what you studied before you went to bed.

Eating a light, well-balanced meal that is high in protein (eggs, milk, yogurt, meat, fish, nuts, or peanut butter) will keep you full longer than carbohydrates (breads, candy, or pastries). When time is short, don't skip breakfast—grab a quick meal such as a few tablespoons of peanut butter, a banana, or a high-protein granola bar.

## Make the Most of Last-Minute Cramming

*Cramming*—studying intensively and around the clock right before an exam—often results in information going into your head and popping right back out when the exam is over. *If learning is your goal, cramming will not help you reach it.* The reality, however, is that you are likely to cram for tests, especially midterms and finals, from time to time in your college career. Use these hints to make the most of this study time:

- *Focus on crucial concepts.* Summarize the most important points and try to resist reviewing notes or texts page by page.

- *Create a last-minute study sheet to review right before the test.* Write down key facts, definitions, and formulas on a single sheet of paper or on flash cards. If you prefer visual notes, use think links to map out ideas and supporting examples.

- *Arrive early.* Review your study aids until you are asked to clear your desk.

After your exam, evaluate how cramming affected your performance. Did it help, or did it load your mind with disconnected details? Did it increase or decrease your anxiety when the test began? Then evaluate how cramming affected your recall. Within a few days, you will probably remember very little—a reality that will work against you in advanced courses that build on this knowledge and in careers that require it. Think ahead about how you can start studying earlier to prepare for your next exam.

# How Can You Work Through Test Anxiety?

Some students experience incapacitating stress, known as test anxiety, before and during exams, especially midterms and finals. Test anxiety can cause sweating, nausea, dizziness, headaches, and fatigue. It can reduce your ability to concentrate, make you feel overwhelmed, and cause you to "blank out" during the exam. As a result, test anxiety often results in lower grades that do not reflect what you really know. The following strategies, which tap your emotional intelligence, will help you control reactions that may get in the way of your performance.

TEST ANXIETY

A bad case of nerves that can make it hard to think or remember during an exam.

# Prepare and Have a Positive Attitude

Being on top of your work from the beginning of the term is the greatest stess reliever. Similarly, creating and following a detailed study plan will build knowledge and a sense of control, as will finding out what to expect on the exam. The following strategies will help you build a positive attitude:

- *See tests as opportunities to learn.* Instead of thinking of tests as contests that you either "win" or "lose," think of them as signposts along the way to mastering material.

- *Understand that tests measure performance, not personal value.* Grades don't reflect your ability to succeed or your self-worth. Whether you get an A or an F, you are the same person.

- *Believe that instructors are on your side.* Your instructors want you to do well, even when they give challenging tests—so contact them if you need help.

- *Seek study partners who challenge you.* Find study partners who inspire you to do your best. Try to avoid people who are also anxious because you may pick up their fears and negativity. (See chapter 1 for more on study groups.)

- *Get tutored.* Many schools offer tutoring help at no charge. Find out what's available and then sign up for sessions.

- *Practice relaxation.* When you feel test anxiety mounting, breathe deeply and slowly, close your eyes, and visualize positive mental images such as getting a good grade. Try to ease muscle tension—stretch your neck, tighten and then release your muscles.

- *Shut out negative vibrations.* If you arrive at the testing room early for a last-minute review, pick a seat far away from others who are nervously discussing the test.

- *Practice positive self-talk.* Tell yourself that you can do well and that it is normal to feel anxious, particularly before an important exam.

- *Remind yourself of your goals.* Connecting the test to your long-term goals will help you calm down as you focus on what's important.

Math exams are a special problem for many students. Dealing with the anxieties associated with these exams will be examined in the *Get Focused!* end-of-part section on pages 275–278 where you will find stress-management, studying, and exam-taking techniques.

Finally, a good attitude involves expecting different test-taking challenges from those you experienced in high school. College exams may ask you to critically analyze and apply material in ways that you never did before. For example, your history instructor may ask you to place a primary source in its historical context. Prepare for these challenges as you study by continually asking critical-thinking questions.

## Test Anxiety and the Returning Student

If you're returning to school after years away, you may wonder how well you will handle exams. To deal with these feelings, focus on what you have learned through life experience, including the ability to handle work and family pressures. Without even knowing it, you may have developed the time-management, planning, organizational, and communication skills needed for college success.

In addition, your life experiences will give real meaning to abstract classroom ideas. For example, workplace relationships may help you understand social psychology concepts, and refinancing your home mortgage may help you grasp a key concept in economics—how the actions of the Federal Reserve Bank influence interest rate swings.

Studying for a test with children underfoot is a reality for many students who are also parents. This student manages his 3-year-old while pursuing a degree from home.

Parents who have to juggle child care with study time can find the challenge especially difficult before a test. Here are some suggestions that might help:

- *Find help.* Join a babysitting cooperative, switch off with a neighbor, post a sign for a part-time babysitter at the local high school.

- *Plan activities.* With younger children, have a supply of games, books, and videos. Give young artists a box of markers and unlimited paper. Then tell them to draw scenes of their family, their home, their friends—all in brilliant color.

- *Explain the time frame.* Tell school-aged children your study schedule and test date. Then promise them a reward for cooperating.

# What General Strategies Can Help You Succeed on Tests?

Even though every test is different, there are general strategies that will help you handle almost all tests, including short-answer and essay exams.

## Choose the Right Seat

Your goal is to choose a seat that will put you in the right frame of mind and minimize distractions. Find a seat near a window, next to a wall, or in the front row so you can look into the distance. Know yourself: For many students, it's smart to avoid sitting near friends.

### Successful Intelligence Connections Online

Listen to author Sarah Kravits describe how to use analytical, creative, and practical intelligence to overcome the anxiety you feel before a big test.

Go to the *Keys to Success* Companion Website at www.prenhall.com/carter to listen or download as a podcast.

## Write Down Key Facts

Before you even look at the test, write down key information, including formulas, rules, and definitions, that you don't want to forget. (Use the back of the question sheet so your instructor knows that you made these notes after the test began.)

## Begin with an Overview

Although exam time is precious, spend a few minutes at the start gathering information about the questions—how many there are in each section, what types, and their point values. Use this information to schedule your time. For example, if a two-hour test is divided into two sections of equal value—an essay section with four questions and a short-answer section with 60 questions—you might spend an hour on the essays (15 minutes per question) and an hour on the short-answer section (one minute per question).

Take level of difficulty into account as you parcel out your time. For example, if you think you can get through the short-answer questions in 45 minutes and sense that the writing section will take longer, you can budget an hour and a quarter for the essays.

## Read Test Directions

Reading test directions carefully can save you trouble. For example, although a history test of 100 true/false questions and one essay may look straightforward, the directions may tell you to answer 80 of the 100 questions or that the essay is optional. If the directions indicate that you are penalized for incorrect answers—meaning that you lose points instead of simply not gaining points—avoid guessing unless you're fairly certain.

When you read directions, you may learn that some questions or sections are weighted more heavily than others. For example, the short-answer questions may be worth 30 points, whereas the essays are worth 70. In this case, it's smart to spend more time on the essays.

## Mark Up the Questions

QUALIFIERS

Words and phrases that can alter the meaning of a test question and that require careful attention.

Mark up instructions and key words to avoid careless errors. Circle qualifiers, such as *always*, *never*, *all*, *none*, *sometimes*, and *every*; verbs that communicate specific instructions; and concepts that are tricky or need special attention.

## Take Special Care on Machine-Scored Tests

Use the right pencil (usually a #2) on machine-scored tests, and mark your answer in the correct space, filling it completely. (Use a ruler or your pencil as a straightedge to focus on the correct line for each question.) Periodically, check the answer number against the question number to make sure they match. If you mark the answer to question 4 in the space for question 5, not only will your response to question 4 be wrong, but also your responses to all subsequent questions will be off by a line. When you plan to return to a question and leave a space blank, put a small dot next to the number on the answer sheet. Neatness counts on these tests because the computer may misread stray pencil marks or partially erased answers.

## Work from Easy to Hard

Begin with the easiest questions and answer them as quickly as you can without sacrificing accuracy. This will boost your confidence and leave more time for questions that require greater focus and effort. Mark tough questions as you reach them, and return to them after answering the questions you know.

## Watch the Clock

Some students are so concerned about time that they rush through the test and have time left over. If this happens to you, spend the remaining time checking your work instead of leaving early. If, on the other hand, midway through the test you realize that you are falling behind, try to evaluate the best use of the remaining time. Being flexible will help you handle the crunch.

## Take a Strategic Approach to Questions You Cannot Answer

Even if you are well prepared, you may be faced with questions you do not understand or cannot answer. What do you do in this situation?

- If your instructor is proctoring the exam, ask for clarification. Sometimes a simple rewording will make you realize that you really know the material.

- If this doesn't work, skip the question and come back to it later. Letting your subconscious mind work on the question sometimes makes a difference.

- Use what you do know about the topic to build logical connections that may lead you to the answer. Take a calculated risk by using your analytical intelligence.

- Try to remember where the material was covered in your notes and text. Creating this kind of visual picture may jog your memory about content as well.

- Start writing—even if you think you're going in the wrong direction and not answering the question that was asked. The act of writing about related material may help you recall the targeted information. You may want to do this kind of "freewriting" on a spare scrap of paper, think about what you've written, and then write your final answer on the test paper or booklet. Put yourself out there.

- If you think of an answer right before the bell, write on the paper that you only have minutes left, so you are answering in outline form. While most instructors will deduct points for this approach, they may also give partial credit because you showed that you know the material.

## Master the Art of Intelligent Guessing

When you are unsure of an answer on an objective test, you can leave it blank or guess. As long as you are not penalized for incorrect answers, guessing may help you. When you use what you know to figure out what you don't know, you have a reasonable chance of guessing right.

When you check your work at the end of the test, decide whether you would make the same guesses again. Because your first instincts are usually best, chances are that you will leave your answers alone. However, you may notice something that changes your mind—a qualifier that affects meaning, for example—or you may recall information that you couldn't remember the first time around.

## Be Prepared for Open-Book Exams

From time to time, you may encounter an *open-book* exam—an exam during which you have permission to access a particular set of materials, often including textbooks and readings. It's tempting to think that this type of exam will be a breeze—but don't be fooled. Put your preparation into high gear for any open-book exam, as many of them tend to be *harder* than a regular exam because of the fact that you can refer to your books.

The exam strategies you've been reading about—watch the clock, answer easy questions first, and so on—all apply to any open-book exam. Testtakingtips.com offers these additional specific tips:

- Be as familiar with the materials as you can, so you don't spend precious exam time wading through pages looking for a key fact.

- Know exactly what materials you are permitted to use, and bring everything on the list.

- If permitted, mark or flag important information in your materials for use as you proceed through the exam and/or write key points or formulas on a separate sheet.

- Don't rely too heavily on quoting your materials to support your key points. Prioritize your own voice.

## Maintain Academic Integrity

Cheating as a strategy to pass a test or get a better grade robs you of the opportunity to learn, which, ultimately, is your loss. Cheating also jeopardizes your future if you are caught. You may be seriously reprimanded—or even expelled—if you violate your school's code of academic integrity. Remember too that cheating in school may damage your ability to get a job.

In recent years, cheating has become high-tech, with students using their cell phones, MP3 players, personal digital assistants (PDAs), graphing calculators, and Internet-connected laptops to share information through text messaging or to search the Internet. Because this type of cheating can be difficult to discover when exams are administered in large lecture halls, some instructors ban all electronic devices from the room.

The *Get Focused!* end-of-part section on pages 405–409 asks you to react to specific cheating situations. Its goal: to communicate that the person who cheats is the one who stands to lose the most.

# How Can You Master Different Types of Test Questions?

Every type of test question has a different way of finding out how much you know about a subject. For (objective questions,) you choose or write a short answer, often making a selection from a limited number of choices. Multiple-choice, fill-in-the-blank, matching, and true/false questions fall into this category. (Subjective questions) demand the same information recall as objective questions, but they also require you to plan, organize, draft, and refine a response. All essay questions are subjective.

Key 7.1 shows samples of real test questions from Western civilization, geometry, Spanish, and biology college texts published by Pearson Education. Included are multiple-choice, true/false, fill-in-the-blank, matching, essay questions, and exercises. Problems and applications are also included for geometry. Analyzing the types, formats, and complexity of these questions will help you gauge what to expect when you take your exams.

As you review the questions on geometry in Key 7.1, look also at the Multiple Intelligence Strategies for Test Preparation on page 223. Harness the strategies that fit your learning strengths to prepare for geometry exams.

*OBJECTIVE QUESTIONS*
Short-answer questions that test your ability to recall, compare, and contrast information and to choose the right answer from a limited number of choices.

*SUBJECTIVE QUESTIONS*
Essay questions that require written responses that tap your personal knowledge and perspective.

**KEY 7.1**

## Real test questions from real college texts.

From chapter 29, "The End of Imperialism," in *Western Civilization: A Social and Cultural History,* 2nd edition.[3]

■ **MULTIPLE-CHOICE QUESTION**
India's first leader after independence was:
A. Gandhi      B. Bose      C. Nehru      D. Sukharno      (answer: C)

■ **FILL-IN-THE-BLANK QUESTION**
East Pakistan became the country of _____ in 1971.
A. Burma      B. East India      C. Sukharno      D. Bangladesh      (answer: D)

■ **TRUE/FALSE QUESTION**
The United States initially supported Vietnamese independence.      T      F      (answer: false)

■ **ESSAY QUESTION**
Answer one of the following:
1. What led to Irish independence? What conflicts continued to exist after independence?
2. How did Gandhi work to rid India of British control? What methods did he use?

From chapter 2, "Geometric Shapes and Measurement," in *College Geometry: A Problem-Solving Approach with Applications,* 2nd edition.[4]

■ **EXERCISES/PROBLEMS**
• All squares are kites, but not all kites are squares. What additional conditions must be satisfied for a kite to be a square?
(answer: Equiangular—all right angles)

• In the following figure, find one example of the following angles.
a. supplementary      b. complementary      c. right      d. adjacent      e. acute      f. obtuse

*(continued)*

*(Geometry answers)*

a. ∠1 and ∠2, ∠3 and ∠4, ∠1 and ∠3, ∠2 and ∠4, ∠6 and ∠9
b. ∠7 and ∠10, ∠5 and ∠8, ∠5 and ∠7, ∠8 and ∠10
c. ∠9 or ∠6
d. ∠1 and ∠2, ∠2 and ∠4, ∠4 and ∠3, ∠3 and ∠1, ∠5 and ∠6, ∠6 and ∠7, ∠7 and ∠10, ∠10 and ∠9, ∠9 and ∠8, ∠8 and ∠5
e. ∠1, ∠4, ∠7, ∠10, ∠8, ∠5
f. ∠2, ∠3

### ▣ APPLICATIONS

• The bed of a gravel truck has the shape shown next where the lateral faces are rectangles. Describes the shape as completely as possible.

*(answer: right trapezoidal prism)*

### ▣ TRUE/FALSE

• A circle is the set of all points in a plane that are the same distance from a fixed point.    *T    F*
• A parallelogram with four congruent sides is a rhombus.    *T    F*    *(answers: T, T)*

From *Mosaicos: Spanish as a World Language,* 3rd edition.[5]

### ▣ MATCHING QUESTIONS

You are learning new words and your teacher asks you to think of an object similar to or related to the words he says. His words are listed below. Next to each word, write a related word from the list below.

| el reloj | el cuaderno | el pupitre | una computadora |
|---|---|---|---|
| el televisor | la tiza | el lápiz | la mochila |

1. el escritorio  _____
2. el bolígrafo  _____
3. la videocasetera  _____
4. la pizarra  _____
5. el libro  _____

*(answers: 1. el pupitre; 2. el lápiz;*
*3. el televisor; 4. la tiza; 5. el cuaderno)*

### ▣ ESSAY QUESTION

Your mother always worries about you and wants to know what you are doing with your time in Granada. Write a short letter to her describing your experience in Spain. In your letter, you should address the following points:

1. What classes you take
2. When and where you study
3. How long you study every day
4. What you do with your time (mention three activities)
5. Where you go during your free time (mention two places)

From chapter 13, "DNA Structure and Replication," in *Biology: A Guide to the Natural World,* 2nd edition.[6]

### ▣ MULTIPLE-CHOICE QUESTION

What units are bonded together to make a strand of DNA?
A. chromatids    B. cells    C. enzymes    D. nucleotides    E. proteins    *(answer: D)*

### ▣ TRUE/FALSE QUESTION

Errors never occur in DNA replication, because the DNA polymerases edit out mistakes.    T    F    *(answer: false)*

### ▣ FILL-IN-THE-BLANK QUESTION

In a normal DNA molecule, adenine always pairs with _____ and cytosine always
pairs with _____.    *(answers: thymine; guanine)*

### ▣ MATCHING QUESTIONS

Match the scientists and the approximate time frame  (decades of their work) with their achievements.

| Column 1 | Column 2 |
|---|---|
| _____ 1. Modeled the molecular structure of DNA | _____ A. George Beadle and Edward Tatum, 1930s and 1940s |
| _____ 2. Generated X-ray crystallography images of DNA | _____ B. James Watson and Francis Crick, 1950s |
| _____ 3. Correlated the production of one enzyme with one gene | _____ C. Rosalind Franklin and Maurice Wilkins, 1950s |

*(answers: 1–B; 2–C; 3–A)*

# MULTIPLE INTELLIGENCE STRATEGIES

## FOR TEST PREPARATION

**APPLY DIFFERENT INTELLIGENCES TO PREPARING FOR A GEOMETRY EXAM.**

| INTELLIGENCE | USE MI STRATEGIES *to improve test preparation* | APPLY MI TEST-PREP STRATEGIES *to study for a test on geometric shapes and measurement* * |
|---|---|---|
| Verbal-Linguistic | • Write test questions your instructor might ask. Answer the questions and then try rewriting them in a different format (essay, true/false, and so on).<br>• Underline important words in review or practice questions. | • Underline important vocabulary words in the chapter. Then make a set of flash cards, with the word on one side and the definition on the other. Test yourself. |
| Logical-Mathematical | • Logically connect what you are studying with what you know. Consider similarities, differences, and cause-and-effect relationships.<br>• Draw charts that show relationships and analyze trends. | • Create a table that highlights the similarities and differences among polygons, circles, and three-dimensional shapes. Use columns to note qualities such as number of sides, number of angles, measurement of angles, formulas that apply consistently, and special features (for example, in a rectangle, all angles are right angles). |
| Bodily-Kinesthetic | • Use text highlighting to take a hands-on approach to studying.<br>• Create a sculpture, model, or skit to depict a tough concept that will be on the test. | • Use pencils, popsicle sticks, pipe cleaners, containers, or other materials to create the shapes on which you will be tested. |
| Visual-Spatial | • Make charts, diagrams, or think links illustrating concepts.<br>• Make drawings related to possible test topics. | • Draw illustrations that represent all of the postulates (statements assumed to be true) in the chapter. |
| Interpersonal | • Form a study group to prepare for your test.<br>• In your group, come up with possible test questions. Then use the questions to test each other's knowledge. | • With a study partner, work through the exercise set on polygons and circles. Try either working through problems together or having partners "teach" problems to each other. |
| Intrapersonal | • Apply concepts to your own life; think about how you would manage.<br>• Brainstorm test questions and then take the sample "test" you developed. | • Reread the "Geometry Around Us" material in your text to reinforce your understanding of how geometry functions in the real world. Write two additional ideas about how geometry relates to your world. |
| Musical | • Recite text concepts to rhythms or write a song to depict them.<br>• Explore relevant musical links to reading material. | • Write a song that helps you remember the types of triangles and their definitions. |
| Naturalistic | • Try to notice similarities and differences in objects and concepts by organizing your study materials into relevant groupings. | • Create a table or visual organizer that arranges all of the types of two- and three-dimensional shapes into logical groupings. |

* For information on geometric shapes and measurement, see Gary L. Musser, Lynn E. Trimpe, and Vikki R. Maurer, *College Geometry: A Problem-Solving Approach with Applications,* 2nd ed., Upper Saddle River, NJ: Pearson/Prentice Hall, 2008.

Note that some suggestions are repeated in the following sections, in order to reinforce the importance of these suggestions and their application to different types of test questions.

## Multiple-Choice Questions

Multiple-choice questions are the most popular type of question on standardized tests. Examples of these questions are on page 225. The following analytical and practical strategies will help you answer them:

**Read the directions carefully.** Directions tell you precisely what to do. For example, whereas most test items ask for a single correct answer, some give you the option of marking several choices that are correct.

**Read each question thoroughly and try to think of the answer before looking at the choices.** Then read the choices and make your selection. When the answer you thought of matches one of the choices, it is most likely correct. Do not second-guess!

**Underline key words and phrases.** If the question is complicated, try to break it down into small sections that are easy to understand.

**Make sure you read every word of every answer.** Instructors have been known to include answers that are right, except for a single word. Focus especially on qualifying words such as *always, never, tend to, most, often,* and *frequently*. Look also for negatives in a question ("Which of the following is *not* . . . ").

**Once you read every word, take the question on face value.** Don't spend time "reading between the lines" to figure out what the instructor is *really* asking.

**If you don't know the answer, eliminate answers that you know or suspect are wrong.** If you can leave yourself with two possible answers, you will have a 50-50 chance of making the right choice. To narrow down, ask these questions about each of the choices:

- *Is the choice accurate on its own terms?* If there's an error in the choice—for example, a term that is incorrectly defined—the answer is wrong.

- *Is the choice relevant?* An answer may be accurate, but unrelated to the question.

- *Are there any qualifiers?* Absolute qualifiers like *always, never, all, none,* or *every* often signal an exception that makes a choice incorrect. For example, the statement "Normal children *always* begin talking before the age of 2" is untrue (most normal children begin talking before age 2, but some start later). Analysis has shown that choices containing conservative qualifiers like *often, most, rarely,* or *may sometimes be* are often correct.

- *Do the choices give clues?* Does a puzzling word remind you of a word you know? Do any parts of an unfamiliar word—its prefix, suffix, or root—ring a bell?

**When questions are linked to a reading passage, read the questions first.** This will help you focus on the information you need to answer the questions.

## True/False Questions

Read true/false questions carefully to evaluate what they are asking. If you're stumped, guess (unless you're penalized for wrong answers). Some examples of true/false questions are on page 225.

Look for qualifiers in true/false questions—such as *all, only,* and *always* (the absolutes that often make a statement false) and *generally, often, usually,* and *sometimes* (the conservatives that often make a statement true)—that can make a true statement false and vice versa. For example, "The grammar rule 'I before E except after C' is *always* true" is false, whereas "The grammar rule 'I before E except after C' is *usually* true" is true. The qualifier makes the difference.

Be sure to read *every* word of a true/false question to avoid jumping to an incorrect conclusion. Common problems in reading too quickly include missing negatives (*not, no*) that would change your response and deciding on an answer before reading the complete statement.

## Matching Questions

Matching questions ask you to match the terms in one list with the terms in another list, according to the directions. For example, the directions may tell you to match a communicable disease with the microorganism that usually causes it. The following strategies will help you handle these questions.

**Make sure you understand the directions.** The directions tell you whether each answer can be used only once (common practice) or more than once.

**Work from the column with the longest entries.** The column on the left usually contains terms to be defined or questions to be answered, while the column on the right has longer definitions or answers. Reading the items on the right only once will save time as you work to match them with the shorter phrases on the left.

**Start with the matches you know.** On your first run-through, mark these matches with a penciled line. When you can use an answer only once, you may have to make changes if you reconsider a choice.

**Finally, tackle the matches you're not sure of.** On your next run-through, focus on the more difficult matches. If one or more phrases seem to have no correct answer and you can use answers only once, consider the possibility that one of your sure-thing answers is wrong.

## Fill-in-the-Blank Questions

Fill-in-the-blank questions, also known as sentence-completion questions, ask you to supply one or more words or phrases to complete the sentence. Some examples are below. The following strategies will help.

---

**Here are examples of fill-in-the-blank questions you might encounter in an introductory astronomy course[9] (correct answers follow questions):**

1. A _____ is a collection of hundreds of billions of stars. *(galaxy)*
2. Rotation is the term used to describe the motion of a body around some _____. *(axis)*
3. The solar day is measured relative to the sun; the sidereal day is measured relative to the _____. *(stars)*
4. On December 21, known as the _____ _____, the sun is at its _____ _____.
   *(winter solstice; southernmost point)*

---

**Be logical.** Insert your answer; then reread the sentence to be sure it is factually and grammatically correct. Consider thinking of the right answer *before* looking at the choices, then finding the choice that most closely matches.

**Note the length and number of the blanks.** These are clues but not absolute guideposts. If two blanks appear together, the instructor is probably looking for a two-word answer. If a blank is longer than usual, the correct response may require additional space. However, if you are certain of an answer that doesn't seem to fit the blanks, trust your knowledge.

**If there is more than one blank and the blanks are widely separated, treat each one separately.** Answer each as if it were a separate sentence-completion question.

**Think outside the box.** If you can think of more than one correct answer, consider putting them both down. Your instructor may be impressed by your assertiveness and creativity.

**If you are uncertain, guess.** Have faith that after hours of studying, your guess is not completely random.

# Essay Questions

Essay questions ask you to express your knowledge and views in a less structured way than short-answer questions. With freedom of thought and expression comes the challenge to organize your ideas and write well under time pressure.

The following steps will help improve your responses to essay questions. The process is basically a less extensive version of the writing process—you plan, draft, revise, and edit your response (see chapter 8). The primary differences here are that you are writing under time pressure and that you are working from memory.

**1. Start by reading the questions.** Decide which to tackle (if there's a choice). Use critical thinking to identify exactly what the question is asking.

Essay questions require you to budget some planning time when you think through how you will spend the time allotted for the test. This student works through an essay question on a final exam.

**2. Map out your time.** Use the techniques you learned earlier in this chapter to schedule your time, remembering that things don't always go as planned. Try to remain flexible if an answer takes longer than expected.

**3. Focus on action verbs.** Verbs, like those in Key 7.2 on the next page, tell you what to do to answer the question. Underline them and use them to guide your writing.

**4. Plan.** Think carefully about what the question is asking and what you know about the topic. On a piece of scrap paper, create an informal outline or a think link to map your ideas and supporting evidence. Then develop a thesis statement that defines your content and point of view. If necessary—and if you have the time—reorganize your planning notes into an exact writing road map.

*The biggest mistake students make in answering essay questions is to skip the planning stage and start writing without thinking through their answers.* Not only does planning result in a better essay, it also reduces stress. Instead of scrambling for ideas as you write, you are carrying out an organized plan.

To answer question three in the box of sample essay questions below, one student created the planning outline shown in Key 7.3. Notice how abbreviations and shorthand help the student write quickly (see chapter 6 for shorthand notes strategies).

---

**Here are some examples of essay questions you might encounter in an interpersonal communication course. In each case, notice the action verbs from Key 7.2.**

1. Summarize the role of the self-concept as a key to interpersonal relationships and communication.

2. Explain how internal and external noise affects the ability to listen effectively.

3. Describe three ways that body language affects interpersonal communication.

**KEY 7.2** Focus on action verbs on essay tests.

ANALYZE—Break into parts and discuss each part separately.

COMPARE—Explain similarities and differences.

CONTRAST—Distinguish between items being compared by focusing on differences.

CRITICIZE—Evaluate the issue, focusing on its problems or deficiencies.

DEFINE—State the essential quality or meaning.

DESCRIBE—Paint a complete picture; provide the details of a story or the main characteristics of a situation.

DIAGRAM—Present a drawing, chart, or other visual.

DISCUSS—Examine completely, using evidence and often presenting both sides of an issue.

ELABORATE ON—Start with information presented in the question, and then add new material.

ENUMERATE/LIST/IDENTIFY—Specify items in the form of a list.

EVALUATE—Give your opinion about the value or worth of something, usually by weighing positive and negative effects, and justify your conclusion.

EXPLAIN—Make the meaning of something clear, often by discussing causes and consequences.

ILLUSTRATE—Supply examples.

INTERPRET—Explain your personal views and judgments.

JUSTIFY—Discuss the reasons for your conclusions or for the question's premise.

OUTLINE—Organize and present main and subordinate points.

PROVE—Use evidence and logic to show that something is true.

REFUTE—Use evidence and logic to show that something is not true or how you disagree with it.

RELATE—Connect items mentioned in the question, showing, for example, how one item influenced the other.

REVIEW—Provide an overview of ideas and establish their merits and features.

STATE—Explain clearly, simply, and concisely.

SUMMARIZE—Give the important ideas in brief, without comments.

TRACE—Present a history of the way something developed, often by showing cause and effect.

**5. Draft.** Your first draft on an exam is usually the one you hand in. If you plan effectively, you should have enough material to construct a suitable answer. Use the following guidelines as you draft your answer:

- Spend the bulk of your time developing your thesis and supporting evidence and logic. Most instructors do not expect fully developed introductions or conclusions.

# Write to the Verb

Focusing on the action verbs in essay test instructions can mean the difference between giving instructors what they want and answering off the mark. Try this exercise.

- Start by choosing a topic you learned about in this text—for example, the concept of successful intelligence or different barriers to listening. Write your topic here:

  _____

  _____

- Put yourself in the role of instructor. Write an essay question on this topic, using one of the action verbs in Key 7.2 to frame the question. For example, "List the three aspects of successful intelligence," or "Analyze the classroom-based challenges associated with internal barriers to listening." Write your question here:

  _____

  _____

- Now choose three other action verbs from Key 7.2. Use each one to rewrite your original question:

  1. _____

  2. _____

  3. _____

- Finally, analyze how each new verb changes the focus of the essay:

  1. _____
     _____

  2. _____
     _____

  3. _____
     _____

- Start by stating your thesis, and then get right to the evidence that backs it up.
- Pay close attention to how you organize your ideas and how well you support them with evidence. Try to structure your essay so that each paragraph presents an idea that supports the thesis.

Create an informal outline during essay tests.

Roles of BL in IC
1. To contradict or reinforce words
   — e.g., friend says "I'm fine"
2. To add shades of meaning
   — saying the same sentence in 3 diff. ways
3. To make lasting 1st impression
   — impact of nv cues and voice tone greater than words
   — we assume things abt person based on posture, eye contact, etc.

- Use clear language and tight logic to link ideas to your thesis and to create transitions between paragraphs.
- Look back at your outline periodically to make sure you cover everything.
- Wrap it up with a short, to-the-point conclusion.

Pay attention to the test directions when drafting your answer. Your essay may need to be of a certain length, for example, or may need to take a certain form (for example, a particular format such as a business letter). Finally, write on only one side of the page so that the grader can easily read your response.

**6. Revise.** Take a few moments to evaluate your word choice, paragraph structure, and style. Although you may not have the time or opportunity to rewrite your entire answer, you can certainly improve it with minor deletions or additions in the margin. If you find a problem in your work—an idea without support, for example, or some unnecessary information—add the new material in the margins and cross out what you don't need. When adding material, you can indicate with an arrow where it fits or note that inserts can be found on separate pages. If you have more than one insert, label each to avoid confusion (Insert #1, Insert #2). Be neat as you make changes.

As you check over your essay, ask yourself these questions:

- Have I answered the question?
- Does my essay begin with a clear thesis statement, and does each paragraph start with a strong topic sentence that supports the thesis?

- Have I provided the support necessary in the form of examples, statistics, and relevant facts to prove my argument?
- Is my logic sound and convincing?
- Have I covered all the points in my original outline?
- Is my conclusion an effective wrap-up?
- Does every sentence effectively communicate my point?

**7. Edit.** Check for mistakes in grammar, spelling, punctuation, and usage. No matter your topic, correct language leaves a positive impression and reduces problems that may lower your grade.

Key 7.4 shows the student's completed response to the essay question on body language, including the word changes and inserts she made while revising the draft.

Neatness is crucial. No matter how good your ideas are, if your instructor can't read them your grade will suffer. If your handwriting is a problem, try printing or skipping every other line, and be sure to write on only one side of the page. Students with illegible handwriting might ask to take the test on a computer.

The purpose of a test is to see how much you know, not merely to get a grade. Embrace this attitude to learn from your mistakes.

# How Can You Learn from Test Mistakes?

In life—and on exams—people learn most from their mistakes. With exam in hand, use the following strategies to reduce the likelihood of making the same errors again. (If your instructor posts grades but does not hand exams back, ask to see your paper.)

**Try to identify patterns in your mistakes.** Ask yourself global questions that may help you identify correctable patterns:

- *Can you identify your biggest problems?* Did you get nervous, misread the question, fail to study enough, study incorrectly, focus on memorizing material instead of on understanding and applying it?
- *Did your instructor's comments clarify what you failed to do?* Did your answer lack specificity? Did you fail to support your thesis with concrete examples? Was your analysis weak?
- *Were you surprised by the questions?* For example, did you expect them all to be from the lecture notes and text instead of from your notes, text, and supplemental readings?
- *Did you make careless errors?* Did you misread the question or directions, blacken the wrong box on the answer sheet, skip a question, write illegibly?

QUESTION: Describe three ways that body language affects interpersonal communication.

Body language plays an important role in interpersonal communication and helps shape the impression you make, ~~,~~ [*, especially when you meet someone for the first time*] Two of the most important functions of body language are to contradict and reinforce verbal statements. When body language contradicts verbal language, the message ~~conveyed~~ [*delivered*] by the body is dominant. For example, if a friend tells you that she is feeling "fine," but her posture is slumped, [*her eye contact minimal,*] and her facial expression troubled, you have every reason to wonder whether she is telling the truth. If the same friend tells you that she is feeling fine and is smiling, walking with a bounce in her step, and has direct eye contact, her body language is ~~telling the truth.~~ [*accurately reflecting and reinforcing her words.*]

The nonverbal cues that make up body language also have the power to add shades of meaning. Consider this statement: "This is the best idea I've heard all day." If you were to say this three different ways—in a loud voice while standing up; quietly while sitting with arms and legs crossed and looking away; and while ~~maintening~~ [*maintaining*] eye contact and taking the receiver's hand—you might send three different messages.

Finally, the impact of nonverbal cues can be greatest when you meet someone for the first time. [*Although first impressions emerge from a combination of nonverbal cues, tone of voice, and choice of words, nonverbal elements (cues and tone) usually come across first and strongest.*] When you meet someone, you tend to make assumptions based on nonverbal behavior such as posture, eye contact, gestures, and speed and style of movement.

In summary, nonverbal communication plays a ~~crusial~~ [*crucial*] role in interpersonal relationships. It has the power to send an accurate message that may ~~destroy~~ [*belie*] the speaker's words, offer shades of meaning, and set the tone of a first meeting.

- **Did you make conceptual or factual errors?** Did you misunderstand a concept? Did you fail to master facts or concepts? Did you skip part of the text or miss classes in which ideas were covered?

Honest answers will help you change the way you study for the next exam.

**Rework the questions you got wrong.** Based on instructor feedback, try to rewrite an essay, recalculate a math problem from the original question, or redo questions following a reading selection. If you discover a pattern of careless errors, redouble your efforts to be more careful, and save time to double-check your work from now on.

**After reviewing your mistakes, fill in your knowledge gaps.** If you made mistakes because you didn't understand important concepts, develop a plan to learn the material.

**Talk to your instructor.** Focus on specific mistakes on objective questions or a weak essay. The fact that you care enough to review your errors will leave a positive, lasting impression. If you are not sure why you were marked down on an essay, ask what you could have done better. If you feel that an essay was unfairly graded, ask for a rereading. When you use your social intelligence and approach your instructor in a nondefensive way, you are likely to receive help.

**Rethink the way you studied.** Make changes to avoid repeating your errors. Use the varied techniques in *Keys to Success* to study more effectively so that you can show yourself and your instructors what you are capable of

# Learn from Your Mistakes

*get practical!*

Look at an exam on which your performance fell short. If possible, choose one that contains different types of objective and subjective questions. With the test and the answer sheet in hand, use your analytical thinking skills to answer the following questions and learn from your mistakes:

- Identify the types of questions on which you got the most correct answers (for example, matching, essay, multiple-choice):

  _____

- Identify the types of questions on which you made the greatest number of errors:

  _____

- Analyze your errors to identify patterns—for example, did you misread test instructions or ignore qualifiers that changed meaning? What did you find?

  _____

  _____

- Finally, list two practical steps you are prepared to take during your next exam to avoid the same problems:

  Action 1: _____

  Action 2: _____

doing. The earlier in the term you make positive adjustments the better, so make a special effort to analyze and learn from early test mistakes.

**If you fail a test, don't throw it away.** Use it to review troublesome material, especially if you will be tested on it again. You might also want to keep it as a reminder that you can improve if you have the will to succeed. When you compare a failure to later successes, you'll see how far you've come.

# Successful Intelligence Wrap-Up

Tests ask you to show what you know to someone who will judge your performance. However, far more important than the information a test gives to an instructor is the information it gives to you, the test taker. Tests can be your road map to subject mastery, showing you what you have learned, what you are still learning, and what stumps you. Here's how you have built skills in chapter 7:

## Analytical

You examined test-preparation techniques with an eye toward what works best for you. You investigated specific ways to maximize your chances of answering objective and subjective test questions correctly. In the *Get Analytical* exercise, you wrote a series of original essay questions, analyzing the effect that different action verbs had on what the questions were asking. You considered the potential positive effects from a careful analysis of test mistakes.

## Creative

With the *Get Creative* exercise, you produced your own pretest that will help you assess if you have mastered crucial material. In reading about test anxiety, you encountered a different perspective of tests as opportunities to learn rather than contests that you win or lose. The scheduling and study techniques may have inspired you to create a personal study schedule and regimen that help you make the most of your time.

## Practical

You gathered specific test-preparation techniques. You learned specific ways to calm test anxiety and to attack objective test questions. You expanded your knowledge of how to use planning tools, such as a key word outline, to help you write test essays. You deepened your understanding of how examining test mistakes helps you learn from experience. In the *Get Practical* exercise, you explored your mistakes on a particular test and identified steps you will take to avoid the same mistakes in the future.

# hart ducha

## (hahrt doo-cha)

In Polish, *hart ducha* literally means "strength of spirit" or "strength of will" to overcome life's challenges. In college, instructors challenge you on tests to demonstrate what you know and what you can do. Both before and during each test, your success depends on your *hart ducha*. With strength of will, you can commit to spending hours learning, reviewing, thinking about, and memorizing course material instead of cramming at the last minute. Think carefully about your approach because it determines far more than your exam grade. It determines what you will get out of your education.

There are no shortcuts to test success. Only old-fashioned hard work, driven by a powerful strength of will, will enable you to reach your academic potential.[10]

---

"The Five P's of Success: Prior preparation prevents poor performance."

JAMES A. BAKER III, FORMER SECRETARY OF STATE
AND WHITE HOUSE CHIEF OF STAFF

## SUCCESSFUL INTELLIGENCE

*Think, Create, Apply*

Prepare effectively for tests. Take a careful look at your performance on and preparation for a recent test.

**Step 1. Think it through:** *Analyze how you did.* Were you pleased or disappointed with your performance and grade? Why?

_____

_____

Thinking about your performance, look at the problems listed below. Circle those that you feel were a factor in this exam. Fill in the empty spaces with problems not listed.

- Incomplete preparation
- Fatigue
- Feeling rushed during the test
- Shaky understanding of concepts
- Poor guessing techniques
- Feeling confused about directions
- Test anxiety
- Poor essay organization or writing
- _____
- _____
- _____

Now for each problem you identified, think about why you made mistakes.

**Step 2. Think out of the box:** *Be creative about test-preparation strategies.* If you had absolutely no restrictions on time or access to materials, how would you have prepared for this test to improve your performance? Describe briefly what your plan would be and how it would minimize the problems you encountered.

_____

_____

Now think back to your actual test preparation. What techniques did you use and how much time did you spend?

_____

_____

How does what you would do under ideal circumstances differ from what you actually did?

_____

_____

**Step 3. Make it happen:** *Improve preparation for the next exam.* Think about the practical actions you will take the next time you face a similar test. Write your answers here.

Actions I took this time, but do not intend to take next time:

_____

_____

Actions I did not take this time, but intend to take next time:

_____

_____

# TEAMWORK

## *Create Solutions Together*

Test study group. Form a study group with two or three other students. When your instructor announces the next exam, ask each study group member to record everything he or she does to prepare for the exam, including things like these:

- Learning what to expect on the test (topics and material that will be covered, types of questions that will be asked)
- Examining old tests
- Creating and following a study schedule and checklist
- Using SQ3R to review material
- Taking a pretest
- Getting a good night's sleep
- Doing last-minute cramming
- Mastering general test-taking strategies
- Mastering strategies for handling specific types of test questions

After the exam, come together to compare preparation strategies. What important differences can you identify in the routines followed by group members? How did learning styles play a role in those differences? How do you suspect that different routines affected test performance and outcome? On a separate piece of paper or on a computer file, for your own reference, write down what you learned from the test-preparation habits of your study mates that may help you as you prepare for upcoming exams.

# WRITING

*Record your thoughts on a separate piece of paper, in a journal, or on a computer file.*

**Journal entry: Test anxiety.** Do you experience test anxiety? Describe how tests generally make you feel (you might include an example of a specific test situation and what happened). Identify your specific test-taking fears, and brainstorm ideas for how to overcome fears and self-defeating behaviors.

**Real-life writing: Ask your instructor for feedback on a test.** Nearly all students have been in the position of believing that the response they wrote on an essay exam was marked down unfairly. The next time this happens to you—when you have no idea why you lost points or disagree with the instructor's assessment of your work—draft a respectful e-mail to your instructor explaining your position and asking for a meeting to discuss the essay. (See e-mail etiquette guidelines in Quick Start to College.) Use clear logic to defend your work and refer back to what you learned in class and in the text. It is important to address specifically any comments or criticisms the instructor made on the test paper. Before sending the e-mail, analyze your argument: Did you make your case effectively, or was the instructor correct? When you have the meeting, the work you did on the e-mail will prepare you to defend your position.

# PERSONAL PORTFOLIO

*Complete the following in your electronic portfolio or on separate paper.*

**On-the-job testing.** You may encounter different tests throughout your career. For example, if you are studying to be a nurse, you will be now tested on subjects like anatomy and pharmacology. After you graduate you will be required to take certification and recertification exams that gauge your mastery of the latest information in different aspects of nursing.

Some postgraduate tests are for entry into the field; some test proficiency on particular equipment; some move you to the next level of employment. Choose one career you are thinking about and investigate what tests are involved as you advance through different career stages. Write down everything you find out about each test, including the following:

- What it tests you on
- When, in the course of pursuing this career, you would need to take the test
- What preparation is necessary for the test, including continuing education courses, special training, or graduate degrees
- Whether the test needs to be retaken at any time (for instance, airline pilots usually need to be recertified every few years)

Next, write a short essay on how you plan to use the test-taking skills you learned in this chapter to do well on these tests. Among the ideas you may want to touch on are these:

- How you are learning to deal with test anxiety before important exams
- Your growing skill in working under pressure

- Your understanding of the five P's of test success: *prior preparation prevents poor performance*
- Your growing ability to memorize information
- Your developing analytical ability to solve difficult problems
- Your increased use of studying schedules and other practical aids

## Suggested Readings

Browning, William G. *Cliffs Memory Power for Exams*. Lincoln, NE: Cliffs Notes, 1990.

Frank, Steven. *Test Taking Secrets: Study Better, Test Smarter, and Get Great Grades*. Holbrook, MA: Adams Media, 1998.

Fry, Ron. *"Ace" Any Test*, 5th ed. Florence, KY: Thomson Delmar Learning, 2004.

Hamilton, Dawn. *Passing Exams: A Guide for Maximum Success and Minimum Stress*. New York: Continuum International, 2003.

Kesselman-Turkel, Judy, and Franklynn Peterson. *Test Taking Strategies*. Madison: University of Wisconsin Press, 2004.

Luckie, William R., and Wood Smethurst. *Study Power: Study Skills to Improve Your Learning and Your Grades*. Cambridge, MA: Brookline Books, 1997.

Meyers, Judith N. *Secrets of Taking Any Test: Learn the Techniques Successful Test-Takers Know*. New York: Learning Express, July 2000.

## Internet and Podcast Resources

Palm Beach Community College (list of sites offering information on test-taking skills): **www.pbcc.edu/x6838.xml**

TestTakingTips.com (tips to improve your test-taking and study skills): **www.testtakingtips.com**

University of North Dakota—Study Strategies Homepage: **www.d.umn.edu/student/loon/acad/strat**

Prentice Hall Student Success SuperSite: **www.prenhall.com/success**

## Endnotes

[1] From Ben Gose, "Notes from Academe: Living It Up on the Dead Days," *Chronicle of Higher Education*, June 7, 2002 (http://chronicle.com/weekly/v48/i39/39a04801.htm).

[2] From "Students Speak," MEDPREP: Medical/Dental Education Preparatory Program, Southern Illinois University School of Medicine (www.siumed.edu/medprep/studentsspeak.html).

[3] Western civilization test items from Margaret L. King, *Western Civilization: A Social and Cultural History*, 2nd ed., Upper Saddle River, NJ: Pearson Education, 2003. Questions from *Instructor's Manual and Test Item File* by Dolores Davison Peterson. Used with permission.

[4] Geometry exercises from Gary L. Musser, Lynn E. Trimpe, and Vikki R. Maurer, *College Geometry: A Problem-Solving Approach with Applications*, 2nd ed., Upper Saddle River, NJ: Pearson/Prentice Hall, 2008, pp. 99–101. Used with permission.

[5] Spanish test items from Matilde Olivella de Castells, Elizabeth Guzmán, Paloma Lupuerta, and Carmen García, *Mosaicos: Spanish as a World Language*, 3rd ed., Upper Saddle River, NJ: Prentice Hall, 2002. Questions from *Testing Program* by Mark Harpring. Used with permission.

[6] Biology test items from David Krogh, *Biology: A Guide to the Natural World*, 2nd ed., Upper Saddle River, NJ: Prentice Hall, 2002. Questions from *Test Item File* edited by Dan Wivagg. Used with permission.

[7] From Gary W. Piggrem and Charles G. Morris, *Test Item File* for *Understanding Psychology*, 3rd ed., 1996. Reprinted by permission of Pearson Education, Inc., Upper Saddle River, NJ.

[8] Ibid.

[9] From Eric Chaisson and Steve McMillan, *Astronomy Today*, 3rd ed., 1999. Reprinted by permission of Pearson Education, Inc., Upper Saddle River, NJ.

[10] Christopher J. Moore, *In Other Words: A Language Lover's Guide to the Most Intriguing Words Around the World*, New York: Walker, 2004, p. 45.

# RESEARCHING AND WRITING
## *Gathering and Communicating Ideas*

*"When a man dies and goes to heaven, Saint Peter points to an individual, mentioning that he was a great poet. The man looks at Saint Peter, incredulous. 'Excuse me,' he says, 'but I knew that man. He was . . . a humble shoemaker. He never went to school or learned how to write.' 'Precisely so,' responds Saint Peter. Never given the chance to develop his skills, the man's . . . talent went to waste."*

ROBERT J. STERNBERG

Research and writing, powerful tools that engage successful intelligence, are at the heart of your education and are essential to academic and career success. Through library and Internet research, you gather and analyze information from sources all over the world. Through writing, you analyze ideas, think creatively about what they mean, and communicate information and perspectives to others.

*In this chapter you explore answers to the following questions.*

- How can you make the most of your college library? 242
- How can you find reliable information on the Internet? 247
- What is the writing process? 252
- Successful Intelligence Wrap-Up 268

## Analytical

- Analyzing how to use library and Internet sources
- Evaluating the reliability of Internet sources
- Evaluating your writing purpose and crafting a thesis that reflects it
- Evaluating how to organize ideas and choose effective words

## Creative

- Developing a personal approach to Internet and library research
- Brainstorming to develop writing topics
- Using prewriting strategies to narrow topic ideas

## Practical

- How to use a keyword search of library and Internet sources
- How to plan, draft, revise, and edit a paper
- How to avoid plagiarism

# How Can You Make the Most of Your College Library?

In this information age, when researchers have at their disposal a vast array of electronic resources, college libraries are more valued than ever for their role in helping you make intelligent information choices. With expanded and enhanced offerings linked to the Internet and to stacks of books, journals, and other tangible resources, the library is the "brain" of your college. It is your challenge to use analytical, creative, and practical skills to find accurate, reliable information in every medium.

Realizing the value of library resources starts with the awareness that when you use the library's electronic databases, you will have an easier time finding information than if you used the Internet alone. Your library subscribes to many specialized databases that link you to full-text articles, books, and other information. You won't have access to these databases without plugging in to your library account.

Although most students are drawn to the Internet first when researching, this chapter will give you reasons to believe that the library is the best place to begin your research. Your instructors know this and will expect to see library research citations in your work. Start here to become more familiar with what your library has to offer.

## How can I become more confident about my writing?

College papers are a challenge. I don't think my topic ideas are original, and I feel that my vocabulary is not that advanced. If a professor assigns a topic I know nothing about, I don't have as much interest as with something familiar.

One of the reasons I don't like to write is because I don't like researching. I never know where to begin because there's so much to choose from. Once I pull information together, I can't expand on an idea without being redundant or going off on tangents. How can I become a better writer?

Beverly Andre
Triton College, Continuing Education Program
River Grove, Illinois

Raymond Montolvo Jr.
Writers Program
University of
Southern California
Los Angeles, California

### Concentrate on improving your skills instead of worrying about your grade.

I suggest a two-pronged approach to better writing. The first step is to read. Read novels, the newspaper, and nonfiction articles. Reading helps you learn to organize your thoughts and increases your vocabulary. If you want to focus on a specific area of study, read publications in that area. Create folders for pieces of writing that you like. For example, make a copy of a business letter that you think is well written, and refer to it when you need to write a similar correspondence.

Second, ask your instructor what he or she thinks you need to work on. Focus your energy on understanding the assignment and strengthening technical skills such as sentence structure and grammar. Another tip is to read what you've written out loud, sentence by sentence, and think about how you could say it better.

If you don't know where to begin your research, start with what feels comfortable. If you are at ease with computers, use the Internet. If you prefer libraries, start by asking the reference librarian for assistance. Once you read something that relates to your topic, it will refer you to something else.

Finally, your instructor's goal is to help you improve as a writer. Keeping this in mind will help you concentrate and do your best work. Don't get frustrated by setbacks. Your writing will improve over time, and the more writing you do the better you will be. Set goals you can attain. Finishing a paper to the best of your ability will build your confidence as much as getting a good grade.

## Start with a Road Map

The better you know the "road map" of your library, the less time you'll spend searching for elusive resources. Here are some key resources:

- **Circulation desk.** All publications are checked out at the circulation desk, which is usually near the library entrance.

- **Reference area.** Here you'll find reference books, including encyclopedias, directories, dictionaries, almanacs, and atlases. You'll also find information specialists who can direct you to sources. Computer terminals, containing the library's catalog of holdings, as well as online bibliographic and full-text databases, are usually part of the reference area.

- **Book area.** Books—and, in many libraries, magazines and journals in bound or boxed volumes—are stored in the *stacks*. A library with *open*

*stacks* allows you to search for materials. In a *closed-stack* system, a staff member retrieves materials for you.

- **Periodicals area.** Here you'll find recent issues of popular and scholarly magazines, journals, and newspapers.

- **Audiovisual materials areas.** Many libraries have special locations where you can study nonprint materials including video, art and photography, and recorded music collections.

- **Electronic library resources.** Computer terminals, linked to college databases and the Internet, may be scattered throughout the library or clustered in specific areas. Most schools have network systems that allow access to online library materials via personal computers. In addition, an increasing number of colleges have wireless Wi-Fi systems that allow students to conduct research via their computer, cell phone, or PDA while sitting in a classroom or even under a tree.

Almost all college libraries offer orientation sessions on how to find what you need. To learn what your library offers, take a real or virtual tour and sign up for training.

*KEYWORD SEARCH*

*Natural-language words and phrases that are used to search a computer data bank in order to track down specific information.*

## Learn How to Conduct an Information Search

Use a practical, step-by-step method that takes you from general to specific sources. At any point in your search, you can conduct a keyword search—a method in which you use a topic-related *keyword*, any natural-language word or phrase, as a point of reference to locate other information. To narrow your topic and reduce the number of *hits* (resources pulled up by your search), add more keywords. For example, instead of searching through the broad category "art," focus on "French art" or, more specifically, "19th century French art."

Key 8.1 provides tips for using the keyword system, including how to use "or," "and," and "not" to narrow searches with what is called *Boolean logic.*

 **KEY 8.1**

### Perform an effective keyword search.

| IF YOU ARE SEARCHING FOR... | DO THIS | EXAMPLE |
| --- | --- | --- |
| A word | Type the word normally. | Aid |
| A phrase | Type the phrase in its normal word order (use regular word spacing) or surround the phrase with quotation marks. | financial aid or "financial aid" |
| Two or more keywords without regard to word order | Type the words in any order, surrounding the words with quotation marks. Use *and* to separate the words. | "financial aid" and "scholarships" |
| Topic A or topic B | Type the words in any order, surrounding the words with quotation marks. Use *or* to separate the words. | "financial aid" or "scholarships" |
| Topic A but not topic B | Type topic A first within quotation marks, and then topic B within quotation marks. Use *not* to separate the words. | "financial aid" not "scholarships" |

## Start with General Reference Works

These works cover topics in a broad, nondetailed way and are often available in print, online, or on CD-ROM. Examples of general reference works include encyclopedias, almanacs, dictionaries, biographical references (such as *Webster's Biographical Dictionary*), and bibliographies (such as *Books in Print*). Scan these sources for a topic overview and more specialized sources.

## Search Specialized Reference Works

Turn next to specialized reference works, including encyclopedias and dictionaries that focus on a narrow field (such as the *Encyclopedia of American History*), for more specific facts. The short summaries in these volumes focus on critical ideas and introduce keywords you can use to conduct additional research. Bibliographies that accompany the articles point to the works of recognized experts.

## Browse Through Books and Articles on Your Subject

Search the computerized library catalog by author, title, or subject to find information about where in your library to locate books and other materials on your topic. Periodicals include journals, magazines, and newspapers. Journals target readers with specialized knowledge (while *Newsweek* may run a general-interest article on AIDS research, for example, the *Journal of the American Medical Association* may print the original scientific study). *Periodical indexes* such as the *Reader's Guide to Periodical Literature* lead you to specific articles that are available in print, on line, and on CD-ROM.

> PERIODICALS
>
> Magazines, journals, newspapers, and online publications that are published on a regular basis throughout the year.

> JOURNALS
>
> Periodicals that are intended for readers with in-depth knowledge.

## Ask the Librarian

Librarians, also known as *media specialists* and *information technologists,* can assist you in locating unfamiliar or hard-to-find sources, navigating catalogs and databases, uncovering research shortcuts, and dealing with pesky computers and other equipment. Know what you want to accomplish before you ask a question. The more specific your inquiry, the more likely the librarian will be able to help you. In addition, use your emotional and social intelligence to frame your question in a way that is likely to encourage help. Being friendly and courteous and looking the librarian in the eye when you speak will go a long way. When you can't get to the library in person, technology enables librarians at many schools to answer questions via cell phone, e-mail, and instant-messaging.

Librarians can lead you to a variety of online reference sources, such as those listed in Key 8.2.

The library is an indispensable tool in your efforts to gather information—the foundation of knowledge. Chad Clunie, a political science major at Indiana University's Southeast Campus, is driven to use the library by the "quest for

College libraries provide a myriad of resources and services. Many students, like this one, spend time in the library both to access materials and to find study environments that suit them.

KEY 8.2 Become familiar with online reference sources to improve your research efficiency.

| IF YOU WANT TO SEARCH ... | VISIT THIS INTERNET ADDRESS |
|---|---|
| Copyrighted books in print | Amazon.com: *www.amazon.com*<br>Barnes and Noble: *www.barnesandnoble.com* |
| Encyclopedia entries | Encarta: *http://encarta.msn.com* |
| Print and electronic media | Arts & Letters Daily: *http://aldaily.com* (links to conventional and new media including weblogs) |
| Magazine and newspaper articles | Newslink: *http://newslink.org* |
| Academic publications | Google Scholar: *http://scholar.google.com* (search engine with access to academic journals and other sources) |
| Book contents | Google Book Search: *http://books.google.com* (access to thousands of scanned books) |
| Weblogs | QuackTrack: *http://quacktrack.com* (browsable blog index) |
| Primary sources in U.S. history, politics, and culture | Library of Congress: *http://loc.gov* (scanned manuscripts, maps, photos and recordings)<br><br>Library of Congress American Memory: *http://memory.loc.gov/ammem* (the written and spoken words, sound recordings, still and moving images, and sheet music that document the American experience) |
| Federal legislation | Thomas—Legislative information on the Internet: *http://thomas.loc.gov* |
| Biographies | Biographical Dictionary: *www.s9.com/biography*<br>Biography.com: *www.biography.com/search*<br>Biography Center: *www.biography-center.com* |
| Maps | Google Earth: *http://earth.google.com*<br>Perry-Castañeda Library Map Collection: *www.lib.utexas.edu/maps*<br>Maptech MapServer: *http://mapserver.maptech.com* |
| Country profiles | Atlapedia Online: *www.atlapedia.com/online/country_index.htm* |
| U.S. population and economic data | U.S. Census Bureau, U.S. Department of Commerce: *www.census.gov* |
| U.S. historical documents | The Avalon Project: *http://yale.edu/lawweb/avalon/avalon.htm* (documents from colonial period to today) |
| Company information | Thomas Register: *www.thomasnet.com* |
| European primary sources | EuroDocs: *http://eudocs.lib.byu.edu/index.php/Main_Page* (historical sources from two dozen European countries) |

knowledge." As an officer in the student branch of the American Civil Liberties Union, Chad uses library resources to formulate debates on current topics such as same-sex marriage and the Patriot Act. "There's so much to learn," says Chad. "There's no way of knowing it all."[1]

# How Can You Find Reliable Information on the Internet?

The Internet, a computer network that links organizations and people around the world, can connect you to billions of information sources. Unlike your college library collection or library subscription databases—evaluated and selected for usefulness and reliability by educated librarians—Internet resources are not necessarily evaluated or overseen by anyone. As a result, Internet research depends on your analytical judgment.

Most Internet information is displayed on *Web sites*, cyberspace locations developed by companies, government agencies, organizations, and individuals. *Blogs* (also known as *weblogs*), interactive journal-like entries on specific topics that are created and maintained by individual users, enable readers to respond to postings and engage in cyberspace conversations with others who are interested in the topic. Currently, there are more than 100 million Web sites, up from just 18,000 in 1995, and 60 million blogs.[2]

## Start with Search Engines

*Search engines* are tools for finding information on the Internet. Using a keyword search, you gain access to Web sites, blogs, and other resources. With the power of the search engine to access the Internet comes the potential for an enormous list of "hits" unless you carefully limit your keyword search. Among the most popular and effective search engines are Google (*www.google.com*), Yahoo! (*www.yahoo.com*), AltaVista (*www.altavista.com*), HotBot (*www.hotbot.com*), Ask (*www.ask.com*), Excite (*www.excite.com*), Go.com (*www.go.com*), and Lycos (*www.lycos.com*).

Search engines aimed at academic audiences are the Librarian's Index to the Internet (*www.lii.org*) and InfoMine (*www.infomine.com*). The advantage of using academic directories is that you know someone has screened the sites and listed only those that have been determined to be reliable, regularly updated, and reputable.

*Meta search engines*, which compare results across different search engines, include Dogpile.com, Search.com, Mamma.com, Webmetasearch.com, and KartOO.com.

## Use a Search Strategy

The World Wide Web has been called "the world's greatest library, with all its books on the floor." With no librarian in sight, you need to master a practical basic Internet search strategy that will help you evaluate the flood of online sources. Follow these steps:

INTERNET SEARCH STRATEGY
A practical, step-by-step method that helps you locate accurate, reliable online sources.

1. *Think carefully about what you want to locate.* University of Michigan professor Eliot Soloway recommends phrasing your search

in the form of a question—for example, *What vaccines are given to children before age 5?* Then he advises identifying the important words in the question (*vaccines, children, before age 5*) as well as other related words (*polio, shot, pediatrics,* and so on). This will give you a collection of terms to use in different combinations as you search.[3]

2. *Use a search engine to isolate sites under your desired topic or category.* Save the sites that look useful. Most Internet software programs have a "bookmark" or "favorites" feature for recording sites you want to visit again.

3. *Explore these sites to get a general idea of what's out there.* Usually, in academic research, you will need to go beyond the search engine's listings. Use what you find there to notice useful keywords and information locations.

4. *Use your keywords in a variety of ways to uncover more possibilities:*
   - Vary word order if you are using more than one keyword (for example, search under both "*education, college, statistics*" and "*statistics, education, college*").
   - Limit your search through Boolean operators, such as "and," "not," and "or."

5. *Evaluate the number of links that appear.* If there are too many, narrow your search by using more, or more specific, keywords ("*Broadway*" could become "*Broadway*" AND "*fall season*" AND "*2008*"). If there are too few links, broaden your search by using fewer or different keywords.

6. *When you think you are done, start over.* Choose another search engine and search again. Different systems access different sites.

## Use Critical Thinking to Evaluate Every Source

Your Internet research is only as strong as your analytical thinking. Robert Harris, professor and author of *WebQuester: A Guidebook to the Web,* has developed an easy-to-remember system for evaluating Internet information called the CARS test for information quality (Credibility, Accuracy, Reasonableness, Support). Use the information in Key 8.3 to question any source you find as you conduct research.[4]

Educational and government sites are more likely to be evaluated for accuracy and reliablility than other sites. You can identify these sites by looking at the *URL (universal resource locator)*—the string of text and numbers that identifies an Internet site. Look for URLs ending in *.edu* (originating at educational institutions) and *.gov* (originating at government agencies). If you are unsure of the credibility of a source, ask your instructor.

Some popular information sites sometimes have reliability problems. For example, the online encyclopedia Wikipedia, which allows all readers to create or edit articles, is plagued by incorrect information or glaring omissions. Knowing that Wikipedia's information is often written by non-experts will raise your level of critical analysis and encourage you to cross-check the information in other places. Because of Wikipedia's problems, some colleges have banned its use in research papers.

KEYS TO SUCCESS

**KEY 8.3** Use the CARS test to determine information quality on the Internet.

| CREDIBILITY | ACCURACY | REASONABLENESS | SUPPORT |
|---|---|---|---|
| Examine whether a source is believable and trustworthy. | Examine whether information is correct—i.e., factual, comprehensive, detailed, and up-to-date (if necessary). | Examine whether material is fair, objective, moderate, and consistent. | Examine whether a source is adequately supported with citations. |
| *What are the author's credentials?*<br><br>Look for education and experience; title or position of employment; membership in any known and respected organization; reliable contact information; biographical information; and reputation. | *Is it up-to-date, and is that important?*<br><br>If you are searching for a work of literature, such as Shakespeare's play *Macbeth*, there is no "updated" version. However, if you want reviews of its latest productions in major theaters, you will need to note when material was created. For most scientific research, you will need to rely on the most updated information you can find. | *Does the source seem fair?*<br><br>Look for a balanced argument, accurate claims, and a reasoned tone that does not appeal primarily to your emotions. | *Where does the information come from?*<br><br>Look at the site, the sources used by the person or group who compiled the information, and the contact information. Make sure that the cited sources seem reliable and that statistics are documented. |
| *Is there quality control?*<br><br>Look for ways in which the source may have been screened. For example, materials on an organization's Web site have most likely been reviewed and approved by several members; information coming from an academic journal has to be screened by several people before it is published. | *Is it comprehensive?*<br><br>Does the material leave out any important facts or information? Does it neglect to consider alternative views or crucial consequences? Although no one source can contain all of the available information on a topic, it should still be as comprehensive as is possible within its scope. | *Does the source seem objective?*<br><br>While there is a range of objectivity in writing, you want to favor authors and organizations who can control their bias. An author with a strong political or religious agenda or an intent to sell a product may not be a source of the most truthful material. | *Is the information corroborated?*<br><br>Test information by looking for other sources that confirm the facts in this information—or, if the information is opinion, sources that share that opinion and back it up with their own citations. One good strategy is to find at least three sources that corroborate each other. |

*(continued)*

| CREDIBILITY | ACCURACY | REASONABLENESS | SUPPORT |
|---|---|---|---|
| *Is there any posted summary or evaluation of the source?* | *For whom is the source written, and for what purpose?* | *Does the source seem moderate?* | *Is the source externally consistent?* |
| You may find abstracts of sources (summary), or a recommendation, rating, or review from a person or organization (evaluation). Either of these—or, ideally, both—can give you an idea of credibility before you decide to examine a source in depth. | Looking at what the author wants to accomplish will help you assess whether it has a bias. Sometimes biased information will not be useful for your purpose; sometimes your research will require that you note and evaluate bias (such as if you were to compare Civil War diaries from Union soldiers with those from Confederate soldiers). | Do claims seem possible, or does the information seem hard to believe? Does what you read make sense when compared to what you already know? While wild claims may turn out to be truthful, you are safest to check everything out. | Most material is a mix of both current and old information. External consistency refers to whether the old information agrees with what you already know. If a source contradicts something you know to be true, chances are higher that the information new to you may be inconsistent as well. |
| *Signals of a potential lack of credibility:* | *Signals of a potential lack of accuracy:* | *Signals of a potential lack of reasonableness:* | *Signals of a potential lack of support:* |
| Anonymous materials, negative evaluations, little or no evidence of quality control, bad grammar or misspelled words | Lack of date or old date, generalizations, one-sided views that do not acknowledge opposing arguments | Extreme or emotional language, sweeping statements, conflict of interest, inconsistencies or contradictions | Statistics without sources, lack of documentation, lack of corroboration using other reliable sources |

*Source:* Robert Harris, Ev aluating Internet Research Sources," November 17, 1997, VirtualSalt (www.virtualsalt.com/evalu8it.htm).

## Know When to Use the Library and When to Use the Internet

The Internet is a modern reality—but it has not, as some predicted, replaced the printed word. Savvy researchers combine Internet and library research to find information. As a general rule, you should consider heading to the library first in the following situations:

- When you are conducting in-depth research, requiring an historical perspective (Older information is more likely to be available at the library than on the Web.)
- When you want to use your library's subscription databases
- When you want to verify the authenticity of what you discover on the Internet
- When you need personal, face-to-face help from a librarian
- When you feel more comfortable navigating the established library system than the tangle of Internet sites

# Google (Yes, It's a Verb)

Although Google accesses 6 billion documents and has the capacity to return 750,000 Internet links in a third of a second, Leon Botstein, president of Bard College, warns of the pitfalls: "In general, Google overwhelms you with too much information, much of which is hopelessly unreliable or beside the point. It's like looking for a lost ring in a vacuum bag. What you end up with mostly are bagel crumbs and dirt."[6]

With this warning in mind, use your creativity and analysis to complete the following:

- Choose a common topic—for example, apples, kitchen sinks, snowflakes. Google the topic to see how many Web sites you access. Write that number here:

  _____

  Now spend 10 minutes scanning the Web listings. How many different topics did your search uncover other than the topic you intended?

  _____

- Pick two of the off-the-topic links you found and write a thesis statement for a paper that would require you to use these leads in your research. Be creative.

  _____

  _____

- In all likelihood, your thesis statement makes little sense. What does this tell you about the need for critical thinking when using Google and other search engines?

  _____

  _____

  _____

- Finally, open your mind to the creative possibilities your research uncovered. Write down two new ideas inspired by the Web sites about your topic:

  1. _____

  2. _____

The limitations of Internet-only research also make it smart to combine Internet and library research. Search engines can't find everything, in part because not all sources are in digital format. The Internet also prioritizes current information. Furthermore, some digital sources that are not part of your library's subscription offerings cost money.

Your need for solid research skills doesn't stop at graduation—especially in a workplace dominated by information and media. "Work projects may involve interviewing people, researching on the web, library research, taking a look at costs, providing input on support levels, and more . . ." says Victor Yipp of Commonwealth Edison. "These basic skills—being inquisitive and using the library, the Internet, and other people to uncover information—will do well for you in school and later on in life."[5]

Library and Internet research is often done as a step in writing a research paper. The success of your paper depends on the quality of your research and your ability to communicate what you know in writing.

# What Is the Writing Process?

The writing process for research papers and essays involves a series of steps that take you from identifying your topic to finalizing your work. The four main parts of the process are planning, drafting, revising, and editing. Analytical, creative, and practical thinking play important roles throughout.

## Planning

It is during the six-step planning process that you think about how to tackle the assignment and develop writing and research strategies. Although these steps are listed in sequence, in real life they often overlap.

### Pay Attention to Logistics

Start planning with these practical questions to determine the feasibility of different topics:

1. *How much depth does my instructor expect?* Does she want a basic introduction or a more sophisticated, high-level presentation?

2. *How much time do I have to write the paper?* Consider your other course assignments as well as personal responsibilities, such as part-time work.

3. *How long should the paper be?* Going too far above or below the number of pages your instructor specifies can count against you.

4. *What kind of research is needed?* Your topic and purpose may determine your research sources, and some sources are harder to get than others.

5. *Is it a team project or am I researching and writing alone?* If you are working with others, determine what each person will do and whether others can deliver their work on time.

Answering questions like these will help you decide on a topic and depth of coverage.

## Open Your Mind to Topic Ideas Through Brainstorming

Start the process of choosing a paper topic with *brainstorming*—a creative technique to generate ideas without judging their worth (see chapter 4):

- Begin by writing down anything on the assigned subject that comes to mind, in no particular order. To jump-start your thoughts, scan your text and notes, check library or Internet references, or meet with your instructor to discuss ideas.

- Next, organize that list into a logical outline or think link that helps you see the possibilities more clearly.

Key 8.4 shows a portion of an outline constructed from a brainstorming list. The assignment (for an introduction to business class) is to choose an aspect of business ethics and write a short expository research paper on it. Since the student's research is only preliminary, many ideas are in question form.

The *Multiple Intelligence Strategies* table on page 254 is designed to help harness different learning strategies for a business course. Specifically, the table will suggest different research and note-taking strategies for learning the topic of market segmentation.

**KEY 8.4** Brainstorming leads to topic ideas and sets the stage for organizing your thoughts.

Topic: <u>Business Ethics</u>

— What are business ethics?
— Recent scandals that raised ethical issues
   — Enron
   — WorldCom
— Who is responsible—the individual or the corporation?
— How do companies encourage ethical business practices?
   — Some companies have written codes of ethics
   — Codes are based on core ethical values that remain constant even as the environment changes
   — Codes of ethics only work if they are part of the corporate culture
— Why do people act unethically in business?
   — The bottom-line culture puts pressure on managers to show increasing profits every quarter.
   — Corporate cultures stress workers out to the point that they no longer ask whether actions are right or wrong.
   — People have such expensive lifestyles that they are willing to cut ethical corners to keep their jobs and earn large bonuses.

# MULTIPLE INTELLIGENCE STRATEGIES

## FOR RESEARCHING AND WRITING

### APPLY DIFFERENT INTELLIGENCES TO WRITING A PAPER IN MARKETING.

| INTELLIGENCE | USE MI STRATEGIES *to become a better researcher and writer* | APPLY MI RESEARCHING AND WRITING STRATEGIES *to a paper on market segmentation for a marketing course* |
|---|---|---|
| Verbal-Linguistic | • Read many resources and take comprehensive notes. Summarize the main points.<br>• Interview someone about the topic and take notes. | • As preparation for your draft, summarize in writing the similarities and differences among geographic, demographic, psychographic, and behavioral marketing. * |
| Logical-Mathematical | • Take notes on 3X5 cards and organize them by topics and subtopics.<br>• Outline the steps you will take to complete your paper. | • As you gather information, create a table comparing and contrasting 10 different factors in demographic marketing: age, gender, family size, family life cycle, income, occupation, education, religion, race, and nationality. |
| Bodily-Kinesthetic | • Spread your note cards on a desk in the order you intend to use the information.<br>• Sit in the library in the section where the books for your topic are located. Flip through pages of relevant books. | • To learn more about behavioral marketing, create an experiment to find out the benefits people want when they buy toothpaste. Compile your findings on note cards. Then logically arrange the cards until patterns emerge and you can answer questions like these: Do people make purchases because of price, decay prevention, the promise of whiter teeth, or taste? Take notes on your findings. |
| Visual-Spatial | • Use a think link or another visual organizer to map out your main topic and subtopics. Use different colors for different subtopics.<br>• Pay attention to photos, tables, and charts in research sources. Consider using them in your paper. | • Create a visual aid for inclusion in your paper that covers gender segmentation. Use different colored highlighters to help you focus on the characteristics of men's versus women's consumer behavior. |
| Interpersonal | • Discuss research findings with a classmate.<br>• Work as peer editors with another classmate. Read each other's early drafts and offer constructive feedback. | • Interview members of your family to learn what motivates their buying behaviors. Take thorough research notes so you can incorporate the information into your paper. |
| Intrapersonal | • Mull over the assigned paper topic. Decide whether you have mastered the material and are ready to begin writing.<br>• Brainstorm different thesis statements, using different research. | • Think about your own buying patterns. Include your personal observations in your paper as examples. |
| Musical | • Recite key research concepts to rhythms to improve recall.<br>• Explore relevant musical links to your topic. | • Create a song from your research on how attitudes toward products affect purchases. Your goal is to remember how enthusiastic, positive, indifferent, negative, and hostile attitudes impact buying decisions. |
| Naturalistic | • Try to notice similarities and differences in concepts by organizing research into relevant groupings.<br>• Consider using one or more relevant groupings as the foundation for your paper. | • Rewrite your draft to link market segmentation variables in different ways based on your personal buying behaviors. Focus on similarities and differences that may not have been obvious before you thought of your personal experiences. |

* For information on market segmentation, see Philip Kotler and Gary Armstrong, *Principles of Marketing, 12th ed.*, Upper Saddle River, NJ: Prentice Hall, 2008.

## Narrow Your Topic Through Prewriting Strategies

(Prewriting strategies,) including brainstorming, freewriting, and asking journalists' questions,[7] help you decide which possible topic you would most like to pursue. Use them to narrow your topic, focusing on the specific sub-ideas and examples from your brainstorming session.

**Brainstorming.** The same creative process you used to generate ideas will help you narrow your topic. Write down your thoughts about the possibilities you have chosen, do some more research, and then organize your thoughts into categories, noticing patterns that appear. See if any of the sub-ideas or examples might make good topics. Asking critical-thinking questions can spark ideas and help you focus on what to write.

**Freewriting.** When you *freewrite,* you jot down whatever comes to mind without censoring ideas or worrying about grammar, spelling, punctuation, or organization. Freewriting helps you think creatively and gives you an opportunity to piece together what you know about a sub-idea to see if you want to pursue it.

**Asking journalists' questions.** When journalists start working on a story, they ask themselves: Who? What? Where? When? Why? How? Asking these questions about sub-ideas will help you choose a writing topic.

> → PREWRITING STRATEGIES
>
> Techniques for generating ideas about a topic and finding out how much you already know before you start researching and writing.

| | |
|---|---|
| Who? | To whom do companies have an ethical responsibility? Who maintains ethical standards within corporations? |
| What? | What are business ethics? What is the difference between acting unethically and acting illegally, or are they the same? What is the impact of business codes of ethics on behavior? What companies have these codes, and what impact have they had on behavior? |
| When? | When is the best time for companies to address ethics problems—before or after they occur? |
| Where? | Do companies all over the country have ethics problems, or is the problem centered in certain geographic areas or industries? |
| Why? | Why do ethics problems surface? Why do companies make so many mistakes in handling ethics problems? |
| How? | How do companies train employees to act ethically? How do companies maintain their ethical standards in an ever-changing business environment? |

Prewriting helps you develop a topic that is broad enough for investigation but narrow enough to handle. Prewriting also helps you identify what you know and what you don't know. If an assignment involves more than you already know, you need to do research.

## Conduct Research and Make Notes

Research develops in stages as you narrow and refine your ideas. In the first brainstorming-for-ideas stage, look for an overview that can lead to a working thesis statement. In the second stage, track down information that fills in gaps. Ultimately, you will have a body of information that you can evaluate to develop and implement your final thesis.

As you research, create source notes and content notes on index cards. These help you organize your work, keep track of your sources, and avoid plagiarism.

- *Source notes* are preliminary notes, usually taken on index cards. Each should include the author's name; the title of the work; the edition (if any); the publisher, year, and city of publication; issue and/or volume number when applicable (such as for a magazine); and page numbers consulted. Notes on Internet sources should reference the Web site's complete name and address, including the numbers and characters that make up the URL. Include a short summary and critical evaluation for each source.

- *Content notes* written on large index cards, in a notebook, or on your computer are taken during a thorough reading and provide an in-depth look at sources. Use them to record the information you need to write your draft. To supplement your content notes, make notations— marginal notes, highlighting, and underlining—directly on photocopies of sources.

THESIS STATEMENT

A statement that is the central core of your paper around which arguments will be based.

AUDIENCE

The readers of your work for whom your purpose and content must be clear.

## Write a Working Thesis Statement

Next, organize your research and write a thesis statement—the organizing principle of your paper. Your thesis declares your specific subject and point of view and reflects your *writing purpose* (to inform or persuade) and audience. Here is an example from the paper on business ethics:

| | |
|---|---|
| **Topic** | Business ethics |
| **Purpose** | To inform |
| **Audience** | Instructor who assumes the position of an uninformed reader |

**Thesis statement** In an environment where so many executives are behaving badly and where corporate reputations are being tarnished, companies are struggling with how to set expectations of ethical behavior. Most major corporations, including Texas Instruments and Johnson & Johnson, now believe that creating a corporate code of ethics is a critical first step in the process of sensitizing employees to how they should act under normal circumstances and during crises.

Consider this to be your *working thesis*, because it may change as you continue your research and develop your draft. Be ready and willing to rework your writing—and your thesis—one or more times before you hand in your paper.

## Write a Working Outline or Think Link

The final planning step is creating a working outline or think link to use as a loose structural guide. As you draft, your ideas and direction may change, so be ready to rework your thesis to reflect new material and thoughts.

**Successful Intelligence Connections Online**

Listen to author Sarah Kravits describe how to use analytical, creative, and practical intelligence to manage your time and tasks when working through a writing project.

Go to the *Keys to Success* Companion Website at www.prenhall.com/carter to listen or download as a podcast.

# Drafting

You may write many versions of the assignment until you are satisfied. Each version moves you closer to saying exactly what you want in the way you want to say it. The main challenges you face at the first-draft stage include these:

- Finalizing your thesis
- Defining an organizational structure
- Integrating source material into the body of your paper to fit your structure
- Finding additional sources to strengthen your presentation
- Choosing the right words, phrases, and tone
- Connecting ideas with logical transitions
- Creating an effective introduction and conclusion
- Checking for plagiarism
- Creating a list of works cited

Don't aim for perfection in a first draft. Trying to get every detail right too early in the writing process may shut the door on ideas before you even know they are there.

## Freewriting Your Rough Draft

Use everything that you developed in the planning stage as the raw material for freewriting a rough draft. For now, don't think about your introduction, conclusion, or organizational structure. Simply focus on what you want to say. Only after you have written down your thoughts should you begin to shape your work. Many people start with the introduction because it is the beginning of the paper, while others save the introduction for last to make sure it reflects the final product.

## Writing an Introduction

The introduction tells readers what the paper contains and includes the thesis statement. Look on the next page at the introduction for the paper on business ethics. The thesis statement is underlined at the end of the paragraph:

Open to the business section of any newspaper and you are likely to find at least one story of a corporate executive on trial and facing jail or a company paying huge fines or court settlements to the government, consumers, or investors. In the last few years, stories of alleged wrongdoing at Enron, WorldCom, Tyco International, Computer Associates, Sotheby's, and Adelphi Communications, to name just a few, have been front-page news. In an environment where so many executives are behaving badly and where corporate reputations are being tarnished, companies are struggling with how to set expectations of ethical behavior. Most major corporations, including Texas Instruments and Johnson & Johnson, now believe that creating a corporate code of ethics is a critical first step in the process of sensitizing employees to how they should act under normal circumstances and during crises.

## Creating the Body of a Paper

The body of the paper contains your central ideas and supporting *evidence*, which underpins your thesis with facts, statistics, examples, and expert opinions. Try to find a structure that helps you organize your ideas and evidence into a clear pattern. Several organizational options are presented in Key 8.5.

 KEY 8.5

## Find the best way to organize the body of the paper.

| ARRANGE IDEAS . . . | HOW TO DO IT |
| --- | --- |
| . . . by time | Describe events in order or in reverse order. |
| . . . according to importance | Start with the idea that carries the most weight and move to less important ideas. Or move from the least to the most important ideas. |
| . . . by problem and solution | Start with a problem and then discuss solutions. |
| . . . to present an argument | Present one or both sides of an issue. |
| . . . in list form | Group a series of items. |
| . . . according to cause and effect | Show how events, situations, or ideas cause subsequent events, situations, or ideas. |
| . . . through the use of comparisons | Compare and contrast the characteristics of events, people, situations, or ideas. |
| . . . by process | Go through the steps in a process; a "how to" approach. |
| . . . by category | Divide topics into categories and analyze each in order. |

## Writing the Conclusion

A conclusion brings your paper to a natural ending by summarizing your main points, showing the significance of your thesis and how it relates to larger issues, calling the reader to action, or looking to the future. Let the ideas in the body of the paper speak for themselves as you wrap up.

## Avoiding Plagiarism: Crediting Authors and Sources

Using another writer's words, content, unique approach, or illustrations without crediting the author is called plagiarism and is illegal and unethical. The following techniques will help you properly credit sources and avoid plagiarism:

PLAGIARISM

*The act of using someone else's exact words, figures, unique approach, or specific reasoning without giving appropriate credit.*

- *Make source notes as you go.* Plagiarism often begins accidentally during research. You may forget to include quotation marks around a quotation, or you may intend to cite or paraphrase a source but never do. To avoid forgetting, write detailed source and content notes as you research.

- *Learn the difference between a quotation and a paraphrase.* A *quotation* repeats a source's exact words and uses quotation marks to set them off from the rest of the text. A *paraphrase,* a restatement of the quotation in your own words, requires that you completely rewrite the idea, not just remove or replace a few words.

As Key 8.6 illustrates, a paraphrase may not be acceptable if it is too close to the original. To avoid picking up too much of the original quote, read the quote several times, and then use your own words to communicate the thought without looking back at the quote. You are less likely to have problems when you integrate your own analysis into your writing and when you connect ideas from different sources.

- *Use a citation even for an acceptable paraphrase.* Take care to credit any source that you quote, paraphrase, or use as evidence. To credit a source, write a footnote or endnote that describes it, using the format preferred by your instructor.

- *Understand that lifting material off the Internet is plagiarism.* Words in electronic form belong to the writer just as words in print form do. If you cut and paste sections from a source document onto your draft, you are probably committing plagiarism.

Key 8.7 will help you identify what instructors regard as plagiarized work.

Students who plagiarize place their academic careers at risk, in part because the cheating is easy to discover. Increasingly, instructors are using antiplagiarism software to investigate whether strings of words in student papers match those in a database. Make a commitment to hand in your own work and to uphold the highest standards of academic integrity. The potential consequences of cheating are not worth the risk. The *Get Analytical!* exercise on page 262 and the *Get Focused!* section on page 405 at the end of Part III will help you analyze your attitudes about academic integrity and plagiarism.

KEY 8.6

## Avoid plagiarism by learning how to paraphrase.

### QUOTATION

"The most common assumption that is made by persons who are communicating with one another is . . . that the other perceives, judges, thinks, and reasons the way he does. Identical twins communicate with ease. Persons from the same culture but with a different education, age, background, and experience often find communication difficult. American managers communicating with managers from other cultures experience greater difficulties in communication than with managers from their own culture."[3]

### UNACCEPTABLE PARAPHRASE

*(The underlined words are taken directly from the quoted source.)*

When we communicate, we assume that the person to whom we are speaking <u>perceives, judges, thinks, and reasons the way</u> we do. This is not always the case. Although <u>identical twins communicate with ease, persons from the same culture but with a different education, age, background, and experience often</u> encounter communication problems. Communication problems are common among American managers as they attempt to <u>communicate with managers from other cultures</u>. They experience greater communication problems than when they communicate <u>with managers from their own culture.</u>

### ACCEPTABLE PARAPHRASE

Many people fall into the trap of believing that everyone sees the world exactly as they do and that all people communicate according to the same assumptions. This belief is difficult to support even within our own culture as African-Americans, Hispanic-Americans, Asian-Americans, and others often attempt unsuccessfully to find common ground. When intercultural differences are thrown into the mix, such as when American managers working abroad attempt to communicate with managers from other cultures, clear communication becomes even harder.

KEY 8.7

## Plagiarism takes many forms.

Instructors consider work to be plagiarized when you . . .

- Submit a paper from a Web site that sells or gives away research papers
- Buy a paper from a non-Internet service
- Hand in a paper written by a fellow student or a family member
- Copy material in a paper directly from a source without proper quotation marks or source citation
- Paraphrase material in a paper from a source without proper source citation
- Submit the same paper in more than one class, even if the classes are in different terms or even different years

## Citing Sources

You may be asked to submit different kinds of source lists when you hand in your paper:

- The *References list,* also called the *List of Works Cited*, includes only the sources you actually cited in your paper.
- The *Bibliography* includes all the sources you consulted, whether or not they were cited in the paper.
- The *Annotated Bibliography* includes all the sources you consulted as well as an explanation or critique of each source.

Your instructor will tell you which documentation style to use and whether to list footnotes at the end of the paper or the bottom of the page. The general styles of documentation are discipline-specific (for more details, see resource lists at the end of this chapter):

- The Modern Language Association (MLA) format is generally used in the humanities, including history, literature, the arts, and philosophy.
- The American Psychological Association (APA) style is the appropriate format in psychology, sociology, business, economics, nursing, criminology, and social work.
- An alternate documentation style is found in the 15th edition of the *Chicago Manual of Style*, published by the University of Chicago Press.
- The Council of Science Editors (CSE)—formerly called the Council of Biology Editors—style is used to cite scientific sources.
- The Columbia Online Style (COS) is often used to cite online sources.

Consult a college-level writers' handbook for an overview of these documentation styles.

## Solicit Feedback

Because it is difficult to be objective about your own work, asking for someone else's perspective can be a practical help. Talk with your instructor about your draft, or ask a study partner to read it and answer specific analytical questions like these:

- Is my thesis clear and does my evidence back it up?
- Are the ideas logically connected?
- Are there places where my writing style, choice of words, paragraph structure, or transitions detract from what I am trying to say?
- Am I missing anything?

  Be open-minded about the comments you receive. Consider each carefully, and then make a decision about what to change.

Feedback from an instructor, classmate, or writing center tutor can be invaluable as you revise your writing. These students catch a moment to review each other's work.

## Avoid Plagiarism

Complete the following to explore your views on the growing problem of plagiarism:

- Why is plagiarism considered an offense that involves both stealing and lying? Describe how you look at it:

  _____

  _____

  _____

- Citing sources indicates that you respect the ideas of others. List two additional ways in which accurate source citation strengthens your writing and makes you a better student:

  1. _____

  2. _____

- What specific penalties for plagiarism are described in your college handbook? Explain whether you feel that these penalties are reasonable or excessive and whether they will keep students from plagiarizing:

  _____

  _____

  _____

- Many experts believe that researching on the Internet is behind many acts of plagiarism. Do you agree? Why or why not?

  _____

  _____

- How do you react when others plagiarize and you don't? Does it affect how you feel about them?

  _____

  _____

# Revising

When you revise, you critically evaluate the content, organization, word choice, paragraph structure, and style of your first draft. You evaluate the strength of your thesis and whether your evidence proves it, and you look for logical holes. You can do anything you want at this point to change your work. You can move information from the end of your paper up front, tweak your thesis to reflect the evidence you presented, or choose a different organizational structure. This is also the time to incorporate ideas from peer reviewers or your instructor.

Key 8.8 shows a paragraph from the first draft of the business ethics paper, with revision comments added.

**KEY 8.8**  Incorporate revision comments to strengthen your paper.

---

Like Texas Instruments, Johnson & Johnson developed a code of ethics that ~~written in plain English,~~

~~employees rely on to make decisions.~~ *is a cornerstone of its corporate culture* A simple one-page document that has

*(add more detail here)* been in place for more than 60 years, "Our Credo," as the code is called, states

J & J's ethical responsibilities to ~~everyone it does business with.~~ *customers, employees, communities, stockholders* It has been trans-

lated into 36 languages for employees, customers, suppliers, governments, and

shareholders *to consult* in every market in which it operates, from North America

to the far reaches of Africa, Europe, Latin America, the Middle East, and *the*

Asia/Pacific *region* (add footnote—*Johnson & Johnson: Our Credo*).

When Johnson & Johnson updated its credo in the mid-1970s, executives

examined every word and phrase to make sure ~~they still applied~~ *it continued to represent company values.* "These meetings

infused the values in the minds of all of us managers," explained Bob Kniffin,

*who was* Vice President of External Affairs, *at the time.* J & J's managers had no way of knowing that

the exercise they were engaged in would ~~give them the skills~~ *prepare them* to handle ~~a~~ *one of the most* difficult

challenge *ever faced by an American company.* Only a few years later, many of the same executives who ~~examined~~ *scrutinized* the

company's credo struggled with how to protect consumers, company employees

and shareholders when bottles of Tylenol were poisoned on store shelves and

innocent people died.

Engage your analytical thinking skills to evaluate the content and form of your paper. Ask yourself these questions as you revise:

- Does the paper fulfill the requirements of the assignment?
- Do I prove my thesis?
- Will my audience understand my thesis and how I've supported it?
- Does the introduction prepare the reader and capture attention?
- Is the body of the paper organized effectively?
- Does each paragraph have a *topic sentence* that is supported by the rest of the paragraph? (See chapter 5 for more on topic sentences.)
- Is each idea and argument developed, explained, and supported by examples?
- Are my ideas connected to one another through logical transitions?
- Do I have a clear, concise, simple writing style?
- Does the conclusion provide a natural ending without introducing new ideas?

## Check for Clarity and Conciseness

Now check for sense, continuity, and clarity. Focus also on tightening your prose and eliminating wordy phrases. Examine once again how paragraphs flow into one another by evaluating the effectiveness of your *transitions*—the words, phrases, or sentences that connect ideas. Make your transitions signal what comes next.

## Editing

Editing comes last, after you are satisfied with your thesis, ideas, organization, and writing style. It involves correcting technical mistakes in spelling, grammar, and punctuation, as well as checking for consistency in such elements as abbreviations and capitalization. If you use a computer, start with the grammar-check and spell-check features to find mistakes, realizing that you still need to check your work manually. Look also for *sexist language,* which characterizes people according to gender stereotypes and often involves the male pronouns *he* or *his* or *him.*

Peer editing can sharpen your writing. Kristina Torres, a senior at Susquehanna University in Pennsylvania, is convinced that her relationship with Adam Cole helped make her a better writer. She has worked with Adam for more than three years to fine-tune her work. In one case, Adam helped Kristina cut a 40-page paper in half. "It's hard to do that on your own," she said, "because you get really attached to a line or a section. You need to have someone who can help you step back and take another look at it."[8]

*Proofreading,* the last editing stage, involves reading every word for accuracy. Look for technical mistakes, run-on sentences, and sentence fragments. Look for incorrect word usage and unclear references. A great way to check your work is to read it out loud.

Your final paper reflects all the hard work you put in during the writing process. Ideally, when you are finished, you have a piece of work that

# Revise and Edit with the Help of a Checklist

*get practical!!*

When finishing a paper, you have a lot to keep track of. To avoid forgetting important steps, try using a checklist like the one below to organize your work.

| Date due | Task | Is it complete? |
|---|---|---|
| | Check the body of the paper for clear thinking and adequate evidence. | |
| | Finalize introduction and conclusion. | |
| | Check spelling, usage, and grammar. | |
| | Check paragraph structure. | |
| | Make sure language is familiar and concise. | |
| | Check punctuation and capitalization. | |
| | Check transitions. | |
| | Eliminate sexist language. | |
| | Get feedback from peers and/or instructors. | |

- Use this checklist for your next paper. Then respond: Did it help you stay focused on tasks and organize your time? Did it help you do your best work?

_____

_____

- On separate sheets, use what you learned in this chapter to create two additional checklists—one for planning your paper and the other for writing your first draft.

shows your writing and thinking ability and clearly communicates and proves your thesis. Key 8.9, the final version of the business ethics paper, is a product of this writing process. The reference sources follow APA style.

KEY 8.9

## Follow the writing process to produce a well-crafted paper.

### Codes of Ethics Encourage Companies to Do What Is Right

Open to the business section of any newspaper and you are likely to find at least one story of a corporate executive on trial and facing jail or a company paying huge fines or court settlements to the government, consumers, or investors. In the last few years, stories of alleged wrongdoing at Enron, WorldCom, Tyco International, Computer Associates, Sotheby's, and Adelphi Communications, to name just a few, have been front-page news. In an environment where so many executives are behaving badly and where corporate reputations are being tarnished, companies are struggling with how to set expectations of ethical behavior. Most major corporations, including Texas Instuments and Johnson & Johnson, now believe that creating a corporate code of ethics is a critical first step in the process of sensitizing employees to how they should act under normal circumstances and during crises.

Business ethics, like personal ethics, are based on values that define actions as right or wrong, good or bad, proper or improper. Sometimes ethical decisions are clear—for example, almost no one would argue that it is ethically wrong for an auto maker to hide a major safety defect in order to avoid the cost of recalling thousands of vehicles—but often they are not. (Should the same manufacturer issue a recall if the defect is likely to affect only 1 in 10,000 cars?) Business decisions in today's complex, competitive marketplace often involve choices that put a company's morals to the test.

The Josephson Institute of Ethics defines six key concepts to help managers evaluate competing choices (Josephson Institute of Ethics, 2002). These are trustworthiness (honesty, integrity, promise-keeping, loyalty), respect (civility, courtesy and decency, dignity and autonomy, tolerance and acceptance), responsibility (accountability, pursuit of excellence, self-restraint), fairness (procedural fairness, impartiality, equity), caring (compassion, consideration, giving, sharing, kindness), and citizenship (law abiding, community service, protection of environment). These pillars are among the factors that underlie the ethics codes at Texas Instruments and Johnson & Johnson.

Texas Instruments places ethics at the core of its corporate culture. First published 45 years ago, TI's code sets ethical expectations, based on principles and values, for employees to consider every time they make a decision or take action. To encourage adherence to the highest ethical standards, TI gives each employee a business-card sized "Ethics Test" to carry at all times (Texas Instruments, 1988). The test—with seven clear bullet points—is based on TI's core principles and on legal and societal values:

- Is the action legal?
- Does it comply with our values?
- If you do it, will you feel bad?
- How will it look in the newspaper?
- If you know it's wrong, don't do it!
- If you're not sure, ask.
- Keep asking until you get an answer.

To support employees who face ethics-related challenges in an ever-changing and increasingly competitive business environment, TI established an ethics office in the late 1980s. The function of the office is to make sure business practices continue to reflect company values, to communicate and reinforce ethical expectations to every employee, and to give employees feedback on ethics-related problems (Texas Instruments, 1988).

Like Texas Instruments, Johnson & Johnson developed a code of ethics, written in plain English, that is a cornerstone of its corporate culture. A simple one-page document that has been in place for more than 60 years, "Our Credo," as the code is called, states J & J's ethical responsibilities to its customers, its employees, the communities in which it operates, and its stockholders. It has been translated into 36 languages for employees, customers, suppliers, governments, and shareholders to consult in every market in which it operates, from North America to the far reaches of Africa, Europe, Latin America, the Middle East, and the Asia/Pacific region (Johnson & Johnson, 2004).

McNamara (1999) describes Johnson & Johnson's updating of its credo in the mid-1970s along with subsequent events. Executives examined every word and phrase to make sure it continued to represent company values. "These meetings infused the values in the minds of all of us managers," explained Bob Kniffin, who was Vice President of External Affairs at the time. J & J's managers had no way of knowing that the exercise they were engaged in would prepare them to handle one of the most difficult challenges ever faced by an American company: Only a few years later, many of the same executives who scrutinized the company's credo struggled with how to protect consumers, company employees, and shareholders when bottles of Tylenol were poisoned on store shelves and innocent people died.

Experts inside and outside the company believed that the examination of the company's credo that had taken place in these meetings guided J & J's decision to recall every bottle of Tylenol and repackage the product at a cost of $100 million. According to Kniffin, who was a key player in the crisis, the ethical road was set before the crisis began. "In a crisis, there's no time for moral conclusions," he said. Those must be done beforehand (quoted in McNamara, 1999).

Corporate codes of ethics are effective only if they are followed. (Even Enron had a code of ethics that was set aside by the board of directors to allow the company to complete unscrupulous deals.) While products and marketing strategies change frequently to meet competitive pressures, core values never change, nor does the expectation (in companies like TI and J & J) that managers will weigh business decisions and actions against these values. The old joke about "business ethics" being a contradiction in terms does not apply at these companies—not only because they have taken the time to institutionalize a code of ethics and to use it to evaluate job candidates, but also because employees are expected to follow its guidelines, even when it hurts the bottom line. When employees choose to break the law, they are dismissed and the authorities are notified. This happened to J & J in 2007 when the head of its medical devices unit was believed to have made improper payments to secure business abroad (Seelye, 2007).

Taking the idea of a written ethics code to another dimension, financial services companies are considering adopting an industry-wide code to set uniform standards of right and wrong for every company (Berman, 2005). That would mean that even in the toughest competitive situations—where millions of dollars in commissions were up for grabs—everyone would be playing by the same ethical rules.

## References

Berman, D. K. (2005, March 10). Does Wall Street finally need an ethics code? *Wall Street Journal,* p. C1.

Johnson & Johnson. (2004). Our credo. Retrieved February 16, 2005, from *http://www.jnj.com/our_company/ our_credo/index.htm*

Josephson Institute of Ethics. (2002). The six pillars of character. In *Making ethical decisions* [Electronic version]. Retrieved February 22, 2005, from *http://www.josephsoninstitute.org/MED/MED-intro+toc.htm*

McNamara, C. (1999). *Complete guide to ethics management: An ethics toolkit for managers* [Electronic version]. Retrieved February 16, 2005, from *http://www.managementhelp.org/ethics/ethxgde.htm*

Seelye, K. Q. (2007, February 13). J & J says improper payments were made. *New York Times,* p. D1.

Texas Instruments. (1988). The TI ethics quick test. Retrieved March 4, 2005, from *http://www.ti.com/corp/docs/company/citizen/ethics/quicktest.shtml*

The writing skills you develop in college will be reflected in the documents you give prospective employers, and these, in turn, will impact the success of your job search. June Brown, of Olive Harvey College, explains how good writing is at the center of your efforts:

The written documents you leave with a company may be your most lasting calling card. If your documents are incorrect, messy, or poorly organized, they will leave a negative impression. No matter how well you do in a face-to-face meeting, your cover letter, résumé, and other work-related documents are a record that memorializes who you are. Make sure it is your best work.[9]

# Successful Intelligence Wrap-Up

At their heart, researching and writing are about communicating information. When you research, you tap the knowledge of others in the hope of learning something new and valuable. When you write, others read your information and perspective and learn from you. Here's how you have built skills in chapter 8:

## Analytical

You discovered how to select and use the best combination of library and Internet sources for research assignments. You explored how to analyze the reliability of specific Internet sources. In the *Get Analytical* exercise, you analyzed your views on plagiarism. In reading the section on writing, you examined the parts and sequence of the writing process.

## Creative

In the *Get Creative* exercise, you used creative skills to explore the pros and cons of Internet searching. You considered how to brainstorm topic ideas for a research paper. Considering creative prewriting strategies, such as freewriting and asking journalists' questions, may have inspired new ideas about how you will develop your thesis the next time you write.

## Practical

You solidified your understanding of how to conduct a keyword information search of library and Internet sources, and sharpened your sense of when to prioritize each type of source. You went through the steps in the writing process including planning, drafting, revising, and editing. In the *Get Practical* exercise, you used a checklist to make sure you took care of all tasks related to a paper. In the section on plagiarism, you explored specific rules for proper citation.

# *meraki*
# μερακι
## *(meh-ra-kee)*

In Greece, when someone says you are acting with *meraki,* he is a giving you a compliment. It means that you are putting your heart, soul, creativity, and intelligence into a task so that your work reflects what's inside you. While the word is traditionally used to describe cooking a wonderful meal and setting an elaborate table, you can use it to refer to accomplishing results that are at your highest level and are uniquely yours.

As a researcher and writer, set a goal of filling your work with your thoughts and analysis, your creativity and organizational ability, your tenacity and skill in tracking down information, and your special way with language. Know in advance that no one else will hand in writing that is exactly like yours, and no one else will experience your satisfaction when the writing hits the mark.[10]

"How can I know what I think until I read what I write?"

*NEW YORK TIMES* COLUMNIST JAMES RESTON, DURING
THE 1962 NEWSPAPER STRIKE

## SUCCESSFUL INTELLIGENCE
### Think, Create, Apply

Be a planner. Engage analytical, creative, and practical skills as you work through the planning stage of writing.

**Step 1. Think it through:** *Analyze your writing goal.* Imagine that you have been asked to write an essay on a time when you turned a difficulty into an opportunity. First, write a brief description of your topic:

_____

_____

Next, think about your purpose and audience. How might you frame your purpose if you were writing to a person who is going through a tough time and needs inspiration or an instructor who wanted to know what you learned from a difficult experience? Write your purpose and intended audience here:

_____

_____

_____

_____

**Step 2. Think out of the box:** *Prewrite to create ideas.* On a separate sheet of paper or a computer file, use prewriting strategies to start the flow of ideas:

- Brainstorm your ideas.
- Freewrite.
- Ask journalists' questions.

Step 3. **Make it happen:** *Write a thesis statement.* With the thesis statement, you make your topic as specific as possible and you clearly define your purpose. Write your thesis statement here:

_____

_____

_____

# TEAMWORK
## Create Solutions Together

**Team research.** Join with three other classmates and decide on two relatively narrow research topics that interest all of you and that you can investigate by spending no more than an hour in the library. The first topic should be current and in the news—for example, food-borne illnesses, body piercing do's and don'ts, or the social meaning of reality TV. The second topic should be more academic and historical—for example, the polio epidemic in the 1950s, the Irish potato famine, or South African apartheid.

Working alone, team members will use the college library, including subscription databases, and the Internet to research both topics. Set a research time limit of one hour per topic. The goal should be to collect a list of sources for later investigation. When everyone is finished, the group should come together to discuss the research process. Ask each other questions such as these:

- What research tools did you use to investigate each topic?
- How did your research differ from topic to topic? Why?
- How did your use of library and Internet resources differ from topic to topic?
- Which research techniques yielded the best results? Which led to dead ends?

Next, compare the specific results of everyone's research. Analyze each source for what it is likely to yield in the form of useful information. Finally, come together as a group and discuss what you learned that might improve your approach to library and Internet research.

# WRITING
## Journal and Put Skills to Work

*Record your thoughts on a separate piece of paper, in a journal, or on a computer file.*

**Journal entry: Learning from other writers.** Identify a piece of powerful writing that you recently read. (It could be a work of literature, a biography, a magazine or newspaper article, or even a section from one of your college texts.) Describe, in detail, why it was powerful. Did it make you feel something, think something, or take action? Why? What can you learn about writing from this piece that you can apply to your own writing?

You see a need for a student organization that does not exist at your school. Using your research and writing skills, draft a proposal to the dean of student affairs that accomplishes the following goals:

- States your thesis that students would benefit from the new student organization
- States at least two specific arguments to support your thesis
- Reflects evidence you collected by surveying students who share your interest and by searching the Web for other colleges that have such an organization.
- States what the organization needs from the school—for example, a place to meet or an academic advisor

Use the stages in the writing process to perfect your proposal, and then ask others to read it over. Finally, consider sending it. Stay open to the possibility of a positive response.

## PERSONAL PORTFOLIO
*Prepare for Career Success*

**Writing sample: A job interview cover letter.** To secure a job interview, you will have to write a letter describing your background and explaining your value to the company. For your portfolio, write a one-page, three-paragraph cover letter to a prospective employer. Be creative—you may use fictitious names, but select a career and industry that interest you. Use the format shown in Key 8.10. It should include the following:

- **Introductory paragraph:** Start with a statement that convinces the employer to read on. You might name a person the employer knows who told you to write or refer to something positive about the company that you read in the newspaper or on the Internet. Identify the position for which you are applying, and tell the employer that you are interested in working for the company.
- **Middle paragraph:** Sell your value. Try to convince the employer that hiring you will help the company in some way. Center your "sales effort" on your experience in school and the workplace. If possible, tie your qualifications to the needs of the company. Refer indirectly to your enclosed résumé.
- **Final paragraph:** Close with a call to action. Ask the employer to call you, or tell the employer to expect your call to arrange an interview.

Exchange your first draft with a classmate. Read each other's letters and make marginal notes to improve impact and persuasiveness, writing style, grammar, punctuation, and spelling. Discuss and then make corrections. Create a final draft for your portfolio.

**KEY 8.10** A cover letter should express your job interest and summarize why you are a strong candidate.

First name Last name
1234 Your Street
City, ST 12345

November 1, 2008

Ms. Prospective Employer
Prospective Company
5432 Their Street
City, ST 54321

Dear Ms. Employer:

On the advice of Mr. X, career center advisor at Y College, I am writing to inquire about the position of production assistant at KWKW Radio. I read the description of the job and your company on the career center's employment-opportunity bulletin board, and I would like to apply for the position.

I am a senior at Y College and will graduate this spring with a degree in communications. Since my junior year when I declared my major, I have wanted to pursue a career in radio. For the last year I have worked as a production intern at KCOL Radio, the college's station, and have occasionally filled in as a disc jockey on the evening news show. I enjoy being on the air, but my primary interest is production and programming. My enclosed résumé will tell you more about my background and experience.

I would be pleased to talk with you in person about the position. You can reach me anytime at 555/555-5555 or by e-mail at xxxx@xx.com. Thank you for your consideration, and I look forward to meeting you.

Sincerely,

*Sign Your Name Here*

First name Last name

Enclosure(s) *(use this notation if you have included a résumé or other item with your letter)*

## Suggested Readings

American Psychological Association. *Publication Manual of the American Psychological Association*, 5th ed. Washington, DC: American Psychological Association, 2001.

Becker, Howard S. *Tricks of the Trade: How to Think About Your Research While You're Doing It*. Chicago: University of Chicago Press, 1998.

Booth, Wayne C., Gregory G. Columb, and Joseph M. Williams. *The Craft of Research*. Chicago: University of Chicago Press, 1995.

Cameron, Julia. *The Right to Write: An Invitation into the Writing Life*. New York: Putnam, 1999.

Gibaldi, Joseph, and Phyllis Franklin. *MLA Handbook for Writers of Research Papers*, 6th ed. New York: Modern Language Association of America, 2003.

LaRocque, Paula. *Championship Writing: 50 Ways to Improve Your Writing*. Oak Park, IL: Marion Street Press, 2000.

Markman, Peter T., and Roberta H. Markman. *10 Steps in Writing the Research Paper*, 5th ed. New York: Barron's, 1994.

Strunk, William Jr., and E. B. White. *The Elements of Style*, 4th ed. New York: Allyn & Bacon, 2000.

Troyka, Lynn Quitman. *Simon & Schuster Handbook for Writers*, 7th ed. Upper Saddle River, NJ: Prentice Hall, 2005.

Walker, Janice R., and Todd Taylor. *The Columbia Guide to Online Style*, 2nd ed. New York: Columbia University Press, 2006.

Walsch, Bill. *Lapsing into a Comma: A Curmudgeon's Guide to the Many Things That Can Go Wrong in Print—and How to Avoid Them.* New York: Contemporary Books, 2000.

Williams, Joseph M. *Style: Ten Lessons in Clarity and Grace.* Chicago: University of Chicago Press, 2003.

## Internet and Podcast Resources

American Psychological Association—Style Tips: **www.apastyle.org/previoustips.html**

Chicago Manual of Style Online: **www .chicagomanualofstyle.org/home.html**

Columbia Manual Press—*Columbia Guide to Online Style:* **www.columbia.edu/cu/cup/ cgos2006/basic.html**

Council of Science Editors—*Scientific Style and Format* official CSE style manual: **www.councilscienceeditors.org**

Grammar Girl's Quick and Dirty Tips for Better Writing (podcasts from QDnow.com): **http://grammar.qdnow.com**

Hamilton College—Nesbitt-Johnson Writing Center (includes handout on common writing mistakes, tips for peer review, grammer and style, source citation, writing for specific disciplines): **www.hamilton.edu/academics/Resource/WC/ index.html**

How to Organize a Research Paper and Document It with MLA Citations (specific citation rules from the Modern Language Association): **www.geocities.com/Athens/Oracle/4184**

Modern Language Association—What Is MLA Style? **www.mla.org/style**

Online Writing Lab—Purdue University: **http://owl.english.purdue.edu**

Plagiarism.org—The Learning Center (online resource concerned with the growing problem of Internet plagiarism): **www.plagiarism.org**

A Student's Guide to Research with the WWW (a tutorial on Web searching, Web page evaluation, and research strategies, developed at St. Louis University): **www.slu.edu/departments/ english/research**

Prentice Hall Student Success Supersite: **www.prenhall.com/success**

## Endnotes

[1] Indiana University Web Site, "Amazing Student, Chad Clunie: On a Knowledge Quest," (http://excellence.indiana.edu/clunie; no longer available).

[2] Andrea L. Foster, "Information Navigation 101," *Chronicle of Higher Education*, March 9, 2007. (http://chronicle.com/free/v53/i27/27a03801 .htm); and Duncan Riley, "World Wide Blog Count for May: Now over 60 Million Blogs, *Blog Herald*, May 25, 2005 (www.blogherald.com/ 2005/05/25/world-wide-blog-count-for-may- now-over-60-million-blogs).

[3] Lori Leibovich, "Choosing Quick Hits over the Card Catalog," *New York Times*, August 10, 2001, p. 1.

[4] Robert Harris, "Evaluating Internet Research Sources," VirtualSalt, November 17, 1997 (www.virtualsalt.com/evalu8it.htm).

[5] *Keys to Lifelong Learning Telecourse* (videocassette), directed by Mary Jane Bradbury, Intrepid Films, 2000.

[6] David Hochman, "In Searching We Trust," *New York Times*, March 14, 2004, Section 9, p. 1.

[7] Analysis based on Lynn Quitman Troyka, *Simon & Schuster Handbook for Writers*, Upper Saddle River, NJ: Prentice Hall, 1996, pp. 22–23.

[8] Thomas Bartlett, "Undergraduates Heed the Writer's Muse: English Departments Add Programs as More Students Push to Write Fiction and Poetry," *Chronicle of Higher Education*, March 15, 2002 (http://chronicle.com/weekly/v48/i27/ 2703901.htm).

[9] *Keys to Lifelong Learning Telecourse.*

[10] Christopher J. Moore, *In Other Words: A Language Lover's Guide to the Most Intriguing Words Around the World,* New York: Walker, 2004, p. 103.

# get focused!
## time and math tests

## Do the "Next Thing To Do"

Of the set of tasks required to accomplish an academic responsibility, one task is always at the top of the to-do list at any given time. If you have a test in a week, for example, your next task might be to study chapters 1 through 4 in your text. If you have a lab project due in two weeks, your next task might be to perform a particular experiment.

Deciding on, and doing, the "next thing to do" both boosts schedule awareness and inspires action. Examine your syllabi for the courses you are taking right now. Find the next responsibility pending for each course—a reading assignment, a paper, a project, a quiz, a test. Then, focus on the *next thing to do* for each. Use the accompanying table to record the information and note when the next thing is done. Use the momentum you gain to move through subsequent tasks until you successfully accomplish each responsibility.

| Course | Responsibility pending (include date or due date) | Next task related to this responsibility | Done? |
|---|---|---|---|
| Example: Healthcare Management | 10-page paper due November 12 | Write draft of thesis statement and turn in to the TA | ✓ |
| | | | |
| | | | |
| | | | |
| | | | |
| | | | |
| | | | |
| | | | |
| | | | |
| | | | |
| | | | |

# Slay the Math Anxiety Dragon

A special form of test anxiety, math anxiety is based on common misconceptions about math, such as the notion that people are born with or without an ability to think quantitatively or that men are better at math than women. Students who feel they can't do math may give up without asking for help. On exams, they may experience a range of physical symptoms—including sweating, nausea, dizziness, headaches, and fatigue—that reduce their ability to concentrate and leave them feeling defeated.

The material in this segment is designed to help you deal with the kind of math-related anxiety that affects your grades on exams. As you learn concrete ways to calm your nerves and special techniques for math tests, you will feel more confident in your ability to succeed.

These test-taking tips supplement what you learned in chapter 7, "Test Taking: Showing What You Know," where you studied test taking in depth and generalized test anxiety. That chapter also includes valuable information on test preparation, general test taking strategies, strategies for handling different types of test questions, and learning from test mistakes.

## Gauge Your Level of Math Anxiety

Use the accompanying questionnaire to get an idea of your math anxiety level.

---

### ARE YOU ANXIOUS ABOUT MATH?

*Rate each of the following statements on a scale of 1 (Strongly Disagree) to 5 (Strongly Agree).*

1. _____ I cringe when I have to go to math class.

2. _____ I am uneasy about going to the board in a math class.

3. _____ I am afraid to ask questions in math class.

4. _____ I am always worried about being called on in math class.

5. _____ I understand math now, but I worry that it's going to get really difficult soon.

6. _____ I tend to zone out in math class.

7. _____ I fear math tests more than any other kind.

8. _____ I don't know how to study for math tests.

9. _____ It's clear to me in math class, but when I go home it's like I was never there.

10. _____ I'm afraid I won't be able to keep up with the rest of the class.

**SCORING KEY:**

| | |
|---|---|
| 40–50 | Sure thing, you have math anxiety. |
| 30–39 | No doubt! You're still fearful about math. |
| 20–29 | On the fence. |
| 10–19 | Wow! Loose as a goose! |

*Source:* Ellen Freedman, *Do You Have Math Anxiety? A Self-Test,* 1997 (www.mathpower.com/anxtest.htm).

---

The best way to overcome math test anxiety is through practice. Keeping up with your homework, attending class, preparing well for tests, and doing extra problems will help you learn the material and boost your confidence.

Following are 10 additional ways to reduce math anxiety and do well on tests:

**Ten Ways to Reduce Math Anxiety**

1. Overcome your negative self-image about math by remembering that even Albert Einstein wasn't perfect.
2. Ask questions of your teachers and your friends, and seek outside assistance.
3. Math is a foreign language—practice it often.
4. Don't study mathematics by trying to memorize information and formulas.
5. READ your math textbook.
6. Study math according to your personal learning style.
7. Get help the same day you don't understand something.
8. Be relaxed and comfortable while studying math.
9. "TALK" mathematics. Discuss it with people in your class. Form a study group.
10. Develop a sense of responsibility for your own successes and failures.

*Source:* Adapted from Ellen Freedman, *Ten Ways to Reduce Math Anxiety*, 1997 (www.mathpower.com/reduce.htm).

## Use Special Techniques for Math Tests

Use the general test-taking strategies presented in chapter 7 as well as the following techniques to achieve better results on math exams:

- *Read through the exam first.* When you first get an exam, read through every problem quickly and make notes on how you might attempt to solve the problems.

- *Analyze problems carefully.* Categorize problems according to type. Take the "givens" into account, and write down any formulas, theorems, or definitions that apply before you begin. Focus on what you want to find or prove.

- *Estimate before you begin, to come up with a "ballpark" solution.* Work the problem and check the solution against your estimate. The two answers should be close. If they're not, recheck your calculations. You may have made a calculation error.

- *Break the calculation into the smallest possible pieces.* Go step-by-step and don't move on to the next step until you are clear about what you've done so far.

- *Recall how you solved similar problems.* Past experience can provide valuable clues.

- *Draw a picture to help you see the problem.* Visual images such as a diagram, chart, probability tree, or geometric figure may help clarify your thinking.
- *Be neat.* Sloppy numbers can mean the difference between a right and a wrong answer. A 4 that looks like a 9 will be marked wrong.
- *Use the opposite operation to check your work.* Work backward from your answer to see if you are right.
- *Look back at the question to be sure you did everything.* Did you answer every part of the question? Did you show all required work?

## Decide How Well These Techniques Work for You

Use what you just learned about yourself and math to answer the following questions:

- What did you learn from the math anxiety questionnaire? Describe your current level of math anxiety:

  _____

  _____

- If you are afraid of math, what effect do you think it will have on your future?

  _____

  _____

  _____

- Which suggestions for reducing math anxiety are you likely to use? How do you think they will help you feel more comfortable with math?

  _____

  _____

  _____

  _____

- Which suggestions for improving your performance on math tests are you likely to use?

  _____

  _____

  _____

  _____

- In what other ways can you improve your math performance?

  _____

  _____

  _____

PART
III

# Creating Life Success

**RELATING TO OTHERS**
*Communicating in a Diverse World*

*"Successfully intelligent people question assumptions and encourage others to do so. We all tend to have assumptions about the way things are or should be . . . but creatively intelligent people question many assumptions that others accept, eventually leading others to question those assumptions as well."*

ROBERT STERNBERG

**F**or many students, the college experience brings exposure to new and diverse values, lifestyles, backgrounds, and people. Being open to what is new and different around you can inspire you to question your thinking and beliefs, and ultimately can lead to building respect for others and strong teamwork skills. In this chapter, you will investigate how analytical, creative, and practical abilities can help you build the cultural competence and communication and relationship skills that add to your success as a person and as a student.

*In this chapter you explore answers to the following questions:*

- How can you develop cultural competence? 282
- How can you communicate effectively? 290
- How do you make the most of personal relationships? 297
- *Successful Intelligence Wrap-Up 302*

| Analytical | Creative | Practical |
|---|---|---|
| • Evaluating the assumptions that underlie prejudice and stereotypes<br>• Analyzing how you communicate with others<br>• Examining how you manage conflict and criticism | • Brainstorming ways to defuse conflict and anger<br>• Taking risks that build relationships<br>• Creating new ideas about what diversity means | • How to relate to others with cultural competence<br>• How to communicate effectively<br>• How to criticize constructively |

# How Can You Develop Cultural Competence?

As you read in chapter 1, diversity exists both within each person and among all people. You may work with people from different backgrounds. You may encounter all kinds of people as you attend religious services, buy groceries, swim at a pool, or socialize. You may experience diversity within your family—often the kind of diversity that is not visible. Even if friends or family members share your racial and ethnic background, they may differ in how they learn, the way they communicate, or their sexual orientation.

Interacting successfully with all kinds of people is the goal of *cultural competence*. As you learned in chapter 2, cultural competence refers to the ability to understand and appreciate differences among people and adjust your behavior in ways that enhance, rather than detract from, relationships and communication. According to the National Center for Cultural Competence, to develop cultural competence you must act upon the following five steps:[1]

1. Value diversity.

2. Identify and evaluate personal perceptions and attitudes.

3. Be aware of what happens when different cultures interact.

4. Build knowledge about other cultures.

5. Use what you learn to adapt to diverse cultures as you encounter them.

### How can I adjust to a new society and connect to people in my community?

I came to the U.S. a little over two and a half years ago from Afghanistan. I am a biology student aiming to go to medical school. My goal is to join the team of doctors called "Doctors Without Borders" and help people in underdeveloped countries.

I like hanging out with friends from different backgrounds. However, I want to be myself and not to have to meet the expectations of U.S. college students in order to make friends. How can I connect to my community without losing myself and my culture?

Nisar Nikzad
Community College
of Denver
Denver, Colorado

## PRACTICAL ANSWERS

Afsaneh Nahavandi
Professor of Management
and Director of Freshman
Programs
Arizona State University West

### Incorporate both your home country culture and U.S. culture into who you are.

The challenge to adapt and to integrate is called *acculturation*. I faced a similar situation when I came to the U.S. from Iran to go to college. You already possess three characteristics essential to successful acculturation. First, you are aware of cultural differences and you approach them without negative judgment. Second, you are also aware of your own culture and have a desire to preserve it. Third, you have recognized that adaptation does not happen overnight, and you are willing to put in the work and resolve conflicts.

Your goal is to bring U.S. culture and your home culture together and create a new culture of sorts for yourself. The first step is to continue learning about the U.S. Although it may appear that there is a uniform culture among American college students, there actually are considerable differences in beliefs, values, and behaviors. Additionally, although we each may have a dominant culture, we are all part of many different cultures. You are Afghani, American, male, part of the medical profession (or planning to be), and so forth.

The other thing you can do is to talk to your friends here about your country, religion, language, family, and so forth. You are likely to find them eager to learn, although sometimes their early assumptions may be simplistic. You will change as a result of your experiences; you are likely to feel more "American," but you will also change those around you and they will become a little more "Afghani." This give and take will enrich both you and those around you.

As you develop cultural competence, you heighten your ability to analyze how people relate to one another. Most important, you develop practical skills that enable you to connect to others, bridging the gap between who you are and who they are.[2]

## Value Diversity

Valuing diversity means having a basic respect for, and acceptance of, the differences among people. Every time you meet someone new, you have a choice about how to interact. You won't like everyone you meet, but if you value diversity, you will choose to treat people with tolerance and respect, avoiding assumptions about them and granting them the right to think, feel, and believe without being judged. Being open-minded in this way will help your relationships thrive, as shown in Key 9.1.

## Identify and Evaluate Personal Perceptions and Attitudes

Whereas people may value the *concept* of diversity, attitudes and emotional responses may influence how they act when they confront the *reality* of diversity in their own lives. As a result, many people have prejudices that lead to damaging stereotypes.

### Prejudice

Almost everyone has some level of (prejudice) resulting in the prejudging of others, usually on the basis of characteristics such as gender, race, sexual orientation, disability, or religion. People judge others without knowing anything about them because of factors like these:

- *Influence of family and culture:* Children learn attitudes—including intolerance, superiority, and hate—from their parents, peers, and community.

- *Fear of differences:* It is human to fear the unfamiliar and to make assumptions about it.

- *Experience:* One bad experience with a person of a particular race or religion may lead someone to condemn all people with the same background.

PREJUDICE

*A preconceived judgment or opinion formed without just grounds or sufficient knowledge.*

### Stereotypes

Prejudice is usually based on (stereotypes)— assumptions made, without proof or critical thinking, about the characteristics of a person or group of people. Stereotyping emerges from factors such as these:

- *Desire for patterns and logic:* People often try to make sense of the world by using the labels, categories, and generalizations that stereotypes provide.

- *Media influences:* The more people see stereotypical images—the airhead beautiful blonde, the jolly fat man—the easier it is to believe that stereotypes are universal.

- *Laziness:* Labeling group members according to a characteristic they seem to have in common takes less energy than asking questions that illuminate the qualities of individuals.

STEREOTYPE

*A standardized mental picture that represents an oversimplified opinion or uncritical judgment.*

Stereotypes derail personal connections and block effective communication, because pasting a label on a person makes it hard for you to see the real person underneath. Moreover, language derived from stereotypical ideas is often damaging. This was demonstrated in 2007 when radio and television talk show host Don Imus labeled the members of the Rutgers women's basketball team

**KEY 9.1**

## Approaching diversity with an open mind builds relationships.

| Your role | Situation | Closed-minded actions | Open-minded actions |
|---|---|---|---|
| **Fellow student** | For an assignment, you are paired with a student old enough to be your mother. | You assume the student will be clueless about the modern world. You think she might preach to you about how to do the assignment. | You get to know the student as an individual. You stay open to what you can learn from her experiences and knowledge. |
| **Friend** | You are invited to dinner at a friend's house. When he introduces you to his partner, you realize that he is gay. | You are turned off by the idea of two men in a relationship. You make an excuse to leave early. You avoid your friend after that. | You have dinner with the two men and make an effort to get to know more about them, individually and as a couple. |
| **Employee** | Your new boss is of a different racial and cultural background from yours. | You assume that you and your new boss don't have much in common. You think he will be distant and uninterested in you. | You rein in your stereotypes. You pay close attention to how your new boss communicates and leads. You adapt to his style and make an effort to get to know him better. |

**KEY 9.2**

## Both positive and negative stereotypes mask uniqueness.

| Positive stereotype | Negative stereotype |
|---|---|
| Women are nurturing. | Women are too emotional for business. |
| African Americans are great athletes. | African Americans struggle in school. |
| Hispanic Americans are family oriented. | Hispanic Americans have too many kids. |
| White people are successful in business. | White people are cold and power hungry. |
| Gay men have a great sense of style. | Gay men are sissies. |
| People with disabilities have strength of will. | People with disabilities are bitter. |
| Older people are wise. | Older people are set in their ways. |
| Asian Americans are good at math and science. | Asian Americans are poor leaders. |

with a racial slur. Consequently, his show was pulled from the air. Even stereotypes that seem "positive" may not be true and may get in the way of perceiving uniqueness. Key 9.2 lists some "positive" and "negative" stereotypes.

Use your analytical abilities to question your own ideas and beliefs, weed out the narrowing influence of prejudice and stereotyping, and discover problems that need addressing. Giving honest answers to questions like the following is an essential step in the development of cultural competence:

- How do I react to differences?

- What prejudices or stereotypes come to mind when I see people, in real life or the media, who are a different color than I am? From a different culture? Making different choices?

- Where did my prejudices and stereotypes come from?
- Are these prejudices fair? Are these stereotypes accurate?
- What harm can having these prejudices and believing these stereotypes cause?

With the knowledge you build as you answer these questions, move on to the next stage: Looking carefully at what happens when people from different cultures interact.

## Be Aware of Opportunities and Challenges That Occur When Cultures Interact

Interaction among people from different cultures can promote learning, build mutual respect, and broaden perspectives. However, as history has

### get creative!

## Expand Your Perception of Diversity

Being able to respond to people as individuals requires that you become more aware of the diversity that is not always on the surface. Start by examining your own uniqueness. Brainstorm 10 words or phrases that describe *you*. The challenge: Keep references to your ethnicity or appearance (brunette, Cuban American, wheelchair dependent, and so on) to a minimum, and fill the list with characteristics others can't see at a glance (laid-back, only child, 24 years old, drummer, marathoner, interpersonal learner, and so on).

1. _____
2. _____
3. _____
4. _____
5. _____

6. _____
7. _____
8. _____
9. _____
10. _____

Next, pair up with a classmate whom you do not know well. List on a separate sheet of paper any characteristics you know about him or her—chances are most of them will be visible. Then talk with the classmate, and both of you should round out your lists about each other with what you have discovered from your conversation. Finally, answer the questions below:

What stands out to you about what you learned about your classmate, and why?

_____

What about your description of yourself would you like people to focus on more often, and why?

_____

shown, such interaction can also produce problems caused by lack of understanding, prejudice, and stereotypical thinking. At their mildest, these problems create roadblocks that obstruct relationships and communication. At their worst, they set the stage for acts of discrimination and hate crimes.

## Discrimination

Federal law says that you cannot be denied basic opportunities and rights because of your race, creed, color, age, gender, national or ethnic origin, religion, marital status, potential or actual pregnancy, or potential or actual illness or disability (unless the illness or disability prevents you from performing required tasks and unless accommodations are not possible). Despite these legal protections, discrimination is common and often appears on college campuses. Students may not want to work with students of other races. Members of campus clubs may reject prospective members because of religious differences. Outsiders may harass students attending gay and lesbian alliance meetings. Instructors may judge students according to their weight, accent, or body piercings.

*DISCRIMINATION*

*Actions that deny people equal employment, educational, and housing opportunities, or treat people as second-class citizens.*

## Hate crimes

When prejudice turns violent, it often manifests itself in *hate crimes*—crimes motivated by a hatred of a specific characteristic thought to be possessed by the victim—usually directed at people based on their race, ethnicity, or religious or sexual orientation. Because hate crime statistics include only reported incidents, they tell just a part of the story—many more crimes likely go unreported by victims fearful of what might happen if they contact authorities.

Focusing on the positive aspect of intercultural interaction starts with awareness of the ideas and attitudes that lead to discrimination and hate crimes. With this awareness, you will be better prepared to push past negative possibilities and open your mind to positive ones.

# Build Cultural Knowledge

The successfully intelligent response to discrimination and hate, and the next step in your path toward cultural competence, is to gather knowledge. You have a personal responsibility to learn about people who are different from you, including those you are likely to meet on campus.

What are some practical ways to begin?

- *Read* newspapers, books, magazines, and Web sites that expose you to different perspectives.

- *Ask questions* of all kinds of people, about themselves and their traditions.

- *Observe* how people behave, what they eat and wear, how they interact with others.

- *Travel internationally* to unfamiliar places where you can experience different ways of living.

- *Travel locally* to equally unfamiliar, but nearby, places where you will encounter a variety of people.

- *Build friendships* with fellow students or coworkers you would not ordinarily approach.

Many college campuses have students reflecting an enormous variety of cultures, values, and backgrounds. Just interacting with others different from you can build your cultural knowledge.

Some colleges have international exchange students who can help you appreciate the world's cultural diversity. When Yiting Liu left China to study mathematics and economics at a U.S. college, she knew little about the United States. Dorothy Smith, her African American roommate, helped her adjust. "Yiting didn't know much about race relations when she first got to America," explains Dorothy, "but from hanging around us, she's been able to get an interpretive experience." Also, says Dorothy, when Yiting "first came here, she was an outsider. She didn't know what the taboos were. Now she's able to cross into different groups."[3]

Building knowledge also means exploring yourself. Talk with family, read, seek experiences that educate you about your own cultural heritage. Then share what you know with others.

## Adapt to Diverse Cultures

Here's where you take everything you have gathered—your value of diversity, your self-knowledge, your understanding of how cultures interact, your information about different cultures—and put it to work with practical actions. As you question, you can define actions and solutions that improve how you relate to others, and perhaps even change how people relate to one another on a larger scale. Choose actions that feel right to you, that cause no harm, and that may make a difference, however small.

Dr. Martin Luther King Jr. believed that careful thinking could change attitudes. He said:

> The tough-minded person always examines the facts before he reaches conclusions: in short, he postjudges. The tender-minded person reaches conclusions before he has examined the first fact; in short, he prejudges and is prejudiced. . . . There is little hope for us until we become tough minded enough to break loose from the shackles of prejudice, half-truths, and down-right ignorance.[4]

Let the following suggestions inspire your own creative ideas about what else you can do in your daily life to improve how you relate to others.

**Look past external characteristics.** If you meet a woman with a disability, get to know her. She may be an accounting major, a daughter, and a mother. She may love baseball, politics, and science fiction novels. These characteristics—not just her physical person—describe who she is.

**Put yourself in other people's shoes.** Attend a meeting about an issue that people in your community face but that is unfamiliar to you. Ask questions about what other people feel, especially if there's a conflict. Offer information and friendship to someone new who is adjusting to your school community.

**Adjust to cultural differences.** When you understand someone's way of being and put it into practice, you show respect and encourage communication. If a friend's family is formal at home, dress appropriately and behave formally when you visit. If an instructor maintains a lot of personal space, keep a respectful distance when you visit during office hours. If a study group member takes offense at a particular kind of language, avoid it when you meet.

**Help others in need.** Newspaper columnist Sheryl McCarthy wrote about an African American man who, in the midst of the 1992 Los Angeles riots, saw an Asian American man being beaten and helped him to safety: "When asked why he risked grievous harm to save an Asian man he didn't even know, the African-American man said, 'Because if I'm not there to help someone else, when the mob comes for me, will there be someone there to save me?'"[5]

**Stand up against prejudice, discrimination, and hate.** When you hear a prejudiced remark or notice discrimination taking place, ask yourself questions about how to encourage a move in the right direction. Then act. You may choose to make a comment, or to get help by approaching an authority such as an instructor or dean. Sound the alarm on hate crimes—let authorities know if you suspect that a crime is about to occur, join campus protests, support organizations that encourage tolerance.

**Recognize that people everywhere have the same basic needs.** Everyone loves, thinks, hurts, hopes, fears, and plans. When you are trying to find common ground with diverse people, remember that you are united first through your essential humanity.

When people use analytical, creative, and practical thinking to work through problems, changes can happen. After a gay tutor left a university job rather than face harassment, his friends organized an intercollegiate meeting on intolerance. Chandra J. Johnson, assistant to the president at the University of Notre Dame, asked participants to examine themselves:

> This is an opportunity to see how our own biases have been formed. . . . We are not born with notions of racism. These kinds of social ills have been projected onto us. . . . These things are very, very real and people's spirits are destroyed every day as a result of a bias or a misconception.[6]

Ada Maxwell, a student attendee at the meeting, stressed that talking about intolerance is the key to eliminating it: "It doesn't have to be taboo," she said. "Half of the education . . . is the classes and the professors . . . but the other half—and it's a really important half—is what you can learn from other people. Your thinking can change and other people's thinking can change."[7]

Working toward understanding is key when it comes to this kind of problem solving. As Paul Barrett Jr., political science major at Earlham College, puts it:

> As a black male, I am faced with situations very different from that of a white male, a white female, a black female, an Asian-American male, and so on. We must have the ability to approach situations with a panoramic perspective rather than the narrow scope of our own worlds. Is that not the very essence of diversity? Is it not the ability to at least try to understand differences in culture and understand what makes a person act or think the way that he or she does?[8]

So far, this chapter has focused on the need to accept and adapt to diversity in its many forms. Just as there is diversity in skin color and ethnicity, there is also diversity in the way people communicate. Effective communication helps people of all cultures understand one another and make connections.

## Make a Difference

Connect with other cultures by rewriting three strategies in the "Adapt to Diverse Cultures" section on pages 288–289 as specific actions to which you commit. For example, "Help others in need" might become "Sign up to tutor in the Writing Center." Circle or check the number when you have completed each task or, if it is ongoing, when you have begun the change.

1. _____

2. _____

3. _____

# How Can You Communicate Effectively?

Spoken communication that is clear promotes success at school, at work, and in personal relationships. Successfully intelligent communicators analyze and adjust to communication styles, learn to give and receive criticism, analyze and make practical use of body language, and work through communication problems. Note that language barriers may arise with cross-cultural communication. When speaking with someone who is struggling with your language, make the conversation easier by choosing words the person is likely to know, avoiding slang expressions, being patient, and using body language to fill in what words can't say. Also, invite questions—and ask them yourself—so that you both can be as clear as possible.

## Adjust to Communication Styles

When you speak, your goal is for listeners to receive the message as you intended. Problems arise when one person has trouble "translating" a message coming from someone using a different communication style. Your knowledge of the Personality Spectrum dimensions (see chapter 3) will help you understand and analyze the ways diverse people communicate.

## Identifying Your Styles

Following are some communication styles that tend to be associated with the four dimensions in the Personality Spectrum. No one style is better than another. Successful communication depends on understanding your personal style and becoming attuned to the styles of others. As you read, keep in mind that these are generalizations—individuals will exhibit a range of variations within each style.

**Thinker-dominant communicators focus on facts and logic.** As speakers, they tend to rely on logical analysis to communicate ideas and prefer quantitative concepts to those that are conceptual or emotional. As listeners, they often do best with logical messages. Thinkers may also need time to process what they have heard before responding. Written messages—on paper or via e-mail—are often useful for these individuals because writing can allow for time to put ideas together logically.

**Organizer-dominant communicators focus on structure and completeness.** As speakers, they tend to deliver well-thought-out, structured messages that fit into an organized plan. As listeners, they often appreciate a well-organized message that defines practical tasks in concrete terms. As with Thinkers, a written format is often an effective form of communication to or from an Organizer.

**Giver-dominant communicators focus on concern for others.** As speakers, they tend to cultivate harmony, analyzing what will promote closeness in relationships. As listeners, they often appreciate messages that emphasize personal connection and address the emotional side of an issue. Whether speaking or listening, Givers often favor in-person talks over written messages.

**Adventurer-dominant communicators focus on the present.** As speakers, they focus on creative ideas, tending to convey a message as soon as the idea arises and move on to the next activity. As listeners, they appreciate up-front, short, direct messages that don't get sidetracked. Like Givers, Adventurers tend to communicate and listen more effectively in person.

What is your style? Use this information as a jumping-off point for your self-exploration. Just as people tend to demonstrate characteristics from more than one Personality Spectrum dimension, communicators may demonstrate different styles.

## Put Your Knowledge of Communication Style to Use

Analyze your style by thinking about the communication styles associated with your dominant Personality Spectrum dimensions. Compare them to how you tend to communicate and how others seem to respond to you. Then, use creative and practical thinking skills to decide what works best for you as a communicator.

**Speakers adjust to listeners.** Listeners may interpret messages in ways you never intended. Think about practical solutions to this kind of problem as you read the following example involving a Giver-dominant instructor and a Thinker-dominant student (the listener):

*Instructor:* Your essay didn't communicate any sense of your personal voice.

*Student:* What do you mean? I spent hours writing it. I thought it was on the mark.

- *Without adjustment:* The instructor ignores the student's need for detail and continues to generalize. Comments like "You need to elaborate," "Try writing from the heart," or "You're not considering your audience" might confuse or discourage the student.
- *With adjustment:* Greater logic and detail will help. For example, the instructor might say, "You've supported your central idea clearly, but you didn't move beyond the facts into your interpretation of what they mean. Your essay reads like a research paper. The language doesn't sound like it is coming directly from you."

**Listeners adjust to speakers.** As a listener, improve understanding by being aware of stylistic differences and translating the message into one that makes sense to you. The following example of an Adventurer-dominant employee speaking to an Organizer-dominant supervisor shows how adjusting can pay off:

*Employee:* I'm upset about the e-mail you sent me. You never talked to me directly and you let the problem build into a crisis. I haven't had a chance to defend myself.

- *Without adjustment:* If the supervisor is annoyed by the employee's insistence on direct personal contact, he or she may become defensive: "I told you clearly what needs to be done. I don't know what else there is to discuss."
- *With adjustment:* In an effort to improve communication, the supervisor responds by encouraging the in-person exchange that is best for the employee: "Let's meet after lunch so you can explain to me how you believe we can improve the situation."

In addition to the Personality Spectrum dimensions, Multiple Intelligences theory can also provide clues about communication style. The *Multiple Intelligence Strategies* table on page 298 presents different communication strategies suggested for use in a study group for a criminal justice course.

Although adjusting to communication styles helps you speak and listen more effectively, you also need to understand, and learn how to effectively give and receive, criticism.

## Know How to Give and Receive Criticism

CONSTRUCTIVE
CRITICISM

Criticism that promotes improvement or development.

Criticism can be either *constructive* or *unconstructive.* Constructive criticism is a practical problem-solving strategy, involving goodwill suggestions for improving a situation. In contrast, unconstructive criticism focuses on what went wrong, doesn't offer alternatives that might help solve the problem, and is often delivered negatively, creating bad feelings.

When offered constructively, criticism can help bring about important changes. Consider a case in which someone has continually been late to study group sessions. The group leader can comment in one of two ways. Which comment would encourage you to change your behavior?

- *Constructive:* The group leader talks privately with the student, saying, "I've noticed that you've been late a lot. We count on you, because our success depends on what each of us contributes. Is there a problem that is keeping you from being on time? Can we help?"

- *Unconstructive:* The leader watches the student arrive late and says, in front of everyone, "If you can't start getting here on time, there's really no point in your coming."

At school, instructors criticize classwork, papers, and exams. On the job, criticism may come from supervisors, coworkers, or customers. No matter the source, constructive comments can help you grow as a person. Be open to what you hear, and remember that most people want you to succeed.

**Offering constructive criticism.** When offering constructive criticism, use the following strategies to be effective:

- *Criticize the behavior rather than the person.* Avoid personal attacks. "You've been late to five group meetings" is much preferable to "You're lazy."
- *Define the problematic behavior specifically.* Try to focus on the facts, substantiating with specific examples and minimizing emotions. Avoid additional complaints—people can hear criticisms better if they are discussed one at a time.

# Give Constructive Criticism

- Think of a situation in your life that could be improved if you were able to offer constructive criticism to a friend or family member. Describe the situation and name the improvement you seek:

  _____
  _____

- Now imagine that you have a chance to speak to this person. First describe the setting—time, place, atmosphere—where you think you would be most successful:

  _____
  _____

- Next develop your "script." Keeping in mind what you know about constructive criticism, analyze the situation and decide on what you think would be the best approach. Use a separate sheet of paper to freewrite what you would say. Keep in mind the goal you want your communication to achieve.

- Finally, if you can, make your plan a reality. Will you do it?   Yes___ No___

- If you do have the conversation, note here: Was it worth it?   Yes___No___

- *Suggest new approaches and offer help.* Talk about practical ways of handling the situation. Work with the person to develop creative options. Help the person feel supported.

- *Use a positive approach and hopeful language.* Express the conviction that changes will occur and that the person can turn the situation around.

**Receiving criticism.** When you find yourself on criticism's receiving end, use the following techniques to handle it constructively:

- *Analyze the comments.* Listen carefully, then evaluate what you heard. What does it mean? What is the intent? Try to let unconstructive comments go without responding.

- *Request suggestions on how to change your behavior.* Ask, "How would you like me to handle this in the future?"

- *Summarize the criticism and your response to it.* Make sure everyone understands the situation.

- *Use a specific strategy.* Use problem-solving skills to analyze the problem, brainstorm ways to change, choose a strategy, and take practical action to make it happen.

Criticism, as well as other thoughts and feelings, may be communicated nonverbally. You will become a more effective communicator if you understand body language.

## Understand Body Language

Body language has an extraordinary capacity to express people's real feelings through gestures, eye movements, facial expressions, body positioning and posture, touching behaviors, vocal tone, and use of personal space. Why is it important to know how to analyze body language?

**Nonverbal cues shade meaning.** What you say can mean different things depending on body positioning or vocal tone. The statement "That's a great idea" sounds positive. However, said while sitting with your arms and legs crossed and looking away, it may communicate that you dislike the idea. Said sarcastically, the tone may reveal that you consider the idea a joke.

**Culture influences how body language is interpreted.** For example, in the United States, looking away from someone may be a sign of anger or distress; in Japan, the same behavior is usually a sign of respect.

**Nonverbal communication strongly influences first impressions.** First impressions emerge from a combination of verbal and nonverbal cues. Nonverbal elements, including tone of voice, posture, eye contact, and speed and style of movement, usually come across first and strongest.

Although reading body language is not an exact science, the following practical strategies will help you use it to improve communication:

- *Pay attention to what is said through nonverbal cues.* Focus on your tone, your body position, and whether your cues reinforce or contradict your words. Then do the same for those with whom you are speaking. Look for the level of meaning in the physical.

- *Adjust behavior based on cultural differences.* In cross-cultural conversation, discover what seems appropriate by paying attention to what the other person does and by noting how others react to what you do. Then consider making changes based on your observations.

- *Adjust body language to the person or situation.* What body language might you use when making a presentation in class? Meeting with your advisor? Confronting an angry coworker? Think through how to use your physicality to communicate successfully.

One of the biggest barriers to successful communication is conflict, which can result in anger and even violence. With effort, you can successfully manage conflict and stay away from those who cannot.

When you share an interest with someone, you may find that communication flows and personal differences fade into the background. These students, both interested in television, work together to learn how to operate broadcasting equipment.

## Manage Conflict

Conflicts, both large and small, arise when there is a clash of ideas or interests. You may have small conflicts with a housemate over a door left unlocked. You may have major conflicts with your partner about finances or with an instructor about a failing grade. Conflict, as unpleasant as it can be, is a natural element in the dynamic of getting along with others. Prevent it when you can—and when you can't, use problem-solving strategies to resolve it.

### Conflict-Prevention Strategies

The following two strategies can help you to prevent conflict from starting in the first place.

**Send "I" messages.** "I" messages help you communicate your needs rather than attacking someone else. Creating these messages involves some simple rephrasing: "You didn't lock the door!" becomes "I felt uneasy when I came to work and the door was unlocked." Similarly, "You never called last night" becomes "I was worried when I didn't hear from you last night."

"I" statements soften the conflict by highlighting the effects that the other person's actions have on you, rather than focusing on the other person or the actions themselves. These statements help the receiver feel freer to respond, perhaps offering help and even acknowledging mistakes.

**Be assertive.** Most people tend to express themselves in one of three ways— aggressively, assertively, or passively. *Aggressive* communicators focus primarily on their own needs and can become impatient when needs are not satisfied. *Passive* communicators focus primarily on the needs of others and often deny themselves power, causing frustration. *Assertive* communicators are able to declare and affirm their opinions while respecting the rights of others to do the same. Assertive behavior strikes a balance between aggression and passivity and promotes the most productive communication. Key 9.3 contrasts the characteristics of these three.

## KEY 9.3   Assertiveness fosters successful communication.

| Aggressive | Assertive | Passive |
|---|---|---|
| Blaming, name-calling, and verbal insults: "You have created this mess!" | Expressing oneself and letting others do the same: "I have thoughts about this—first, what is your opinion?" | Feeling that one has no right to express anger: "No, I'm fine." |
| Escalating arguments: "You'll do it my way, no matter what it takes." | Using "I" statements to defuse arguments: "I am uncomfortable with that choice and want to discuss it." | Avoiding arguments: "Whatever you want to do is fine." |
| Being demanding: "Do this." | Asking and giving reasons: "Please consider doing it this way, and here's why . . ." | Being noncommittal: "You don't have to do this unless you really want to, but . . ." |

What can aggressive and passive communicators do to move toward a more assertive style? Aggressive communicators might take time before speaking, use "I" statements, listen to others, and avoid giving orders. Passive communicators might acknowledge anger, express opinions, exercise the right to make requests, and know that their ideas and feelings are important.

### Successful Intelligence Connections Online

Listen to author Sarah Kravits discuss analytical, creative, and practical ways to manage conflict.

Go to the *Keys to Success* Companion Web site at www.prenhall.com/carter to listen or download as a podcast.

## Conflict Resolution

All too often, people deal with conflict through *avoidance* (a passive tactic that shuts down communication) or *escalation* (an aggressive tactic that often leads to fighting). Conflict resolution demands calm communication, motivation, and careful thinking. Use analytical, creative, and practical thinking skills to apply the problem-solving plan from chapter 4.

Trying to calm anger is an important part of resolving conflict. All people get angry at times—at people, events, and themselves. However, excessive anger can contaminate relationships, stifle communication, and turn friends and family away.

## Manage Anger

Strong emotions can get in the way of happiness and success. It is hard to concentrate on American history when you are raging over being cut off in traffic or can't let go of your anger with a friend. Psychologists report that angry outbursts may actually make things worse. When you feel yourself losing control, try some of these practical anger-management techniques:

- *Relax.* Breathe deeply. Slowly repeat a calming phrase or word like "Take it easy" or "Relax."

- *Change your environment.* Take a break from what's upsetting you. Go for a walk, go to the gym, see a movie. Come up with some creative ideas about what might calm you down.

- *Think before you speak.* When angry, most people tend to say the first thing that comes to mind, even if it's hurtful. Inevitably, this escalates the hard feelings and the intensity of the argument. Instead, wait until you are in control before you say something.

- *Do your best to solve a problem, but remember that not all problems can be solved.* Instead of blowing up, think about how you can handle what's happening. Analyze a challenging situation, make a plan, resolve to do your best, and begin. If you fall short, you will know you made an effort and be less likely to turn your frustration into anger.
- *Get help if you can't keep your anger in check.* If you consistently lash out, you may need the help of a counselor. Many schools have mental health professionals available to students.

Your ability to communicate and manage conflict has a major impact on your relationships with friends and family. Successful relationships are built on self-knowledge, good communication, and hard work.

# How Do You Make the Most of Personal Relationships?

Personal relationships with friends, classmates, spouses and partners, and parents can be sources of great satisfaction and inner peace. Good relationships can motivate you to do your best in school, on the job, and in life. When relationships fall apart, however, nothing may seem right. You may be unable to eat, sleep, or concentrate. Relationships have enormous power.

## Use Positive Relationship Strategies

Here are some strategies for improving personal relationships:

**Prioritize personal relationships.** You devote time and energy to education, work, and sports. Relationships benefit from the same investment. In addition, spending time with people you like can relieve stress.

**Spend time with people you respect and admire.** Life is too short to hang out with people who bring you down or encourage you to ignore your values. "Try to nurture at least one friendship in each class," advises a Palo Alto College student. "If you know negative people who will try to discourage you and crush your spirit, avoid them. . . . You need nurturing and positivity."[9]

**If you want a friend, be a friend.** If you treat others with the kind of loyalty and support that you appreciate, you are likely to receive the same in return.

**Work through tensions.** Negative feelings can fester when left unspoken. Get to the root of a problem by discussing it, compromising, forgiving, and moving on.

**Take risks.** It can be frightening to reveal your deepest dreams and frustrations, to devote yourself to a friend, or to fall in love. However, if you open yourself up, you stand to gain the incredible benefits of companionship, which for most people outweigh the risks.

# MULTIPLE INTELLIGENCE STRATEGIES

## FOR COMMUNICATION

**APPLY DIFFERENT INTELLIGENCES TO IMPROVE A CRIMINAL JUSTICE STUDY GROUP.**

| INTELLIGENCE | USE MI STRATEGIES *to improve communication* | APPLY MI COMMUNICATION STRATEGIES *to learn about the U.S. court system**  |
|---|---|---|
| Verbal-Linguistic | • Find opportunities to express your thoughts and feelings to others—either in writing or in person.<br>• *Listening* to words is at least as important as speaking them. | • Divide your group or pair into two parts. One person or subgroup should teach the historical development of the state court system. The other should teach the historical development of the federal court system. |
| Logical-Mathematical | • Allow yourself time to think through a problem before discussing it. Write out an argument on paper and rehearse it.<br>• When communicating with others whose styles are not as logic-focused, ask specific questions to learn the facts you need. | • Ask these questions to evaluate the effectiveness of the state and federal court systems: What works well? Where are the breakdowns? What improvements could you suggest? |
| Bodily-Kinesthetic | • Have an important talk while walking, running, or performing a task that does not involve concentration.<br>• Work out to burn off excess energy before having an important discussion. | • Assign roles for group members to set up a courtroom "set" in the classroom. Choose a case to recreate and perform a "mock trial" to illustrate an example of how a trial works in a state or federal court. |
| Visual-Spatial | • Make a drawing or diagram of points you want to communicate during an important discussion.<br>• If you are in a formal classroom or work setting, use visual aids to explain your main points. | • In a pair or group, each individual or group half draws a diagram—one showing the structure of the state court system, and one showing the structure of the federal court system. |
| Interpersonal | • If you tend to dominate group conversation, focus more on listening.<br>• If you tend to prioritize listening to others, work on becoming more assertive about expressing your opinion. | • Select a landmark Supreme Court case. In a pair or group, each person or half of the group should argue one side of the case. Give everyone time to communicate clearly. |
| Intrapersonal | • Be as clear as possible when expressing what you know about yourself, and recognize that not all communicators may be self-aware.<br>• When you have a difficult encounter, take time alone to decide how to communicate more effectively next time. | • Select the court system topic or segment that you know you will comprehend best. Suggest that you handle that topic or segment when the group divides up material for each group member to learn and present to the others. |
| Musical | • Before communicating difficult thoughts or feelings, work through them by writing a poem or song.<br>• Be sensitive to the rhythms of a conversation. Sense when to voice your opinion and when to hang back. | • Create a song or rhythmic mnemonic device together that helps you remember the vocabulary associated with the court system, such as *appeal, jurisdiction,* and *judicial review.* |
| Naturalistic | • Use your ability to recognize patterns to evaluate communication situations. Employ patterns that work well and avoid those that do not.<br>• When appropriate, make an analogy from the natural world of plants or animals to clarify a point in a conversation. | • In a pair or group, talk through the process of how a trial moves from the lowest state level all the way to the Supreme Court. Make a time line that shows the pattern of how the case progresses. |

* For information on the federal court system, see Frank Schmalleger, *Criminal Justice Today: An Introductory Text for the Twenty-first Century,* Upper Saddle River, NJ: Prentice Hall, 2005.

**Find a pattern that suits you.** Some students date exclusively and commit early. Some students prefer to socialize in groups. Some students date casually. Be honest with yourself—and others—about what you want in a relationship.

**If a relationship fails, find ways to cope.** When an important relationship becomes strained or breaks up, analyze the situation and choose practical strategies to help you move on. Some people need time alone; others need to be with friends and family. Some seek counseling. Some throw their energy into school or exercise. Some cry. Whatever you do, believe that in time you will emerge from the experience stronger.

## Manage Communication Technology

Modern technology has revolutionized the way people communicate with one another. Not even 30 years ago the telephone, U.S. mail, and telegrams were the only alternatives to speaking in person. Today, in addition to those existing methods, you can call or text on a mobile phone; you can write a note via e-mail or instant message, from a computer or a PDA such as a BlackBerry or Treo; you can communicate through Internet-based venues such as blogs and chat rooms; and you can learn about one another by frequenting social networking sites such as MySpace or Facebook.

© Jason Stitt—Fotolia.com

Younger students, who grew up with technology, tend to use it most. A recent Kaiser Family Foundation study found that 8- to 18-year-olds averaged 6½ hours a day in various media interactions, including texting, cell phones, and networking sites. AOL reports that among Americans aged 16–21, 66% prefer instant-messaging to e-mail.[10]

Communication technologies have many advantages. You can communicate faster, more frequently, and with more people at one time than ever before. You can be instant-messaging several friends at once while talking on your regular phone, texting on your cell phone, and answering periodic e-mails. You can also communicate with more control and initiative than you may have in person, which may help you build confidence for face-to-face situations.

However, there are drawbacks. It's easy to misunderstand the tone or meaning of instant messages (IMs), e-mails, and text messages. Many of these communication methods are addictive—you might look up at the clock and realize you've spent 3 hours IM-ing your friends instead of studying for an upcoming test. In addition, spending too much time communicating electronically can limit your real-time personal connections and ultimately derail relationships. Finally, revealing too much about yourself on social networking sites may come back to haunt you. Increasingly, employers are checking MySpace and Facebook for information about prospective job candidates.[11] Before posting words or images, consider whether you may regret your action later on. Once this information is in cyberspace, you cannot pull it back.

Ultimately, students will all have their own personal communication "recipe," consisting of how much they want to communicate and what methods of communication suit them best. The best way for you to create your ideal recipe is to analyze situations carefully, think creatively, and make practical decisions about how to move forward. How do you prefer to communicate with others? What forms of communication do you overuse, and what are the effects? Keep everything in moderation, and let modern communication methods *enhance* in-person interaction rather than replace it.

## Avoid Destructive Relationships

On the far end of the spectrum are relationships that turn destructive. Colleges see their share of violent incidents. The more informed you are, the less likely you are to add to the sobering statistics.

### Sexual Harassment

Both men and women can be victims, although the most common targets are women. Sexual harassment basically consists of two types:

- *Quid pro quo harassment* refers to a request for a sexual favor or activity in exchange for something else: "If you don't do X for me, I will fail you/fire you/make your life miserable."

- *Hostile environment harassment* indicates any situation where sexually charged remarks, behavior, or items cause discomfort. Examples include lewd jokes and pornography.

If you feel degraded by anything that goes on at school or work, address the person whom you believe is harassing you, or speak to a dean or supervisor.

### Violence in Relationships

Statistics indicate that violent relationships among students are increasing.[12] Consider the following:

- One in five college students has experienced and reported at least one violent incident while dating, from being slapped to more serious violence.

- In three of four violent relationships, problems surface after the couple has dated for a while.

- In six of ten cases, drinking and drugs are associated with the violence.

Women in their teens and twenties are more likely to be victims of domestic violence than older women. Here's why: First, when trouble occurs, students are likely to turn to friends rather than counselors or the law. Second, peer pressure makes them uneasy about leaving the relationship. And finally, some inexperienced women may believe that the violence is normal.[13]

Analyze your situation and use problem-solving skills to come up with practical options. If you see warning signs such as controlling behavior, unpredictable mood swings, personality changes associated with alcohol and drugs, and outbursts of anger, consider ending the relationship. If you are being abused, call a shelter or abuse hotline or seek counseling at school or at a community center. If you need medical attention, go to a clinic or hospital emergency room. If you believe that your life is in danger, get out and obtain a restraining order that requires your abuser to stay away from you.

### Rape and Date Rape

Any intercourse or anal or oral penetration by a person against another person's will is defined as rape. Rape is primarily an act of rage and control, not a sexual act. Acquaintance rape, or *date rape,* refers to sexual activity during an arranged social encounter that is against one partner's will, including situations where one partner is too drunk or drugged to give consent. Odorless, tasteless drugs like Rohypnol, GHB, and Ketamine are sometimes used by date rapists to sedate victims and are difficult to detect in a drink.

Prevention is the first line of defense. Communicate—clearly and early—what you want and don't want to do. Keep a cell phone handy. Avoid alcohol or drugs that might make it difficult for you to stay aware. Maintain control of your drink at all times (drink from a container you open yourself, or watch your drink being mixed, and avoid open-source containers like punch bowls or trash cans). When on a date with someone who seems unstable, stick to safe, public places.

If you are raped, whether by an acquaintance or a stranger, seek medical attention immediately. Next, talk to a close friend or counselor. Consider reporting the incident to the police or to campus officials. Whether or not you take legal action, continue to get help through counseling, a rape survivor group, or a hotline.

## Choose Communities That Enhance Your Life

Personal relationships often take place within *communities,* or groups that include people who share your interests—for example, sororities and fraternities, athletic clubs, and political groups. The presence of the Internet has added chat rooms, blogs, and newsgroups to the scope of social communities available to you. Some colleges even put their Facebooks online and have school-sponsored online communities.

© Bart van der Putten—Fotolia.com

So much of what you accomplish in life is linked to your network of personal contacts. If you affiliate with communities that are involved in positive activities, you are more likely to surround yourself with responsible and character-rich people who may become your friends and colleagues. You may find among them your future spouse or partner, your best friend, a person who helps you land a job, your doctor, accountant, real estate agent, and so on.

Finding and working with a community of people with similar interests can have positive effects in personal relationships and in workplace readiness, as Eastern Kentucky University student Kasey Doyle explains:

> During my sophomore year, a friend persuaded me to join a service sorority on campus. I was hesitant at first, but once I began to get involved, I realized that I had missed out on many opportunities. Not only have I made many friends, I have also become more outgoing and personable. . . . I found a place where I fit in.
>
> Joining this organization also prepared me for my major and my job at [the campus newspaper] *The Progress.*
>
> As a reporter, you are expected to be outgoing and personable, and before joining an organization, I was extremely shy. I'm definitely not timid anymore, and I have matured and become more self-confident.[14]

If you find yourself drawn toward communities that encourage negative and even harmful behavior, such as gangs or groups that haze pledges, stop and think. Analyze why you are drawn to these groups. Resist the temptation to join. If you are already involved and want out, stand up for yourself and be determined.

# Successful Intelligence Wrap-Up

As you go through life, you have a choice—often many times a day—about how to relate to people and ideas that cross your path. When you make a successfully intelligent choice, considering a new person or perspective with an open and questioning mind, you give yourself the opportunity to learn and grow. Here's how you have built skills in chapter 9:

## Analytical

In the section about cultural competence, you gathered the tools you need to analyze your attitudes toward people, cultures, and values that differ from yours. You explored the ways in which you and others communicate and the effects of various styles. You examined various responses to criticism, conflict, and anger, using the *Get Analytical* exercise to analyze how to use constructive criticism to improve a specific personal situation.

## Creative

In the *Get Creative* exercise, you used brainstorming techniques to broaden your perspective on your own diversity as well as that of a classmate. You expanded your range of ideas for how to accept and support different people and cultures. The section on communication may have inspired ideas about ways to communicate with others that promote understanding, make the best of criticism, and minimize conflict.

## Practical

You considered practical strategies for avoiding prejudice, stereotyping, and discrimination. In the *Get Practical* exercise, you applied strategies for adapting to diverse cultures to your own life in specific, practical ways. You reinforced your knowledge of practical strategies for communicating effectively with others, nurturing personal relationships, and staying safe in your interpersonal interactions.

# *taraadin*
## *(tah-rah-den)*

The Arabic word *taraadin* includes the concept of "compromise" but contains another level of meaning. Specifically, it refers to a "win-win" solution to a problem, an agreement that brings positive effects to everyone involved.[15]

With the cultural competence that enables you to accept and adjust to the diverse people around you, you have the knowledge necessary to come up with win-win solutions. With the ability to analyze communication and think practically about how to make the best of opportunities to communicate, you have the power to make those solutions happen. Not every problem can be resolved happily for all concerned, but when you can bring about *taraadin* in your life, you will benefit as much as those around you.

"We cannot live for ourselves alone. Our lives are connected by a thousand invisible threads, and along these sympathetic fibers, our actions run as causes and return to us as results."

AUTHOR HERMAN MELVILLE

# PERSONAL TRIUMPH CASE STUDY
## ADJUSTING TO COLLEGE AFTER SERVING IN THE MILIT

VICTOR OZUNA,
STUDENT AT SAN DIEGO STATE UNIVERSITY, SAN DIEGO, CALIFORNIA

*Connecting with others can be difficult, especially if you start out feeling exceptionally different. Victor Ozuna enlisted in the Navy after high school and was deployed to Iraq in 2003. After his tour of duty, at 23 years old, Victor went from walking the battlefields of Iraq to walking the campus of San Diego State University in less than a month. Read this account, then answer the questions on page 305.*

 His hobbies include working out at the gym, playing tennis, and spending time with family and friends. He has pulled an "all nighter" studying into the early hours of the morning, and is flushed with panic at the thought of a pop quiz. In many ways Victor Ozuna is a typical college student; but before attending SDSU he lived a reality that most of his peers will never know.

"I was 17 when I enlisted in the Navy. My parents had to sign a waiver for me to enlist," Victor said.

"One of the reasons I decided to join the Navy was to do construction as a Seabee. I've always enjoyed construction and I admired my father, who was a great handyman. Plus, I always wanted to serve my country." Victor was trained as a combat engineer with the U.S. Navy Seabees, where he was part of a construction battalion that provided engineering and construction support to U.S. troops during major combat operations.

In 2003, Victor was deployed to Iraq. "I was one of the first (American troops) to cross the Kuwait–Iraqi border. And I was one of the first to come home," he said.

Prior to his deployment to Iraq, Victor began thinking about college after a Navy superior suggested he consider a career in construction engineering. "I was stationed in Greece when I first visited the SDSU Web site," Victor said. "I saw that they offered a construction engineering program. I went from conducting urban combat operations in Iraq to a classroom."

Victor said it was tough for him to relate to other students when he first arrived at the university. "I was ready to quit college after my first week. No one wanted to hear about the war. No one talked about it. It was like it wasn't happening. I felt like nobody cared, and that the war was in vain. I saw people dying. To think of people dying in vain. . . ."

Someone did care.

While Victor was working part-time in the SDSU Veteran's Affairs Office, his supervisor showed interest in Victor's story. "The fact that she actually cared, and noticed the war, that was a big factor for me continuing as a student at SDSU."

Victor also credits his military training. "The main thing I got out of the military was discipline," he said. "Discipline is what kept me in college."

Today, he participates in a Combat Veteran Support Group at the San Diego VA Outpatient Clinic where he meets with other local students who served in Iraq. Victor has also become involved with campus organizations. He is a member of SDSU's Civil Engineering Honor Society, Chi Epsilon, and is the vice president of the student chapter of Associated General Contractors of America at SDSU. Last spring, he began an internship with a construction company, where he works as a field engineer.

Victor has come a long way from the first-time freshman who thought he wasn't college material. He's had to make several transitions in his young life and has faced each one courageously. "A new transition is hard for anyone. I went through a lot of them," he said. "They're unavoidable in life; but the better you handle them, the more successful you will be overall."

Victor has witnessed tragedy, lived fear, and experienced what the majority of his 18-to-23-year-old classmates have only read about in textbooks or seen in video games. Although he described his transition from soldier to student as "difficult," he found the strength to persevere.

By Jessica E. Gonzales. Reprinted by permission of San Diego State University, Division of Student Affairs.

*Abigail Holtz, the student artist who created this drawing, also took an unconventional educational route after high school. She enrolled at the Academy of Art University for a year and then attended community college full-time while working 50-hour weeks to support herself. Now a senior majoring in economics at Tufts University, Abby's journey gave her the confidence to believe in her own strengths and in her ability to take a different road. For more of Abby's story, please visit www.prenhall.com/carter.*

# SUCCESSFUL INTELLIGENCE

*Think, Create, Apply*

**Learn from the experiences of others.** Look back to Victor Ozuna's Personal Triumph on page 304. After you've read his story, relate his experience to your own life by answering the following questions on a separate sheet of paper or on a computer file:

**Step 1. Think it through:** *Analyze your experience and compare it to Victor's.* When in your life have you felt like an outsider, and how does this relate to Victor's experience? What was his key to finding his place in his new world? What was yours?

**Step 2. Think out of the box:** *Create a challenge.* Think about the activities and organizations at your school with which you would most feel "at home." Then imagine that none of those are available—and that you are required to get involved with three organizations or activities that interest you but that you would not naturally choose. How would you challenge yourself? Name your three choices and describe what you think you could gain from your experiences.

**Step 3. Make it happen:** *Use practical strategies to connect with others.* Choose one of those organizations or activities from your list of three. Now take steps toward trying it out. Contact a person involved with the organization or activity and ask for details—when the group meets, what they do, what the time commitment may be, what the benefit would be. Consider joining in the coming term, making an effort to get to know others who are involved.

# TEAMWORK

## Create Solutions Together

**Problem solving close to home.** Divide into groups of two to five students. Assign one group member to take notes. Discuss the following questions, one at a time:

1. What are the three largest problems your school or community faces with regard to how people get along with and accept others?

2. What could we do to deal with these three problems?

3. What can each individual student do to make improvements? (Talk specifically about what you think you can do.)

When all groups have finished, gather as a class and hear each group's responses. Observe the variety of problems and solutions. Notice whether more than one group came up with one or more of the same problems. If there is time, one person in the class, together with your instructor, could gather the responses to question 3 into an organized document that you can send to your school or local paper.

# WRITING

## Journal and Put Skills to Work

*Record your thoughts on a separate piece of paper, in a journal, or on a computer file.*

**Journal entry: Your experience with prejudice.** Have you ever been discriminated against, or encountered any other type of prejudice? Have you been on the other end and acted with prejudice yourself? Describe what happened, your feelings about the situation, and any action that you have taken as a result.

**Real-life writing: Improve communication.** Few students make use of the wealth of ideas and experience that academic advisors can offer. Think of a question you have—regarding a specific course, major, or academic situation— that your advisor might help you answer. Craft an e-mail in appropriate language to your advisor, and send it. Then, to stretch your communication skills, rewrite the same e-mail twice more: once in a format you would send to an instructor, and once in a format appropriate for a friend. Send either or both of these if you think the response would be valuable to you.

# PERSONAL PORTFOLIO

## Prepare for Career Success

*Complete the following in your electronic portfolio or on separate sheets of paper.*

**Compiling a résumé.** What you have accomplished in various work and school situations will be important for you to emphasize on a résumé when you apply for jobs. Your roles at work, in school, at home, and in the community help you gain knowledge and experience.

To start, use two sheets of paper or a computer to brainstorm. On one electronic page or sheet of paper, list your education and skills information. On another, list job experience. For each job, record job title, the dates of

employment, and the tasks you performed. Be as detailed as possible—
write down everything you remember. When you compile your résumé, you
will make this material more concise. Update this list periodically as you
gain experience and accomplishments.

Using the information you have gathered and Key 9.4 as your guide,
draft a résumé.

 KEY 9.4

## Set yourself apart with an attractive, clear résumé.

# Désirée Williams

237 Custer Street, San Francisco, CA 94101 • 650/555-5252 (w) or 415/555-7865 (h)
• fax: 707/555-2735 • e-mail: desiree@zzz.com

---

**EDUCATION**

---

*2005 to present* | San Francisco State University, San Francisco, CA

Pursuing a B.A. in the Spanish BCLAD (Bilingual, Cross-Cultural Language Acquisition Development) Education and Multiple Subject Credential Program. Expected graduation: June 2008.

---

**PROFESSIONAL EMPLOYMENT**

---

*10/06 to present* | **Research Assistant, Knowledge Media Lab**

Developing ways for teachers to exhibit their inquiry into their practice of teaching in an online, collaborative, multimedia environment.

*5/05 to present* | **Webmaster/Web Designer**

Work in various capacities at QuakeNet, an Internet Service Provider and Web Commerce Specialist in San Mateo, CA. Designed several sites for the University of California, Berkeley, Graduate School of Education, as well as private clients such as A Body of Work and Yoga Forever.

*9/05 to 6/06* | **Literacy Coordinator**

Coordinated, advised, and created literacy curriculum for an America Reads literacy project at Prescott School in West Oakland. Worked with non-reader 4th graders on writing and publishing, incorporating digital photography, Internet resources, and graphic design.

*8/05* | **Bilingual Educational Consultant**

Consulted for Children's Television Workshop, field-testing bilingual materials. With a research team, designed bilingual educational materials for an ecotourism project run by an indigenous rain forest community in Ecuador.

*1/05 to 6/06* | **Technology Consultant**

Worked with 24 Hours in Cyberspace, an online worldwide photojournalism event. Coordinated participation of schools, translated documents, and facilitated public relations.

---

**SKILLS**

---

*Languages:* | Fluent in Spanish.
Proficient in Italian and Shona (majority language of Zimbabwe).

*Computer:* | Programming ability in HTML, Javascript, Pascal, and Lisp. Multimedia design expertise in Adobe Photoshop, Netobjects Fusion, Adobe Premiere, Macromedia Flash, and many other visual design programs.

*Personal:* | Perform professionally in Mary Schmary, a women's a cappella quartet. Have climbed Mt. Kilimanjaro.

Remember that there are many ways to construct a résumé; consult other resources, such as those listed in the Internet resources, for different styles. You may want to reformat your résumé according to a style that your career counselor or instructor recommends. Also, if you already have a specific career focus, that career area may favor a particular style of résumé. Ask questions to be sure.

Keep your résumé draft in hard copy and on a computer hard drive or disk. When you need to submit a résumé with a job application, update the draft and print it out on high-quality paper.

Here are some general tips for writing a résumé:

- Always put your name and contact information at the top. Make it stand out.

- State an objective if it is appropriate—for instance, if your focus is specific or you are designing this résumé for a particular interview or career area.

- List your postsecondary education, starting from the latest and working backward. This may include summer school, night school, seminars, and accreditations.

- List jobs in reverse chronological order (most recent job first). Include all types of work experience (full-time, part-time, volunteer, internship, and so on).

- When you describe your work experience, use action verbs and focus on what you have accomplished, rather than on the description of assigned tasks.

- Include keywords that are linked to the description of the jobs for which you will be applying (see page 244 for more on keywords).

- List references on a separate sheet. You may want to put "References upon request" at the bottom of your résumé.

- Use formatting (larger font sizes, different fonts, italics, bold, and so on) and indents selectively to help the important information stand out.

- Get several people to look at your résumé before you send it out. Other readers will have ideas that you haven't thought of and may find errors that you have missed.

## Suggested Readings

Blank, Carla, and the Before Columbus Foundation. *Rediscovering America: The Making of Multicultural America, 1900–2000.* New York: Three Rivers Press, 2003.

Dublin, Thomas, ed. *Becoming American, Becoming Ethnic: College Students Explore Their Roots.* Philadelphia: Temple University Press, 1996.

Furlong, Gary. *The Conflict Resolution Toolbox.* Hoboken, NJ: Wiley, 2005.

Hockenberry, John. *Moving Violations.* New York: Hyperion, 1996.

Howard, Kim, and Annie Stevens. *Out & About Campus: Personal Accounts by Lesbian, Gay, Bisexual & Transgender College Students.* New York: Alyson Publications, 2000.

Levey, Marc, Michael Blanco, and W. Terrell Jones. *How to Succeed on a Majority Campus: A Guide for Minority Students.* Belmont, CA: Wadsworth, 1997.

Qubein, Nido R. *How to Be a Great Communicator: In Person, on Paper, and at the Podium.* New York: Wiley, 1996.

Schuman, David. *Diversity on Campus*. Dubuque, IA: Kendall/Hunt, 2001.

Tannen, Deborah. *You Just Don't Understand: Women and Men in Conversation*. New York: Perennial Currents, 2001.

Tannen, Deborah. *Conversational Style: Analyzing Talk Among Friends*. New York: Oxford University Press, 2005.

Tatum, Beverly Daniel. *"Why Are All the Black Kids Sitting Together in the Cafeteria?" and Other Conversations About Race: A Psychologist Explains the Development of Racial Identity*. Philadelphia: Basic Books, 2003.

Terkel, Studs. *Race: How Blacks and Whites Think and Feel About the American Obsession*. New York: Free Press, 2005.

Watkins, Boyce D. *Everything You Ever Wanted to Know About College: A Guide for Minority Students*. Camillus, NJ: Blue Boy, 2004.

## Internet and Podcast Resources

Association of American Colleges and Universities—AAC&U Podcasts (podcasts about on-campus diversity): **www.aacu.org/Podcast/DL06_podcasts.cfm**

*The Black Collegian* Online: **www.black-collegian.com**

Cultural Competency Web page (information from the Center for Effective Collaboration and Practice): **http://cecp.air.org/cultural**

Latino USA (with podcasts available on the Web site): **www.latinousa.org**

The Sociology of Race and Ethnicity (Web page with multiple links to other resources, created by Michael C. Kearl): **www.trinity.edu/mkearl/race.html**

Prentice Hall Student Success SuperSite: **www.prenhall.com/success**

## Endnotes

[1] "Conceptual Frameworks/Models, Guiding Values and Principles," National Center for Cultural Competence, 2002 (www11.georgetown.edu/research/gucchd/nccc/foundations/frameworks.html).

[2] Information in the sections on the five stages of building competency is based on Mark A. King, Anthony Sims, and David Osher, "How Is Cultural Competence Integrated in Education?" n.d., Center for Effective Collaboration and Practice (http://cecp.air.org/cultural/Q_integrated.htm).

[3] Jen Lin-Liu, "China's 'Harvard Girl': A College Student Has Become an Example for a New Style of Raising Children," *Chronicle of Higher Education*, May 30, 2003 (http://chronicle.com/weekly/v49/i38/38a04001.htm).

[4] Martin Luther King Jr., from his sermon "A Tough Mind and a Tender Heart," *Strength in Love*, Philadelphia: Fortress Press, 1986, p. 14.

[5] Sheryl McCarthy, *Why Are the Heroes Always White?* Kansas City, MO: Andrews McMeel, 1995, p. 137.

[6] Quoted in Doug Gavel, "Students Speak Out at Hate Crime Forum," *Harvard University Gazette*, February 15, 2001 (www.news.harvard.edu/gazette/2001/02.15/01-hatecrime.html).

[7] Ibid.

[8] Paul Barrett Jr., "Solutions Offered to Address Racism on Campus," *Earlham Word Online*, November 20, 1998. (http://word.cs.earlham.edu/issues/XIII/112098/opin91.html).

[9] From student essay submitted by the First Year Experience students of Patty Parma, Palo Alto College, San Antonio, Texas, January 2004.

[10] Betsy Israel, "The Overconnecteds," *New York Times* Education Life, November 5, 2006, p. 20.

[11] Ibid.

[12] Tina Kelley, "On Campuses, Warnings About Violence in Relationships," *New York Times*, February 13, 2000, p. 40.

[13] Ibid.

[14] Kasey Doyle, "Getting Involved on Campus Important," *Eastern Progress Online*, November 4, 2004 (http://media.www.easternprogress.com/media/storage/paper419/news/2004/11/04/Perspective/Getting.Involved.On.Campus.Important-792180.shtml).

[15] Christopher J. Moore, *In Other Words: A Language Lover's Guide to the Most Intriguing Words Around the World*, New York: Walker, 2004, p. 69.

**PERSONAL WELLNESS**

*Taking Care of Yourself*

> *"Successfully intelligent people have the ability to delay gratification. People who are unable to delay gratification seek rewards for achieving short-term goals but miss the larger rewards they could receive from accomplishing more important, long-term goals."*

ROBERT STERNBERG

**H**ow well you do in school is directly related to your physical and mental health, in large part because healthy people are more able to manage life's stresses as they arise. The more capable you are of managing stress, the more energy you will have to perform well academically.

This chapter examines ways to manage stress through health maintenance, handle stress-related health issues, and make effective decisions about drugs, alcohol, tobacco, and sex. Approach all the topics in this chapter with successful intelligence. Analyze your situations and choices, brainstorm creative options, and take practical actions that work for you.

*In this chapter you explore answers to the following questions:*

- How can focusing on health help you manage stress? 312
- How can you make effective decisions about alcohol, tobacco, and drugs? 324
- How can you make effective decisions about sex? 331
- Successful Intelligence Wrap-Up 335

| Analytical | Creative | Practical |
|---|---|---|
| • Evaluating how you react to stress | • Brainstorming healthy ways to have fun | • How to work toward healthier personal habits |
| • Analyzing how your sleep and eating patterns affect you | • Creating new eating habits | • How to seek support for stress and health issues |
| • Analyzing the effects of alcohol, tobacco, and drug use | • Coming up with ways to fit exercise into your day | • How to make effective decisions about substances and sex |

# How Can Focusing on Health Help You Manage Stress?

As you learned in chapter 2, *stress* refers to the physical or mental strain that occurs when your body reacts to pressure. The kind of pressure that produces stress comes from situations like heavy workloads (final exam week), excitement (being a finalist for the lead in a play), change (new school, new courses), being short on time (working 20 hours a week at a job and finding time to study), or illness (having a head cold that wipes you out for a week).

Stress doesn't come just from negative events. When psychologists T. H. Holmes and R. H. Rahe measured the intensity of people's reaction to specifi changes and the levels of stress related to them, they found that people experience both positive and negative events as stressors (see their Social Readjustment Rating Scale in Key 10.1).

For example, whereas some events like the death of a relative are clearly negative, other stressors, like getting married or even taking a vacation, are generally positive.

At their worst, stress reactions can make you physically ill. However, stress can also supply the heightened readiness you need to do well on tests, finish assignments on time, prepare for a class presentation, or befriend new people. Your goal is to find a manageable balance. Key 10.2 on page 315, based on research

### How can I manage the stress of leaving old friends and familiar places?

I started high school with my best friend since seventh grade, and our big plan was to star on the freshman basketball team. Then, in October of that year, my friend went into cardiac arrest and passed away. After more than two years, I've opened up to people again, and my two best friends and I are like brothers. Now that we've graduated, though, it scares me to think that we could grow apart. How do I adapt to being away from old friends and fitting into my college community?

Randy Ust
University of Mary
Bismarck, North Dakota

## PRACTICAL ANSWERS

### Get involved . . . broaden your horizons and talk to people.

Tracy Ust
St. Cloud State University
St. Cloud, Minnesota

I am an RA (Resident Advisor). In training, we learn how to deal with any situation that may arise in the residence halls and how to help college feel like home for students. One of my first duties is to hold a meeting where I meet my residents, and they meet one another. I share tips to help them reduce the stress of being in a new situation.

The most important thing I tell them is to get involved. Look for clubs or sports (at the intramural, club, or collegiate levels) that interest you. Try a couple of different things to see what you like most, but try not to overload yourself with activities and let your studies slack.

Another way to begin to fit in is to reach out to people. If you live in a dorm, keep your room doors open, go to planned activities together, and be friendly—others will be friendly back! On campus you can talk to people while you are in line at the cafeteria, get to know your chemistry lab partners, or introduce yourself to someone new in the student union. Broaden your horizons and talk to people different from yourself.

Remember that your old friends are no more than a mouse click or a phone call away. They'll be there for you any time. Make the effort to continue to be friends—it'll pay off. Finally, you can always ask your RA or other older students for advice. They will help you find ways to reduce stress and to take advantage of all the opportunities and people in your new community.

conducted by Robert M. Yerkes and John E. Dodson, shows that stress can be helpful or harmful, depending on how much you experience.

Being as physically and mentally healthy as possible is a crucial stress-management tool. You are making a difference in your health, recent studies say, by simply being in school. Scientists and researchers who study aging report that statistically, more education is linked to longer life. Some potential causes for this link may be that education teaches cause-and-effect thinking, helping people to plan ahead and make better choices for their health, and that educated people tend to be better equipped to delay gratification, reducing risky behavior.[1]

No one is able to make healthy choices and delay gratification all the time. However, you can pledge to do your best. Focus on your physical health through what you eat, how you exercise, how much you sleep, reviewing your vaccinations, and taking steps to stay safe. Focus on your

DELAY GRATIFICATION
To forgo an immediate pleasure or reward in order to gain a more substantial one later.

**KEY 10.1**

## Use the Holmes-Rahe scale to find your "stress score."

To find your current "stress score," add the values of the events that you experienced in the past year. The higher the number, the greater the stress. Scoring over 300 points puts you at high risk for developing a stress-related health problem. A score between 150 and 299 reduces your risk by 30%, and a score under 150 means that you have only a small chance of a problem.

| EVENT | VALUE | EVENT | VALUE |
|---|---|---|---|
| Death of spouse or partner | 100 | Son or daughter leaving home | 29 |
| Divorce | 73 | Trouble with in-laws | 29 |
| Marital separation | 65 | Outstanding personal achievement | 28 |
| Jail term | 63 | Spouse begins or stops work | 26 |
| Personal injury | 53 | Starting or finishing school | 26 |
| Marriage | 50 | Change in living conditions | 25 |
| Fired from work | 47 | Revision of personal habits | 24 |
| Marital reconciliation | 45 | Trouble with boss | 23 |
| Retirement | 45 | Change in work hours, conditions | 20 |
| Changes in family member's health | 44 | Change in residence | 20 |
| Pregnancy | 40 | Change in schools | 20 |
| Sex difficulties | 39 | Change in recreational habits | 19 |
| Addition to family | 39 | Change in religious activities | 19 |
| Business readjustment | 39 | Change in social activities | 18 |
| Change in financial status | 38 | Mortgage or loan under $10,000 | 17 |
| Death of a close friend | 37 | Change in sleeping habits | 16 |
| Change to different line of work | 36 | Change in # of family gatherings | 15 |
| Change in # of marital arguments | 35 | Change in eating habits | 15 |
| Mortgage or loan over $10,000 | 31 | Vacation | 13 |
| Foreclosure of mortgage or loan | 30 | Christmas season | 12 |
| Change in work responsibilities | 29 | Minor violation of the law | 11 |

*Source:* Reprinted from *Journal of Psychosomatic Research, 11*(2), T. H. Holmes and R. H. Rahe, "The Social Readjustment Rating Scale," 1967, with permission from Elsevier.

mental health by recognizing mental health problems related to stress or other causes, and understanding ways to get help.

## Food and Eating Habits

Making intelligent choices about what you eat can lead to more energy, better general health, and an improved quality of life. However, this is easier said than done, for two reasons in particular. One is that the *food environment* in which most people live—characterized by an overabundance of unhealthful food choices combined with the fact that the cheapest choices are often not the best—does not support people's efforts to choose well.[2]

The second reason is that college life can make it tough to eat right. Students spend hours sitting in class or studying and tend to eat on the run, build social events around food, and eat as a reaction to stress. Many new

**KEY 10.2** Stress levels can help or hinder performance.

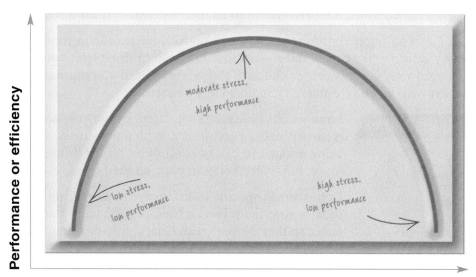

**Stress or anxiety**

(y-axis: **Performance or efficiency**)

moderate stress, high performance

low stress, low performance

high stress, low performance

*Source:* From *Your Maximum Mind* by Herbert Benson M.D., copyright © 1987 by Random House, Inc. Used by permission of Times Books, a division of Random House, Inc.

students find that the "freshman 15"—referring to 15 pounds that people say freshmen tend to gain in the first year of school—is an unpleasant reality.

## Take Practical Actions for Healthy Eating

The two key ideas for healthy eating are *balance* (varying your diet) and *moderation* (eating reasonable amounts). It can be tough, however, to eat in a balanced and moderate way when unbalanced and overly generous food choices are consistently available to you. To incorporate these concepts into your day-to-day life, break them down into specific actions like the following.

**Target your ideal weight.** Your college health clinic has charts of ideal weight ranges for men and women with different body builds and heights. You can also find this information on Internet sites such as the Centers for Disease Control, which has a calculator for body mass index, or BMI, at www.cdc.gov/nccdphp/dnpa/bmi/index.htm.

BODY MASS INDEX (BMI)

A number calculated from your weight and height, which provides a reliable indicator of body fatness.

**Vary what you eat.** Make sure your food choices go beyond one or two food groups. Focus especially on getting a variety of vegetables and fruits into your daily diet. The new government-generated "food pyramid" recommends amounts of food in particular food groups; you can find it at www.mypyramid.gov.

**Evaluate your eating habits.** Evaluate a day's food intake by writing down everything that you ate during the previous day and calculating the total calories. You may even want to log in a week's worth of eating. Then, go to MyPyramid.gov and create a food guide customized to your age, gender, and habitual level of physical activity. If your eating habits fall short of your ideal plan, make changes in your eating and exercise to move in a more healthful direction.

**Limit fat and cholesterol.** Watch the fat and cholesterol content of your food choices. When you cook with fats, use "good" fats like olive and canola oils. When you can, minimize your intake of fried foods and foods that contain *trans fats* (an unsaturated fat, usually produced when plant oils are partially hydrogenated, which has been shown to increase the risk of heart disease).

**Cut down on sugar consumption.** Try to limit foods that contain mostly empty calories, like candy and sugar soda. Try fresh or dried fruit when you need something sweet, or choose a sugar-free treat. If you normally eat dessert with lunch or dinner, try to do so less frequently.

**Limit alcohol consumption.** Don't be fooled—alcohol is surprisingly calorie-heavy. With a non-lite beer averaging about 150 calories and sweet mixed drinks even more, heavy drinkers can pack on the pounds quickly.

**Define small, specific tasks.** Pledge to stop drinking soda or to give up French fries. Record your plans on paper so they become real. Check in with yourself to note your progress.

**Reduce portion size.** A "serving" of cooked pasta is about one-half cup, for example, and cheese about 1.2 ounces. Read packaging carefully—that big bag of M & M's that you split with a friend, for example, is actually 10 servings, not 2! Many restaurants in the United States serve supersized portions that could feed two or three people. When you eat out, don't feel obligated to clear your plate. Take home what you don't finish, or ask for a half portion when you order.

**Snack smart.** Avoid high-fat, high-sugar foods. Choose snacks with fewer than 200 calories, such as a frozen fruit juice bar or a container of low-fat fruit yogurt.

**Plan your meals.** Try to eat at regular times and in a regular location. Attempt to minimize late-night eating sprees during study sessions. Avoid skipping meals, since it may make you more likely to overeat later.

**Identify "emotional triggers" for your eating.** If you eat to relieve stress or handle disappointment, try substituting a positive activity. If you are upset about a course, spend more time studying, talk with your instructor, or write in your journal.

**Get help.** If you need to lose weight, find a support group, such as Weight Watchers or an on-campus organization, that can help you stay on target.

**Set reasonable goals.** Losing weight and keeping it off will take time and patience. Start by aiming to lose 5% to 10% of your current weight; for example, if you weigh 200 pounds, your weight-loss goal is 10 to 20 pounds. Work toward your goal at a pace of approximately 1 to 2 pounds a week. When you reach it, set a new goal if you need to, or begin a maintenance program.

**Get your school to help students make better choices.** If it's tough to achieve your goals at your school, become an activist for a "healthy food environment." Advocate for menu improvement and more nutritious choices in the dining halls. Ask to have nutrition information posted in eating areas. See if vending machines can be updated with more healthful options and fewer junk foods.

## Understand the Effects of Obesity

The term *obese* refers to having a BMI of 30 or more (*overweight* refers to having a BMI of 25–29). Obesity is a serious problem in the United States, as these statistics indicate:

- The overweight and the obese make up the majority of the population, with 66% of the U.S. population currently falling into these two groups.[3]

- Between 1994 and 2004, the number of Americans considered obese rose from 23% to 32% of the population.[4]

Obesity is a major risk factor in the development of adult-onset diabetes, coronary heart disease, high blood pressure, stroke, cancer, and other illnesses. In addition, obese people often suffer social and employment discrimination and may find daily life difficult. Studies have shown that overweight job applicants tend to be reviewed more negatively during interviews, and that overweight employees tend to be paid less than normal-weight people in the same jobs and have a reduced chance of promotion.[5]

Use the BMI calculator to see if you would be considered either overweight or obese. If you would, consider taking specific actions to improve your health, such as consulting health professionals, enrolling in a reputable and reasonable weight-loss program, and incorporating a regular exercise plan into your life. Striving for the goal of reducing your BMI will improve not only your physical well-being but your mental health as well, and perhaps even your job prospects.

# Exercise

Being physically fit enhances your general health, increases your energy, and helps you cope with stress. During physical activity, the brain releases *endorphins*, chemical compounds that have a positive and calming effect on the body.

College athletes use daily exercise as a stress reliever. Larisa Kindell, a senior and co-captain of Wesleyan University's swimming team, credits her athletic routine with helping her balance her life. "If I didn't have swimming, a place to release my academic stress, I don't think I'd be as effective in the classroom or studying at night," she said. Swimming has taught her "discipline, time management, and motivation" and has contributed to her academic success.[6]

Always check with a physician before beginning an exercise program, and adjust your program to your physical needs and fitness level. If you don't currently exercise, walking daily is a good way to begin. If you exercise frequently and are already in good shape, you may prefer a more intense workout.

## Types of Exercise

There are three general categories of exercises. The type you choose depends on your exercise goals, available equipment, your time and fitness level, and other factors.

- *Cardiovascular training* strengthens your heart and lung capacity. Examples include running, swimming, in-line skating, aerobic dancing, and biking.

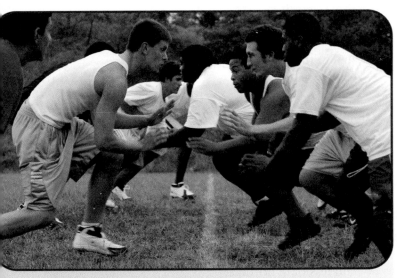

There are many ways to get exercise in college. Some students, like these, participate in sports teams, sports clubs, or intramurals for the social experience as well as the workout.

- *Strength training* strengthens different muscle groups. Examples include using weight machines and free weights and doing push-ups and abdominal crunches.
- *Flexibility training* increases muscle flexibility. Examples include stretching and yoga.

Some exercises, such as lifting weights or biking, fall primarily into one category. Others, like power yoga, combine elements of two or all three. For maximum benefit, try alternating exercise methods through *cross-training* (alternating types of exercise and combining elements from different types of exercise). For example, if you lift weights, use a stationary bike for cardiovascular work and build stretching into your workout.

## Make Exercise a Priority

Busy students often have trouble getting to the gym, even when there is a fully equipped athletic center on campus. Use these ideas to help make exercise a priority, even in the busiest weeks:

- Walk to classes and meetings. When you reach your building, use the stairs.
- Use your school's fitness facilities.
- Play team recreational sports at school or in your community.
- Take up swing or ballroom dancing.
- Find activities you can do outside of a club, such as running or pickup basketball.
- Work out with friends or family to combine socializing and exercise.

Being fit is a lifelong pursuit that is never "done." Furthermore, because your body is constantly changing, reevaluate your exercise program on a regular basis to maximize its benefits.

## Sleep

College students are often sleep deprived. While research indicates that students need eight to nine hours of sleep a night to function well, studies show that students average six to seven hours—and often get much less.[7] Inadequate sleep hinders your ability to concentrate, raises stress levels, and makes you more susceptible to illness. It can also increase your risk of auto accidents. According to Dr. Tracy Kuo at the Stanford Sleep Disorders Clinic, "A sleepy driver is just as dangerous as a drunk driver."[8]

Students, overwhelmed with responsibilities, often feel that they have no choice but to prioritize schoolwork over sleep. Michelle Feldman, a sophomore at Syracuse University, stays up regularly until 4:00 a.m. getting her reading and studying done. Fellow Syracuse student Brian Nelson, a junior aiming to complete a triple major, only manages two hours a night as he works to keep up with the 24 credits he's taking in one term.[9]

For the sake of your health and your GPA, find a way to get the sleep you need. Gauge your needs by first analyzing how you feel. If you are groggy in the morning, doze off during the day, or regularly need caffeine to make it through your classes, you may be sleep deprived. Sleep expert Gregg D. Jacobs has the following practical suggestions for improving sleep habits:[10]

- *Reduce consumption of alcohol and caffeine.* Caffeine may keep you awake, especially if you drink it late in the day. Alcohol causes you to sleep lightly, making you feel less rested when you awaken.

- *Exercise regularly.* Regular exercise, especially in the afternoon or early evening, promotes sleep.

- *Take naps.* Studies have shown that taking short afternoon naps can reduce the effects of sleep deprivation.

- *Be consistent.* Try to establish somewhat regular times to wake up and go to bed.

- *Complete tasks an hour or so before sleep.* Give yourself a chance to wind down.

- *Establish a comfortable sleeping environment.* Wear something comfortable, turn down the lights, and keep the room cool. Use earplugs, soft music, or a white noise machine if you're dealing with outside distractions.

Sleep is crucial for both stress reduction and normal development. The *Multiple Intelligence Strategies* table on page 336 presents different strategies for managing the stress of writing a final paper in a human development course, many of which involve time-management tools that will help a student avoid writing the whole paper during a last-minute all-nighter.

## Review Your Immunizations

Immunizations are not just for kids. Adults often need them to prevent diseases in particular circumstances or because they didn't receive a full course of shots as children. Following is immunization information from the Centers for Disease Control (CDC) that may prevent major illness or literally save your life. If you think you need any of these vaccines, check with your doctor or the college health service:[11]

- The CDC recommends that college freshmen living in dormitories receive the *meningococcal meningitis* vaccine. This vaccine prevents the spread of a bacterial infection that can quickly kill even healthy young adults and often leaves survivors with permanent, serious disabilities. Meningococcal bacteria are spread through direct contact (such as sharing a glass) or indirect contact (such as sneezing) with infected individuals. Outbreaks are linked to close living situations, such as those common in college dormitories and military barracks.

- For women under the age of 26, the new *human papillomavirus* (HPV) vaccine is recommended. Three doses are required within a six-month period. The vaccine prevents HPV infections, which have been linked to cervical cancer, and are most effective when the woman has never been exposed to HPV. The vaccine is *not* recommended during pregnancy.

- A *tetanus booster* is recommended every 10 years to protect you from bacterial infections related to certain wounds. When untreated, the toxin in tetanus can kill a person.

- Three shots to prevent *hepatitis B* and two shots to prevent *hepatitis A* (both blood diseases) are recommended in childhood. Vaccinations are recommended in college if you have not been immunized. Homosexuals, intravenous drug users, and some health care professionals are at increased risk.

- The *chicken pox* vaccine is recommended for any adult who did not have this illness as a child and who risks exposure. Chicken pox in adults can be severe and painful. Adults who have had chicken pox can also get a secondary outbreak of the virus later in life, which is called "shingles."

- Although it used to be given only to adults who are over 65 or who have weak immune systems, the *influenza* vaccine is now recommended for many adults and children. It is available each year for a few months, starting around mid-October.

- Adults over 65 years of age, and younger adults with chronic illnesses like diabetes, chronic pulmonary disease, or compromised immune systems should get the *pneumococcal polysaccharide* vaccine. This vaccine prevents a serious, often fatal, bacterial cause of pneumonia, bloodstream infections, and meningitis.

- The *measles-mumps-rubella* (MMR) vaccine is recommended for unvaccinated adults born after 1956 as well as adults who received vaccinations between 1963 and 1967.

A common illness, not protected by immunization, is *mononucleosis*. "Mono" is caused by a virus passed in saliva and is related to kissing and sharing drinking cups. Major symptoms—which can last for a few days or a few months—are fever, sore throat, swollen lymph glands, and fatigue. The only treatment is rest, fluids, and a balanced diet. Protect yourself by being careful in your relationships with friends, family, and roommates.

## Stay Safe

© Damien Richard—
Fotolia.com

Staying safe is another part of staying well and reducing stress. Crime is a reality on campus as it is in any community. Alcohol- and drug-related offenses may occur more frequently than other crimes on campus. By law, colleges are required to report crime statistics yearly. Check www. securityoncampus.org for a link to statistics by school and for other helpful information.

Making intelligent choices is a crucial part of staying safe. Take the following practical measures to prevent incidents that jeopardize your well-being.

KEYS TO SUCCESS

**320**

**Be aware of safety issues.** Every college has its particular issues—problematic areas of the campus, particular celebrations that get out of hand, bad habits such as students propping open security doors. With awareness, you can steer clear of problems and even work to improve them.

**Avoid situations that present clear dangers.** Don't walk or exercise alone at night, especially in isolated areas. Don't work or study alone in a building. If a person looks suspicious, contact someone who can help.

**Avoid drugs or overuse of alcohol.** Anything that impairs judgment makes you vulnerable to assault. Avoid driving while impaired or riding with someone who has taken drugs or alcohol.

**Avoid people who make you uneasy.** If a fellow student gives you bad feelings, avoid situations that place you alone together. Speak to an instructor if you feel threatened.

**Be cautious about giving out personal information online.** If you have a MySpace or Facebook page, be careful about the text and photos you post. If you feel that someone is harassing you by e-mail or IM, contact an advisor or counselor who can help you address the problem.

It is not enough to have a healthy body. Your well-being also depends on a healthy mind.

## Recognize Mental Health Problems

Staying positive about who you are, making hopeful plans for the future, and building resilience to cope with setbacks will all help you target

# Find Health Resources

*get practical!*

What resources does your school offer to support your efforts to stay healthy? Write down names, locations, phone numbers, hours, and any other pertinent information for the following:

- Free counseling offered to students: _____

  _____

- Exercise facility: _____

  _____

- Other resource: _____

  _____

Finally, if you don't already have plans to work out there, make a trip to the exercise facility of your choice this week and see what it has to offer.

positive mental health. However, some people experience emotional disorders that make it more difficult than usual to cope with life's stressful situations. If you recognize yourself in any of the following descriptions, take practical steps to improve your health. Most student health centers and campus counseling centers provide both medical and psychological help or referrals for students with emotional disorders.

## Depression

Almost everyone has experienced sadness after setbacks such as the end of a relationship or failing a course. However, as many as 10% of Americans will experience a major depression, going beyond temporary blues, at some point in their lives. A *depressive disorder* is an illness, not a mental state that can be escaped by trying to "snap out of it." It is also fairly common among college students; the American Psychological Association reports that in a recent survey, nearly half of all college students reported that they had experienced a level of depression that affected their ability to function, and almost 15% had depressive episodes that fulfilled the clinical criteria for a diagnosis of depression.[12]

Depression is "an illness that involves the body, mood, and thoughts."[13] This illness requires a medical evaluation and is treatable. Depression can have a genetic, psychological, physiological, or environmental cause, or a combination. Key 10.3 shows possible causes of depression as well as some typical symptoms.

If you recognize some of these symptoms in yourself, seek evaluation from a professional who can help you get the treatment you need. Most student health centers and campus counseling centers provide both medical and psychological help or referrals for students with emotional disorders. For some people, adequate sleep, a regular exercise program, a healthy diet, and the passage of time are enough to lessen stress and ease the disorder.

 KEY 10.3

## Know the causes and symptoms of depression.

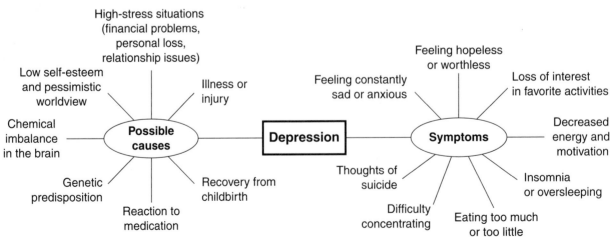

*Source: Depression,* National Institutes of Health publication 02-3561, National Institutes of Health, 2002.

For others, medication is important. Either way, helpful coping strategies include the following:[14]

- Do your best and let go of unreasonable expectations.
- Try to be with others as much as possible rather than alone.
- Don't expect your mood to change right away; feeling better takes time.
- Try to avoid making major life decisions until your condition improves.
- Seek out activities that help you feel better.
- Let family and friends help you.

At its worst, depression can lead to suicide. SAVE (Suicide Awareness Voices of Education) lists these suicide warning signs:[15]

- Statements about hopelessness or worthlessness: "The world would be better off without me."
- Loss of interest in people, things, or activities.
- Preoccupation with suicide or death.
- Making final arrangements such as visiting or calling family and friends and giving things away.
- Sudden sense of happiness or calm. (A decision to commit suicide often brings a sense of relief that convinces others that the person "seemed to be on an upswing.")

If you recognize these symptoms in someone you know, begin talking with the person about his or her feelings. Then do everything you can to convince the individual to see a doctor or mental health professional. Don't keep your concerns a secret; sound an alarm that may save a life. If you recognize these symptoms in yourself, know that you can find help if you reach out.

## Eating Disorders

Millions of people develop serious and sometimes life-threatening eating disorders every year, including anorexia nervosa, bulimia, and binge eating disorder. Because these disorders are relatively common on college campuses, student health and counseling centers generally offer medical and psychological help, including referrals to trained specialists.[16]

**Anorexia nervosa.** Anorexia nervosa is the most rare of the eating disorders. Recent research found that 0.9% of women and 0.3% of men report having anorexia nervosa at some point during their lifetime. People with anorexia nervosa restrict their eating and become dangerously underweight. They may also engage in overexercising, vomiting, and abuse of diuretics and laxatives. Anorexia-induced starvation may cause loss of menstrual periods in women and impotence in men. Other effects of anorexia nervosa include hair loss, loss of cognitive functioning, organ and bone damage, heart damage, and death. The most effective treatments for anorexia nervosa typically involve individual psychotherapy, medical interventions to restore weight, and sometimes pharmacological treatment. Anorexia nervosa tends to run in families and is often linked to characteristics such as excessive anxiety and perfectionism.

**Bulimia nervosa.** In the general population, 1.5% of women and 0.5% of men report having bulimia nervosa sometime during their lifetime. People with bulimia engage in "binge episodes," which involve eating excessive amounts of foods and feeling out of control. Following the binge, the person feels remorseful and attempts to purge the calories through self-induced vomiting, laxative abuse, excessive exercise, or fasting. Because these purging methods are largely ineffective, people with bulimia nervosa are usually normal weight or slightly overweight. Negative effects of bulimia can include tooth enamel erosion, damage to the esophagus and digestive tract, and electrolyte imbalance, which can lead to heart failure. Bulimia nervosa is also thought to have a genetic component, although research suggests that it can be "contagious" when young women living together begin to emulate each other's behavior.

**Binge eating disorder.** Binge eating disorder is the most common of the eating disorders, affecting 3.5% of women and 2% of men at some point during their lives. People with binge eating disorder eat large amounts of food and feel out of control, similar to those with bulimia, but they do not purge after a binge episode. They also tend to eat unusually fast, eat in secret, eat until they feel uncomfortably full, and feel ashamed of their eating behavior. Individuals with binge eating disorder are typically overweight and are more likely to struggle with other psychiatric illnesses than overweight people who do not binge-eat. Binge eaters may suffer from health problems associated with obesity.

The stresses of college lead some students to experiment with alcohol, tobacco, and other potentially addictive substances. Although these substances may alleviate stress temporarily, they have potentially serious consequences.

# How Can You Make Effective Decisions About Alcohol, Tobacco, and Drugs?

Abusing alcohol, tobacco, and drugs adds significantly to stress levels and can cause financial struggles, emotional traumas, family and financial upheaval, health problems, and even death. As you read the information in this section, think about the effects of your actions on yourself and others, and continually look for new and better ways to make positive, life-affirming choices.

## Alcohol

Alcohol is a depressant that slows vital body functions and is the most frequently abused drug on campus. Even a few drinks affect thinking and muscle coordination. Heavy drinking can damage the liver, the digestive system, and brain cells and can impair the central nervous system. Prolonged use also leads to addiction, making it seem impossible to quit. In addition, alcohol contributes to the deaths of 100,000 people every year through both alcohol-related illnesses and accidents involving drunk drivers.[17]

Of all alcohol consumption, binge drinking is associated with the greatest problems, and is consistently an issue on college campuses. Here are statistics from recent surveys:

- Of respondents 18–25 years of age, 41.9% reported binge drinking in the month before the National Survey on Drug Use and Health

ADDICTION
The compulsive need for a habit-forming substance.

BINGE DRINKING
Having five or more drinks (for men) or four or more (for women) at one sitting

(NSDUH). Of respondents 26–34 years of age, 32.9% reported binge drinking in the month before the survey.[18]

- In one survey, 8 of 10 students who do not binge-drink reported experiencing such "secondhand effects" as vandalism, sexual assault or unwanted sexual advances, or interrupted sleep or study.[19]

- Students who binge-drink are more likely to miss classes or work, perform poorly in class and on academic projects, experience physical problems (memory loss, headache, stomach issues), become depressed, and engage in unplanned or unsafe sexual activity.[20]

From what Darra Clark, a freshman at a large university in the Southwest, has seen, it is not possible to be a successful student if you drink too much. You can't do well in school and have friends if you "get drunk and stoned out of your gourd every night," she explains. "I think that the whole drinking scene is probably the thing I've found most appalling about college (our student handbook specifically outlaws beer funnels, for example). The problem, of course, is that drinking becomes a really hard behavior to regulate. . . . Drinking and drugs have done some awful things to some of the kids I've seen around here."[21]

If you drink, think carefully about the effects on your health, safety, and academic performance. The *Get Analytical* exercise on page 329, a self-test, will help you analyze your habits. If you think you have a problem, use your creative and practical thinking skills to come up with a viable solution. The information on addiction on pages 330–331 introduces possible options.

## Tobacco

The NSDUH found that nearly 30.6% of full-time college students reported smoking at least once in the month before they were surveyed, and 42.7% of students attending less than full-time had smoked at least once within the previous month.[22]

When people smoke they inhale nicotine, a highly addictive drug found in all tobacco products. Nicotine's immediate effects may include an increase in blood pressure and heart rate, sweating, and throat irritation. Long-term effects may include the following:

- High blood pressure

- Bronchitis and emphysema

- Stomach ulcers

- Heart disease

- For pregnant women, increased risk of infants with low birth weight, premature births, or stillbirths

- Damage to the cells that line the air sacs of the lungs, potentially leading to lung cancer or mouth, throat, and other cancers (lung cancer causes more deaths in the United States than any other type of cancer)[23]

SECONDHAND SMOKE

Smoke in the air exhaled by smokers or given off by cigarettes, cigars, or pipes.

In recent years, the health dangers of (secondhand smoke) have been recognized. Simply being around smokers on a regular basis causes about 3,000 lung cancer deaths per year in nonsmokers.[24] This awareness has led many colleges (and local jurisdictions) to ban smoking in classrooms and other public spaces and even in dorm rooms. More and more companies, aware of the risk, are banning smoking in the workplace or even refusing to hire people who smoke.[25]

If you want to quit smoking, your best bet may be to combine medicine with emotional support and habit change. Practical suggestions include these strategies:[26]

- Try a nicotine replacement strategy such as a patch or nicotine gum, and be sure to use it consistently.

- Get support and encouragement from a health care provider, a telephone-based support program such as the American Cancer Society's Quitline, a support group such as Nicotine Anonymous, and friends and family.

- Avoid situations that increase your desire to smoke, such as places or events where other smokers gather.

- Find other ways to lower stress and occupy your hands, such as exercise or a hobby you enjoy.

- Set goals. Set a quit date and tell friends and family. Make and keep medical appointments.

The positive effects of quitting—increased life expectancy, lung capacity, and energy—may inspire any smoker to consider making a lifestyle change. Quitting provides financial benefits as well, even if you quit later in life. *MSN Money* reports that "a 40-year-old pack-a-day smoker who quits and puts the savings into a 401(k) earning 9% a year will have $250,000 by age 70." In addition, there are savings connected to health care costs, cleaning costs (home and car), dental costs, and insurance costs (health and life insurance agencies charge smokers a higher rate).[27]

In order to assess the level of your potential addiction, you may want to take the self-test in the *Get Analytical* exercise on page 329, replacing the words "alcohol" or "drugs" with "cigarettes" or "smoking." Think about your results, weigh your options, and make a responsible choice.

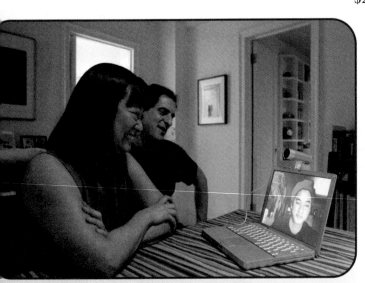

Connecting with family at home can help to alleviate stress, reinforce values, and renew support systems. This student checks in with his parents using online video chat software.

## Drugs

Illicit drug use is a perennial problem on college campuses. The NSDUH reports that more than 37% of college students surveyed had used illicit drugs in the year prior to the survey.[28] College students may use drugs to relieve stress, to be accepted by peers, or just to try something new.

In most cases, the negative consequences of drug use outweigh any temporary high. Drug use violates federal, state, and local laws, and you may be arrested, tried, and imprisoned for possessing even a small amount of drugs. You can jeopardize your reputation, your student status, and your ability to get a job if you are caught using drugs or if drug use impairs your performance. Finally, long-term drug use can damage your body and mind. Key 10.4 has comprehensive information about the most commonly used illicit drugs.

KEY 10.4

Drugs have potent effects on the user.

| DRUG | DRUG CATEGORY | USERS MAY FEEL ... | POTENTIAL PHYSICAL EFFECTS | DANGER OF DEPENDENCE |
|---|---|---|---|---|
| **Cocaine** (also called *coke, blow, snow*) and **crack cocaine** (also called *crack* or *rock*) | Stimulant | Alert, stimulated, excited, energetic, confident | Nervousness, mood swings, sexual problems, stroke or convulsions, psychoses, paranoia, coma at large doses | Strong |
| **Alcohol** | Depressant | Sedated, relaxed, loose | Impaired brain function, impaired reflexes and judgment, cirrhosis, impaired blood production, greater risk of cancer, heart attack, and stroke | Strong with regular, heavy use |
| **Marijuana and hashish** (also called *pot, weed, herb*) | Cannabinol | Euphoric, mellow, little sensation of time, paranoid | Impaired judgment and coordination, bronchitis and asthma, lung and throat cancers, anxiety, lack of energy and motivation, hormone and fertility problems | Moderate |
| **Heroin** (also called *smack, dope, horse*) and **codeine** | Opiate | Warm, relaxed, without pain, without anxiety | Infection of organs, inflammation of the heart, convulsions, abscesses, risk of needle-transmitted diseases such as hepatitis and HIV | Strong, with heavy use |
| **Lysergic acid diethylamide (LSD)** (also called *acid, blotter, trips*) | Hallucinogen | Heightened sensual perception, hallucinations, distortions of sight and sound, little sense of time | Impaired brain function, paranoia, agitation and confusion, flashbacks | Insubstantial |
| **Hallucinogenic mushrooms** (also called *shrooms, magic mushrooms*) | Hallucinogen | Strong emotions, hallucinations, distortions of sight and sound, "out of body" experience | Paranoia, agitation, poisoning | Insubstantial |
| **Glue, aerosols** (also called *whippets, poppers, rush*) | Inhalants | Giddy, light-headed, dizzy, excited | Damage to brain, liver, lungs, and kidneys; suffocation; heart failure | Insubstantial |

*(continued)*

KEY 10.4

## Continued

| DRUG | DRUG CATEGORY | USERS MAY FEEL . . . | POTENTIAL PHYSICAL EFFECTS | DANGER OF DEPENDENCE |
|---|---|---|---|---|
| **Ecstasy** *(also called X, XTC, vitamin E)* | Stimulant | Heightened sensual perception, relaxed, clear, fearless | Fatigue, anxiety, depression, heart arrhythmia, hyperthermia from lack of fluid intake during use | Insubstantial |
| **Ephedrine** *(also called chi powder, zest)* | Stimulant | Energetic | Anxiety, elevated blood pressure, heart palpitations, memory loss, stroke, psychosis, insomnia | Strong |
| **Gamma hydroxyl butyrate (GHB)** *(also called G, liquid ecstasy, goop)* | Depressant | Uninhibited, relaxed, euphoric | Anxiety, vertigo, increased heart rate, delirium, agitation | Strong |
| **Ketamine** *(also called K, Special K, vitamin K)* | Anesthetic | Dreamy, floating, having an "out of body" sensation, numb | Neuroses, disruptions in consciousness, reduced ability to move | Strong |
| **OxyContin** *(also called Oxy, OC, legal heroin)* | Analgesic (containing opiate) | Relaxed, detached, without pain or anxiety | Overdose death can result when users ingest or inhale crushed time-release pills, or take them in conjunction with alcohol or narcotics | Moderate, with long-term use |
| **Anabolic steroids** *(also called roids, juice, hype)* | Steroid | Increased muscle strength and physical performance, energetic | Stunted growth, mood swings, male-pattern baldness, breast development (in men) or body hair development (in women), mood swings, liver damage, insomnia, aggression, irritability | Insubstantial |
| **Methamphetamine** *(also called meth, speed, crank)* | Stimulant | Euphoric, confident, alert, energetic | Seizures, heart attack, strokes, vein damage (if injected), sleeplessness, hallucinations, high blood pressure, paranoia, psychoses, depression, anxiety, loss of appetite | Strong, especially if taken by smoking |

*Source:* "Drug Facts," n.d., SafetyFirst, Drug Policy Alliance (www.safety1st.org/drugfacts.html).

You are responsible for analyzing the potential consequences of what you introduce into your body. Ask questions like the following:

- Why do I want to do this?
- Am I taking drugs to escape from other problems?
- What positive and negative effects might my behavior have?
- Why do others want me to take drugs, and what do I really think of these people?
- How would my drug use affect the people in my life?

# Evaluate Your Substance Use

## GET ANALYTICAL!

Even one yes answer may indicate a need to look carefully at your habits. Three or more yes answers indicates that you may benefit from discussing your use with a counselor.

## WITHIN THE LAST YEAR:

(Y) (N) 1. Have you tried to stop drinking or taking drugs but found that you couldn't do so for long?

(Y) (N) 2. Do you get tired of people telling you they're concerned about your drinking or drug use?

(Y) (N) 3. Have you felt guilty about your drinking or drug use?

(Y) (N) 4. Have you felt that you needed a drink or drugs in the morning— as an "eye-opener"—in order to cope with a hangover?

(Y) (N) 5. Do you drink or use drugs alone?

(Y) (N) 6. Do you drink or use drugs every day?

(Y) (N) 7. Have you found yourself regularly thinking or saying, "I need" a drink or any type of drug?

(Y) (N) 8. Have you lied about or concealed your drinking or drug use?

(Y) (N) 9. Do you drink or use drugs to escape worries, problems, mistakes, or shyness?

(Y) (N) 10. Do you find you need increasingly larger amounts of drugs or alcohol in order to achieve a desired effect?

(Y) (N) 11. Have you forgotten what happened while drinking or using drugs because you had a blackout?

(Y) (N) 12. Have you been surprised by how much you were using alcohol or drugs?

(Y) (N) 13. Have you spent a lot of time, energy, and/or money getting alcohol or drugs?

(continued)

(Y) (N) 14. Has your drinking or drug use caused you to neglect friends, your partner, your children, or other family members, or caused other problems at home?

(Y) (N) 15. Have you gotten into an argument or a fight that was alcohol or drug related?

(Y) (N) 16. Has your drinking or drug use caused you to miss class, fail a test, or ignore schoolwork?

(Y) (N) 17. Have you rejected planned social events in favor of drinking or using drugs?

(Y) (N) 18. Have you been choosing to drink or use drugs instead of performing other activities or hobbies you used to enjoy?

(Y) (N) 19. Has your drinking or drug use affected your efficiency on the job or caused you to fail to show up at work?

(Y) (N) 20. Have you continued to drink or use drugs despite any physical problems or health risks that your use has caused or made worse?

(Y) (N) 21. Have you driven a car or performed any other potentially dangerous tasks while under the influence of alcohol or drugs?

(Y) (N) 22. Have you had a drug- or alcohol-related legal problem or arrest (possession, use, disorderly conduct, driving while intoxicated, etc.)?

*Source:* Adapted from the Criteria for Substance Dependence and Criteria for Substance Abuse in the *Diagnostic and Statistical Manual of Mental Disorders*, 4th ed., published by the American Psychiatric Association, Washington, DC, 1994; and from materials titled "Are You an Alcoholic?" developed by Johns Hopkins University.

Use the self-test to assess your relationship with drugs. If you believe you have a problem, read the following section on steps that can help you get your life back on track.

## Facing Addiction

People with addictions have lost control. If you think you may be addicted, take the initiative to seek help. Because substances often cause physical and chemical changes and psychological dependence, habits are tough to break and quitting may involve a painful withdrawal. Asking for help isn't an admission of failure but a courageous move to reclaim your life.

Even one yes answer on the self-test may indicate that you need to evaluate your alcohol or drug use and to monitor it more carefully. If you answered yes to three or more questions, you may benefit from talking to a professional about your use and the problems it may be causing.

Working through substance-abuse problems can lead to restored health and self-respect. Helpful resources like the following can help you generate options and develop practical plans for recovery:

- *Counseling and medical care.* You can find help from school-based, private, government-sponsored, or workplace-sponsored resources. Ask your school's counseling or health center, your personal physician, or a local hospital for a referral.

- *Detoxification ("detox") centers.* If you have a severe addiction, you may need a controlled environment where you can separate yourself completely from drugs or alcohol.

- *Support groups.* Alcoholics Anonymous (AA) is the premier support group for alcoholics. AA has led to other support groups for addicts, such as Overeaters Anonymous (OA) and Narcotics Anonymous (NA). Many schools have AA, NA, or other group sessions on campus.

Another important aspect of both physical and mental health involves being comfortable with your sexuality and making wise sexual decisions. Choosing birth control and avoiding sexually transmitted infections have short- and long-term consequences for the rest of your life.

# How Can You Make Effective Decisions About Sex?

What sexuality means to you and the role it plays in your life are your own business. However, the physical act of sex goes beyond the private realm. Individual sexual conduct can result in an unexpected pregnancy or in contracting or passing on a *sexually transmitted infection (STI)*. These consequences affect everyone involved in the sexual act and, often, their families as well.

Your self-respect depends on making choices that maintain health and safety—yours as well as those of the person with whom you are involved. Analyze sexual issues carefully, weighing the positive and negative effects of your choices. Ask questions like the following:

- Is this what I really want? Does it fit with my values?

- Do I feel ready or do I feel pressured? Does this choice cause stress for me?

- Is this the right person/moment/situation? Does my partner truly care for me and not just for what we might be doing? Will this enhance or damage our emotional relationship?

- Do I have what I need to prevent pregnancy and exposure to STIs? If not, is having unprotected sex worth the risk?

## Birth Control

Using birth control is a choice, and it is not for everyone. For some, using any kind of birth control goes against religious or personal beliefs. Others may want to have children. Many sexually active people, however, choose one or more methods of birth control.

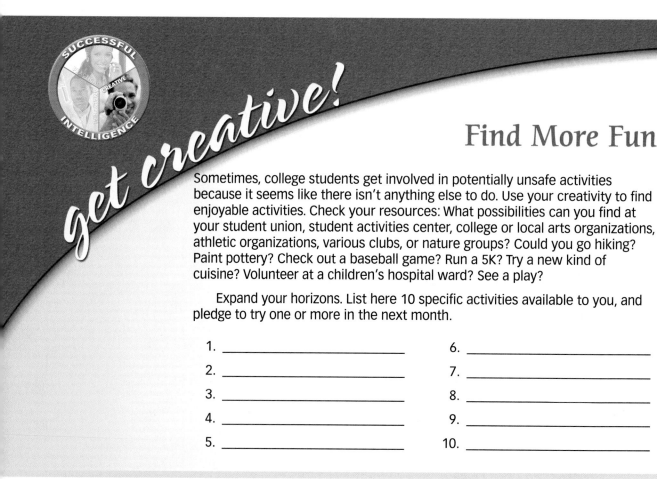

## get creative!

### Find More Fun

Sometimes, college students get involved in potentially unsafe activities because it seems like there isn't anything else to do. Use your creativity to find enjoyable activities. Check your resources: What possibilities can you find at your student union, student activities center, college or local arts organizations, athletic organizations, various clubs, or nature groups? Could you go hiking? Paint pottery? Check out a baseball game? Run a 5K? Try a new kind of cuisine? Volunteer at a children's hospital ward? See a play?

Expand your horizons. List here 10 specific activities available to you, and pledge to try one or more in the next month.

1. _____
2. _____
3. _____
4. _____
5. _____

6. _____
7. _____
8. _____
9. _____
10. _____

Evaluate the pros and cons of each birth control option for yourself and your partner. Consider cost, ease of use, reliability, comfort, and protection against STIs. Communicate with your partner and together make a choice that is comfortable for both of you. For more information, check your library, the Internet, or a bookstore; talk to your doctor; or ask a counselor at the student health center. Key 10.5 on page 334 describes established methods, with effectiveness percentages and STI prevention based on proper and regular use.

## Sexually Transmitted Infections

STIs spread through sexual contact (intercourse or other sexual activity that involves contact with the genitals). All are highly contagious. The only birth control methods that offer protection are the male and female condoms (latex or polyurethane only), which prevent skin-to-skin contact. Most STIs can also spread to infants of infected mothers during birth. Have a doctor examine any irregularity or discomfort as soon as you detect it. Key 10.6 on page 334 describes common STIs.

### AIDS and HIV

The most serious STI is AIDS (acquired immunodeficiency syndrome), which is caused by the human immunodeficiency virus (HIV). Not everyone who tests positive for HIV will develop AIDS, but AIDS has no cure and results in eventual death. Key 10.7 shows some current statistics on AIDS.

KEY 10.5

# Make an educated decision about birth control.

| METHOD | APPROXIMATE EFFECTIVENESS | PREVENTS STIs? | DESCRIPTION |
|---|---|---|---|
| **Abstinence** | 100% | Only if no sexual activity occurs | Just saying no. No intercourse means no risk of pregnancy. However, alternative modes of sexual activity can still spread STIs. |
| **Condom** | 85% (95% with spermicide) | Yes, if made of latex | A sheath that fits over the penis and prevents sperm from entering the vagina. |
| **Diaphragm, cervical cap, or shield** | 85% | No | A bendable rubber cap that fits over the cervix and pelvic bone inside the vagina (the cervical cap and shield are smaller and fit over the cervix only). The diaphragm and cervical cap must be fitted initially by a gynecologist. All must be used with a spermicide. |
| **Oral contraceptives ("the Pill")** | 99% with perfect use, 92% for typical users | No | A dosage of hormones taken daily by a woman, preventing the ovaries from releasing eggs. Side effects can include headache, weight gain, and increased chances of blood clotting. Various brands and dosages; must be prescribed by a gynecologist. |
| **Injectable contraceptives (Depo-Provera)** | 97% | No | An injection that a woman must receive from a doctor every few months. Possible side effects may resemble those of oral contraceptives. |
| **Vaginal ring (NuvaRing)** | 92% | No | A ring inserted into the vagina that releases hormones. Must be replaced monthly. Possible side effects may resemble those of oral contraceptives. |
| **Spermicidal foams, jellies, inserts** | 71% if used alone | No | Usually used with diaphragms or condoms to enhance effectiveness, they have an ingredient that kills sperm cells (but not STIs). They stay effective for a limited period of time after insertion. |
| **Intrauterine device (IUD)** | 99% | No | A small coil of wire inserted into the uterus by a gynecologist (who must also remove it). Prevents fertilized eggs from implanting in the uterine wall. May or may not have a hormone component. Possible side effects include increased or abnormal bleeding. |
| **Tubal ligation** | Nearly 100% | No | Surgery for women that cuts and ties the fallopian tubes, preventing eggs from traveling to the uterus. Difficult and expensive to reverse. Recommended for those who do not want any, or any more, children. |
| **Vasectomy** | Nearly 100% | No | Surgery for men that blocks the tube that delivers sperm to the penis. Like tubal ligation, difficult to reverse and only recommended for those who don't want any, or any more, children. |
| **Rhythm method** | Variable | No | Abstaining from intercourse during the ovulation segment of the woman's menstrual cycle. Can be difficult to time and may not account for cycle irregularities. |
| **Withdrawal** | Variable | No | Pulling the penis out of the vagina before ejaculation. Unreliable, because some sperm can escape in the fluid released prior to ejaculation. Dependent on a controlled partner. |

*Source:* "Birth Control," 2005, MayoClinic.com (www.mayoclinic.com/health/birth-control/BI99999).

**KEY 10.6** To stay safe, know these facts about sexually transmitted infections.

| DISEASE | SYMPTOMS | HEALTH PROBLEMS IF UNTREATED | TREATMENTS |
|---------|----------|------------------------------|------------|
| **Chlamydia** | Discharge, painful urination, swollen or painful joints, change in menstrual periods for women | Can cause pelvic inflammatory disease (PID) in women, which can lead to sterility or ectopic pregnancies; infection; miscarriage or premature birth. | Curable with full course of antibiotics; avoid sex until treatment is complete. |
| **Gonorrhea** | Discharge, burning while urinating | Can cause PID, swelling of testicles and penis, arthritis, skin problems, infections. | Usually curable with antibiotics; however, certain strains are becoming resistant to medication. |
| **Genital herpes** | Blisterlike itchy sores in the genital area, headache, fever, chills | Symptoms may subside and then reoccur, often in response to high stress levels; carriers can transmit the virus even when it is dormant. | No cure; some medications, such as Acyclovir, reduce and help heal the sores and may shorten recurring outbreaks. |
| **Syphilis** | A genital sore lasting one to five weeks, followed by a rash, fatigue, fever, sore throat, headaches, swollen glands | If it lasts over four years, it can cause blindness, destruction of bone, insanity, or heart failure; can cause death or deformity of a child born to an infected woman. | Curable with full course of antibiotics. |
| **Human Papilloma Virus (HPV, or genital warts)** | Genital itching and irritation, small clusters of warts | Can increase risk of cervical cancer in women; virus may remain in body and cause recurrences even when warts are removed. | Treatable with drugs applied to warts or various kinds of wart removal surgery. Vaccine (Gardasil) newly available; most effective when given to women before exposure to HPV. |
| **Hepatitis B** | Fatigue, poor appetite, vomiting, jaundice, hives | Some carriers will have few symptoms; others may develop chronic liver disease that may lead to other diseases of the liver. | No cure; some will recover, some will not. Bed rest may help ease symptoms. Vaccine is available. |

**KEY 10.7**

## AIDS and HIV continue to spread in the United States.

- At the end of 2003, it was estimated that more than 1 million persons were living with HIV/AIDS in the U.S., with more than 20% unaware of the infection and having no formal diagnosis.

- The year 2005 brought more than 45,000 newly diagnosed AIDS patients. About 7,000 of these were individuals under the age of 30.

- Approximately 58% of newly infected men in 2005 contracted HIV from male-to-male sexual contact, 18% through injection drug use, and 16% through high-risk heterosexual contact.

- Approximately 71% of newly infected women in 2005 contracted HIV through high-risk heterosexual contact, and 28% through injection drug use.

- At the end of 2005, it was estimated that more than 450,000 persons in the U.S. were living with AIDS.

*Source:* "Basic Statistics," 2005, Centers for Disease Control and Prevention (www.cdc.gov/hiv/topics/surveillance/basic.htm).

HIV can lie undetected in the body for up to 10 years before surfacing, and a carrier can spread it during that time. Medical science continues to develop drugs to combat AIDS and its related illnesses. The drugs can cause severe side effects, however, and none are cures.

HIV is transmitted through two types of bodily fluids: fluids associated with sex (semen and vaginal fluids) and blood. People have acquired HIV through sexual relations, by sharing hypodermic needles for drug use, and by receiving infected blood transfusions. You cannot become infected unless one of those fluids is involved. Therefore, it is unlikely you can contract HIV from toilet seats, hugging, kissing, or sharing a glass.

## Protecting Yourself

The best defense against AIDS or other STIs is not having sex or being in a long-term monogamous relationship with someone who has tested negative. Condoms are the next best choice. The U.S. Department of Health and Human Services reports: *"There's absolutely no guarantee even when you use a condom.* But most experts believe that the risk of getting AIDS and other sexually transmitted diseases can be greatly reduced if a condom is used properly. . . . Sex with condoms *isn't* totally 'safe sex,' but it *is* 'less risky' sex."[29]

Always use a latex condom, because natural skin condoms may let the virus pass through. Avoid petroleum jelly, which can destroy latex. Be wary of "safe sex fatigue," which leads young and healthy people to be less vigilant about using condoms for every sexual encounter. Although some people dislike using condoms, it's a small price to pay for preserving your life.

To be safe, have an HIV test done at your doctor's office or at a government-sponsored clinic. Your school's health department may also administer HIV tests, and home HIV tests are available over the counter. Consider requiring that any sexual partner be tested as well. If you are infected, first inform all sexual partners and seek medical assistance. Then, contact support organizations in your area or call the National AIDS Hotline at 1-800-342-AIDS.

# Successful Intelligence Wrap-Up

College pressures can be enormous—but successfully intelligent thinking gives you the power to manage your wellness in the face of those pressures. If you do your best to make choices that have a positive impact, you have a strong chance of enjoying physical and mental health over the long haul. Here's how you have built skills in chapter 10:

## Analytical

You examined the effect that stress has on performance. You analyzed how eating, exercise, and sleeping patterns can affect your health. You used the *Get Analytical* exercise to examine your relationship with drugs, alcohol, and tobacco. You explored the pros and cons of choices regarding substances and sex.

# MULTIPLE INTELLIGENCE STRATEGIES
## FOR STRESS MANAGEMENT

**APPLY DIFFERENT INTELLIGENCES TO REDUCE THE STRESS OF WRITING A FINAL PAPER IN HUMAN DEVELOPMENT.**

| INTELLIGENCE | USE MI STRATEGIES *to manage stress* | APPLY MI STRESS-MANAGEMENT STRATEGIES *to handle a final paper on the stages of physical development in infancy* * |
|---|---|---|
| Verbal-Linguistic | • Keep a journal of what situations, people, or events cause stress.<br>• Write letters or e-mail friends about your problems. | • Early in the writing process, summarize in writing the different reflex reactions common in normal newborns. |
| Logical-Mathematical | • Think through problems using a problem-solving process, and devise a detailed plan.<br>• Analyze the negative and positive effects that may result from a stressful situation. | • Analyze the functions of each of the six different states of being in infants: crying, waking activity, alert activity, drowsiness, irregular sleep, and regular sleep. |
| Bodily-Kinesthetic | • Choose a physical activity that helps you release tension—running, yoga, team sports—and do it regularly.<br>• Plan physical activities during free time—go for a hike, take a bike ride, go dancing with friends. | • When you need a break from writing or research, re-create the classic experiment to test infants' depth perception, known as the "visual cliff." |
| Visual-Spatial | • Enjoy things that appeal to you visually—visit an exhibit, see an art film, shoot photos with your camera.<br>• Use a visual organizer to plan out a solution to a stressful problem. | • Create a visual aid comparing the development of a full-term infant with that of a premature infant. |
| Interpersonal | • Talk with people who care about you and are supportive.<br>• Shift your focus by being a good listener to others who need to talk about their stresses. | • Interview the parents of a premature infant to learn about the special challenges the family faced during the first year. |
| Intrapersonal | • Schedule down time when you can think through what is causing stress.<br>• Allow yourself five minutes a day of meditation where you visualize a positive way in which you want a stressful situation to resolve. | • Separate your scheduled working times over a period of weeks so that you have time to contemplate individual development topics in between sessions. |
| Musical | • Listen to music that relaxes, inspires, and/or energizes you.<br>• Write a song about what is bothering you. | • Listen to lullabies from different countries. Compare and contrast melody and rhythm. Link observations to what you know about infants' auditory systems. |
| Naturalistic | • See if the things that cause you stress fall into categories that can give you helpful ideas about how to handle situations.<br>• If nature is calming for you, interact with it—spend time outdoors, watch nature-focused TV, read books or articles on nature or science. | • Visit the newborns at your local hospital during visiting hours. Search for common characteristics—for example, reflex responses and state of wakefulness or sleep. Create a chart to report your findings. |

* For information on the newborn, see Robert S. Feldman, *Child Development*, 4th ed., Upper Saddle River, NJ: Prentice Hall, 2007.

## Creative

Considering ways to incorporate more healthful behaviors into your life may have inspired new ideas about how to eat, exercise, adjust your schedule, or manage stress. In the *Get Creative* exercise, you brainstormed new ideas about how to have fun in safe and positive ways. You explored creative ways to handle substance problems.

## Practical

You gathered a wealth of eating, exercise, and sleeping strategies from which you can choose those that work best for you. In the *Get Practical* exercise, you tracked down resources in your college and community that can support your personal wellness efforts. You considered practical ways to get help if your mental health demands it. You noted specific ways to adjust, if necessary, your use of alcohol, drugs, and tobacco.

# *zhongyong (Mandarin)* 中庸
## *(djung-yung)*

This long-standing Chinese concept can be loosely translated as "the doctrines of the mean" (*zhong* means "middle" and *yong* means "normal"). In other words, it recommends that one live moderately, using common sense to avoid extremes. It is similar to the phrase often attributed to the Greek philosopher Socrates: "Everything in moderation."[30]

*Zhongyong* applies to every aspect of your personal wellness. If you avoid extremes in your actions and choices, if you use common sense to make practical and intelligent decisions about how you live, you will have the best chance to manage stress and maintain good health. And remember, when you do swing too far, there is no shame in asking for help. Maintaining balance challenges people regardless of wealth, fame, or level of accomplishment, and trained and caring people stand ready to help bring balance back. Here's to your wellness.

---

"When we change our perception we gain control. . . . When we commit to action, to actually doing something rather than feeling trapped by events, the stress in our life becomes manageable."

GREG ANDERSON, CANCER SURVIVOR AND FOUNDER
OF THE AMERICAN WELLNESS PROJECT

## SUCCESSFUL INTELLIGENCE

### *Think, Create, Apply*

**Take steps toward better health.** Put your successful intelligence to work in improving your physical health.

**Step 1. Think it through:** *Analyze your habits.* Pick a topic—eating, drinking, sleeping, sexual activity—that is an issue for you. To examine why it is a problem, identify behaviors and attitudes and note their positive and negative effects.

*Example:*  Issue: binge drinking

Behavior: I binge-drink probably three times a week.

Attitude: I don't think it's any big deal. I like using it to escape.

Positive effects: I have fun with my friends. I feel confident, accepted, social.

Negative effects: I feel hung over and foggy the next day. I miss class. I'm irritable.

*Your turn:*  Issue: _____

Behavior: _____

Attitude: _____

Positive effects: _____

Negative effects: _____

Question to think about: Is it worth it?

**Step 2. Think out of the box:** *Brainstorm ways to change.* First think about what you want to be different, and why. Then come up with changes you could make. For example, the binge drinker might consider cutting back on one drinking outing a week and investigating one new social activity that does not involve drinking. Be creative!

*How you might change your behavior:* _____

*How you might change your attitude:* _____

*Positive effects you think these changes would have:* _____

**Step 3. Make it happen:** *Put a practical health improvement plan into action.* Choose two actions to take—one that would improve your attitude and one that would improve your behavior—that you think would have the most positive effect for you. Commit to these actions with specific plans and watch the positive change happen.

*Attitude improvement plan:* _____

*Behavior improvement plan:* _____

# TEAMWORK
## Create Solutions Together

**Actively dealing with stress** By yourself, look back at the Holmes-Rahe scale on page 314. Note the stressors you have experienced in the past year and tally your "stress score." In a discussion with your class, identify the four stressors from the scale most commonly experienced by the members of the class. Divide into four groups according to the stressor each student would identify as most important (redistribute some people if the group sizes are unbalanced). Each group should discuss its assigned stressor and its effects on people. Then, as a group, brainstorm solutions and strategies, making sure to include ones that relate to wellness (eating, sleeping, exercise, substances). List your best coping strategies and present them to the class. Groups may want to make extra copies of the lists so that every member of the class has four, one for each stressor.

# WRITING
## Journal and Put Skills to Work

*Record your thoughts on a separate piece of paper, in a journal, or in a computer file.*

**Journal entry: Addiction.** Discuss how you feel about addiction in any form—to alcohol, drugs, food, sex, the Internet, gambling— whether or not you have had direct or indirect experience with it. If it has affected you directly or through your relationship to an addicted person, you may want to use the experience as an example if you are comfortable doing so.

**Real-life writing: Health on campus.** Think about what you consider to be the most significant health issue at your school—safety, alcohol or drug abuse, smoking, weight management, and so on. Write a 500-word editorial for your school paper on the topic, describing the details of the problem and proposing one or more solutions. For example, if weight control is a problem, you might suggest changing the contents of the drink vending machines in the student union. When you are done, consider submitting your editorial to the paper (have an instructor or peer review it before you send it in).

# PERSONAL PORTFOLIO

*Prepare for Career Success*

*Complete the following in your electronic portfolio or on separate sheets of paper.*

**Wellness at work.** In the working world, mental and physical health is a big issue. One reason is that many companies are putting pressure on their employees to do more in less time. Resulting issues such as increased work burdens, additional tasks, late nights, and keeping your cell phone on for work calls on weekends or at off hours create an environment that places workers under a great deal of stress. Another reason is that health care costs are on the rise for companies, in terms of both paying for health insurance and dealing with the cost of lost work time when employees are out sick. Two specific actions will help you manage your health and work situation effectively:

1. Make sure that, for any current or prospective job, you understand the company's health-related policies. On a sheet of paper, write down answers to the following questions if you have a job right now, or keep the questions handy for when you do enter the workplace:

   - What health care is available for full-time employees? Part-time? Freelance?

   - What is the policy regarding sick days—how many per year? Paid or unpaid?

   - In what ways does the company promote wellness for employees? Clinic care, wellness programs, discounts on insurance for specific criteria?

2. Come up with plans to address minor health issues that may not be enough to justify staying home from work or school, but still hamper your functioning.

In the table that follows, enter drugstore or home remedies that can help you in each of these situations (use the blank row to enter any health situation you encounter that is not listed here). Make sure they are in your medicine cabinet, and always stick to the dosage recommended on the packaging. If a problem worsens or continually recurs, make an appointment with a health professional to discuss it.

| Problem | Helpful home remedy | Helpful drugstore item |
|---|---|---|
| Head cold | | |
| Twisted knee or ankle | | |
| Burned hand | | |
| Stomach problem | | |
| Sleep deprivation | | |
| Sinus headache | | |
| | | |

Finally, name where you can go on campus for health issues and include the phone number or e-mail: _____

## Suggested Readings

Addis, Michael E., and Christopher R. Martell. *Overcoming Depression One Step at a Time: The New Behavioral Activation Approach to Getting Your Life Back.* Oakland, CA: New Harbinger Publications, 2004.

Brownell, Kelly. *The LEARN Program for Weight Management,* 10th ed. Dallas: Lifestyle, 2004.

Duyff, Roberta Larson. *The American Dietetic Association's Complete Food and Nutrition Guide.* Hoboken, NJ: Wiley, 2006.

Gifford, Allen L., Kate Lorig, Diana Laurent, and Virginia Gonzales. *Living Well with HIV and AIDS.* Boulder, CO: Bull, 2005.

Grayson, Paul A., and Philip W. Meilman. *Beating the College Blues.* New York: Checkmark Books, 1999.

Kadison, Richard D., and Theresa Foy DiGeronimo. *College of the Overwhelmed: The Campus Mental Health Crisis and What to Do About It.* San Francisco: Jossey-Bass, 2004.

Kuhn, Cynthia, Scott Swartzwelder, and Wilkie Wilson. *Buzzed: The Straight Facts About the Most Used and Abused Drugs from Alcohol to Ecstasy,* 2nd ed. New York: Norton, 2003.

*Mayo Clinic Family Health Book: The Ultimate Home Medical Reference,* 3rd ed. New York: HarperResource, 2003.

Selkowitz, Ann. *The College Student's Guide to Eating Well on Campus.* Bethesda, MD: Tulip Hill Press, 2000.

## Internet and Podcast Resources

American Cancer Society (general information, prevention, and early detection tips): **www.cancer.org**

The Body—The Complete AIDS/HIV Resource: **www.thebody.com/safesex.html**

Centers for Disease Control and Prevention (disease prevention and health information): **www.cdc.gov**

Dietary Guidelines for Americans (from the U.S. Department of Health and Human Services): **www.health.gov/dietaryguidelines**

Go Ask Alice—Columbia University's Health Q&A Internet Service: **www.goaskalice.columbia.edu**

Living Healthy podcasts: **www.livinghealthy podcast.com**

MayoClinic.com (medical information from the world-renowned medical center): **www.mayoclinic.com**

Nicotine Addiction podcast: **www.podcastdirectory .com/podshows/71927**

Sexual Health Network: **www.sexualhealth.com**

Straight Talk on Alcohol and Other Drugs: **http://alcoholandotherdrugs.com**

Think MTV—It's Your Sex Life (MTV's sexual health Web site): **www.mtv.com/thinkmtv/ sexual_health**

Prentice Hall Student Success SuperSite: **www .prenhall.com/success**

# Endnotes

[1] Gina Kolata, "A Surprising Secret to a Long Life: Stay in School," *New York Times,* January 3, 2007, pp. A1, A16.

[2] Information in this section based on materials from Dr. Marlene Schwartz of the Rudd Center for Food Policy and Obesity at Yale University.

[3] Centers for Disease Control, National Center for Health Statistics, "Prevalence of Overweight and Obesity Among Adults: United States, 2003–2004," January 30, 2007 (www.cdc.gov/nchs/products/pubs/pubd/hestats/overweight/overwght_adult_03.htm).

[4] Ibid.

[5] Yale University, Rudd Center for Food Policy and Obesity, "Employment," 2005 (www.yaleruddcenter.org/default.aspx?id=77).

[6] Quoted in Jennifer Jacobson, "How Much Sports Is Too Much? Athletes Dislike Conferences' Efforts to Give Players More Time to Be Students," *Chronicle of Higher Education,* December 6, 2002 (http://chronicle.com/weekly/v49/i15a03801.htm).

[7] CBS News, "Help for Sleep-Deprived Students," April 19, 2004 (www.cbsnews.com/stories/2004/04/19/health/main612476.shtml).

[8] "College Students' Sleep Habits Harmful to Health, Study Finds," *The Daily Orange,* September 25, 2002 (www.dailyorange.com/news/2002/09/25/Feature/College.Students.Sleep.Habits.Harmful.To.Health.Study.Finds-280340.shtml).

[9] Ibid.

[10] Gregg Jacobs, "Insomnia Corner," Talk About Sleep, 2004 (www.talkaboutsleep.com/sleepdisorders/insomnia_corner.htm); also see Herbert Benson and Eileen M. Stuart, *The Wellness Book,* New York: Simon & Schuster, 1992, p. 292.

[11] Information in this section based on materials from the Centers for Disease Control (www.cdc.gov/vaccines/recs/schedules/adult-schedule.htm) and on advice from Dr. Orin Levine, associate professor of epidemiology at Johns Hopkins University.

[12] American Psychiatric Association, "College Mental Health Statistics," n.d. (www.healthyminds.org/collegestats.cfm).

[13] National Institute of Mental Health, *Depression,* Bethesda, MD: National Institute of Mental Health, National Institutes of Health, U.S. Department of Health and Human Services, 2002 (NIH Publication No. 02-3561). p. 2 (www.nimh.nih.gov/publicat/nimhdepression.pdf).

[14] Ibid., p. 18.

[15] SAVE (Suicide Awareness Voices of Education), "Symptoms and Danger Signs," 2005 (www.save.org/depressed/symptoms.html).

[16] McLean Hospital, "First National Survey on Eating Disorders Finds Binge Eating More Common Than Other Eating Disorders," February 1, 2007 (www.mclean.harvard.edu/news/press/current.php?id=103).

[17] J. McGinnis and W. Foege, "Actual Causes of Death in the United States," *Journal of the American Medical Association (JAMA),* 270(18), November 10, 1993, p. 2208.

[18] National Survey on Drug Use and Health (NSDUH), "The NSDUH Report: Binge Alcohol Use Among Persons 12 to 20: 2002 and 2003 Update," August 26, 2005 (www.oas.samhsa.gov/2k5/youthBinge/youthBinge.htm).

[19] Henry Wechsler, George Dowdall, Gretchen Maenner, Jeana Gledhill-Hoyt, and Hang Lee, "Changes in Binge Drinking and Related Problems Among American College Students Between 1993 and 1997," *Journal of American College Health,* 47(2), September 1998, p. 57.

[20] Joel Seguine, "Students Report Negative Consequences of Binge Drinking in New Survey," *The University Record,* University of Michigan, October 25, 1999 (www.umich.edu/~urecord/9900/Oct25_99/7.htm).

[21] Darra Clark, Arizona State freshman's comments on EssayEdge.com, April 6, 2001 (www.essayedge.com/college/admissions/speakout/arizona.shtml).

[22] National Survey on Drug Use and Health (NSDUH): National Results, "Tobacco Use—College Students," 2005 (www.oas.samhsa.gov/NSDUH/2k5NSDUH/2k5results.htm#4.6).

[23] David Stout, "Direct Link Found Between Smoking and Lung Cancer," *New York Times,* October 18, 1996, pp. A1, A19.

[24] *Chicago Tribune,* February 26, 1997, "Secondhand Smoke Blamed in 3,000 Yearly Cancer Deaths" (http://pqasb.pqarchiver.com/chicagotribune/advancedsearch.html).

[25] Hilary Smith, "The High Cost of Smoking," 2007, *MSN Money* (http://moneycentral.msn.com/content/Insurance/Insureyourhealth/P100291.asp).

[26] American Cancer Society, "Guide to Quitting Smoking," October 27, 2006 (www.cancer.org/docroot/PED/content/PED_10_13X_Guide_for_Quitting_Smoking.asp).

[27] Smith, "The High Cost of Smoking."

[28] National Survey on Drug Use and Health (NSDUH), "The NSDUH Report: College Enrollment Status and Past Year Illicit Drug Use Among Young Adults: 2002, 2003, and 2004,"

October 21, 2005 (www.oas.samhsa.gov/2k5/College/college.htm).

[29] U.S. Department of Health and Human Services, "A Condom Could Save Your Life," Publication # 90-4239.

[30] Christopher J. Moore, *In Other Words: A Language Lover's Guide to the Most Intriguing Words Around the World,* New York: Walker, 2004, p. 85.

# MANAGING MONEY AND CAREER

*Reality Resources*

*"Successfully intelligent people realize that the environment in which they find themselves may or may not enable them to make the most of their talents. They actively seek an environment where they can not only do competent work but make a difference."*

ROBERT STERNBERG

**D**ealing with finances and thinking through career plans should be a high priority for every college student. How will you manage your money now and in the future? What careers and work environments will make the most of your strengths while providing the money you need for your chosen lifestyle? This chapter will show you how you can use successful intelligence to make effective decisions about money, careers, job searches, and balancing the demands of work and school.

*In this chapter you explore answers to the following questions:*

- What does money mean in your life? 346
- How can you manage short-term financial goals? 349
- How can you work toward long-term financial goals? 357
- How can you prepare for career success? 361
- How can you conduct an effective job search? 370
- *Successful Intelligence Wrap-Up* 373

| Analytical | Creative | Practical |
|---|---|---|
| • Analyzing your money-related attitudes and goals<br>• Examining your spending and saving patterns<br>• Evaluating your strengths and career interests | • Coming up with day-to-day money-saving ideas<br>• Creating new ways to connect how you learn to career areas<br>• Brainstorming ways to search for a job on the Internet | • How to use a monthly budget<br>• How to save money for short-term and long-term financial goals<br>• How to search for and win a job |

# What Does Money Mean in Your Life?

According to the American Psychological Association, nearly three out of four Americans cite money as the number one stressor in their lives.[1] Adding the high cost of college tuition to the normal list of financial obligations means that, for the vast majority of college students, money is tight. Finances can be especially problematic for self-supporting students who may have to cover living and family expenses while coming up with funds for tuition, books, and other college fees.

The way you handle money and the level of importance it has for you reflects your values, your goals, and your self-image. It influences your career choice and where you choose to live. For example, if your goal is to earn a high salary and you have strong mathematical and business sense, you might choose investment banking as a career. Jobs in this field are generally located in high-priced cities such as New York, Chicago, and London. In contrast, if you are not focused on high earnings and your talents lie in a field with lower annual salaries, you may be able to live comfortably on your earnings in less expensive locations.

Approaching money management with successful intelligence can help relieve money-related stress and increase control. Engage your successful intelligence in this process by analyzing who you are as a money manager and the relationship between your money and your time.

### How can I find a career I will enjoy?

I have always had varied interests, including piano, voice, and Renaissance fairs. I am also motivated to keep a high grade point average. So, when it came time to choose a college, I looked for one whose reputation in academics, particularly the English department, was balanced by opportunities to participate in the arts.

When I chose my major in English, I did so based on a subject that interested me and that would prepare me to participate in a profession that I would like to turn into my career—editing and publishing. I'm wondering if it is enough to excel in my courses or whether there are other ways I should try to grow while at school that will make me a valued employee.

Morgan Packard
Tulane University
New Orleans, Louisiana

## PRACTICAL ANSWERS

Ramona Z. Locke
Vice President
Senior Financial Consultant
Merrill Lynch Private Client
Group, Dallas, Texas

### Use college to discover what you do well; then . . . find the job you are most suited for.

Other than your school affiliation and grades, the strengths that you acquired along the way will be crucial when you graduate and look for a job. People who strictly adhere to the academic route may not have worked often enough in a team environment, for example, which is important in the job market. Also important to businesses today is how flexible you can be to mold and grow into the position which that company is looking to fill. Finally, one of the greatest attributes a person can acquire is to be able to get up in front of a crowd. If you can communicate your ideas, you are likely to be successful.

Life doesn't work within the bounds of a rigid focus. To be successful and happy, you must assimilate all of those situations that come your way and find the benefit in them. My analytical background and nature have helped me in my current career; I have a bachelor's degree in science and a master's in biochemistry and biophysics. I love what I do now, but that doesn't mean that I couldn't do seven other careers and be happy in them too. Use college to discover what you do well; then, when it comes time to leave, find a job you are suited for at that time, staying flexible and open to the next opportunity that comes your way.

## Your Unique Way of Managing Money

The way you interact with money is as unique as you are: You might be a spender or a saver. You might think about money only in the present tense, or you might frequently plan for the future. You might charge everything, only purchase things that you can buy with cash, or do something in between. You might measure your success in life in terms of how much money you have or define your worth in nonmaterial terms.

Influences on who you are as a money manager might include the following:

- *Your values.* You tend to spend money on what you think is most important.

- *Your personality.* Thinkers may focus on planning, Organizers may balance bank accounts down to the penny, Givers may prioritize spending money to help others, Adventurers may spend impulsively and deal with the consequences later.

- *The culture of your family.* Some cultures see money as a collective resource to be shared within families, others prize individual accumulation as a sign of independence.

- *Your family and peer group.* You tend to either follow or react against how your parents and immediate family handle money. Your classmates and friends also influence your attitudes and behavior.

- *Other factors* such as ethnicity, class, level of education, and marital status play a role in how you manage money.

Money coach Connie Kilmark notes that you cannot change how you handle money until you analyze your attitudes and behaviors. "If managing money was just about math and the numbers, everyone would know how to manage their finances sometime around the fifth grade," she says.[2] She encourages her clients to take a hard look at how they feel about money as they work to develop effective money-management attitudes and skills. Once you do the same, you can make real-life money decisions based on what works best for you.

## Money Spent Costs You the Time It Took to Earn It

© Liz Van Steenburgh—Fotolial.com

When you spend money, you exchange the time you spent earning it for a product or service. For example, you are thinking about purchasing a $200 cell phone. If you have a job that pays you $10 an hour after taxes, you would have spent 20 hours of work—a full week at a part-time job—to buy the phone. Ask yourself: Is it worth it? If the answer is no, put the money away and use it for something that is of more value to you. Every hour you work has a value—consider how to exchange those hours for what matters most to you.

This concept can hit home when you look at where your money goes from day to day. Cutting back on regular expenses can make a significant difference (see Key 11.1). If it takes you a month of work to earn $1,000 at your part-time job, you need to decide whether you would rather spend that money on coffee or see it grow in a savings account.

Going to college may cost more hours of work than almost anything else you purchase, and it takes hours away from your day that you might otherwise spend earning money. It is an expensive investment. However, you are spending tuition and time in order to better your chances of long-term financial success. Your finances may be tight now, but they are likely to improve in the years ahead. If you look back at the statistics in Key 1.1 on p. 6, you will recall that college graduates tend to earn more in the workplace than nongraduates. You are making a sound investment in your future.

What you give up to get something, in economic terms, is called "opportunity cost." For most students, the opportunity cost of going to

KEY 11.1

Put your wallet away today; earn money for tomorrow.

| DAY-TO-DAY EXPENSE | APPROXIMATE COST | POTENTIAL SAVINGS |
|---|---|---|
| Gourmet coffee | $4 per day, 5 days a week, totals $20 per week | $80 per month; $960 for the year—invested in a 5% interest account for a year, would amount to over $1,000 |
| Cigarettes | $5 per day, 7 days a week (for a pack-a-day habit), totals $35 per week | $140 per month; $1,680 for the year—invested in a 5% interest account for a year, would amount to over $1,750 |
| Ordering in meals | $15 per meal, twice per week, totals $30 per week | $120 per month; $1,440 for the year—invested in a 5% interest account for a year, would amount to nearly $1,550 |

college is worth it. The *Multiple Intelligence Strategies* table on page 362 is designed to clarify the concept of opportunity cost through descriptions of different budgeting strategies.

Continue to engage your successful intelligence as you use analytical, creative, and practical skills to set and achieve both short- and long-term financial goals.

# How Can You Manage Short-Term Financial Goals?

You make financial decisions nearly every day. Managing your income and expenses, juggling work and school, handling credit card use, and financing your education require frequent money management actions. Look back at chapter 2 where majors exploration was broken down into a series of short-term goals. In like fashion, the following sections will help you think of day-to-day money management in terms of short-term *financial* goals. These goals also support long-term financial goals as they help you manage and save your money.

## Short-Term Goal #1: Learn to Manage Income and Expenses Through Budgeting

Creating a practical monthly (budget) that works requires that you tap every aspect of successful intelligence. You gather information about your resources (money flowing in) and expenditures (money flowing out) and *analyze* the difference. Next, you come up with *creative ideas* about how you can make changes. Finally, you take *practical action* to adjust spending or earning so that you come out even or ahead.

BUDGET

A plan to coordinate resources and expenditures; a set of goals regarding money.

Your biggest expense right now is probably the cost of your education, including tuition and room and board. However, that expense may not hit you fully until after you graduate and begin to pay back your student loans. For now, include in your budget only the part of the cost of your education you are paying while you are in school.

## Figure Out Your Income

Add up all of the money you receive during the year—the actual after-tax money you have to pay your bills. Common sources of income include the following:

- Take-home pay from a regular full-time or part-time job during the school year
- Take-home pay from summer and holiday employment
- Money you earn as part of a work-study program
- Money you receive from your parents or other relatives for your college expenses
- Scholarships or grants

If you have savings specifically earmarked for your education, decide how much you will withdraw every month for school-related expenses.

## Figure Out What You Spend

Start by recording every check or electronic withdrawal going toward fixed expenses like rent, phone, and Internet service. Then, over the next month, record personal expenditures in a small notebook. Indicate any expenditure over five dollars, making sure to count smaller expenditures if they are frequent (for example, a bus pass for a month, coffee or lunch purchases per week).

Some expenses, like automobile and health insurance, may be billed only a few times a year. In these cases, convert the expense to monthly by dividing the yearly cost by 12. Common expenses include the following:

- Rent or mortgage
- Tuition that you are paying right now (the portion remaining after all forms of financial aid, including loans, scholarships, and grants, are taken into account)
- Books, lab fees, and other educational expenses
- Regular bills (electric, gas, oil, phone, water)
- Food, clothing, toiletries, and household supplies
- Child care
- Transportation and auto expenses (gas, maintenance)
- Credit cards and other payments on credit (car payments)
- Insurance (health, auto, homeowner's or renter's, life)
- Entertainment items (cable TV, movies, eating out, books and magazines, music downloads)
- Computer-related expenses, including the cost of your online service
- Miscellaneous unplanned expenses

Use the total of all your monthly expenses as a baseline for other months, realizing that your expenditures will vary depending on what is happening in your life and even the season (for example, the cost to heat your home may be much greater in the winter than in the summer).

## Evaluate the Difference

Focusing again on your current situation, subtract your monthly expenses from your monthly income. Ideally, you have money left over—to save or to spend. However, if you are spending more than you take in, use your analytical thinking skills to ask some focused questions.

**Examine your expenses.** Did you forget to budget for recurring expenses such as the cost of semiannual dental visits? Or was your budget derailed by an emergency expense that you could not foresee, such as a major car repair?

**Examine your spending patterns and priorities.** Did you spend money wisely during the month, or did you overspend on luxuries? If you are using your credit card frequently, are you being hit by high interest payments or late fees?

**Examine your income.** Do you bring in enough to suit your needs? Do you need to look for another source of income—a job or financial aid?

## Adjust Expenses or Earning

After you have analyzed the causes of any budget shortfall, brainstorm solutions that address those causes. Solutions can involve either increasing resources or decreasing spending. To increase resources, consider taking a part-time job, increasing hours at a current job, or finding scholarships or grants. To decrease spending, prioritize your expenditures and trim the ones you don't need to make. In addition, work to save money in small ways on a day-to-day basis. Small amounts can eventually add up to big savings. Here are some suggestions for cutting corners:

- Share living space.
- Rent movies or borrow them from friends or the library.
- Eat at home more often.
- Use grocery and clothing coupons.
- Take advantage of sales, buy store brands, and buy in bulk.
- Find discounted play and concert tickets (students often receive discounts).
- Walk or use public transport.
- Bring lunch from home.
- Shop in secondhand stores or swap clothing with friends.
- Communicate via e-mail or snail mail.
- Ask a relative to help with child care, or create a babysitting co-op.
- Save on the cost of electricity by cutting back on air conditioning and switching to compact fluorescent bulbs (CFLs) in your lamps at home.

Key 11.2 shows a sample budget of an unmarried student living with two other students in off-campus housing with no meal plan. Included are all regular and out-of-pocket expenses with the exception of tuition, which the student will pay back after graduation in student loan payments. In this case, the student is $223 over budget. How would you make up the shortfall?

## How one student mapped out a monthly budget

- Wages: $12 an hour (after taxes) $\times$ 20 hours a week = $240 a week $\times$ 4$\frac{1}{3}$ weeks (one month) = $1,039
- Withdrawals from savings (from summer earnings) made each month = $200
- Total income per month = $1,239

**MONTHLY EXPENDITURES**

| | |
|---|---|
| School-related expenses (books, supplies, any expense not covered by financial aid) | $80 |
| Public transportation | $90 |
| Phone | $72 |
| Food (groceries and takeout) | $305 |
| Credit card payments | $100 |
| Rent (including utilities) | $650 |
| Entertainment (music, movies, tickets to events) | $90 |
| Miscellaneous expenses, including clothing and personal items | $75 |
| **Total monthly spending:** | **$1,462** |
| $1,239 (income) − $1,462 (expenses) = −$223 | *$223 over budget* |

Rely on your dominant multiple intelligences to plan your budget. For example, whereas logical-mathematical learners may take to a classic detail-oriented budgeting plan, visual learners may want to create a budget chart, or bodily-kinesthetic learners may want to make budgeting more tangible by dumping receipts into a big jar and tallying them at the end of the month.

## Short-Term Goal #2:
## Juggle Work and School

With the cost of education rising all the time, the working student has become the norm. In fact, more than two-thirds of college students have some kind of job while in school. Key 11.3 shows the percentages of part-time and full-time college students who work.

Many people want to work and many need to work to pay for school. Use your decision-making skills to gather information about what you need, analyze the potential effects of working, create options, and choose one that works for you.

### Establish Your Needs

Think about what you need from a job before you begin your job hunt. Ask questions like these:

- How much money do I need to make—weekly, per term, for the year?

# Brainstorm Day-to-Day Ways to Save Money

*get creative!*

Think about all the ways you spend money in a month's time. Where can you trim a bit? What expense can you do without? Where can you look for savings or discounts? Can you barter a product or service for one that a friend can provide? Give yourself a day or two to brainstorm a list of ideas on a sheet of paper or computer. Write your five most workable ideas here:

1. _____
2. _____
3. _____
4. _____
5. _____

Give these a try and see how they can help you put some money toward your savings. To make the experiment tangible, put cash into a jar daily or weekly in the amounts that these changes are saving you. See what you have accumulated at the end of one month—and bank it.

 KEY 11.3

## Many students are working while in school.

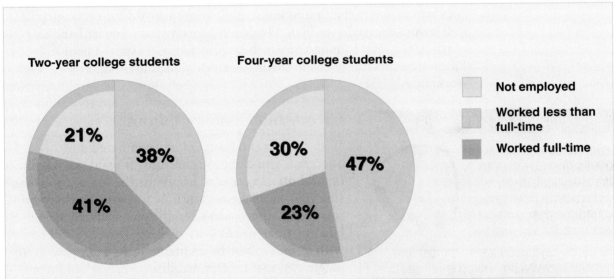

**Two-year college students**

21%
38%
41%

**Four-year college students**

30%
47%
23%

Not employed

Worked less than full-time

Worked full-time

*Source:* U.S. Department of Education, National Center for Educational Statistics, *Profile of Undergraduates in U.S. Postsecondary Educational Institutions: 2003–2004* (NCES 2006-184), June 2006, p. 13.

- What time of day is best for me? Should I consider night or weekend work?
- Can my schedule handle a full-time job, or should I look for part-time work?
- Do I want hands-on experience in a particular field? What do I like and dislike doing?
- Does location matter? Where do I want to work and how far am I willing to commute?
- How flexible a job do I need?
- Can I, or should I, find work at my school or as part of a work-study program?

## Analyze Effects of Working While in School

Working while in school has pros and cons. In addition to the money you earn, your job may have positive effects such as the following:

- General and career-specific experience
- Contacts who might be able to help you in the future
- Enhanced school and work performance (working up to 15 hours a week may encourage students to manage time more effectively and build confidence)

Potential negative effects of working while in school include:

- Time commitment, for the job and perhaps a commute, that reduces available study time
- Reduced opportunity for social and extracurricular activities
- Having to shift gears mentally from work to classroom

Some part-time jobs build skills that you can use after graduation. For example, "techies" on the University of Denver's technology help desk learn to solve computer and Internet problems as they polish their customer-service etiquette. "We're on the front line, so if something goes wrong, we're the first to know, and we get blamed for everything," said technician Andrew Chan. On an average day, each staffer handles nearly 100 contacts, many of which involve angry, frustrated people. Efficient, respectful problem solving is a skill that is useful in any workplace.[3]

### Successful Intelligence Connections Online

Listen to author Sarah Kravits describe how to use analytical, creative, and practical intelligence to find the best possible part-time job for you.

Go to the *Keys to Success* Companion Website at www.prenhall.com/carter to listen or download as a podcast.

## Create and Choose Options

With the information you have gathered and analyzed, you can look carefully at what is available on and off campus and apply for the job or jobs that suit your needs best. Continue to evaluate after you start a job. If it doesn't benefit you as much as you had anticipated, consider making a change, either with in that job or by changing jobs. Your goal is to juggle two major responsibilities—school and work—in order to do well in your studies and meet your expenses.

# Short-Term Goal #3: Manage Credit Card Use

College students often receive dozens of credit card offers. These offers—and the cards that go along with them—are a double-edged sword: They are a handy alternative to cash and can help build a strong credit history if used appropriately, but they also can plunge you into a hole of debt. Recent statistics from a survey of undergraduates illustrate the situation:[4]

- 42% of students in their first year of college hold a credit card. By the final year, 90% of students have at least one, and 56% have four or more.

- Students who hold credit cards carry an average outstanding balance of $2,169.

- Just under half of student credit card holders carry a balance of over $1,000. Nearly 25% of students carry over $3,000 in debt, and 7% carry over $7,000.

- 74% of students report charging school supplies on their cards. Nearly 24% report using their cards to pay tuition.

- 44% of student card holders report that although they pay more than the minimum every month, they always carry a balance. Just 21% report that they pay the full balance due every month.

Often cash-poor, college students charge books and tuition on cards (or "plastic") as well as expenses like car repair, food, and clothes. Before they know it, their debt becomes unmanageable. It's hard to notice trouble brewing when you don't see your wallet taking a hit.

## How Credit Cards Work

Every time you charge a textbook, a present, or a pair of pants, you are creating a debt that must be repaid. The credit card issuer earns money by charging interest, often 18% or higher, on unpaid balances. Here's an example of how quickly debt can mount. Say you have a $3,000 unpaid balance on your card at an annual interest rate of 18%. If you make the $60 minimum payment every month, it will take you *eight years* to pay off your debt, assuming that you make no other purchases. The math—and the effect on your wallet—is staggering:

- Original debt—$3,000

- Cost to repay credit card loan at an annual interest rate of 18% for 8 years—$5,760

- Cost of using credit—$5,760 − $3,000 = $2,760

As you can see, by the time you finish, you will have repaid nearly *twice* your original debt.

To avoid unmanageable debt that can lead to a personal financial crisis, learn as much as you can about credit cards, starting with the important concepts in Key 11.4. Use credit wisely while you are still in school. The habits you learn today can make a difference to your financial future.

**KEY 11.4**

## Learn to be a smart credit consumer.

| WHAT TO KNOW ABOUT . . . | . . . AND HOW TO USE WHAT YOU KNOW |
|---|---|
| *Account balance*—a dollar amount that includes any unpaid balance, new purchases and cash advances, finance charges, and fees. Updated monthly. | Charge only what you can afford to pay at the end of the month. Keep track of your balance. Hold on to receipts and call customer service if you have questions. |
| *Annual fee*—the yearly cost that some companies charge for owning a card. | Look for cards without an annual fee or, if you've paid your bills on time, ask your current company to waive the fee. |
| *Annual percentage rate (APR)*—the amount of interest charged on your unpaid balance, meaning the cost of credit if you carry a balance in any given month. The higher the APR, the more you pay in finance charges. | Shop around (check www.studentcredit.com). Also, watch out for low, but temporary, introductory rates that skyrocket to over 20% after a few months. Look for *fixed* rates (guaranteed not to change). |
| *Available credit*—the unused portion of your credit line, updated monthly on your bill. | It is important to have credit available for emergencies, so avoid charging to the limit. |
| *Cash advance*—an immediate loan, in the form of cash, from the credit card company. You are charged interest immediately and may also pay a separate transaction fee. | Use a cash advance only in emergencies because the finance charges start as soon as you complete the transaction. It is a very expensive way to borrow money. |
| *Credit limit*—the debt ceiling the card company places on your account (e.g., $1,500). The total owed, including purchases, cash advances, finance charges, and fees, cannot exceed this limit. | Credit card companies generally set low credit limits for college students. Many students get around this limit by owning more than one card, which increases the credit available but most likely increases problems as well. |
| *Delinquent account*—an account that is not paid on time or for which the minimum payment has not been met. | Avoid having a delinquent account at all costs. Not only will you be charged substantial late fees, but you also risk losing your good credit rating, affecting your ability to borrow in the future. Delinquent accounts remain part of your credit record for many years. |
| *Due date*—the date your payment must be received and after which you will be charged a late fee. | Avoid late fees and finance charges by mailing your payment a week in advance. |
| *Finance charges*—the total cost of credit, including interest and service and transaction fees. | The only way to avoid finance charges is to pay your balance in full by the due date. |
| *Minimum payment*—the smallest amount you can pay by the statement due date. The amount is set by the credit card company. | Making only the minimum payment each month can result in disaster if you charge more than you can afford. When you make a purchase, think in terms of total cost. |
| *Outstanding balance*—the total amount you owe on your card. | If you carry a balance over several months, additional purchases are hit with finance charges. Pay cash instead. |
| *Past due*—your account is considered "past due" when you fail to pay the minimum required payment on schedule. | Three credit bureaus note past due accounts on your credit history: Experian, Trans Union, and Equifax. You can contact each bureau for a copy of your credit report to make sure there are no errors. |

## Managing Credit Card Debt

Prevention is the best line of defense. To avoid excessive debt, ask yourself questions before charging: Would I buy it if I had to pay cash? Can I pay off the balance in full at the end of the billing cycle? If I buy this, what purchases will I have to forgo?

The majority of American citizens have some level of debt, and many people go through periods when they have a hard time paying bills. Falling behind on payments, however, could result in a poor credit rating that will make it difficult to get a future loan or finance a large purchase. Particular organizations such as the National Foundation for Credit Counseling (*www. nfcc.org*) or American Financial Solutions (1-888-282-5899) can help you solve credit problems. See the end of the chapter for more resources.

Debbie Alford, a student at the University of Central Oklahoma, realized too late how poor financial decisions would affect her future. As a freshman, Debbie charged only "necessities," such as books and tuition, and paid her credit card debt in full when her financial aid check arrived every term. Her debt began to escalate when she started using her cards to cover expenses like car repairs, food, and clothes. At age 23, and only a junior in college, Debbie filed for personal bankruptcy. Looking back, she blames credit card companies for making it so easy to accumulate debt and herself for not understanding the financial hole she was digging.[5]

A few basics will help you stay in control:

- Choose your card wisely—students are often eligible for cards with a lower interest rate, cards with no annual fee, cards with useful rewards, or cards with a grace period (no penalty for late payments up to a certain number of days).

- Pay bills regularly and on time and always make at least the minimum payment.

- If you get into trouble, call the creditor and see if you can pay your debt gradually using a payment plan. Then, going forward, try to avoid what got you into trouble.

> CREDITOR
> A person or company to whom a debt is owed, usually money.

- Cut up a credit card or two if you have too many.

# How Can You Work Toward Long-Term Financial Goals?

Being able to achieve long-term financial goals—buying a car or a house, having money for expenses that go beyond everyday costs, saving money for retirement and for emergencies—requires that you think critically about what you do with your money for the long term.

The short-term goals you just examined—budgeting, working while in school, managing credit use, and finding financial aid—all contribute to your long-term goals because they help you spend wisely and maximize your savings.

## Save and Invest Your Money

Having financial security requires that you live beneath your means—in other words, to spend *less* than you earn. Then the money accumulated can

# Map Out Your Budget

**Step 1:** Estimate your current expenses in dollars per month, using the following table. This may require tracking expenses for a month, if you don't already keep a record of your spending. The grand total is your total monthly expenses.

| Expense | Amount Spent |
| --- | --- |
| Rent/mortgage or room and board payment | $ |
| Utilities (electric, heat, gas, water) | $ |
| Food (shopping, eating out, meal plan) | $ |
| Telephone (land line and mobile phone) | $ |
| Books, lab fees, other educational expenses | $ |
| Loan payments (educational or bank loans) | $ |
| Car (repairs, insurance, payments, gas) | $ |
| Public transportation | $ |
| Clothing/personal items | $ |
| Entertainment | $ |
| Child care (caregivers, clothing/supplies, etc.) | $ |
| Medical care/insurance | $ |
| Other | $ |
| **TOTAL** | $ |

**Step 2:** Calculate your average monthly income. If it's easiest to come up with a yearly figure, divide by 12 to derive the monthly figure. For example, if you have a $6,000 scholarship for the year, your monthly income would be $500 ($6,000 divided by 12).

| Income Source | Amount Received |
| --- | --- |
| Regular work salary/wages (full-time or part-time) | $ |
| Grants or work-study programs | $ |
| Scholarships | $ |
| Assistance from family members | $ |
| Other | $ |
| **TOTAL** | $ |

**Step 3:** Subtract the grand total of your monthly expenses from the grand total of your monthly income:

| | |
|---|---|
| Income per month | $ |
| Expenses per month | – $ |
| **CASH FLOW** | $ |

**Step 4:** If you have a negative cash flow, you can increase income, decrease spending, or both. List here two workable ideas about how you can get your cash flow back in the black:

1. _____

2. _____

go into savings accounts and investments, helping you with regular expenses, long-term financial plans, and emergencies (financial advisors recommend that you have cash in an "emergency fund" amounting to 3–6 months' income). Use the following tools to help your money grow.

## Savings Accounts

The most basic and flexible place to save money is in an account that earns compound interest. Most savings accounts have a fixed rate of *interest*, which is a sum paid for the use of your money while it is in the bank. Here's how compound interest works: If you put $1,000 in an account that carries 5% interest, you will earn $50 over the course of the first year. Your account then holds $1,050. From that point on, interest is calculated on that $1,050, not just on the original $1,000. Imagine this: *If you invested that $1,000 at the age of 22 and put a mere $50 in the account each month, by the time you turned 62 you would have over $100,000.*

The stock market is a viable way to earn money on long-term investments. It is also a career option for students interested in finance. These traders celebrate after a good day on the floor of the New York Stock Exchange.

## Certificates of Deposit (CDs) and Money Market Accounts

CDs deliver a fixed rate of interest on an amount of money that you put away for a specific period of time (3 months, 6 months, one year). Money market accounts also deliver a fixed rate of interest and allow you to withdraw money, but tend to require a minimum balance and restrict you to a certain number of withdrawals per month. Both kinds of accounts earn slightly more than a regular savings account and are good places to put money that you want to be able to use in the near future.

COMPOUND INTEREST

Interest calculated on the principal (original investment) as well as the interest already added to the account.

## Stocks and Bonds

*Stocks* are shares of ownership in a company, and their value fluctuates with the value of the company and may pay dividends to shareholders. *Bonds* are issued by the government and corporations to finance debt for a fixed rate of return. Neither investment is without risk and requires basic knowledge of investments and financial growth strategies. Many people rely on others to provide this expertise when they invest in a *mutual fund* (a security that gives investors access to a predetermined combination of stocks and bonds). Different mutual funds have different combinations of stocks and bonds.

Since all investments carry risk, you have to analyze your investment personality before buying stocks, bonds, or mutual funds. Could you sleep at night if the value of your holdings dropped? Could you pay your bills? The responsibility to manage your finances in a responsible way is yours alone. One guideline is to subtract your age from 100—the result is the percentage of your investment that should be in stocks or all-stock funds, with the rest in fixed-income such as savings, money market accounts, and certificates of deposit.

## Begin Saving for Retirement

With so many workers switching jobs frequently and working freelance, fewer people are retiring with guaranteed retirement income other than Social Security. As more and more large and small employers are reducing or eliminating pension benefits, it is up to individual workers to put away as much money as they can for retirement. Starting early and continuing on a yearly basis gives you the benefit of growth over time.

Full-time workers whose employers offer a 401(k) retirement savings plan should sign up and contribute regularly. A 401(k) plan lets you deposit money tax-free until withdrawal, and your employer will often match your contributions. Everyone else should look into *individual retirement accounts* (IRAs). An IRA is a retirement investing tool that accepts annual contributions up to a maximum amount. Contributions, interest, and dividends are not taxed until withdrawn (with a Roth IRA even withdrawn earnings are untaxed provided the withdrawal isn't early). An IRA holder can withdraw money without penalty any time after 59½ years of age.

IRAs may be your best bet for investment. Key 11.5 shows the extraordinary earning potential of an IRA. There are many different types of IRAs, and the one that is right for you will depend on your employment, your income, and the money you have available to invest. Financial institutions such as banks and investment firms offer IRAs.

## Investigate Effective Ways to Purchase a Home

Owning a home is a big deal. Besides being a major life goal, it is also a significant financial investment, since home values usually *appreciate*, or increase in value, over time (by contrast, even though buying a car is also a major purchase, almost any car *depreciates*, or decreases in value, the instant you drive it off the lot). Furthermore, a home is a

**KEY 11.5** Use an IRA to grow your retirement investment.

| Initial investment and contributions | Investment growth, based on 10% return, after . . . | | |
|---|---|---|---|
| | **10 years** | **25 years** | **40 years** |
| $5000 one-time investment | $12,969 | $54,174 | $226,296 |
| $2000 investment plus $ 2,000 annual contribution | $37,062 | $218,364 | $975,704 |

*Note:* Calculations based on 10% average annual S & P Index growth from 1926 to present, as per "Investment Intelligence," Legg Mason Investor Services, 2007 (http://investorservices.leggmason.com/doc_library/1730.pdf?seq=11).

double-duty investment that provides both financial security and a place to live.

There is much more to know about buying a home than can fit into this chapter. The two most important tasks in preparation for this major goal are to control spending and pay bills on time, so that you can put as much money down on the house as possible and get a favorable mortgage based on your good credit rating. Keep in mind that you should look into different types of mortgages. A fixed-rate mortgage assures you that you will always pay the same rate of interest. An adjustable-rate mortgage (ARM) starts with a low interest rate, but the rate may rise quickly. An interest-only mortgage allows you to pay only the interest on your loan each month, which keeps your payments low but doesn't reduce the principal of the loan unless you pay down the principal separately.

You have been thinking through all kinds of long-term financial investments. In a sense, your career is also a long-term financial investment, because it is likely to be your primary means for earning a living. As you will see next, your earnings are only one factor in choosing a career.

# How Can You Prepare for Career Success?

Your career reflects your values and talents and provides the income you need to support yourself and your family in the years ahead. Choosing the "right" career starts with knowing yourself. It continues with knowing

# MULTIPLE INTELLIGENCE STRATEGIES

## FOR FINANCIAL MANAGEMENT

**APPLY DIFFERENT INTELLIGENCES TO THE CONCEPT OF OPPORTUNITY COST IN ECONOMICS.**

| INTELLIGENCE | USE MI STRATEGIES *to manage your money* | APPLY MI BUDGETING STRATEGIES *to learn about opportunity cost\** |
|---|---|---|
| Verbal-Linguistic | • Talk over your financial situation with someone you trust.<br>• Write out a detailed budget outline. If you can, store it on a computer file so you can update it regularly. | • Clarify the concept of *opportunity cost* (what you sacrifice to get something) with two personal examples: the opportunity cost of a course you are taking and of a purchase you've made or plan to make. |
| Logical-Mathematical | • Focus on the numbers; using a calculator and amounts as exact as possible, determine your income and spending.<br>• Calculate how much money you'll have in 10 years if you start now to put $2,000 in a 5% interest-bearing IRA account each year. | • Compute the estimated opportunity cost of one year of your college education by comparing it to working full-time for the year. Consider all education-related expenses in your computation. Analyze your results. |
| Bodily-Kinesthetic | • Consider putting money, or a slip with a dollar amount, each month in envelopes for various budget items—rent, dining out, etc. When the envelope is empty or the number is reduced to zero, spending stops. | • On slips of paper, write opportunity costs of a choice—for example, buying a new car—and put the slips in a pile. Then, write the benefits of the choice on more slips, and put them in a separate pile. Compare your piles—does the benefit outweigh the cost? |
| Visual-Spatial | • Set up a budgeting system that includes color-coded folders and colored charts.<br>• Create color-coded folders for papers related to financial and retirement goals—investments, accounts, etc. | • In order to see what combination of work time and school time is ideal for you, design a *production possibilities curve* that shows all of the possible combinations. |
| Interpersonal | • Whenever money problems come up, discuss them right away with a family member, partner, or roommate.<br>• Brainstorm a five-year financial plan with one of your friends. | • Meet with a friend to discuss the opportunity cost of different ways to spend your *discretionary income* (money available after you pay your monthly fixed expenses). |
| Intrapersonal | • Schedule quiet time to plan how to develop, follow, and update your budget. Consider financial-management software, such as Quicken.<br>• Think through where your money should go to best achieve your long-term financial goals. | • Schedule down time to think about the opportunity cost of an extracurricular activity with which you are involved. Overall, do you benefit from this experience? If you decide that the cost is too high, change your level of involvement. |
| Musical | • Include a category of music-related purchases in your budget—going to concerts, buying CDs—but keep an eye on it to make sure you don't go overboard. | • Look at what you spend on music-related purchases through one term. Thinking about other ways you could use that money, calculate the opportunity cost of that expense. |
| Naturalistic | • Analyze your spending by using a system of categories. Your system may be based on time (when payments are due), priority (must-pay bills vs. extras), or spending type (monthly bills, education, family expenses). | • Choose a category and total your spending in that category through the year. Think about something else that you would like to do with that amount of money. Is there a more favorable choice you could make in the future? |

\* For information on opportunity cost, see Arthur O'Sullivan, Steven M. Sheffrin, and Stephen J. Perez, *Survey of Economics: Principles, Applications, and Tools,* Upper Saddle River, NJ: Prentice Hall, 2008.

what employers want from workers. As you read this section, keep in mind that all of the of skills you acquire in college—thinking, teamwork, writing, goal setting, and others—prepare you for workplace success.

## Investigate Career Paths

Career possibilities extend far beyond what you can imagine. Ask instructors, relatives, mentors, and fellow students about careers they are familiar with. Explore job listings, occupation lists, assessments, and other information about careers and companies at your school's career center. Check your library for books on careers or biographies of people who worked in fields that interest you. Look at Key 11.6 for the kinds of analytical questions that will aid your search. You may discover several things about job possibilities, including the following:

**A wide array of job possibilities exists for most career fields.** For example, the medical world consists of more than doctors and nurses. Administrators run hospitals, researchers test drugs, pharmacists prepare prescriptions, security experts ensure patient and visitor safety, and so on.

**Within each job, there is a variety of tasks and skills.** You may know that an instructor teaches, but you may not realize that instructors also write, research, study, design courses, give presentations, and counsel. Take your career exploration beyond first impressions to get an accurate picture of the careers that interest you.

Look beyond first impressions when you are investigating salaries. You can earn a good living in fields other than finance, law, and medicine. According to data from the U.S. Department of Labor, other careers with high earnings include electricians, registered nurses, aircraft mechanics, and more.[6] Remember too that even if you earn a high salary, you may not be

**KEY 11.6** Ask questions like these to analyze how a career area or job may fit you.

| | |
|---|---|
| What can I do in this area that I like and do well? | Do I respect the company or the industry? The product or service? |
| What are the educational requirements (certificates or degrees, courses)? | Does this company or industry accommodate special needs (child care, sick days, flex time)? |
| What skills are necessary? | Do I need to belong to a union? What does union membership involve? |
| What wage or salary and benefits can I expect? | Are there opportunities near where I live (or want to live)? |
| What personality types are best suited to this kind of work? | What other expectations exist (travel, overtime, etc.)? |
| What are the prospects for moving up to higher-level positions? | Do I prefer the service or production end of this industry? |

happy unless you enjoy your work. Look up the U.S. Department of Labor's *Occupational Outlook Handbook* or see Salary.com for information on average salaries in different fields.

## Consider Your Personality and Strengths

Because who you are as a learner relates closely to who you are as a worker, your assessment results from chapter 3 will give you helpful clues in the search for the right career. The *Multiple Pathways to Learning* assessment points to information about your natural strengths and challenges, which can lead you to careers that involve these strengths. Review Key 3.7 on p. 86 to see majors and internships that tend to suit different intelligences, and look at Key 11.7 to see how those intelligences may link up with various careers.

 KEY 11.7 Multiple intelligences may open doors to careers.

| Multiple intelligence | Look into a career as . . . |
|---|---|
| Bodily-Kinesthetic | ■ Carpenter or draftsman<br>■ Physical therapist<br>■ Mechanical engineer<br>■ Dancer or actor<br>■ Exercise physiologist |
| Intrapersonal | ■ Research scientist<br>■ Computer engineer<br>■ Psychologist<br>■ Economist<br>■ Author |
| Interpersonal | ■ Social worker<br>■ PR or HR rep<br>■ Sociologist<br>■ Teacher<br>■ Nurse |
| Naturalistic | ■ Biochemical engineer<br>■ Natural scientist (geologist, ecologist, entomologist)<br>■ Paleontologist<br>■ Position with environmental group<br>■ Farmer or farm management |
| Musical | ■ Singer or voice coach<br>■ Music teacher<br>■ Record executive<br>■ Musician or conductor<br>■ Radio DJ or sound engineer |

| Logical-Mathematical | ■ Doctor or dentist |
| | ■ Accountant |
| | ■ Attorney |
| | ■ Chemist |
| | ■ Investment banker |
| Verbal-Linguistic | ■ Author or journalist |
| | ■ TV/radio producer |
| | ■ Literature or language teacher |
| | ■ Business executive |
| | ■ Copywriter or editor |
| Visual-Spatial | ■ Graphic artist or illustrator |
| | ■ Photographer |
| | ■ Architect or interior designer |
| | ■ Art museum curator |
| | ■ Art teacher |
| | ■ Set or retail stylist |

The *Personality Spectrum* assessment in chapter 3 is equally as significant, because it focuses on how you work best with others, and career success depends in large part on your ability to function in a team. Key 11.8 focuses the four dimensions of the Personality Spectrum on career ideas and strategies. Look for your strengths and decide what you may want to keep in mind as you search. Look also at areas of challenge, and try to identify ways to boost your abilities in those areas. Even the most ideal job involves some tasks that are not in your area of comfort.

Use the information in Key 11.8 as a guide, not a label. Although you may not have all the strengths and challenges indicated by your dominant area, thinking through them will still help you clarify your abilities and interests. In addition, remember that you are capable of change, and with focus and effort you can develop your abilities. Use ideas about strengths and challenges as a starting point for your goals about how you would like to grow.

## Build Knowledge and Experience

It's hard to choose the right career path without knowledge or experience. Courses, internships, jobs, and volunteering are four great ways to build both.

**Courses.** Take a course or two in your areas of interest to determine if you like the material and excel. Find out what courses are required for a major in those areas and decide if you are willing to study this material during college.

# Personality Spectrum dimensions indicate strengths and challenges.

| DIMENSION | STRENGTHS ON THE JOB | CHALLENGES ON THE JOB | LOOK FOR JOBS/CAREERS THAT FEATURE . . . |
|---|---|---|---|
| Thinker | Problem solving<br>Development of ideas<br>Keen analysis of situations<br>Fairness to others<br>Efficiency in working through tasks<br>Innovation of plans and systems<br>Ability to look strategically at the future | A need for private time to think and work<br>A need, at times, to move away from established rules<br>A dislike of sameness—systems that don't change, repetitive tasks<br>Not always being open to expressing thoughts and feelings to others | Some level of solo work/think time<br>Problem solving<br>Opportunity for innovation<br>Freedom to think creatively and to bend the rules<br>Technical work<br>Big-picture strategic planning |
| Organizer | High level of responsibility<br>Enthusiastic support of social structures<br>Order and reliability<br>Loyalty<br>Ability to follow through on tasks according to requirements<br>Detailed planning skills with competent follow-through<br>Neatness and efficiency | A need for tasks to be clearly, concretely defined<br>A need for structure and stability<br>A preference for less rapid change<br>A need for frequent feedback<br>A need for tangible appreciation<br>Low tolerance for people who don't conform to rules and regulations | Clear, well-laid-out tasks and plans<br>Stable environment with consistent, repeated tasks<br>Organized supervisors<br>Clear structure of how employees interact and report to one another<br>Value of, and reward for, loyalty |
| Giver | Honesty and integrity<br>Commitment to putting energy toward close relationships with others<br>Finding ways to bring out the best in self and others<br>Peacemaker and mediator<br>Ability to listen well, respect opinions, and prioritize the needs of coworkers | Difficulty in handling conflict, either personal or between others in the work environment<br>Strong need for appreciation and praise<br>Low tolerance for perceived dishonesty or deception<br>Avoidance of people perceived as hostile, cold, or indifferent | Emphasis on teamwork and relationship building<br>Indications of strong and open lines of communication among workers<br>Encouragement of personal expression in the workplace (arrangement of personal space, tolerance of personal celebrations, and so on) |
| Adventurer | Skillfulness in many different areas<br>Willingness to try new things<br>Ability to take action<br>Hands-on problem-solving skills<br>Initiative and energy<br>Ability to negotiate<br>Spontaneity and creativity | Intolerance of being kept waiting<br>Lack of detail focus<br>Impulsiveness<br>Dislike of sameness and authority<br>Need for freedom, constant change, and constant action<br>Tendency not to consider consequences of actions | A spontaneous atmosphere<br>Less structure, more freedom<br>Adventuresome tasks<br>Situations involving change<br>Encouragement of hands-on problem solving<br>Travel and physical activity<br>Support of creative ideas and endeavors |

**Internships.** You can get supervised practical experience in a number of professional fields through an (internship.) Your career center may list summer or year-round internship opportunities.

**Jobs.** You may discover career opportunities while earning money at a part-time job. Someone who takes a third-shift legal proofreading job to make extra cash might discover an interest in law. Someone who answers phones for a newspaper company might be drawn into journalism.

**Volunteering.** Helping others in need can introduce you to careers and increase your experience. Some schools have programs that link you to volunteering opportunities (see chapter 12). You may even be able to find opportunities that mesh with an area of interest. For example, if you are studying accounting, volunteering as a part-time bookkeeper in a shelter will increase your skills while you help those less fortunate than you. Many employers look favorably on volunteering.

*INTERNSHIP*
*A temporary work program in which a student can gain supervised practical experience in a particular professional field.*

## Know What Employers Want

When you apply for a job, it is important to realize that prospective employers look for particular skills and qualities that mark you as a promising candidate. Most employers require you to have a (skillset) that includes specific technical skills, but in the current rapidly changing workplace, more general life skills may be even more crucial to your success. Following are some details about what employers will be looking for.

*SKILLSET*
*A combination of the knowledge, talent, and abilities that are needed to perform a specific job.*

### Big-Picture Skills

In the modern workplace, workers will hold an average of 10 jobs through their most productive working years.[7] The high rate of job and workplace change means that abilities such as successful thinking and teamwork are the most crucial to workplace success. Key 11.9 describes the particular skills and qualities that tell an employer you are likely to be an efficient and effective employee.

### Emotional and Social Intelligence

Employers are also drawn to candidates with high levels of emotional intelligence and social intelligence. According to psychologist Daniel Goleman, *emotional intelligence* can be even more important than IQ and knowledge in job success. As you learned in chapter 1, Goleman defines emotional intelligence as a combination of two factors: *personal competence* (self-management, self-awareness) and *social competence* (awareness of others' feelings, handling relationships with others). Refer to Key 1.4 on p. 21 for more details.

*Social intelligence* focuses even more specifically on your interactions with others. As you read in chapter 1, Goleman uses two factors to define it: *social awareness* (sensing people's emotions, working to understand how people feel, understanding the workings of social interactions) and *social facility* (smooth nonverbal interaction, presenting yourself in ways appropriate to situations, shaping social interactions, acting on your sense of what others need). See Key 1.5 on p. 22 for full descriptions.

**KEY 11.9**    Employers look for candidates with these important skills.

| SKILL | WHY IS IT USEFUL? |
|---|---|
| Communication | Good listening, speaking, and writing skills are keys to working with others, as is being able to adjust to different communication styles. |
| Analytical thinking | An employee who can analyze choices and challenges, as well as assess the value of new ideas, stands out. |
| Creativity | The ability to come up with new concepts, plans, and products helps companies improve and innovate. |
| Practical thinking | No job gets done without employees who can think through a plan for achieving a goal, put it into action, and complete it successfully. |
| Teamwork | All workers interact with others on the job. Working well with others is essential for achieving workplace goals. |
| Goal setting | Teams fail if goals are unclear or unreasonable. Employees and company benefit from setting realistic, specific goals and achieving them reliably. |
| Cultural competence | The workplace is increasingly diverse. An employee who can work with, adjust to, and respect people from different backgrounds and cultures is valuable. |
| Leadership | The ability to influence and motivate others in a positive way earns respect and career advancement. |
| Positive attitude | Other employees will gladly work with, and often advance, someone who completes tasks with positive, upbeat energy. |
| Integrity | Acting with integrity at work—communicating promptly, being truthful and honest, following rules, giving proper notice—enhances value. |
| Flexibility | The most valuable employees understand the constancy of change and have developed the skills to adapt to its challenge. |
| Continual learning | The most valuable employees take personal responsibility to stay current in their fields. |

Your emotional and social intelligence can empower or limit your career success during every single workday. Consider the following scenario: Say you arrive at work distracted by a personal problem and tired from studying late the night before. Your supervisor is overloaded with a major project due that day. The person you work most closely with will be arriving late due to a car problem. In other words, everyone is strung out. What does an emotionally and socially intelligent person do?

- Knowing your mental state, you prioritize your task list so that you can concentrate on what is most pressing and leave the rest for a day when you are more energetic.
- Sensing your supervisor's stress, you put a memo on her desk saying that you are available to support her as she nails down the loose ends on her urgent project.

- You call your coworker on his cell phone while he settles the car problem and let him know the status at work, preparing him to prioritize and to support the supervisor.
- You ask another coworker to bring in a favorite mid-morning snack to keep everyone going on what looks to be a very long day.

The current emphasis on teamwork has heightened the importance of emotional and social intelligence in the workplace. The more adept you are at working comfortably and productively with others, the more likely you are to succeed.

## Expect Change

The working world is always in flux, responding to technological developments, global competition, and other factors. Think about the following as you prepare for your own career.

You will benefit from thinking creatively, taking the initiative, and avoiding assumptions when considering careers. This woman started her own contracting company. Now the president, she stays directly involved. Here she checks the progress on a roofing project.

**Growing and declining career areas.** Rapid workplace change means that a growth area today may be declining tomorrow—witness the sudden drop in Internet company jobs and fortunes in 2001. The U.S. Bureau of Labor Statistics keeps updated data on the status of various career areas. For example, for the period 1998–2008, of the 10 fastest growing occupations identified by the bureau, five are computer-related occupations.

**Workplace trends.** What's happening now? Companies, to save money, are hiring more temporary employees (temps) and fewer full-time employees. Temporary jobs offer flexibility, few obligations, and often more take-home pay, but have limited benefits. Also, in response to the changing needs of the modern workforce, companies are offering more "quality of life" benefits such as telecommuting, job sharing, and on-site child care. You can track these changes by scanning hard-copy or online versions of business-focused publications such as *Fortune, BusinessWeek*, or the *Wall Street Journal*.

**Personal change.** Even difficult personal changes can open doors that you never imagined were there. After a devastating horseback riding accident left him paralyzed from the neck down, Christopher Reeve found new careers as a writer and a public advocate for those suffering from the effects of spinal injury.

Adjusting to changes, both large (leaving an industry for a new career) and small (changing the software you use daily on the job) means putting successful intelligence to work. With the information you collect from newspapers and magazines, Internet sites, and television news, you can analyze what you are facing in the workplace. Based on your analysis you can create options for yourself, either within your own workplace or elsewhere, and take practical action.

With what you know about general workplace success strategies, you can search effectively for a job in a career area that works for you.

# How Can You Conduct an Effective Job Search?

Whether you are looking for a job now or planning ahead for a search closer to graduation, you have choices about how to proceed. Maximize your success by using the resources available to you, knowing the basics about résumés and interviews, and planning strategically.

## Use Available Resources

Use your school's career planning and placement office, your networking skills, classified ads, and online services to help you explore possibilities for career areas or specific jobs.

### Your School's Career Planning and Placement Office

**COOPERATIVE EDUCATION**

*A program, offered by some colleges, that combines credit-earning course work with paid work experience in a field that relates to the course.*

Generally, the career planning and placement office deals with postgraduation job opportunities, whereas the student employment office, along with the financial aid office, has information about working during school. At either location you might find job listings, interview sign-up sheets, and company contact information. The career office may hold frequent informational sessions on different topics. Your school may also sponsor job or career fairs that give you a chance to explore job opportunities. Get acquainted with the career office early in your college career.

If your school has a cooperative education office, it can lead you to job opportunities and can even help you land a job before graduation. Jason Roach, a business computer systems major at New Mexico State University, used the co-op office as a job-referral source. He explains: "The Cooperative Education office works very hard to notify students when companies will be on campus interviewing for jobs. I receive at least ten e-mails a week telling me what company will be on campus and a quick background on the position."[8]

### Networking

**NETWORKING**

*The exchange of information or services among individuals, groups, or institutions.*

The most basic type of networking—talking to people about fields and jobs that interest you—is one of the most important job-hunting strategies. Networking contacts can answer questions regarding job hunting, job responsibilities and challenges, and salary expectations. You can network with friends and family members, instructors, administrators, counselors, alumni, employers, coworkers, and others.

**CONTACT**

*A person who serves as a carrier or source of information.*

You can also network with people you meet through your extracurricular activities. Christine Muñoz, a student at New Mexico State University, chose a campus club that she knew could help her prepare for a business career—the Hispanic Business Student Association (HBSA):

> This term we did several fund-raisers and community service projects. We have biweekly meetings, and we also have socials where we all just get together and hang out. Professional speakers from large

companies come and speak about résumé building skills and interview skills, something that is beneficial to everyone.[9]

### Online Services and Classified Ads

Some of the best job listings are in newspapers. Individual ads describe the position available, including background requirements, and provide contact information. In addition, the Internet has exploded into one of the most fruitful sources of job listings. There are many different ways to hunt for a job on the Web, as follows:

- Look up career-focused and job listing Web sites such as CareerBuilder .com, Monster.com, BilingualCareer.com, JobBank USA, or Futurestep .com. Many sites offer resources on career areas, résumés, and online job searching in addition to job listings.
- Access job search databases such as the Career Placement Registry and U.S. Employment Opportunities.
- Check the Web pages of individual associations and companies, which may post job listings and descriptions.

If nothing happens right away, keep at it. New job postings appear, new people sign on to look at your résumé. Plus, sites change all the time. Search using the keywords "job sites" or "job search" to see what sites are up (QuintCareers.com has a listing of the 50 best job sites).

## Your Résumé, Cover Letter, and Interview

Information on résumés, cover letters, and interviews fills entire books. You'll find specific sources listed at the end of the chapter. To get you started, here are a few basic tips on giving yourself the best possible chance.

### Résumé and Cover Letter

Design your résumé neatly, using a current and acceptable format (books or your career office can show you some standard formats). Make sure all the information is accurate and truthful. Proofread for errors and have someone else proofread it as well. Type or print it on high-quality paper (a heavier bond paper than is used for ordinary copies). Include a brief, to-the-point cover letter along with your résumé that tells the employer what job you are interested in and why he or she should hire you.

Prospective employers often use a computer to scan résumés, selecting the ones that contain keywords relating to the job opening or industry. Résumés without enough keywords probably won't even make it to the human resources desk. When you construct your résumé, make sure to include as many keywords as you can. For example, if you are seeking a computer-related job, list computer programs you use and other specific technical proficiencies. To figure out what keywords you need, check out job descriptions, job postings, and other current résumés.[10]

### The Interview

Be clean, neat, and appropriately dressed. Choose a nice pair of shoes—people notice. Bring an extra copy of your résumé and any other materials that you want to show the interviewer, even if you sent a copy ahead of

## Assess the Cost of Résumé Mistakes

- Take a look at these common résumé errors and miscalculations:
    1. Typos and grammatical errors
    2. Not focused on a goal or target
    3. Focusing on duties and responsibilities of past jobs instead of actions and accomplishments
    4. Using visual gimmicks (colors, graphics, distinctive fonts) to get attention
    5. Making up or exaggerating job or academic information
    6. Getting too personal with information (including personal Web sites)

- Now, put yourself in the interviewer's chair. Choose three of the mistakes and analyze the effect that they would have on your opinion of the applicant. Record specific impressions here:

Mistake #: _____ Effect: _____

_____

Mistake #: _____ Effect: _____

_____

Mistake #: _____ Effect: _____

_____

time. Avoid chewing gum or smoking. Offer a confident handshake. Make eye contact. Show your integrity by speaking honestly about yourself. After the interview, no matter what the outcome, follow up right away with a formal but pleasant thank-you note.

Being on time to your interview makes a positive impression—and being late will almost certainly be held against you. If you are from a culture that does not consider being late a sign of disrespect, remember that your interviewer may not agree.

## Be Strategic

With solid resources to support you and information about how to build a résumé and interview well, you can focus on making a practical, personal plan to achieve your career goals. First, create a time line that can illustrate the steps you plan to take toward a specific career goal you want to explore. Working with an advisor, career office employee, or mentor, establish a time frame and write in the steps when you think they should happen. If your plan is five years long, for example, indicate what you plan to do by the fourth, third, and second years, and then the first year, including a six-month goal and a one-month goal for that first year. Your path may change, of course; use your time line as a guide rather than as an inflexible plan.

After you establish your time frame, focus on details. Make specific plans for pursuing the jobs or careers that have piqued your interest. Set goals that establish whom you will talk to, what courses you will take, what skills you will work on, what jobs or internships you will investigate, and any other research you need to do.

Organize your approach according to what you need to do and when you have to do it. Do you plan to make three phone calls per day? Will you fill out one job application each week? Keep a record—on 3-by-5 cards, in a computer file, or in a notebook—of the following:

- People you contact
- Companies to which you apply
- Jobs you rule out (for example, a job that becomes unavailable)
- Responses to communications (phone calls to you, interviews, written communications), information about the person who contacted you (name, title), and the time and dates of contact

Keeping accurate records enables you to both chart your progress and maintain a clear picture of the process. If you don't get a job now but another opens up at the same company in a few months, well-kept records will enable you to contact key personnel quickly and efficiently.

# Successful Intelligence Wrap-Up

Many money and career decisions are made too quickly or based on criteria that aren't really important—often with troublesome results. As a successfully intelligent thinker, you can buck that trend by planning ahead in ways that will benefit you down the road, enabling you to say, years from now, "I made a good choice." Here's how you have built skills in chapter 11:

## Analytical

You examined what money means in your life and how you manage it. You broke down the step-by-step process of budgeting. You explored the effects of working in school as well as the potential results of working toward long-term financial goals. You looked carefully at what promotes career success, looking specifically at the cost of résumé mistakes in the *Get Analytical* exercise.

## Creative

The material on budgeting may have inspired new ideas about how to manage what you earn and spend. In the *Get Creative* exercise, you brainstormed day-to-day ways to save money. Considering long-term financial goals may have introduced new thoughts about how to plan ahead with your money. As you explored the section on careers and job searches, you may have come up with new career ideas or creative ways to look for a job.

## Practical

You reviewed a step-by-step plan for budgeting month by month, and put some ideas into action by mapping out your personal budget in the *Get Practical* exercise. You gathered specific strategies for managing credit card use. You explored the practical value of committing to save for your near future (major purchases) and far future (retirement). You took in the details of how to perform an effective job search.

# *gotong-royong*
## *(got-ong-roi-ong)*

In Indonesia, the word *royong* refers to working together with others to accomplish something that benefits everyone. When Indonesians use *gotong* in conjunction with *royong*, they are saying that when people come together to "carry a heavy burden," the burden is lightened because it is shared. In a broader sense, the phrase tells us that what is good for the group is more important than what is good for one person.[11]

Keep *gotong-royong* in mind as you make decisions about your money and your work, because your actions have repercussions for those who share your life. When you spend and save your money wisely, you and your family build financial security that will give you personal flexibility in the future. When you make well-considered decisions about jobs and careers, you have the best opportunity to put your strengths to use in an environment where you work.

"Standing still is the fastest way of moving backwards in a rapidly changing world."

LAUREN BACALL

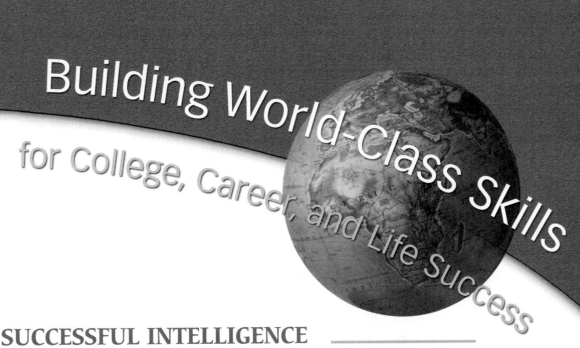

# Building World-Class Skills
## for College, Career, and Life Success

## SUCCESSFUL INTELLIGENCE
*Think, Create, Apply*

Your relationship with money. Getting a handle on money anxiety starts with an honest examination of how you relate to it.

**Step 1. Think it through:** *Analyze yourself as a money manager.* Look back to pages 347–348 for a description of what influences how people handle money. Make some notes about your personal specifics in the following areas.

I most value spending money on: _____
_____

My money "personality" can be described as: _____
_____

My culture tends to view money as: _____
_____

My family and friends tend to handle money in this way: _____
_____

**Step 2. Think out of the box:** *Generate ideas about what you want to do with your money.* If you had enough for expenses and then some, what would you do with the extra? Would you save it, spend it, a little of both? Imagine what you would do if you had an extra $10,000 to spend this year. Describe your plan on a separate sheet of paper.

**Step 3. Make it happen:** *Look for practical ways to move toward the scenario you imagined.* How can you make that $10,000 a reality? You may need to change how you operate as a money manager. You may need to make sacrifices in the short term. Come up with two specific plans here about changes and sacrifices that will move you toward your goal:

1. _____

2. _____

When you put these ideas to work, save or invest the money to reach for your goal.

# TEAMWORK

## Create Solutions Together

**Building interview skills.** Divide into pairs—each student will have a turn interviewing the other about themselves and their career aspirations. Be as interested—and as interesting—as you can. Follow these steps:

1. Independently, take three minutes to brainstorm questions you'll ask the other person. Focus on learning style, interests, and initial career ideas. You might ask questions like these:

   - If you could have any job in the world, what would it be?
   - What do you think would be the toughest part of achieving success in that profession?
   - Who are you as a learner and worker?
   - What sacrifices are you willing to make to realize your dreams?
   - What is your greatest failure, and what have you learned from it?
   - Who is a role model to you in terms of career success?

2. Person A interviews Person B for 5 to 10 minutes and takes notes.

3. Switch roles: Person B interviews Person A and takes notes. You should each use your own questions, which you developed in step 1.

4. Share with each other what interesting ideas stand out to you from the interviews. If you have any, offer constructive criticism to your interviewee about his or her interview skills.

5. Finally, submit your notes to your instructor for feedback.

This exercise will build your ability to glean information from others and to answer questions during an interview. You will use this skill throughout your professional life.

# WRITING

## Journal and Put Skills to Work

*Record your thoughts on a separate piece of paper, in a journal, or in a computer file.*

**Your money personality.** Describe who you are as a money manager, and where you think your behaviors and attitudes came from. What do you buy? Are you careful or reckless? Unattentive or detail-focused? How do you handle credit? How do you feel about how you handle money?

**Real-life writing: Apply for aid.** Start by reading the information on financial aid on pages xxix–xxxviii in Quick Start to College. Then, use Internet or library resources to find two non-federally-funded scholarships, available through your college, for which you are eligible. They can be linked to academic areas of interest, associated with particular talents that you have, or offered by a group to which you or members of your family belong. Get applications for each and fill them out. Finally, write a one-page cover letter for each, telling each committee why you should receive this scholarship. Have someone proofread your work, *send the applications*, and see what happens.

# PERSONAL PORTFOLIO
*Prepare for Career Success*

*Complete the following in your electronic portfolio or on separate sheets of paper.*

**Being specific about your job needs.** As you consider specific job directions and opportunities, begin thinking about a variety of job-related factors that different employers offer and that may affect your job experience and personal life. Among these factors are the following:

- Benefits such as health insurance, vacation, 401(k)
- Integrity of company (its reputation)
- How the company deals with employees
- Promotion prospects or your chances for advancement
- Job stability
- Training and educational opportunities (Does the company offer in-house training or fund job-related coursework?)
- Starting salary
- Quality of employees
- Quality of management
- Nature of the work you will be doing (Will you be required to travel extensively? Will you be expected to work long hours? Will you be working in an office or in the field?)
- Your relationship with the company (Will you be a full-time or part-time employee or an independent contractor?)
- Job title
- Location of your primary workplace
- Company size
- Company's financial performance over time

Think about how important each factor is in your job choice. Then rate each on a scale of 1 to 10, with 1 being the least important and 10 being the most important. As you consider each factor, keep in mind that even if you consider something very important, you may not get it right away if you are just beginning your career.

Finally, consider the results of a survey of college students conducted by the National Association of Colleges and Employers. When asked their top two reasons for choosing an employer, students named *integrity of organization in its dealings with employees* as number one and *job stability* as number two. How do these top choices compare to your own?[12]

# Suggested Readings

Beatty, Richard H. *The Resume Kit,* 5th ed. New York: Wiley, 2003.

Boldt, Laurence G. *How to Find the Work You Love.* New York: Arkana, 2004.

Bolles, Richard Nelson. *What Color Is Your Parachute? 2007: A Practical Manual for Job Hunters and Career Changers.* Berkeley, CA: Ten Speed Press, 2006.

Detweiler, Gerri. *The Ultimate Credit Handbook: How to Cut Your Debt and Have a Lifetime of Good Credit,* 3rd ed. New York: Plume, 2003.

Goleman, Daniel. *Emotional Intelligence.* New York: Bantam Books, 1997.

Goleman, Daniel. *Working with Emotional Intelligence.* New York: Bantam Books, 2000.

Goleman, Daniel. *Social Intelligence: The New Science of Human Relationships.* New York: Bantam Books, 2006.

Kennedy, Joyce Lain. *Job Interviews for Dummies.* Foster City, CA: IDG Books Worldwide, 2000.

MarksJarvis, Gail. *Saving for Retirement Without Living Like a Pauper or Winning the Lottery.* Indianapolis: FT Press, 2007.

Tyson, Eric. *Personal Finance for Dummies.* Foster City, CA: IDG Books Worldwide, 2006.

Walsh, Richard. *The Complete Job Search Book for College Students.* Boston: Adams Media, 2007.

# Internet and Podcast Resources

Career Advice podcasts (from Monster.com): **http://podcast.monster.com**

CollegeGrad.com (advice on résumés, interviews, and internships, plus a database of entry-level jobs): **www.collegegrad.com**

Consumer Credit Counseling Services (help with budgeting, money management, and credit issues): **www.cccsintl.org**

Federal Trade Commission—Credit Cards and Consumer Loans (information for consumers): **www.ftc.gov/bcp/conline/edcams/credit/coninfo_loans.htm**

FinancialAidPodcast.com (daily financial aid news): **www.financialaidpodcast.com**

1st Steps in the Hunt: (daily news for online job hunters): **www.interbiznet.com/hunt**

JobWeb (career information site for college students): **www.jobweb.com**

Monster.com (online job search): **www.monster.com**

The Motley Fool (money and investment advice): **www.fool.com**

Springboard (consumer credit management assistance): **www.ncfe.org**

Student Advantage (information on student discounts): **www.studentadvantage.com**

U.S. Department of Labor, Bureau of Labor Statistics—*Occupational Outlook Handbook:* **www.bls.gov/oco**

WomenWorking.com (success strategies for working women): **www.womenworking.com**

Prentice Hall Student Success SuperSite: **www.prenhall.com/success**

# Endnotes

[1] Cited in Jim Hanson, "Your Money Personality: It's All In Your Head," December 25, 2006, University Credit Union (http://hffo.cuna.org/012433/article/1440/html).

[2] Ibid.

[3] Scott Carlson, "Help-Desk Diary: Tech-Savvy Students Learn People Skills and Patience by Solving Campus Computer Problems," *Chronicle of Higher Education,* June 20, 2003 (http://chronicle.com/weekly/v49/i41a02701.htm).

[4] Nellie Mae, "Undergraduate Students and Credit Cards in 2004," May 2005 (www.nelliemae.com/library/research_12.html).

[5] Eric Hoover, "The Lure of Easy Credit Leaves More Students Struggling with Debt: Consumer Advocates Blame Lenders, Congress, and Some

Colleges," *Chronicle of Higher Education,* June 15, 2001 (http://chronicle.com/weekly/v47/i40/40a03501.htm).

[6]"The Hot Jobs with High Pay," February 2007, Career Prospects in Virginia (www.careerprospects.org/Trends/salary-high.html).

[7]U.S. Department of Labor, Bureau of Labor Statistics, "Number of Jobs Held, Labor Market Activity, and Earnings Growth Among the Youngest Baby Boomers: Results from a Longitudinal Survey," news release, August 25, 2006 (www.bls.gov/news.release/pdf/nlsoy.pdf).

[8]New Mexico State University FAQ, "Does NMSU Do Anything to Help People Get Jobs After They Graduate?" October 2000 (https://www.nmsu.edu/aggieland/students/faq_jobs.html).

[9]New Mexico State University FAQ, "What Kind of Student Clubs and Organizations Are There?" June 1999 (https://www.nmsu.edu/aggieland/students/faq_orgs.html).

[10]ResumeEdge.com, "Resume Keyword Search," 2004 (www.enetsc.com/ResumeTips23.htm).

[11]Christopher J. Moore, *In Other Words: A Language Lover's Guide to the Most Intriguing Words Around the World,* New York: Walker, 2004, p. 91.

[12]Eduardo Porter and Greg Winter, "'04 Graduates Learned Lesson in Practicality," *New York Times,* May 30, 2004, pp. A1, A24.

**CREATING YOUR LIFE**

*Building a Successful Future*

*"Successfully intelligent people are flexible in adapting to the roles they need to fulfill. They recognize that they will have to change the way they work to fit the task and situation at hand, and then they analyze what these changes will have to be and make them."*

ROBERT STERNBERG

This chapter will help you analyze how you fared this term, think through upcoming academic decisions, and connect college to the rest of your life. You will see how the skills and attitudes you acquire in school fuel future success. You will consider your role as a member of broader communities and what it means to be an active participant. You will gather tools that will help you apply the power of successful intelligence to your life now and after college. Finally, you will create a personal mission, exploring how to use it to guide your dreams.

*In this chapter you explore answers to the following questions:*

- How can you continue to activate your successful intelligence? 382
- How will what you've learned in this course bring success? 386
- How can you make a difference in your community? 389
- How can you create and live your personal mission? 394
- Successful Intelligence Wrap-Up 395

| Analytical | Creative | Practical |
|---|---|---|
| • Examining your development of the 20 self-activators | • Creating new ways to continue to learn throughout life | • How to respond to change with flexibility |
| • Analyzing how the skills in this course promote life success | • Brainstorming ways to make a difference locally and globally | • How to preserve the environment and help others |
| • Examining how your character, contributions, and values inform your life goals | • Creating positive thoughts and dreams | • How to construct a personal mission |

# How Can You Continue to Activate Your Successful Intelligence?

Throughout this text you have connected analytical, creative, and practical thinking to academic and life skills. You have put them together in order to solve problems and make decisions. You have seen how these skills, used consistently and balanced, can help you succeed.

You are only just beginning your career as a successfully intelligent learner. You will continue to discover the best ways to use your analytical, creative, and practical thinking skills to achieve goals that are meaningful to you. In chapter 1, you completed a self-assessment to examine your levels of development in Robert Sternberg's 20 self-activators. Here are more details to remind you of these characteristics that will keep you moving ahead toward your goals. According to Sternberg, successfully intelligent people do the following:[1]

1. *They motivate themselves.* They make things happen, spurred on by a desire to succeed and a love of what they are doing.

2. *They learn to control their impulses.* Instead of going with their first quick response, they sit with a question or problem. They allow time for thinking and let ideas surface before making a decision.

3. *They know when to persevere.* When it makes sense, they push past frustration and stay on course, confident that success

### What knowledge will help me succeed in a changing world?

At my school, we are required to focus on an area of interest starting in the second semester of sophomore year. At this point I'm planning on studying acting, with an intent to pursue an acting career after I graduate. However, I want to take time in college to explore other areas. Art history and religion both interest me, although I don't know how I would translate those interests into a career. Outside of the specific training I'll receive in acting, how will what I'm doing in college serve me in a career?

Rachel Faison
Bard College
Annandale-on-Hudson,
New York

## PRACTICAL ANSWERS

Carol Carter
President and Founder
LifeBound, LLC
Denver, Colorado

### Internship experience and exploring your passions will help you achieve success.

If you learn to use your mind to the fullest, you will prepare yourself well for any profession you decide to pursue. The key right now is to develop several skillsets to complement your academic learning so that you will be versatile.

First, work at least two internships before you graduate. You will learn volumes from experiencing the culture and politics in different workplaces and by proving your instincts and skills in the real-world environment. This experience will also help you discover what you like and dislike. Many students select fields that sound good or pay a lot without discovering what succeeding in that field really entails.

Second, build your leadership skills. What organization can you join? What leadership role can you play? How will that organization be different and better because you have been a part of it? Stretch yourself. Sometimes when we move into areas that scare us, we grow the most.

Finally, think carefully about what you love (and don't love) doing. Ask probing questions about your values. What makes you feel purposeful, creative, joyful, and valued? What makes you want to wake up every morning? You may not come up with answers right away, but committing yourself to the process of asking the questions and "holding" the questions will allow you to dig genuinely and deeply for the way that you can make your mark in the world of work.

is in their sights. They also are able to see when they've hit a dead end—and, in those cases, to stop pushing.

4. *They know how to make the most of their abilities.* They understand what they do well and capitalize on it in school and work.

5. *They translate thought into action.* Not only do they have good ideas, but they are able to turn those ideas into practical actions that bring ideas to fruition.

6. *They have a product orientation.* They want results; they focus on what they are aiming for rather than on how they are getting there.

7. *They complete tasks and follow through.* With determination, they finish what they start. They also follow through to make sure all the loose ends are tied and the goal has been achieved.

8. *They are initiators.* They commit to people, projects, and ideas. They make things happen rather than sitting back and waiting for things to happen to them.

9. *They are not afraid to risk failure.* Because they take risks and sometimes fail, they often enjoy greater success and build their intellectual capacity. Like everyone, they make mistakes—but tend not to make the same mistake twice.

10. *They don't procrastinate.* They are aware of the negative effects of putting things off, and they avoid them. They create schedules that allow them to accomplish what's important on time.

11. *They accept fair blame.* They strike a balance between never accepting blame and taking the blame for everything. If something is their fault, they accept responsibility and don't make excuses.

12. *They reject self-pity.* When something goes wrong, they find a way to solve the problem. They don't get caught in the energy drain of feeling sorry for themselves.

13. *They are independent.* They can work on their own and think for themselves. They take responsibility for their own schedule and tasks.

14. *They seek to surmount personal difficulties.* They keep things in perspective, looking for ways to remedy personal problems and separate them from their professional lives.

15. *They focus and concentrate to achieve their goals.* They create an environment in which they can best avoid distraction and they focus steadily on their work.

16. *They spread themselves neither too thin nor too thick.* They strike a balance between doing too many things, which results in little progress on any of them, and too few things, which can reduce the level of accomplishment.

17. *They have the ability to delay gratification.* While they enjoy the smaller rewards that require less energy, they focus the bulk of their work on the goals that take more time but promise the most gratification.

18. *They have the ability to see the forest and the trees.* They are able to see the big picture as well as the important details.

19. *They have a reasonable level of self-confidence and a belief in their ability to accomplish their goals.* They believe in themselves enough to get through the tough times, while avoiding the kind of overconfidence that stalls learning and growth.

20. *They balance analytical, creative, and practical thinking.* They sense what to use and when to use it. When problems arise, they combine all three skills to arrive at solutions.

These characteristics are your personal motivational tools. Consult them when you need a way to get moving. You may even want to post them somewhere in your home, in the front of a notebook, or in your PDA.

Use the following *Get Analytical* exercise to see how you have developed your command of the self-activators over the course of the term.

# Evaluate Your Self-Activators

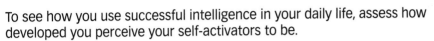

To see how you use successful intelligence in your daily life, assess how developed you perceive your self-activators to be.

| 1 | 2 | 3 | 4 | 5 |
|---|---|---|---|---|
| Not at All Like Me | Somewhat Unlike Me | Not Sure | Somewhat Like Me | Definitely Like Me |

Please circle the number that best represents your answer:

1. I motivate myself well. 1 2 3 4 5

2. I can control my impulses. 1 2 3 4 5

3. I know when to persevere and when to change gears. 1 2 3 4 5

4. I make the most of what I do well. 1 2 3 4 5

5. I can successfully translate my ideas into action. 1 2 3 4 5

6. I can focus effectively on my goal. 1 2 3 4 5

7. I complete tasks and have good follow-through. 1 2 3 4 5

8. I initiate action—I move people and projects ahead. 1 2 3 4 5

9. I have the courage to risk failure. 1 2 3 4 5

10. I avoid procrastination. 1 2 3 4 5

11. I accept responsibility when I make a mistake. 1 2 3 4 5

12. I don't waste time feeling sorry for myself. 1 2 3 4 5

13. I independently take responsibility for tasks. 1 2 3 4 5

14. I work hard to overcome personal difficulties. 1 2 3 4 5

15. I create an environment that helps me to concentrate on my goals. 1 2 3 4 5

16. I don't take on too much work or too little. 1 2 3 4 5

17. I can delay gratification in order to receive the benefits. 1 2 3 4 5

18. I can see both the big picture and the details in a situation. 1 2 3 4 5

19. I am able to maintain confidence in myself. 1 2 3 4 5

20. I can balance my analytical, creative, and practical thinking skills. 1 2 3 4 5

When you complete the assessment, look back at pages 27–28 for your original scores. What development do you see? List five changes that feel significant:

1. _____

2. _____

3. _____

4. _____

5. _____

As you grow, there is always room for improvement. Choose one self-activator that you feel still needs work. Analyze the specific reasons why it remains a challenge. For example, does a need to please others lead to taking on too much work, or is it a lack of taking time to map out responsibilities and time commitments? Write a brief analysis here, and let this analysis guide you as you work to build your strength in this area:

_____

_____

_____

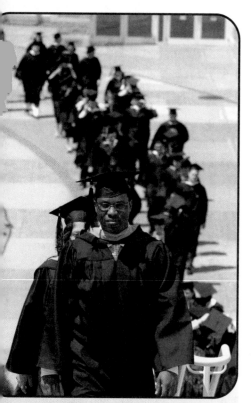

For these graduates of Lafayette College as well as all college graduates, the end of formal schooling is just the beginning of a lifetime of learning.

# How Will What You've Learned in This Course Bring Success?

You leave this course with far more than a final grade, a notebook full of work, and a credit hour or three on your transcript. You leave with a set of skills and attitudes that open the door to lifelong learning, giving you the flexibility to respond to change.

## College Skills Promote Lifelong Learning

Though you will graduate knowing much more than you did when you started college, you are not finished learning. On the contrary—with knowledge in many fields doubling every two to three years and with your personal interests and needs changing every day, what you learn in college is just the beginning of lifelong learning. With the *habit* of learning you will be able to achieve your career and personal goals—those that you set out for yourself today and those that you cannot anticipate now but that will be part of your future.

As you can see in Key 12.1, the attitudes and skills you acquired this term are your keys to success now and in the future. *As you continue in college, remind yourself that you are creating tools that will benefit you in everything you do.* It will renew your motivation.

Start now to make lifelong learning a habit. Lay the foundation by asking questions and being open to new ideas and possibilities. You will build on that foundation when you do the following:

**Investigate new interests.** When information and events catch your attention, take your interest one step further and find out more. Instead of dreaming about it, just do it.

# Attitudes and skills acquired in college are tools for lifelong success.

| ACQUIRED SKILL | IN COLLEGE, YOU'LL USE IT TO ... | IN CAREER AND LIFE, YOU'LL USE IT TO ... |
| --- | --- | --- |
| **Investigating resources** | . . . find who and what can help you have the college experience you want | . . . get acclimated at a new job or in a new town—find the people, resources, and services that can help you succeed |
| **Knowing and using your learning styles** | . . . select study strategies that make the most of your learning styles | . . . select jobs, career areas, and other pursuits that suit what you do best |
| **Setting goals and managing stress** | . . . complete assignments and achieve educational goals; reduce stress by being in control | . . . accomplish tasks and reach career and personal goals; reduce stress by being in control |
| **Managing time** | . . . get to classes on time, juggle school and work, turn in assignments when they are due, plan study time | . . . finish work tasks on time or before they are due, balance duties on the job and at home |
| **Analytical, creative, and practical thinking** | . . . think through writing assignments, solve math problems, analyze academic readings, brainstorm paper topics, work through academic issues, work effectively on team projects | . . . find ways to improve product design, increase market share, present ideas to customers; analyze life issues, come up with ideas, and take practical action |
| **Reading** | . . . read course texts and other materials | . . . read operating manuals, work guidebooks, media materials in your field; read for practical purposes, for learning, and for pleasure at home |
| **Note taking** | . . . take notes in class, in study groups, during studying, and during research | . . . take notes in work and community meetings and during important phone calls |
| **Test taking** | . . . take quizzes, tests, and final exams | . . . take tests for certification in particular work skills and for continuing education courses |
| **Writing** | . . . write essays and reports | . . . write work-related documents, including e-mails, reports, proposals, and speeches; write personal letters and journal entries |
| **Building successful relationships** | . . . get along with instructors, students, and student groups | . . . get along with supervisors, coworkers, team members, friends, and family members |
| **Staying healthy** | . . . stay physically and mentally healthy so that you can make the most of school | . . . stay physically and mentally healthy so that you can be at your best at work and at home |
| **Managing money** | . . . stay on top of school costs and make decisions that earn and save you the money you need | . . . budget the money you earn so that you can pay your bills and save for the future |
| **Establishing and maintaining a personal mission** | . . . develop a big-picture idea of what you want from your education, and make choices that guide you toward those goals | . . . develop a big-picture idea of what you wish to accomplish in life, and make choices that guide you toward those goals |

**Read, read, read.** Reading expert Jim Trelease says that people who don't read "base their future decisions on what they used to know. If you don't read much, you really don't know much. You're dangerous."[2] Decrease the danger to yourself and others by opening a world of knowledge and perspectives through reading. Ask friends which books have changed their lives. Keep up with local, national, and world news through newspapers and magazines.

**Keep on top of changes in your career.** After graduation, continue your education both in your field and in the realm of general knowledge. Stay on top of ideas, developments, and new technology in your field by seeking out continuing education courses. Sign up for career-related seminars. Take single courses at a local college or community learning center. Some companies offer additional on-the-job training or pay for their employees to take courses that will improve their knowledge and skills.

CONTINUING
EDUCATION

*Courses that students can take without having to be part of a degree program.*

**Spend time with interesting people.** When you meet someone new who inspires you and makes you think, keep in touch. Form a study group, a film club, or a walking club. Host a potluck dinner party and invite people from different corners of your life—family, school, work, or neighborhood. Learn something new from everyone you meet.

**Talk to people from different generations.** Younger people can learn from the experienced, broad perspective of those belonging to older generations; older people can learn from the fresh and often radical perspective of those younger than themselves. Communication builds mutual respect.

**Delve into other cultures.** Talk with a friend who has grown up in a culture different from your own. Invite him or her to dinner. Eat food from a country you've never visited. Initiate conversations with people of different races, religions, values, and ethnic backgrounds. Travel internationally and locally. Take a course that deals with some aspect of cultural diversity. Try a term or year abroad. Learn a new language.

**Nurture a spiritual life.** Wherever you find spirituality—in organized religion, family, friendship, nature, music, or anywhere else—it will help you find balance and meaning.

**Experience the arts.** Art is "an adventure of the mind" (Eugène Ionesco, playwright); "a means of knowing the world" (Angela Carter, author); something that "does not reproduce the visible; rather, it makes visible" (Paul Klee, painter); "a lie that makes us realize truth" (Pablo Picasso, painter); a revealer of "our most secret self" (Jean-Luc Godard, filmmaker). Through art you can discover new ideas and shed light on old ones. Seek out whatever moves you—music, visual arts, theater, photography, dance, performance art, film, television, poetry, prose, and more.

**Be creative.** Take a class in drawing, writing, or quilting. Learn to play an instrument. Write poems for your favorite people or stories to read to your children. Concoct a new recipe. Design and build a set of shelves for your home. Create a memoir of your life. Express yourself, and learn more about yourself, through art.

Lifelong learning is the master key that unlocks so many of the doors you encounter on your journey. If you keep it firmly in your hand, you will discover worlds of knowledge—and a place for yourself to continue growing within them.

## Flexibility Helps You Adapt to Change

As a citizen of the 21st century, you are likely to move in and out of school, jobs, and careers in the years ahead. You are also likely to experience important personal changes. How you react to the changes you experience, especially if they are unexpected and difficult, is almost as important as the changes themselves in determining your future success. The ability to "make lemonade from lemons" is the hallmark of people who frequently manage to land on their feet.

Both your ability to learn throughout life and your ability to think analytically, creatively, and practically will help you stay flexible. As planned and unplanned changes arise, you analyze them, create and consider options, make decisions, and take practical actions. With these skills you can adapt to the loss of a job or an exciting job offer, a personal health crisis or a happy change in family status, failing a course or winning an academic scholarship.

Although sudden changes may throw you off balance, the unpredictability of life can open new horizons. Margaret J. Wheatley and Myron Kellner-Rogers, leadership and community experts and founders of the Berkana Institute, explain: People "often look at this unpredictability with resentment, but . . . unpredictability gives us the freedom to experiment. It is this unpredictability that welcomes our creativity."[3] Here are some strategies they recommend for making the most of unpredictable changes:

- *Look for what happens when you meet someone or experience something new.* Be aware of new feelings, insights, or connections that arise. Observe where they lead you.

- *Be willing to be surprised.* Great creative energies can come from the force of a surprise. Instead of turning back to familiar patterns, explore new possibilities.

- *Use your planning as a guide rather than a rule.* If you allow yourself to follow new paths when changes occur, you are able to grow from what life gives you.

- *Focus on what* is *rather than what is supposed to be.* Planning for the future works best when you accept the reality of your situation.

When change affects a community globally or locally, people depend on one another for support. Giving what you can of your time, energy, and resources to those who need help makes you a valued community member.

# How Can You Make a Difference in Your Community?

Everyday life is demanding and sometimes makes it tough to pay attention to anything except your own issues. However, you can make a difference in your community by helping others, being an active citizen, and doing your share for the environment.

COMMUNITY

1. A group of people living in the same locality.
2. A group of people having common interests. 3. A group of people forming a distinct segment of society.

- List 25 things you like about yourself. You can name anything—things you can do, things you think, things you've accomplished, things you like about your physical self, and so on. (Use a separate sheet of paper or a computer file.)

- Next, list 25 things you would like to do in your life. These can be anything from trying Vietnamese food to traveling to the Grand Canyon to working for Teach for America. They can be things you'd like to do tomorrow or things that you plan to do in 20 years. At least five items on this list should involve your current and future education.

- Finally, come up with five things you can plan for the next year that combine what you like about yourself and what you want to do. If you like your strength as a mountain biker and you want to explore a state you've never seen, plan a mountain biking trip to that state. If you like your writing and you want to be a published author, write an essay to submit to a magazine. Be creative. Let everything be possible.

1. _____
2. _____
3. _____
4. _____
5. _____

## You Can Help Others

What you do for others has enormous impact. Giving others hope, comfort, or assistance can improve their ability to cope. Reaching out to others can also enhance your career. Being involved in causes and the community shows caring and community spirit, qualities companies look for in people they hire.

You can help others by volunteering, participating in service-learning, and setting an example in how you live your life.

### Volunteering

Look for a volunteering activity that you can fit into your schedule. Key 12.2 lists organizations that provide volunteer opportunities; you might also look into more local efforts or private clearinghouses that set up smaller projects.

Many schools, realizing the importance of community involvement, sponsor volunteer groups or have committees that organize volunteering opportunities. For example, the University of Virginia has a student volunteer center that connects students to

## KEY 12.2 Look into volunteering opportunities that these organizations offer.

- AIDS-related organizations
- American Red Cross
- Amnesty International
- Audubon Society
- Battered women shelters
- Big Brothers and Big Sisters
- Churches, synagogues, temples, mosques, and affiliated organizations such as the YMCA, YWCA, or JCCA
- Educational support organizations

- Environmental awareness/support organizations such as Greenpeace and Sierra Club
- Health-focused organizations such as the Avon Foundation for Breast Cancer or the Childhood Leukemia Foundation
- Hospitals
- Hotlines
- Kiwanis/Knights of Columbus/Lions Club/Rotary

- Libraries
- Meals on Wheels
- Nursing homes
- Planned Parenthood
- School districts
- Scouting organizations
- Share Our Strength/other food donation organizations
- Shelters and organizations supporting the homeless
- World Wildlife Fund

the surrounding community through projects such as youth mentoring, housing improvement, and a crisis hotline.

The federal government encourages volunteerism through AmeriCorps, a federal volunteer clearinghouse, which offers education-related financial incentives in return for community service. If you work for AmeriCorps and you are enrolled in the National Service Trust, you will receive an award that you can use to pay current tuition expenses or repay student loans. You may work either before, during, or after your college education.

## Service-Learning

The goal of *service-learning* is to provide the community with service and provide students with knowledge gained from hands-on experience.[4] Students in service-learning programs enroll in for-credit courses in which service and related assignments are required. The National Service-Learning Clearinghouse presents the following example of the difference between volunteering and service-learning:

Making a difference in the world often means taking practical action. This group of students, as part of a service organization called Global Routes, helps out on the island of St. Lucia.

> If school students collect trash out of an urban streambed, they are providing a service to the community as volunteers; a service that is highly valued and important. When school students collect trash from an urban streambed, then analyze what they found and possible sources so they can share the results with residents of the neighborhood along with suggestions for reducing pollution, they are engaging in service-learning. In the service-learning example, the students are providing an important service to the community *and,* at the same time, learning about water quality and laboratory analysis, developing an understanding of pollution issues, learning to interpret

science issues to the public, and practicing communications skills by speaking to residents.[5]

Service-learning builds a sense of civic responsibility, helps students learn useful skills through doing, and promotes values exploration and personal change. If you are interested in seeing these benefits firsthand, talk to your advisor about whether your school offers service-learning programs. Service-learning is a win-win situation—everyone has something to gain.

## Setting an Example

The most basic—and perhaps the most important—way you can make a difference is to live your life in a way that sets an example for others. If you make life choices that show a value of learning and hard work, perseverance, commitment, responsibility, and love, you will inspire others to strive for their own personal best.

When you reach for the heights, you also leave an inspiring legacy to any children you have now or may one day have. A 31-year-old returning student and mother of four at Palo Alto College in San Antonio, Texas, is keenly aware of the relationship between what she is doing in school and her children's future. She explains:

> Having waited so long [to go to college] after high school and having a family has put a new perspective and priority on seeking a degree and my goals I want to accomplish in life. Throughout my high school years and even into my twenties, I didn't have any desire to pursue a degree or have any higher ambitions about work. I decided to go back to college after I realized that I could not get a job that paid more than minimum wage.
>
> Hopefully, I am setting a great example for my children. I want them to be confident in their talents and discover their skills. I know that I live in a very stressful environment and everything doesn't go the way I plan for it to go. That is why I try to stay open and flexible to the changes that occur. There is still a lot of spontaneity and it mostly feels like chaos around this house, but it is more of a controlled chaos. And there is always tomorrow.[6]

# You Can Get Involved Locally and Nationally

Being an active citizen is another form of involvement. On a local level, you might take part in your community's debate over saving open space from developers. On a state level, you might contact legislators about building sound barriers along an interstate highway that runs through your town. On a national level, you might write letters to your congressional representative to urge support of a bill that addresses the high cost of health care. Work for political candidates who adopt the views you support, and even consider running for office yourself—in your district, city, state, or nationally.

Most important, vote in every election. Your votes and your actions can make a difference—and getting involved will bring you the power and satisfaction of being a responsible citizen. Having the right to vote places you in a privileged minority—most people around the world have no voice in how they live. In the booklet "Everything You Wanted to Know About Registering to Vote and Voting in the United States," Caty Borum writes:

For some young people, a feeling of being disconnected from government, or that "politicians don't listen to me" is the reason they say they don't vote. But elected officials must be responsive to their constituents, so your vote is actually your way of telling leaders what you care about. There may be many reasons people give for not taking advantage of the right to vote, but it's never too late to actually jump into the game, rather than sitting it out on the sidelines. There are too many issues that affect young people—such as education, jobs, health care, crime and violence—to sit it out on Election Day.

*Here's the bottom line: If you don't vote, someone else is deciding your future for you.* It's that simple. If you have an opinion about the cost of college tuition, jobs, the economy, or tons of other laws and issues that affect you, then you're already involved. Now take advantage of your right to determine your future. What are you waiting for?[7]

## You Can Help to Preserve Your Environment

Your environment is your home. When you do your part to maintain a clean, safe, and healthy place to live, your actions have an impact not only on your immediate surroundings but also on others around you and on the future of the planet. Every recycled bottle, compact fluorescent lightbulb, and reused bag is a step in the right direction. Take responsibility for what you can control—your own habits—and develop practices that contribute to the health of the environment.

**Recycle anything that you can.** Many communities have some kind of recycling program. If you live on campus, your college may have its own program. What you can recycle—plastics, aluminum, glass, newspapers, magazines, other scrap paper—depends on how extensive the program is. Products that use recycled materials are often more expensive, but if they are within your price range, try to reward the company's dedication by purchasing them.

**Respect the outdoors.** Use products that reduce chemical waste. Pick up after yourself. Through volunteering, voicing your opinion, or making monetary donations, support the maintenance of parks and the preservation of natural, undeveloped land. Be creative: One young woman planned a cleanup of a local lakeside area as the main group activity for the guests at her birthday party (she joined them, of course). Everyone benefits when each person takes responsibility for maintaining the fragile earth.

**Reduce your "footprint."** Your *environmental footprint* refers to the effect your day-to-day actions have on the earth and its resources. Every step you take to use less energy or make less trash helps to reduce your footprint. Ways to use less energy include turning off lights and appliances when not in use, using energy-saving lightbulbs and appliances, walking or biking instead of driving, using public transportation, driving an energy-efficient or hybrid automobile, or using alternative energy sources for your home (solar power, wind power). Ways to make less trash include composting, buying products that miminize packaging, and growing food in a garden.

As with helping others, setting an example is a great way to make a difference yourself while inspiring others to make positive changes. Television producer Laurie David and singer-songwriter Sheryl Crow went on a two-week tour of colleges, in a bus powered by bio-diesel fuel, to open a dialogue with students about global warming. Decide how you can set an example in your life.

Your future accomplishments, and those of your family and community, are possible only if the environment continues to sustain life and economic activity. Ensuring a clean environment that supports your hopes and dreams may be part of the larger picture of your personal mission.

# How Can You Create and Live Your Personal Mission?

If the trees are your goals, the forest is the big picture of what you are aiming for in life—your personal mission. To define your mission, craft a *personal mission statement.*

Stephen Covey, author of *The Seven Habits of Highly Effective People,* defines a mission statement as a philosophy outlining what you want to be (character), what you want to do (contributions and achievements), and the principles by which you live (your values). He describes the statement as "a personal constitution, the basis for making major, life-directing decisions."[8]

Here is a mission statement written by Carol Carter, one of the authors of *Keys to Success:*

> My mission is to use my talents and abilities to help people of all ages, stages, backgrounds, and economic levels achieve their human potential through fully developing their minds and their talents. I aim to create opportunities for others through work, service, and family. I also aim to balance work with people in my life, understanding that my family and friends are a priority above all else.

How can you start formulating a mission statement? Try using Covey's three aspects of personal mission as a guide. Think through the following:

- *Character.* What aspects of character do you think are most valuable? When you consider the people you admire most, which of their qualities stand out?

- *Contributions and achievements.* What do you want to accomplish in your life? Where do you want to make a difference?

- *Values.* How do the values you established in your work in chapter 2 inform your life goals? What in your mission could help you live according to what you value most highly? For example, if you value community involvement, your mission may reflect a life goal of holding elected office, which may translate into an interim goal of running for class office at college.

Because what you want out of life changes as you move from one phase to the next—from single person to spouse, from student to working citizen—your personal mission should remain flexible and open to revision. Frame your mission statement carefully so that it reflects your goals and

# Explore Your
# Personal Mission

get practical!!

Imagine yourself sometime in the future looking back at the life you lived. To do this, answer one or more of the following questions on a separate sheet of paper or in a computer file. Use these responses as the basis for writing your personal mission at the end of the chapter (page 399).

1. You are at your retirement dinner. You have had an esteemed career in whatever you ended up doing in your life. Your best friend stands up and talks about the five aspects of your character that have taken you to the top. What do you think they are?

2. You are preparing for a late-in-life job change. Updating your résumé, you need to list your contributions and achievements. What would you like them to be?

3. You have been told that you have one year to live. With family or close friends, you talk about the values that mean the most to you. Based on that discussion, how do you want to spend your time in this last year? What choices will reflect what is most important to you?

charts your course. As Mel Levine says in *Ready or Not, Here Life Comes*, his book on work and life readiness: "An adult must be able to chart her own road maps."[9] Your mission can be the road map for your journey, helping you to infuse your daily activities with integrity and meaning, take responsibility for your actions, and continue to grow.

## Successful Intelligence Wrap-Up

As a lifelong learner, you will always have a new direction in which to grow and a new challenge to face. Seek improvement in your personal, educational, and professional life. Dream big, knowing that incredible things are possible. Live each day to the fullest, using your successful intelligence to achieve your most valued goals. Here's how you have built skills in chapter 12:

### Analytical

You explored how you will continue to use the skills you acquired in this course. With the *Get Analytical* exercise, you examined how you now use successful intelligence in your daily life. You considered the role you play in your community and the effect your actions can have both locally and nationally. You analyzed what you consider important to include in your personal mission.

### Creative

Reading the material about how college skills promote lifelong learning may have inspired new ideas about how you can learn throughout your life. In the *Get Creative* exercise, you brainstormed positive thoughts about yourself as well as plans for the near and far future. The material on making a difference in the community may have sparked thoughts about actions you can take to change your community for the better.

### Practical

You revisited Steinberg's 20 self-activators, practical skills for living with successful intelligence. You explored specific ways to be flexible in the face of change. You noted ways to help others and protect the environment. In the *Get Practical* exercise, you used specific thought-provoking questions to prepare materials that will help you develop a personal mission statement.

# *hozh'q*
## *(hoe-shk)*

The Navajo would translate *hozh'q* as "the beauty of life, as seen and created by a person." The word incorporates many concepts, including health and well-being, balance, and happiness. The Navajo perceive that *hozh'q* can start with one person and extend outward indefinitely, having a unifying effect on other people, on the world, and even on the universe. Because the Navajo consider the unity of experience as the ultimate life goal, *hozh'q* is a way of life.[10]

Think of this concept as you reflect on yourself, your goals, your life-long education, your career, and your personal pursuits. Create your own beauty of life by seeking to improve and grow in the ways that are most meaningful to you. Share your *hozh'q* with others, extending the beauty of life as far as you can. By being true to yourself, a respectful friend and family member, a productive employee, and a contributing member of society, you can change the world.

" . . . the world needs you to be forever the generation of strategic optimists, the generation with more dreams than memories, the generation that wakes up each morning and not only imagines that things can be better but also acts on that imagination every day."

THOMAS L. FRIEDMAN, PULITZER PRIZE–WINNING
*NEW YORK TIMES* COLUMNIST

# PERSONAL TRIUMPH CASE STUDY

## DISCOVERING TALENTS AND HELPING OTHERS

JOE A. MARTIN JR.,
PROFESSOR OF COMMUNICATIONS, UNIVERSITY OF WEST FLORIDA, TALLAHASSEE

*Growing up around people who've been hampered by difficulties can inspire a person to make different choices. Joe Martin made the effort to achieve as a student—but that wasn't enough for him. His main focus now is his life mission to use his abilities to help and inspire others. Read the account, then answer the questions on page 398.*

I grew up in the housing projects of Miami, Florida. My mother didn't finish high school, and no one in my family even considered going to college, including me. My low GPA and SAT scores seemed to indicate I wasn't "college material."

While I was in high school, six of my friends died as a result of crime, drugs, or murder. At least 12 people I knew were in prison, five from my own family. I made a vow that if I survived the projects, I would do something constructive with my life and give something back to the community. I initially wanted to join the military, but after the recruiter told me I wasn't smart enough to go to college, I decided to prove him wrong.

I enrolled in college and, given my academic background, was shocked by my success. I ended up graduating at the top of my class, with a bachelor's degree in public relations, and was voted "Student of the Year" among 10,000 students. Competing against more than 400 other candidates, I landed a job right out of college working for the federal government. Within a year, I was able to move my mother out of the projects and afford almost anything I wanted. Life was great, but I didn't like my job and the person I was becoming.

Around that time, I heard a motivational speaker talk about the need for young professionals to give back to the community. I suddenly realized that I hadn't kept my vow. I was indulging myself, but I didn't have any passion or purpose for what I was doing with my life.

After his presentation, I asked the speaker for advice. I jotted down his suggestions on a napkin and began to implement his ideas. I discovered that I could make money doing what I do best—talking. I became a motivational speaker for students and found that my true passion was teaching. Through teaching, whether on stage or in the classroom, I discovered that I could make a difference in the lives of students who were growing up in poverty as I had.

I've given over 300 presentations and spoken to more than a quarter of a million people about student success. I've written books, recorded audio- and videotapes of my programs, and have my own television show. However, my biggest accomplishment so far has been the creation of a Web site called "Real World University." With the Web site, I'm now able to reach more than 100,000 students a month in 26 different countries.

I believe the reason many students fail is because they have no clue about their gifts and talents or about how they can use those gifts and talents to serve others. Many people are on what I call the "Treadmill Trench" of life—motivated to stay busy, but too scared to live their dreams.

My main question to students is: "If you knew you couldn't fail, what would you attempt to do professionally?" The answer to this question can help anyone find their purpose and passion in life. I also stress to students the importance of meeting a model of success—not someone you'll probably never meet, like Michael Jordan, but someone who is doing what you love to do. Then spend time with that person to find out how they did it. Once students have a clear vision of what they want to become, they're destined to succeed.

*Jen Fisher, the student artist who created this drawing, discovered at an early age that art was what she enjoyed doing most. Like Joe, she realized that working in a career area she was passionate about would help her live life to the fullest. After six post-high-school years of working to save money, she is now pursuing an art degree on her way to becoming a professor of art. For more of Jen's story, please visit www. prenhall.com/carter.*

## SUCCESSFUL INTELLIGENCE

*Think, Create, Apply*

Learn from the experiences of others. Look back to Joe Martin's Personal Triumph on page 397. After you've read his story, relate his experience to your own life by completing the following on a separate sheet of paper or on a computer file:

**Step 1. Think it through:** *Analyze your experience and compare it to Joe's.* What was a "missing piece" in Joe's life and how did he fill it? What do you consider a missing piece in your life, and how do you think you could fill the gap?

**Step 2. Think out of the box:** *Imagine ways to contribute.* Think about the ways in which you could serve. How might your talents and skills give something to others? Brainstorm ideas about how you could use what you do well to help others in your community.

**Step 3. Make it happen:** *Make a practical plan to get involved.* Decide on a specific way to help others, then form a plan to pursue this goal. As you think about your decision, consider your missing piece: Is there a way to contribute that also somehow fills that missing piece? Write down what you intend to do and the specific steps you will take to do it.

## TEAMWORK

*Create Solutions Together*

Giving back. In your group, research volunteering opportunities on campus or in your local area. Each member should choose one possibility to research. Answer questions such as the following: What is the situation or organization? What are its needs? Do any volunteer positions require an application, letters of reference, or background checks? What is the time commitment? Is any special training involved? Are there any problematic or difficult elements to this experience?

When you have the information, meet together so that each group member can describe each volunteering opportunity to the other members. Choose one that you feel you will have the time and ability to try next term. Name your choice and tell why you selected it.

# WRITING

## Journal and Put Skills to Work

*Record your thoughts on a separate piece of paper, in a journal, or on a computer file.*

**Journal entry: Your communities.** Thinking about the definition of community from page 389, list the communities to which you belong—professional, family, spiritual, academic, athletic, political, and so on. Choose one community and write about your interaction with it—what it gives you, what you give to it, and whether you want to change the nature of your involvement. [11]

**Real-life writing: Personal mission.** Thinking about your answers to the *Get Practical* exercise on page 395, draft a personal mission statement here, up to a few sentences long, that reflects what you want to achieve in life. Focus on the practical—on what you want to do and the effects you want to have on the world.

# PERSONAL PORTFOLIO

## Prepare for Career Success

*Complete the following in your electronic portfolio or on separate sheets of paper. When you have finished, read through your entire career portfolio. You have gathered information to turn to again and again on your path to a fulfilling, successful career.*

**Revisit the *Wheel of Successful Intelligence*.** Without looking at your assessments from chapter 1 or the wheel from chapter 4, analyze where you are after completing this course by taking the three assessments again.

---

**Assess yourself as an** analytical **thinker.**

For each statement, circle the number that feels right to you, from 1 for "not at all true for me" to 5 for "very true for me."

1. I recognize and define problems effectively.          1 2 3 4 5

2. I see myself as a "thinker," "analytical," "studious."          1 2 3 4 5

3. When working on a problem in a group setting, I like to break down the problem into its components and evaluate them.          1 2 3 4 5

4. I need to see convincing evidence before accepting information as fact.          1 2 3 4 5

5. I weigh the pros and cons of plans and ideas before taking action.　　1 2 3 4 5

6. I tend to make connections among pieces of information by categorizing them.　　1 2 3 4 5

7. Impulsive, spontaneous decision making worries me.　　1 2 3 4 5

8. I monitor my progress toward goals.　　1 2 3 4 5

9. Once I reach a goal, I evaluate the process to see how effective it was.　　1 2 3 4 5

10. When something goes wrong, I work to find out why.　　1 2 3 4 5

Total your answers here: _____

## Assess yourself as a creative thinker.

For each statement, circle the number that feels right to you, from 1 for "not at all true for me" to 5 for "very true for me."

1. I tend to question rules and regulations.　　1 2 3 4 5

2. I see myself as "unique," "full of ideas," "innovative."　　1 2 3 4 5

3. When working on a problem in a group setting, I generate a lot of ideas.　　1 2 3 4 5

4. I am energized when I have a brand-new experience.　　1 2 3 4 5

5. If you say something is too risky, I'm ready to give it a shot.　　1 2 3 4 5

6. I often wonder if there is a different way to do or see something.　　1 2 3 4 5

7. Too much routine in my work or schedule drains my energy.　　1 2 3 4 5

8. I tend to see connections among ideas that others do not.　　1 2 3 4 5

9. I feel comfortable allowing myself to make mistakes as I test out ideas.　　1 2 3 4 5

10. I'm willing to champion an idea even when others disagree with me.　　1 2 3 4 5

Total your answers here: _____

## Assess yourself as a practical thinker.

For each statement, circle the number that feels right to you, from 1 for "not at all true for me" to 5 for "very true for me."

1. I can find a way around any obstacle.     1 2 3 4 5

2. I see myself as a "doer," the "go-to" person, I "make things happen."     1 2 3 4 5

3. When working on a problem in a group setting, I like to set up the plan and monitor how it is carried out.     1 2 3 4 5

4. Because I learn well from experience, I don't tend to repeat a mistake.     1 2 3 4 5

5. I finish what I start and don't leave loose ends hanging.     1 2 3 4 5

6. I pay attention to my emotions in academic and social situations to see if they help or hurt me as I move toward a goal.     1 2 3 4 5

7. I can sense how people feel, and can use that knowledge to interact with others effectively in order to achieve a goal.     1 2 3 4 5

8. I manage my time effectively.     1 2 3 4 5

9. I find ways to adjust to the teaching styles of my instructors and the communication styles of my peers.     1 2 3 4 5

10. When involved in a problem-solving process, I can see when I'm headed in an ineffective direction and I can shift gears.     1 2 3 4 5

Total your answers here: _____

After you have finished, fill in your new scores in the blank *Wheel of Successful Intelligence* in Key 12.3. Compare this wheel with your previous wheel on page 119. Look at the changes: Where have you grown? How has your self-perception changed?

- Note three *creative ideas* you came up with over the term that aided your exploration or development:

Creative idea: _____

_____

Creative idea: _____

_____

Creative idea: _____

_____

Use this new *Wheel of Successful Intelligence* to evaluate your progress.

Rate yourself in each area of the wheel on a scale of 1 to 10, with 1 being least developed (near the center of the wheel) and 10 being most developed (the outer edge of the wheel). In each area, at the level of the number you choose, draw a curved line and fill in the wedge below that line. Be honest—this is for your benefit only. Finally, look at what your wheel says about the balance in your life. If this were a real wheel, how well would it roll?

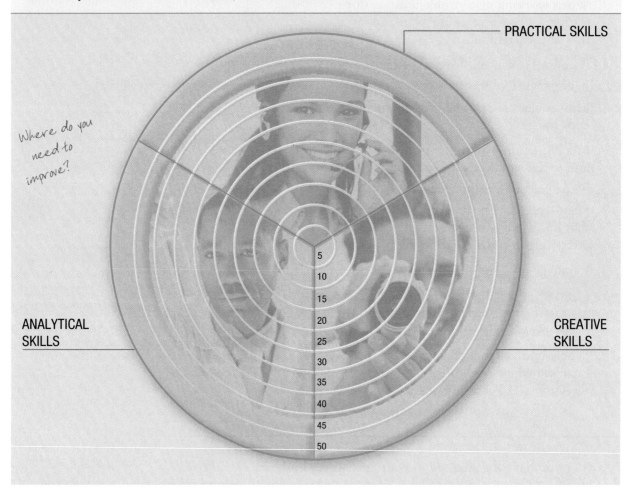

PRACTICAL SKILLS

*Where do you need to improve?*

ANALYTICAL SKILLS

CREATIVE SKILLS

5
10
15
20
25
30
35
40
45
50

*Source:* Based on "The Wheel of Life" model developed by the Coaches Training Institute © Co-Active Space 2000.

- Note three *practical actions* that you took that moved you toward your goals:

Practical action: _____

_____

Practical action: _____

_____

Practical action: _____

_____

Let what you learn from this new wheel inform you about what you have accomplished and what you plan to accomplish. Continue to grow your analytical, creative, and practical skills and use them to manage the changes that await you in the future.

## Suggested Readings

Blaustein, Arthur I. *Make a Difference: America's Guide to Volunteering and Community Service.* San Francisco: Jossey-Bass, 2003.

Gilbert, Daniel. *Stumbling on Happiness.* New York: Vintage, 2007.

Jones, Laurie Beth. *The Path: Creating Your Mission Statement for Work and for Life.* New York: Hyperion, 1998.

Stephan, Naomi. *Fulfill Your Soul's Purpose: Ten Creative Paths to Your Life's Mission.* Nevada City, CA: Blue Dolphin, 2000.

Trask, Crissy. *It's Easy Being Green: A Handbook for Earth-Friendly Living.* Layton, UT: Gibbs Smith, 2006.

Wheatley, Margaret J., and Myron Kellner-Rogers. *A Simpler Way.* San Francisco: Berrett-Koehler, 1999.

## Internet and Podcast Resources

AmeriCorps—Corporation for National and Community Service: **www.americorps.org**

Campus Compact (dedicated to promoting community service, civic engagement, and service-learning in higher education): **www.compact.org**

Cultivate Greatness Leadership Training podcasts: **http://cultivategreatness.com/podcasts**

Freecycle (grassroots network for local trading of free items): **www.freecycle.org**

*The Green Guide* (ideas for environmentally conscious living, published bimonthly by the National Geographic Society): **www.thegreenguide.com**

Hearts & Minds—Information for Change (clearinghouse for volunteer opportunities and civic involvement): **www.change.net/index.htm**

Living Green podcasts from Personal Life Media: **www.personallifemedia.com/podcasts/living-green/living-green-show.html**

Queendom—The Land of Tests (self-tests, personal exploration, and growth): **www.queendom.com**

The Simple Living Network (resources for earth-conscious and simple living): **www.simpleliving.net**

Prentice Hall Student Success SuperSite: **www.prenhall.com/success**

# Endnotes

[1] List and descriptions based on Robert J. Sternberg, *Successful Intelligence*, New York: Plume, 1997, pp. 251–269.

[2] Quoted in Linton Weeks, "The No-Book Report: Skim It and Weep," *Washington Post*, May 14, 2001, p. C8.

[3] Margaret J. Wheatley and Myron Kellner-Rogers, "A Simpler Way," *Weight Watchers Magazine*, 30(3), 1997, pp. 42–44.

[4] "Service-Learning Is . . . ," 2004, National Service-Learning Clearinghouse (www.servicelearning.org/welcome_to_service-learning/service-learning_is/index.php).

[5] Ibid.

[6] From student essay submitted by the First Year Experience students of Patty Parma, Palo Alto College, San Antonio, Texas, January 2004.

[7] Caty Borum, "Everything You Wanted to Know About Registering to Vote and Voting in the United States," 2004, Declare Yourself (www.declareyourself.com/press/voter_guides/voter_guide_download.pdf; no longer available).

[8] Stephen Covey, *The Seven Habits of Highly Effective People*, New York: Simon & Schuster, 1989, pp. 70–144, 309–318.

[9] Mel Levine, *Ready or Not, Here Life Comes*, New York: Simon & Schuster, 2005, p. 10.

[10] Christopher J. Moore, *In Other Words: A Language Lover's Guide to the Most Intriguing Words Around the World*, New York: Walker, 2004, p. 116.

[11] Adapted from Katherine Woodward Thomas, *Calling In the One*, New York: Three Rivers Press, 2004, pp. 298–299.

## Prepare for the End of the Term

Look at your end-of-term responsibilities for each of your courses—a final exam, a final project, a final paper. Get moving to meet these responsibilities by filling in this table and completing its tasks. Check off each task as you complete it.

| Course | Final Project, Paper, or Exam Pending (include date of exam or due date) | Next Task Related to this Responsibility | Done? |
| --- | --- | --- | --- |
|  |  |  |  |
|  |  |  |  |
|  |  |  |  |
|  |  |  |  |
|  |  |  |  |
|  |  |  |  |

## The Challenges and Rewards of Academic Integrity

Academic integrity is about acting ethically. It requires that you submit work that is your own, credit sources accurately, and never cheat on exams or assignments. (See chapter 1 for a discussion of academic integrity and chapter 8 for a discussion of plagiarism.) To follow the principles of academic integrity, you have to understand which specific actions go over the line. Answer the following questions to assess your knowledge and examine what you will and won't do under pressure. This assessment is for you and you alone, so answer honestly.

*Answer each of the following questions on this scale of 1 to 5:*

1 = this is definitely not cheating

2 = this may skirt the edges of cheating, but it's ok to do

3 = I'm not sure

4 = this definitely is cheating, but I would do it if I had to

5 = this definitely is cheating, and I would not do it

1. As part of studying for a math test, you spent hours working through formulas and creating last-minute study notes as text messages on your cell phone. You look at them during the exam. The size of the room and the number of people taking the test with you make you fairly certain that you won't be caught if you are careful.

2. You've been able to handle school and a part-time job until now—final exam crunch time. You look at everything you have to do over the next few weeks and you know that you just can't finish it all. You are under so much pressure to begin studying for exams that you decide to hand in answers to a collaborative assignment that you and your study partner completed together. You do this knowing that your instructor wants *each* of you to complete the answers separately.

3. One of your good friends took the same American government course last year and kept copies of her graded tests. Your course syllabus specifies that the instructor does not make previous exams available, but you decide to look at your friend's material.

4. You're a biology major headed for a career in nursing, but before you graduate you plan to take a few literature and art history courses just for fun. Because these courses have nothing to do with your major or career, you see no problem in doing whatever you can to get a good grade, including cutting and pasting material from the Internet.

5. You never cheat, but it seems that half your class does in one way or another, getting good grades while you struggle to maintain a C+ average. The course is in your academic major, so you need to do well on your upcoming midterm in order to pull your average up to a B. A classmate shows you how to hide tightly wound scrolls of paper, filled with vital facts, under your belt and how to read the scrolls during the test without being noticed. Getting the answers this way doesn't make you happy, but you don't want to be an "honest loser." You decide to look at the scrolls during the exam.

## The Academic Integrity Decision

Each of these questions requires you to make a decision: Should you bend the rules for any number of reasons, or practice academic integrity as defined by your instructor and your school? As you move forward and face real-life "to cheat or not to cheat" situations, use the decision-making model you learned in chapter 4 (see Key 4.8 on page 120) to help you clarify what you think and what you want to do. Here is an example of how you might use this model to make this decision:

Should I cheat on a final exam?

| | | |
|---|---|---|
| **Define the decision:** Whether or not to cheat on a final exam **Examine needs and motives:** I am under pressure to do well on the final. I am also in a constant time crunch. I need a good grade to qualify for the next course in my major. I can't risk failing or getting a D because I'm already in debt and I have to graduate and get a job. | | |

### Choice #1

| Potential positive effects: | Use every way I can think of to cheat on the exam to get the highest possible grade. | Potential negative effects: |
|---|---|---|
| • I will get the grade I need to move ahead. <br><br> • I will be doing what some classmates are already doing, so I won't feel like an "honest fool." <br><br> • Cheating will save me a lot of time that I can use to earn money. | | • If I get caught, I will get in academic trouble. The incident will go on my transcript and I will fail the course. <br><br> • I won't learn the material, and I need to know this stuff for the higher-level course I take next semester. <br><br> • If I get caught, I will be in a worse time crunch because I will have to take the course again. |

### Choice #2

| Potential negative effects: | Cheat in small ways—nothing major. Do only what is absolutely necessary to raise my grade without getting in trouble. | Potential negative effects: |
|---|---|---|
| • I will be "perfecting" the cheating skills I need in the workforce. With so much dishonesty in business, I am convinced that I won't survive if I'm totally honest. | | • Even "minor" cheating undermines learning and reflects poorly on my character. <br><br> • Cheating is cheating. My instructor may throw the book at me if I'm caught. |

| | Choice #3 | |
| --- | --- | --- |
| **Potential positive effects:** | Play it straight and honest—no cheating allowed. | **Potential negative effects:** |
| • I hunker down and actually learn the material so that I come into the test fully prepared.<br><br>• I now have the knowledge I need for the higher-level courses.<br><br>• I can look myself in the mirror and be proud, even if other classmates took the easy way out. | | • I risk getting a lower grade than I would if I cheated.<br><br>• If I fail the test or get a D, I will not qualify for the next course and this will delay my graduation.<br><br>• I will be spending a lot more time studying and won't be able to work as many hours on my job. |
| | **What I did** | |
| **Actual positive effects:** | I decide that it's just not worth it to cheat, so I develop a study and time-management strategy to master the material. | **Actual negative effects:** |
| • I feel that I'm doing the right thing and I don't have to worry about getting into trouble at school.<br><br>• I feel a sense of pride in the process of doing my best to learn the material. | | • I worry a lot more before the exam and lose a lot of sleep while I study.<br><br>• I don't get the A I probably would have gotten had I cheated. |

**Final Evaluation:** Was it a good or bad choice?

Every day when I get up and look in the mirror, I feel better about myself after making this decision. I didn't cut corners and I actually learned the material. I also got a lot better at managing my time. I only wish that I could have gotten an A on my own, instead of a B, especially since a few people I know cheated and got top marks. However, the bottom line is that they probably don't know the stuff and I do.

# Make Your Own Choice

The next time you are tempted to break the rules of academic integrity, use this model to decide what you want to do. *In the end, you are responsible for your own choices and the consequences of your actions.* Now answer these questions:

- Are you more or less likely to cheat after thinking about this *Get Focused!* exercise? Why?

  _____

  _____

- Are you more likely to cheat when you are under time pressure? If you are, what three actions are you going to take to manage your time better throughout the term and particularly before exams?

  1. _____

  2. _____

  3. _____

# INDEX

# Credits and Acknowledgments

Successful intelligence excerpts, chapter-opening quotes, and themes reprinted with permission of Simon & Schuster Adult Publishing Group from SUCCESSFUL INTELLIGENCE by Robert J. Sternberg. Copyright © 1996 by Robert J. Sternberg. Materials extracted and adapted from pp. 12, 19, 127–128, 251–269. Note: from pp. 251–269 material extracted are heading words only.

Excerpts on pages 139, 177, and 188 reprinted by permission of the publisher from MAKING THE MOST OF COLLEGE: STUDENTS SPEAK THEIR MINDS by Richard J. Light, pp. 23–24, 38, 48–49. Cambridge, MA: Harvard University Press, copyright © 2001 by Richard J. Light.

## Photo Credits

All individual photos for Real Questions/Practical Answers and Personal Triumph Case Study features provided by photo subjects.

Photo objects throughout this text from Fotolia and Hemera Technology.

Origami crane icons in chapter 9 (running feet) courtesy of Russ Lappa/Prentice Hall School Division (left) and Prentice Hall School Division (right). Yoga student icon in chapter 10 (running feet) copyright © Lev Dolgatshjov–Fotolia.com.

2, Wyatt McSpadden/*The New York Times*; 9, Phil Marino/*The New York Times*; 22, Tami Chappell/*The New York Times*; 32, © Copyright 2000 PhotoDisc, Inc.; 43, Ruth Fremson/*The New York Times*; 46, C.J. Gunther/*The New York Times*; 64, Tara Todras-Whitehill/*The New York Times*; 79, Nicole Bengiveno/*The New York Times*; 84, Steve Ruark/*The New York Times*; 100, Suzy Allman/*The New York Times*; 105, Angel Franco/*The New York Times*; 117, Michelle Agins/*The New York Times*; 134, Tony Cenicola/*The New York Times*; 142, Joyce Dopkeen/*The New York Times*; 155, Sara Davis/*The New York Times*; 170, Suzanne DeChillo/*The New York Times*; 175, Michelle Agins/*The New York Times*; 190, Jim Wilson/*The New York Times*; 208, Josh Anderson/*The New York Times*; 217, Laura Pedrick/*The New York Times*; 227, Paul Boisvert/*The New York Times*; 240, Don Ipock/*The New York Times*; 245, Jim Wilson/*The New York Times*; 261, Suzanne DeChillo/*The New York Times*; 280, Marilynn Yee/*The New York Times*; 288, Chester Higgins Jr. /*The New York Times*; 295, Laura Pedrick/*The New York Times*; 310, Andrea Mohin/*The New York Times*; 318, Stephen Crowley/*The New York Times*; 326, Michelle Agins/*The New York Times*; 344, © Copyright 2000 PhotoDisc, Inc.; 359, Todd Heisler/*The New York Times*; 369, Rick Scibelli Jr./*The New York Times*; 380, Stephen Crowley/*The New York Times*; 386, Mike Mergen/*The New York Times*; 391, Ruby Washington/*The New York Times*

# FACULTY TRAINING RESOURCES

### PROFESSIONAL DEVELOPMENT IN-SERVICES

For qualified adoptions, instructors using *Keys to Success*, Sixth Edition, can arrange for onsite training sessions. Our authors or professional development faculty trainers can tailor sessions to meet your time constraints and your faculty needs. Contact your local representative for more information about scheduling a session for your campus.

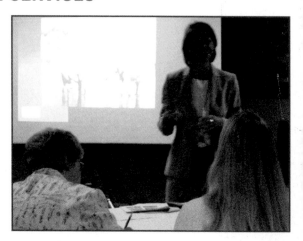

### ONLINE FACULTY TRAINING

All instructors using *Keys to Success*, Sixth Edition, can obtain online faculty training with author Joyce Bishop. See the back cover of this text for more details on this exciting professional development opportunity.

### TRAINING AND CERTIFICATION IN ACADEMIC COACHING

"Learning is based on emotion." *Born to Learn*, Rita Smilkstein. Coaching helps you reach students on all levels to fully engage and motivate them. Training for academic coaching occurs twice a year in Denver, Colorado, or on your campus. This training will help you develop powerful questions that will improve your ability to facilitate your class, teach small groups, or work more effectively with your students one-on-one.

For more information, visit www.lifebound.com or call 1-877-737-8510.